elevate science

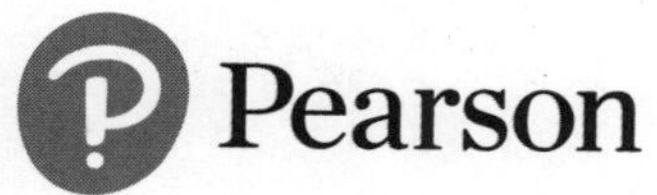

Boston, Massachusetts Chandler, Arizona
Glenview, Illinois New York, New York

You are an author!

This is your book to keep. Write and draw in it! Record your data and discoveries in it! You are an author of this book!

Print your name, school, town, and state below.

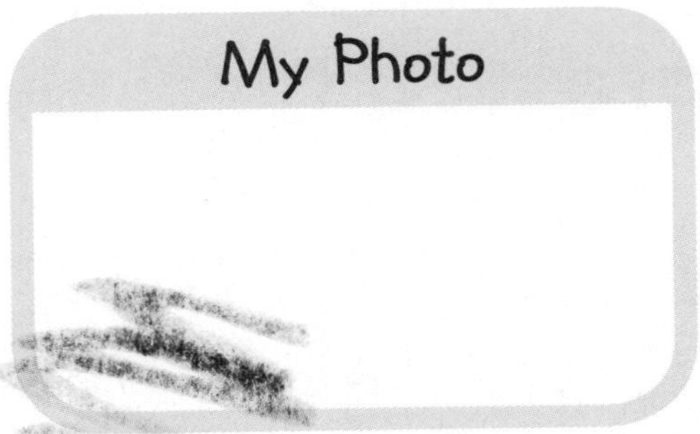

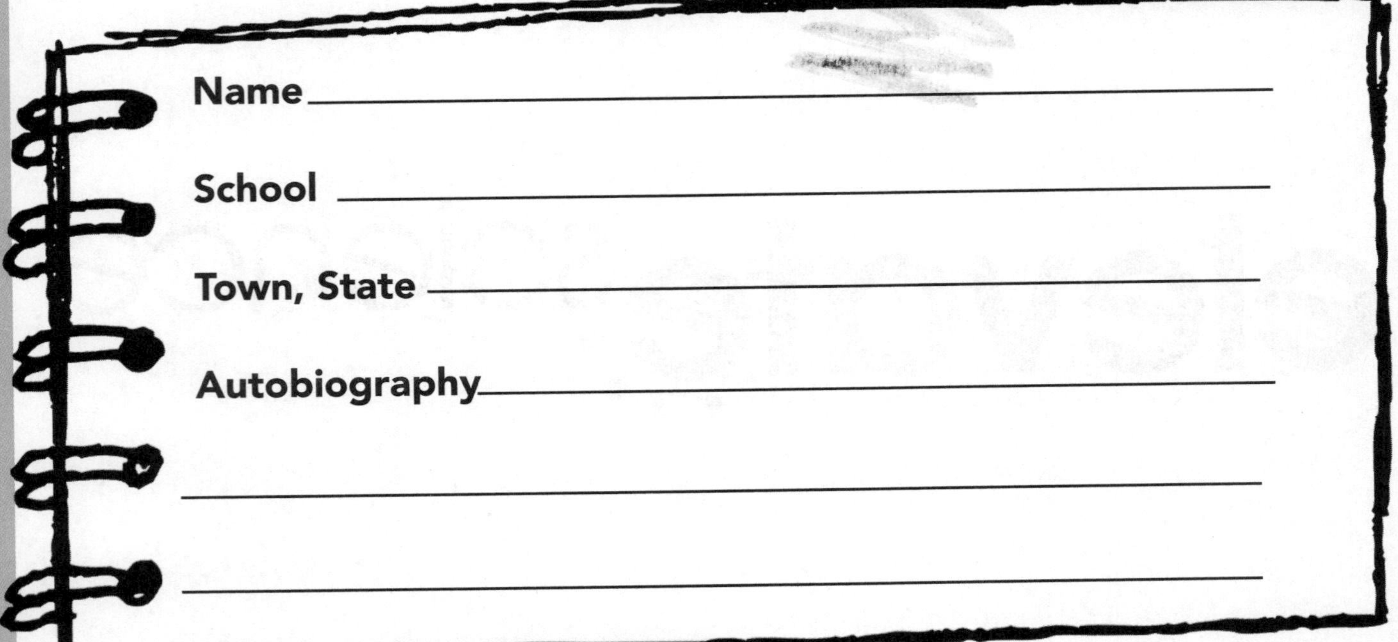

Cover: The cover photo shows an emperor shrimp on a large nudibranch. FCVR: Alex Mustard/Nature Picture Library; BCVR: Marinello/DigitalVision Vectors/Getty Images

Credits appear on pages EM31–EM33, which constitute an extension of this copyright page.

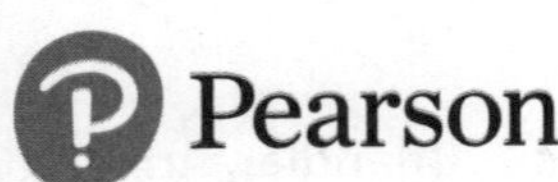

ISBN-13: 978-0-328-94915-1
ISBN-10: 0-328-94915-9
3 18

Program Authors

ZIPPORAH MILLER, EdD
Coordinator for K-12 Science Programs, Anne Arundel County Public Schools.
Zipporah Miller currently serves as the Senior Manager for Organizational Learning with the Anne Arundel County Public School System. Prior to that she served as the K-12 Coordinator for science in Anne Arundel County. She conducts national training to science stakeholders on the Next Generation Science Standards. Dr. Miller also served as the Associate Executive Director for Professional Development Programs and conferences at the National Science Teachers Association (NSTA) and served as a reviewer during the development of Next Generation Science Standards. Dr. Miller holds a doctoral degree from University of Maryland College Park, a master's degree in school administration and supervision from Bowie State University, and a bachelor's degree from Chadron State College.

MICHAEL J. PADILLA, PhD
Professor Emeritus, Eugene P. Moore School of Education, Clemson University, Clemson, South Carolina
Michael J. Padilla taught science in middle and secondary schools, has more than 30 years of experience educating middle grades science teachers, and served as one of the writers of the 1996 U.S. National Science Education Standards. In recent years Mike has focused on teaching science to English Language Learners. His extensive leadership experience, serving as Principal Investigator on numerous National Science Foundation and U.S. Department of Education grants, resulted in more than $35 million in funding to improve science education. He served as president of the National Science Teachers Association, the world's largest science teaching organization, in 2005–2006.

MICHAEL E. WYSESSION, PhD
Professor of Earth and Planetary Sciences, Washington University, St. Louis, Missouri
An author on more than 100 science and science education publications, Dr. Wysession was awarded the prestigious National Science Foundation Presidential Faculty Fellowship and Packard Foundation Fellowship for his research in geophysics, primarily focused on using seismic tomography to determine the forces driving plate tectonics. Dr. Wysession is also a leader in geoscience literacy and education, including being chair of the *Earth Science Literacy Principles*, author of several popular geology *Great Courses* video lecture series, and a lead writer of the *Next Generation Science Standards**.

Reviewers

Program Consultants

Carol Baker
Science Curriculum

Dr. Carol K. Baker is superintendent for Lyons Elementary K-8 School District in Lyons, Illinois. Prior to that, she was Director of Curriculum for Science and Music in Oak Lawn, Illinois. Before that she taught Physics and Earth Science for 18 years. In the recent past, Dr. Baker also wrote assessment questions for ACT (EXPLORE and PLAN), was elected president of the Illinois Science Teachers Association from 2011-2013 and served as a member of the Museum of Science and Industry advisory boards in Chicago. She is a writer of the Next Generation Science Standards. Dr. Baker received her BS in Physics and a science teaching certification. She completed her Master of Educational Administration (K-12) and earned her doctorate in Educational Leadership.

Jim Cummins
ELL

Dr. Cummins's research focuses on literacy development in multilingual schools and the role technology plays in learning across the curriculum. *Elevate Science* incorporates research-based principles for integrating language with the teaching of academic content based on Dr. Cummins's work.

Elfrieda Hiebert
Literacy

Dr. Hiebert is the President and CEO of TextProject, a nonprofit aimed at providing open-access resources for instruction of beginning and struggling readers, and a former primary school teacher. She is also a research associate at the University of California Santa Cruz. Her research addresses how fluency, vocabulary, and knowledge can be fostered through appropriate texts, and her contributions have been recognized through awards, such as the Oscar Causey Award for Outstanding Contributions to Reading Research (Literacy Research Association, 2015), Research to Practice Award (American Educational Research Association, 2013), William S. Gray Citation of Merit Award for Outstanding Contributions to Reading Research (International Reading Association, 2008).

Content Reviewers

Alex Blom, Ph.D.
Associate Professor
Department Of Physical Sciences
Alverno College
Milwaukee, Wisconsin

Joy Branlund, Ph.D.
Department of Physical Science
Southwestern Illinois College
Granite City, Illinois

Judy Calhoun
Associate Professor
Physical Sciences
Alverno College
Milwaukee, Wisconsin

Stefan Debbert
Associate Professor of Chemistry
Lawrence University
Appleton, Wisconsin

Diane Doser
Professor
Department of Geological Sciences
University of Texas at El Paso
El Paso, Texas

Rick Duhrkopf, Ph. D.
Department of Biology
Baylor University
Waco, Texas

Jennifer Liang
University Of Minnesota Duluth
Duluth, Minnesota

Heather Mernitz, Ph.D.
Associate Professor of Physical Sciences
Alverno College
Milwaukee, Wisconsin

Joseph McCullough, Ph.D.
Cabrillo College
Aptos, California

Katie M. Nemeth, Ph.D.
Assistant Professor
College of Science and Engineering
University of Minnesota Duluth
Duluth, Minnesota

Maik Pertermann
Department of Geology
Western Wyoming Community College
Rock Springs, Wyoming

Scott Rochette
Department of the Earth Sciences
The College at Brockport State University of New York
Brockport, New York

David Schuster
Washington University in St Louis
St. Louis, Missouri

Shannon Stevenson
Department of Biology
University of Minnesota Duluth
Duluth, Minnesota

Paul Stoddard, Ph.D.
Department of Geology and Environmental Geosciences
Northern Illinois University
DeKalb, Illinois

Nancy Taylor
American Public University
Charles Town, West Virginia

Safety Reviewers

Douglas Mandt, M.S.
Science Education Consultant
Edgewood, Washington

Juliana Textley, Ph.D.
Author, NSTA books on school science safety
Adjunct Professor
Lesley University
Cambridge, Massachusetts

Teacher Reviewers

Jennifer Bennett, M.A.
Memorial Middle School
Tampa, Florida

Sonia Blackstone
Lake County Schools
Howey In the Hills, Florida

Teresa Bode
Roosevelt Elementary
Tampa, Florida

Tyler C. Britt, Ed.S.
Curriculum & Instructional Practice Coordinator
Raytown Quality Schools
Raytown, Missouri

A. Colleen Campos
Grandview High School
Aurora, Colorado

Ronald Davis
Riverview Elementary
Riverview, Florida

Coleen Doulk
Challenger School
Spring Hill, Florida

Mary D. Dube
Burnett Middle School
Seffner, Florida

Sandra Galpin
Adams Middle School
Tampa, Florida

Rhonda Graham
Science Supervisor
Pittsburgh Public Schools
Pittsburgh, Pennsylvania

Margaret Henry
Lebanon Junior High School
Lebanon, Ohio

Christina Hill
Beth Shields Middle School
Ruskin, Florida

Judy Johnis
Gorden Burnett Middle School
Seffner, Florida

Karen Y. Johnson
Beth Shields Middle School
Ruskin, Florida

Jane Kemp
Lockhart Elementary School
Tampa, Florida

Denise Kuhling
Adams Middle School
Tampa, Florida

Esther Leonard M.Ed. and L.M.T.
Gifted and Talented Implementation Specialist
San Antonio Independent School District
San Antonio, Texas

Kelly Maharaj
Science Department Chairperson
Challenger K—8 School of Science and Mathematics
Elgin, Florida

Kevin J. Maser, Ed.D.
H. Frank Carey Jr/Sr High School
Franklin Square, New York

Angie L. Matamoros, Ph.D.
ALM Science Consultant
Weston, Florida

Corey Mayle
Brogden Middle School
Durham, North Carolina

Keith McCarthy
George Washington Middle School
Wayne, New Jersey

Yolanda O. Peña
John F. Kennedy Junior High School
West Valley City, Utah

Kathleen M. Poe
Jacksonville Beach Elementary School
Jacksonville Beach, Florida

Wendy Rauld
Monroe Middle School
Tampa, Florida

Anne Rice
Woodland Middle School
Gurnee, Illinois

Pat (Patricia) Shane, Ph.D.
STEM & ELA Education Consultant
Chapel Hill, North Carolina

Diana Shelton
Burnett Middle School
Seffner, Florida

Nakia Sturrup
Jennings Middle School
Seffner, Florida

Melissa Triebwasser
Walden Lake Elementary
Plant City, Florida

Michele Bubley Wiehagen
Science Coach
Miles Elementary School
Tampa, Florida

Pauline Wilcox
Instructional Science Coach
Fox Chapel Middle School
Spring Hill, Florida

Topic 1

Solar System

SC.5.E.5.1, SC.5.E.5.2, SC.5.E.5.3

VIDEO

eTEXT

INTERACTIVITY

VIRTUAL LAB

GAME

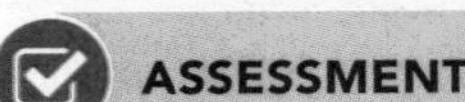
DOCUMENT

ASSESSMENT

Quest

In this **STEM** Quest activity, you meet an astronomical technician who presents you with a design challenge. You need to build a model of the solar system that fits in the lobby of your school.

Like an astronomical technician, you complete activities and labs to design and build your model solar system. You use what you learn in the lessons to make a model solar system that shows the correct size of each planet compared to the other planets.

Find your Quest activities on pages 2–3, 13, 22–23, 32, 34.

Career Connection Astronomical Technicians page 35

The Essential Question

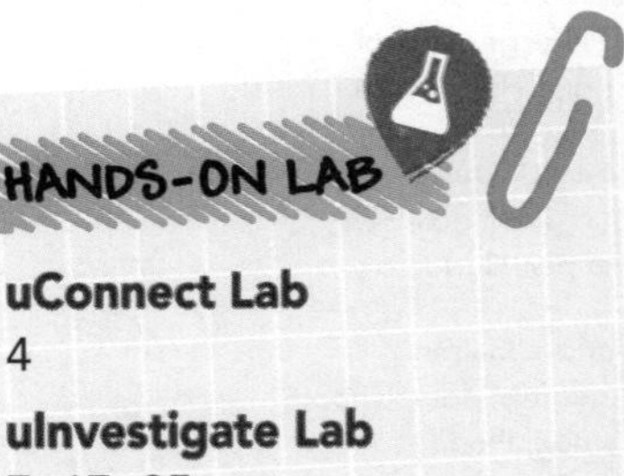

Topic 2

SC.5.E.7.1, SC.5.E.7.2

Earth's Water

VIDEO

eTEXT

INTERACTIVITY

VIRTUAL LAB

GAME

DOCUMENT

ASSESSMENT

Quest

In this Quest activity, you meet a water quality specialist who presents you with a design problem. You need to develop solutions to make unsafe water drinkable.

Like a water quality specialist, you complete activities and labs to learn about sources of freshwater and ways to turn salty ocean water into fresh, drinkable water. You use what you learn in the lessons to decide the best way to provide freshwater to two towns.

Find your Quest activities on pages 44–45, 55, 64–65, 74, 76.

Career Connection Water Quality Specialist page 77

The Essential Question

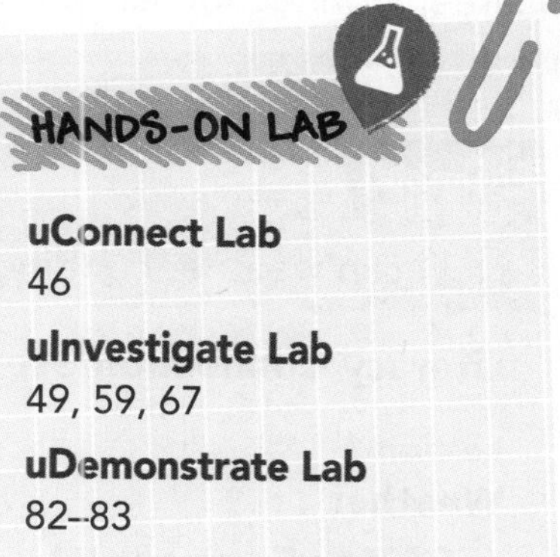

Topic 3

SC.5.E.7.3, SC.5.E.7.4, SC.5.E.7.5, SC.5.E.7.6, SC.5.E.7.7

Weather and Climate

- VIDEO
- eTEXT
- INTERACTIVITY
- VIRTUAL LAB
- GAME
- DOCUMENT
- ASSESSMENT

Quest

In this **STEM** Quest activity, you meet a climatologist who presents you with a challenge. You need to research locations with different weather and write a blog for travelers.

Like a climatologist, you complete activities and labs to look at different weather patterns and forms of precipitation. You use what you learn in the lessons to help travelers decide where to go on a trip and to advise travelers on how to be prepared for severe weather.

Find your Quest activities on pages 86–87, 97, 107, 115, 122–123, 132, 134.

Career Connection Climatologist page 135

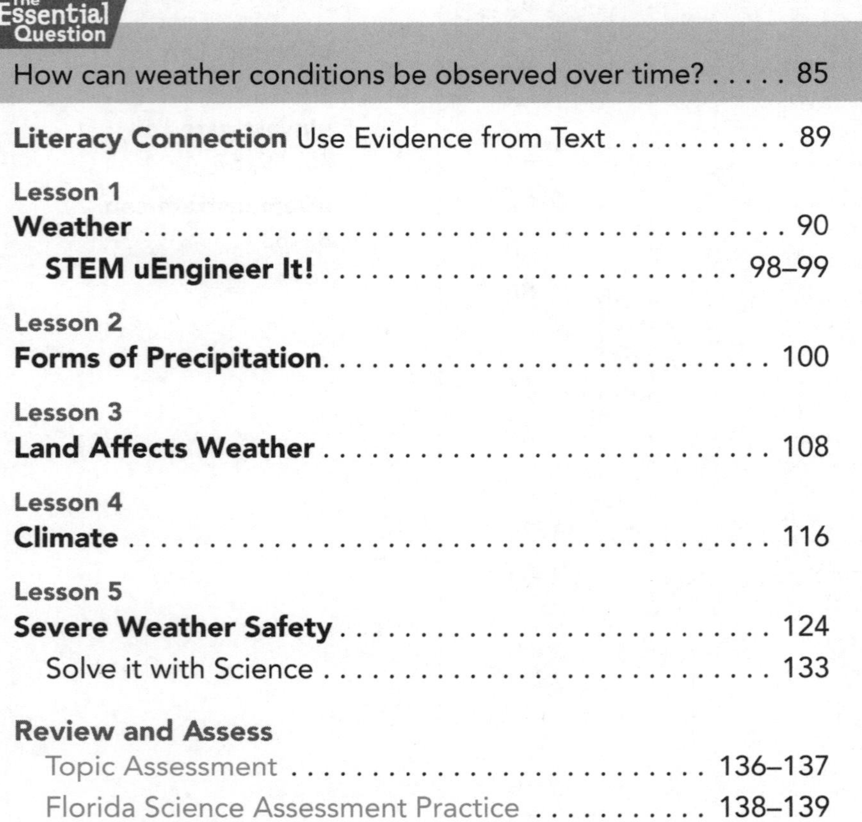

The Essential Question

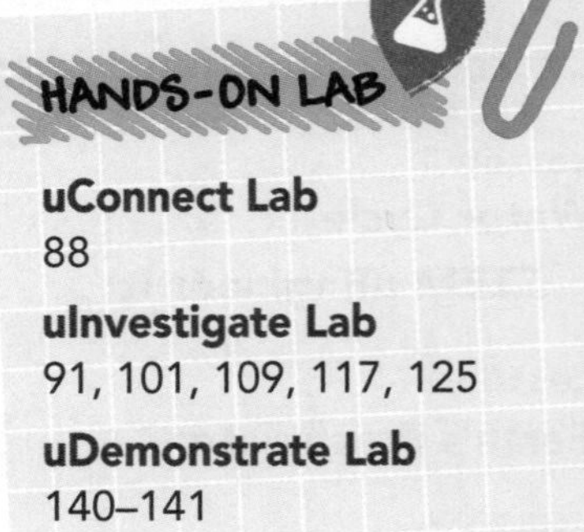

HANDS-ON LAB

Topic 4

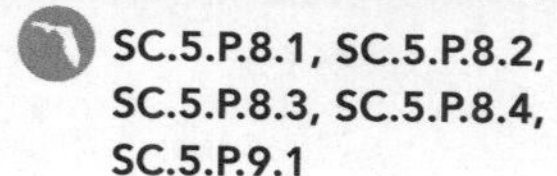
SC.5.P.8.1, SC.5.P.8.2, SC.5.P.8.3, SC.5.P.8.4, SC.5.P.9.1

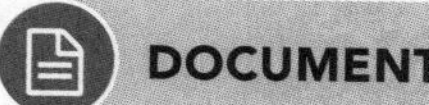

Properties of Matter

Quest

In this **STEM** Quest activity, you meet a materials scientist who presents you with a design problem. You build a model stepping stone so that students can observe a prairie habitat without damaging the plants.

Like a materials scientist, you complete activities and labs to design and build your model stepping stone. You use what you learn in the lessons to help with this design problem.

Find your Quest activities on pages 144–145, 155, 164–165, 173, 180, 192–193, 202–203, 204.

Career Connection Materials Scientist page 205

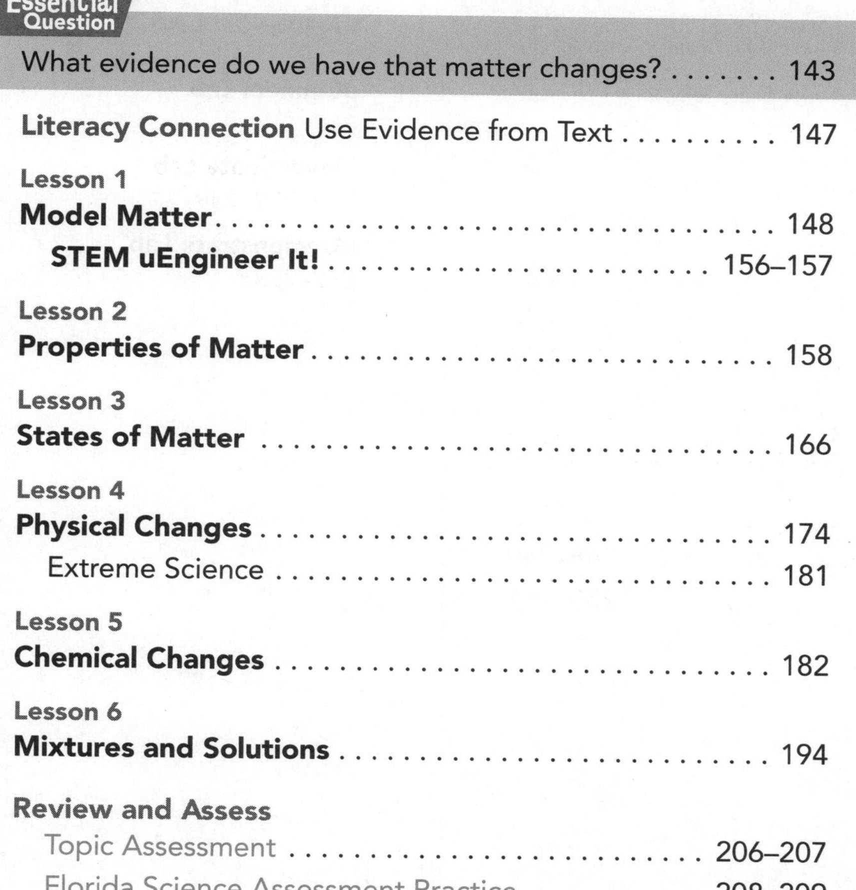

The Essential Question

Topic 5

SC.5.P.10.1, SC.5.P.10.2, SC.5.P.10.3, SC.5.P.10.4, SC.5.P.11.1, SC.5.P.11.2

Forms of Energy

VIDEO

eTEXT

INTERACTIVITY

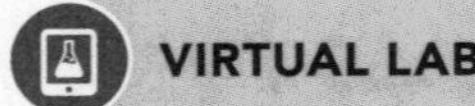
VIRTUAL LAB

GAME

DOCUMENT

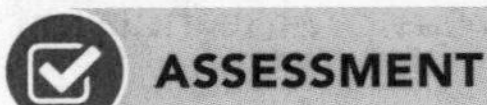
ASSESSMENT

Quest

In this **STEM** Quest activity, you meet a toy designer who presents you with a design problem. You need to design, build, and test a toy that uses electrical energy.

Like a toy designer, you complete activities and labs to design and build your model. You use what you learn in the lessons to build a toy that produces light, sound, or motion and is safe for children from the ages of 5 to 9.

Find your Quest activities on pages 214–215, 227, 234, 244–245, 246.

Career Connection Toy Designer page 247

The Essential Question

Topic 6

SC.5.P.13.1, SC.5.P.13.2, SC.5.P.13.3, SC.5.P.13.4

Forces and Changes in Motion

VIDEO

ASSESSMENT

Quest

In this **STEM** Quest activity, you meet a video game designer who presents you with a design problem. You need to design a video game that demonstrates how forces work.

Like a video game designer, you will think about ways to make the game fun. You use what you learn in the lessons to help the player work through the challenges of the video game.

Find your Quest activities on pages 256–257, 268–269, 277, 286, 288.

Career Connection Video Game Designer page 289

The Essential Question

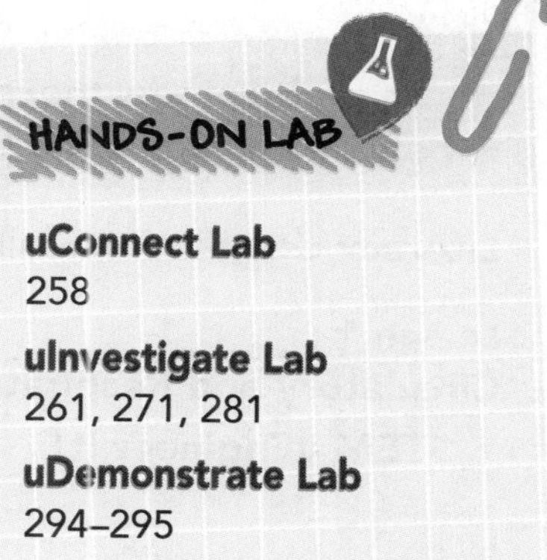

Topic 7

SC.5.L.14.1

Human Body Systems

VIDEO
eTEXT
INTERACTIVITY
VIRTUAL LAB
GAME
DOCUMENT
ASSESSMENT

Quest

In this **STEM** Quest activity, you meet a medical imaging technician who presents you with a design problem. You need to design a remote-controlled micro-camera that can navigate inside the human body.

Like a medical imaging technician, you complete activities and labs to design the remote-controlled camera. You use what you learn in the lessons to determine how to guide your camera.

Find your Quest activities on pages 298–299, 309, 319, 326–327, 336, 338.

Career Connection Medical Imaging Technician page 339

The Essential Question

HANDS-ON LAB

Topic 8

SC.5.L.14.2, SC.5.L.15.1, SC.5.L.17.1

Diversity and Independence

VIDEO
eTEXT
INTERACTIVITY
VIRTUAL LAB
GAME
DOCUMENT
ASSESSMENT

Quest

In this **STEM** Quest activity, you meet a nature photographer who presents you with a design problem. You will solve a human problem by using what you learn about plants and animals.

Like her, you look carefully at plants and animals. You will complete activities and labs and use what you learn to solve a human problem.

Find your Quest activities on pages 348–349, 360–361, 369, 377, 384, 393, 396.

Career Connection Nature Photographer page 397

The Essential Question

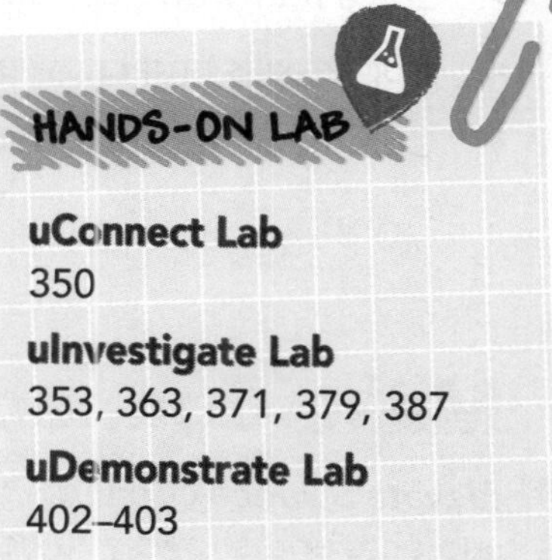

Elevate your thinking!

Elevate Science for Florida takes science to a whole new level and lets you take ownership of your learning. Explore science in the world around you. Investigate how things work. Think critically and solve problems! *Elevate Science* helps you think like a scientist, so you're ready for a world of discoveries.

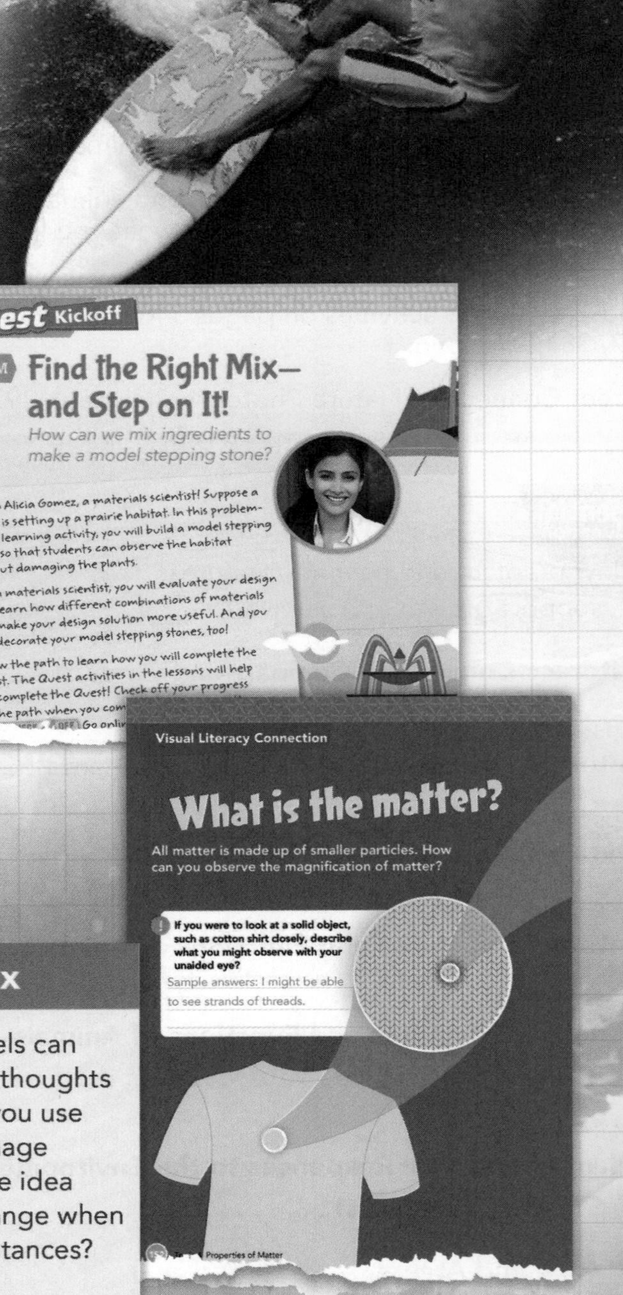

Quest Kickoff

STEM Find the Right Mix—and Step on It!

How can we mix ingredients to make a model stepping stone?

Hi, I'm Alicia Gomez, a materials scientist! Suppose a school is setting up a prairie habitat. In this problem-based learning activity, you will build a model stepping stone so that students can observe the habitat without damaging the plants.

Like a materials scientist, you will evaluate your design and learn how different combinations of materials can make your design solution more useful. And you can decorate your model stepping stones, too!

Follow the path to learn how you will complete the Quest. The Quest activities in the lessons will help you complete the Quest! Check off your progress on the path when you com...

Visual Literacy Connection

What is the matter?

All matter is made up of smaller particles. How can you observe the magnification of matter?

If you were to look at a solid object, such as cotton shirt closely, describe what you might observe with your unaided eye?

Sample answers: I might be able to see strands of threads.

Properties of Matter

Explore Your World

Explore real-life scenarios with engaging Quests that dig into science topics in Florida and around the world. You can:

- Solve real-world problems
- Apply skills and knowledge
- Communicate solutions

Make Connections

Elevate Science connects science to other subjects and shows you how to better understand the world through:

- Mathematics
- Reading and Writing
- Literacy

Math ▸ Toolbox

Use Models Models can help you represent thoughts or ideas. How can you use the blocks in the image below to explain the idea that particles rearrange when they form new substances?

MAFS.K12.MP.4.1

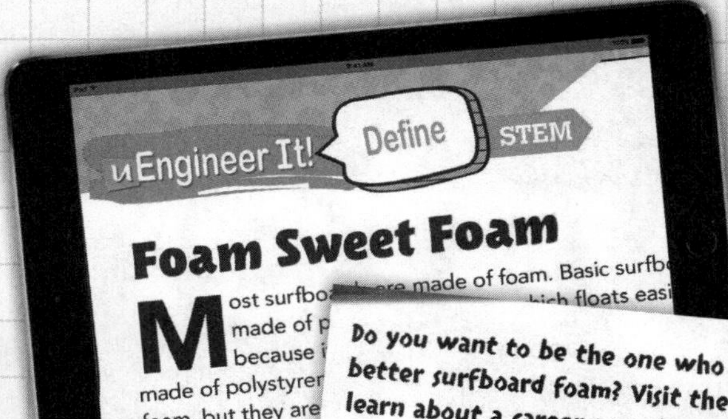

Build Skills for the Future

- Master the Engineering Design Process
- Apply critical thinking and analytical skills
- Learn about STEM careers

Focus on Reading Skills

Elevate Science creates ongoing reading connections to help you develop the reading skills you need to succeed. Features include:

- Leveled Readers
- Literacy Connection Features
- Reading Checks

Literacy ▸ Toolbox

Use Evidence from Text
Water is formed by the combination of atoms of two different elements—hydrogen and o... smallest partic... atom or a mole... you think so?

LAFS.5.W.3...

READING CHECK **Use Evidence from Text** Why do you think aerogels could be used to clean up oil spills in your community? Underline the important facts from the text that support your claim with evidence.

Enter the Lab Zone

Hands-on experiments and virtual labs help you test ideas and show what you know in performance-based assessments. Scaffolded labs include:

- STEM Labs
- Design Your Own
- Open-ended Labs

Explore the Next Generation Sunshine State Science Standards for:

- Connecting Concepts to make connections
- Nature of Science standards to build inquiry skills
- Big Ideas, Benchmarks, and standards to master content

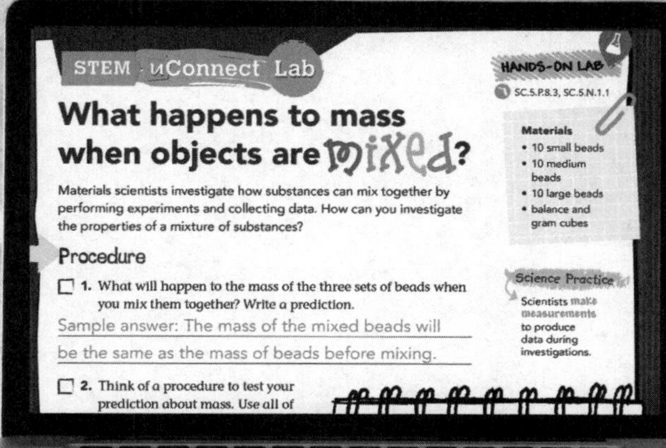

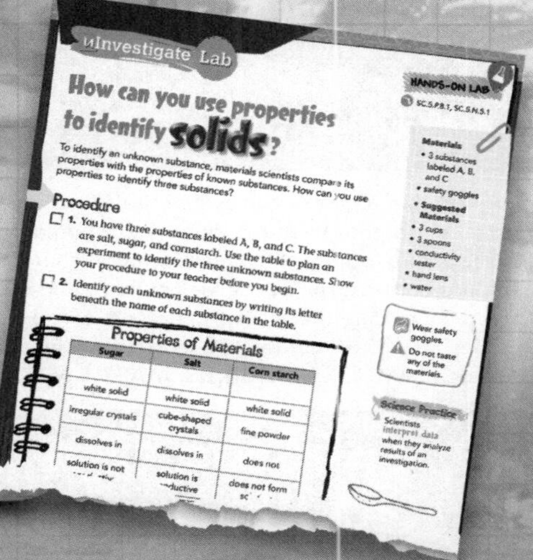

Topic 1

Solar System

SC.5.E.5.1 Recognize that a galaxy consists of gas, dust, and many stars, including any objects orbiting the stars. Identify our home galaxy as the Milky Way. **SC.5.E.5.2** Recognize the major common characteristics of all planets and compare/contrast the properties of inner and outer planets. **SC.5.E.5.3** Distinguish among the following objects of the Solar System—Sun, planets, moons, asteroids, comets—and identify Earth's position in it. (Also: **SC.5.N.1.1, SC.5.N.2.1, LAFS.5.RI.1.3, MAFS.5.NBT.2.6**)

Go Online to access your digital course.

VIDEO

eTEXT

INTERACTIVITY

VIRTUAL LAB

GAME

ASSESSMENT

The Essential Question

What is Earth's place in space?

Show What You Know

Earth is among many planets in our solar system. There are four planets in the inner solar system and four planets in the outer solar system. What makes Earth an inner solar system planet?

____

____

____

Quest Kickoff

STEM Keeping the Planets in Order

How can you model your own solar system?

Hello! I am Kelsey Patton, an astronomical technician. Your school could use a new model of our solar system. I am organizing a small group to help make the model. I think you would be a great addition to our group. Would you join our group?

In this problem-based learning activity, you and your classmates will be the chief advisors. You will guide the team in designing and building the model. One of your challenges will be making a model that fits in your lobby and that shows the correct size of each planet compared to the other planets!

Follow the path to discover how to complete the Quest. The Quest activities in the lessons will help you complete the Quest. Check off your progress on the path when you complete an activity with a QUEST CHECK OFF. Go online for more Quest activities.

Quest Check-In 1

Lesson 1

Apply what you learned in this lesson to make a large poster of the Milky Way Galaxy.

SC.5.E.5.1 Recognize that a galaxy consists of gas, dust, and many stars, including any objects orbiting the stars. Identify our home galaxy as the Milky Way.

SC.5.E.5.2 Recognize the major common characteristics of all planets and compare/contrast the properties of inner and outer planets.

SC.5.E.5.3 Distinguish among the following objects of the Solar System—Sun, planets, moons, asteroids, comets—and identify Earth's position in it.

VIDEO

Watch a video about an astronomical technician.

Quest Check-In Lab 3

Lesson 3

Use what you learned about Jupiter, Saturn, Uranus, and Neptune to build a model of the outer planets for your solar system model.

Quest Findings

Put your model solar system together, including any supporting visuals. Then write a supplemental information sheet that lists the important details of each planet.

Quest Check-In Lab 2

Lesson 2

Use your knowledge of Mercury, Venus, Earth, and Mars to build a model of the inner planets for your solar system model.

uConnect Lab

HANDS-ON LAB

SC.5.E.5.3, SC.5.N.1.1

How big is the sun?

Materials

- modeling clay

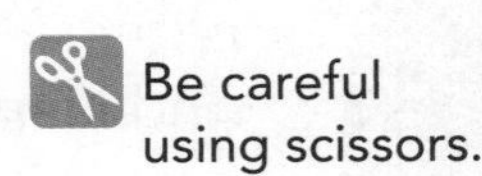

Be careful using scissors.

Astronomers investigate the scale and proportions of objects in space using models. How can you use a model to see how large the sun is compared to other objects in the solar system?

Science Practice

Scientists **use models** to support an argument.

Procedure

☐ **1.** The solar system contains the sun and the planets and their moons. Based on what you already know, make a model of our solar system with the modeling clay.

☐ **2.** Research how much of the total mass of the solar system is taken up by the sun.

☐ **3.** Identify any changes you should make to your model based on data you collected in step 2. Rebuild your model.

Analyze and Interpret Data

4. Use Evidence What changes did you make in your second model? What evidence do you have to support those changes?

Use Text Features

LAFS.5.RI.1.3

GAME

Practice what you learn with the Mini Games.

One important reading skill is to recognize and use text features. Here are some examples of how to use text features when reading.

- Look for headings and subheadings. These are the titles that start a new section.
- Note how the sections of text are divided.
- Get information from graphs, tables, illustrations, labels, photos, and captions.

Read the following text. Look for text features that will help you understand the information.

A Very Old System

Our solar system is estimated to be about 4.6 billion years old. It formed from a giant cloud of dust and gas. This cloud slowly collapsed in on itself from the pull of gravity. During this collapse, what we know today as the sun and the eight planets and their moons were all formed. Many other smaller objects were also formed. All of the objects in our solar system move around the sun. Our understanding of the solar system is not very old. Most of what we know about it has come from scientists using telescopes. Telescopes were first used to study the solar system in the year 1609. Scientists are still making new discoveries about our solar system all the time.

READING CHECK **Use Text Features** What does the title *A Very Old System* tell you about the text?

____

____

____

Lesson 1

Parts of a Galaxy

I can...

Explain that galaxies are made of gas, dust, stars, and many more objects.

Identify the Milky Way as my home galaxy.

Explain how the apparent brightness of stars is related to their distance from Earth.

Literacy Skill

Use Text Features

Vocabulary

galaxy
Milky Way
star

Academic Vocabulary

apparent

VIDEO

Watch a video about star brightness.

SC.5.E.5.1 Recognize that a galaxy consists of gas, dust, and many stars, including any objects orbiting the stars. Identify our home galaxy as the Milky Way. (Also **SC.5.N.1.1, SC.5.N.2.1, LAFS.5.RI.1.3**)

LOCAL-TO-GLOBAL Connection

The sun, the only star in our solar system, provides energy for life on Earth. Scientists know a lot about the sun. Over time, they have discovered the existence of many billions of stars throughout outer space. Our galaxy, the Milky Way, is one of more than 2 trillion galaxies in the observable universe. The Milky Way Galaxy has at least 100 billion stars in it. That is a lot of stars!

Our sun is huge! It has about one million times the volume of Earth. When was the last time you chewed a piece of gum from a gumball machine? Think of the sun as a gumball machine. It would take more than 1 million Earth gumballs to fill the sun gumball machine!

Relate Describe how the Milky Way Galaxy and our sun are related.

____

____

____

____

uInvestigate Lab

SC.5.E.5.1, SC.5.N.1.1

How are distance and brightness related?

Materials
- flashlight
- black construction paper
- meterstick

Scientists study how far stars are from Earth and how bright they look in the night sky. How can you investigate the relationship between light brightness and distance?

Avoid shining light directly into someone's eyes.

Procedure

☐ **1.** Write a hypothesis about how light brightness and distance are related.

____

____

Science Practice
Scientists **use evidence** to support a scientific argument.

☐ **2.** Make a plan to test your hypothesis. Have your teacher approve your plan before you begin.

☐ **3.** Record your data. Rank brightness from 1 to 4, with 1 being the brightest and 4 being the least bright.

Distance of flashlight from paper (cm)	Brightness rank

Analyze and Interpret Data

4. Use Evidence How does distance affect the brightness of an object, such as a star in the night sky? Use your data.

____

____

uBe a Scientist

Light Sky, Dark Sky
Work with an adult. Stand in a brightly lit outdoor area at night. Look at the night sky. Then stand in a place that is dark. Look at the sky again. Can you see more or fewer stars than before? Can you see the Milky Way? How do city lights affect the number of stars you see?

Lights in the Night Sky

Have you ever been outdoors when the sun sets? At first, you do not see any stars. Then as the sun disappears below the horizon, a few bright stars appear. The apparent size of stars is very small. **Apparent** means the way something seems. Even though stars in the sky appear to be small, they are actually huge. Stars also have apparent brightness. Some stars appear to be brighter than others. A small star can appear brighter in the sky than a more distant galaxy. A **galaxy** is a huge system that includes gas, dust, billions of stars, and objects orbiting the stars.

Infer Why do you think stars in the night sky appear to be small when they are really large?

____

____

____

Galaxies

If the sky is very dark, you may see what looks like a faint band of light crossing the sky. This band of light is a galaxy known as the Milky Way. The **Milky Way** is a galaxy made up of gas, dust, and stars. Our solar system is part of the Milky Way. Our solar system includes the sun, Earth, planets, moons, and smaller objects such as asteroids and comets. The universe has more than a trillion galaxies. A few galaxies can be seen without a telescope, but most are so far away that they look like points of light.

Using telescopes, astronomers have learned that galaxies have different sizes and shapes. Irregular galaxies have no particular shape. Elliptical galaxies are oval shaped. About three-fourths of the galaxies that have been discovered are spiral galaxies. They have bright, bulging middles and thin arms that fan out from the center. The stars in the arms of the galaxy are circling the central bulge of the galaxy. They look like pinwheels. Our Milky Way is a spiral galaxy. However, because we are inside the Milky Way, it does not look like a spiral from our point of view.

Identify What is Earth's home galaxy?

____

____

Quest Connection

Think of what you know so far about the Milky Way Galaxy. Why is it important to make a poster of the Milky Way before you make your model of the solar system?

____

____

____

Literacy ▸ Toolbox

Use Text Features This image helps to illustrate part of the text. Underline the section of text that this image best helps the reader understand.

 LAFS.5.RI.1.3

Visual Literacy Connection

What is the structure of a spiral galaxy?

Spiral galaxies, such as the Milky Way, have a certain shape and are made of stars, gas, and dust. There are three main structures in a spiral galaxy: the bulge, disk, and spiral arms.

Bulge
The bulge is near the center of the galaxy. It is a round structure and is mostly made of old stars, gas, and dust.

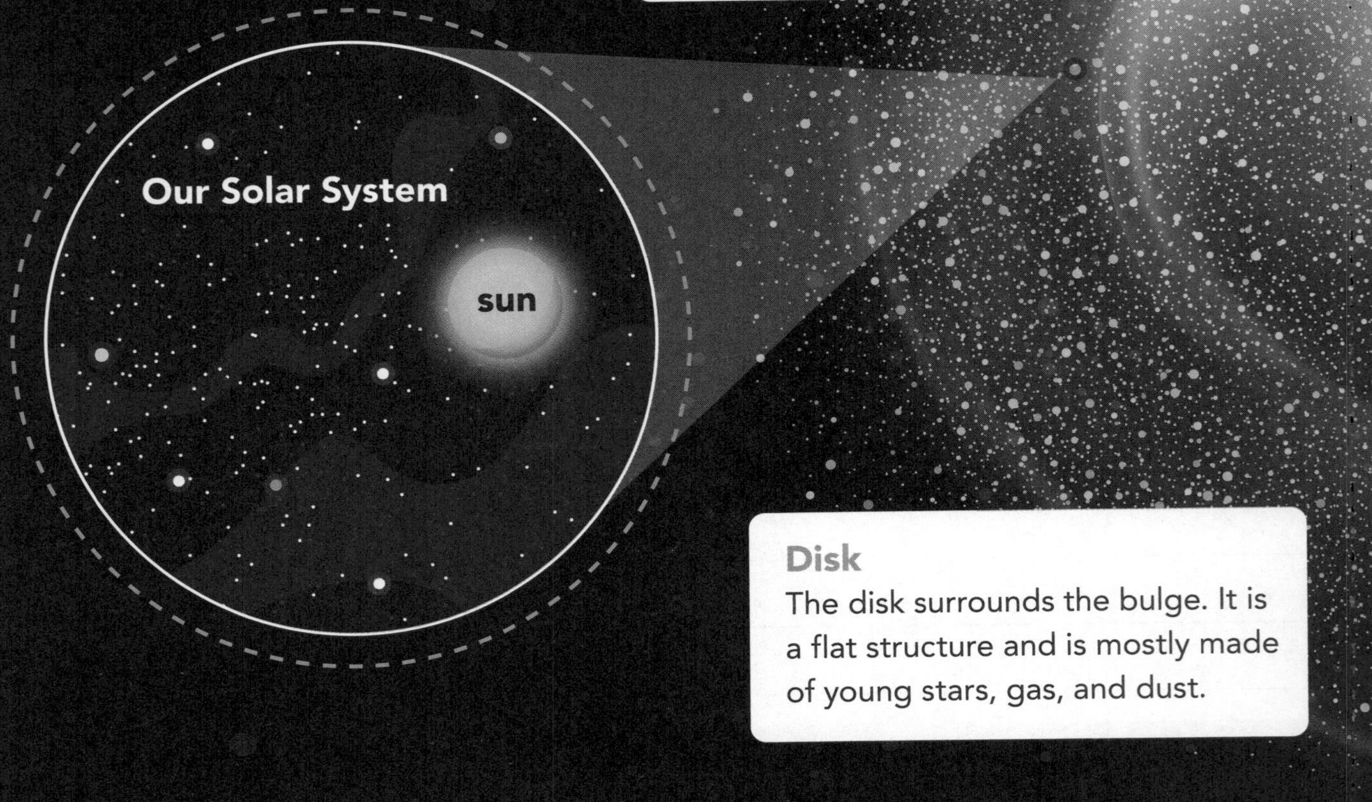

Our Solar System

sun

Disk
The disk surrounds the bulge. It is a flat structure and is mostly made of young stars, gas, and dust.

INTERACTIVITY

Complete an activity on the parts of a galaxy.

Spiral arms

The spiral arms begin at the bulge and curve around in the disk, which gives the galaxy a spiral shape. Spiral arms contain a lot of gas, dust, and some young stars.

Describe how you could make a 3-D model of a spiral galaxy.

____

____

____

____

____

____

Our Star

A **star** is a huge ball of very hot matter that gives off energy. The temperature inside our star, the sun, is extremely high, and the sun gives off large amounts of energy. The sun is an average-sized star compared to the many billions of other stars in the Milky Way. Many of the stars you see in the night sky are actually bigger and brighter than our sun! The sun appears bigger and brighter than other stars because it is much closer to Earth.

Our sun is only a very small part of the Milky Way Galaxy. Suppose the picture of a building represents the Milky Way. Draw an object next to it that could represent the sun on the same scale.

Lesson 1 Check

1. **Recognize** What are four different kinds of materials that make up a galaxy?

____

2. **Develop a Logical Argument** Max claims that the star, Sirius, is closer to Earth than the star Arcturus because it appears brighter in the sky. Use evidence to evaluate his claim.

____

____

____

Milky Way

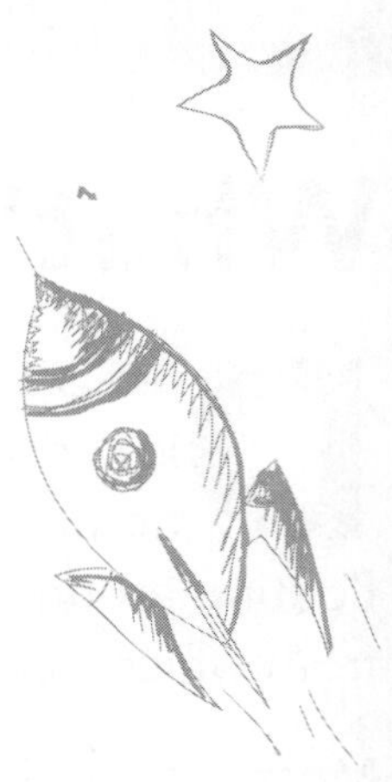

The first step in assembling your solar system model is to make a large poster of the Milky Way Galaxy. This can be the background for your solar system model.

1. Review the important parts of a galaxy.

____

____

2. **Recall** When you make your poster, what shape should the Milky Way Galaxy be?

____

____

3. Sketch your poster. Include all the parts you plan to show on your poster. Identify the locations where you will place labels and descriptions.

4. Make your poster of the Milky Way.

QUEST CHECK OFF

uEngineer It! Model STEM

SC.5.E.5.1, SC.5.N.2.1

VIDEO

Watch a video about observatory telescopes.

What's with the dust?

Dust is everywhere—even in outer space. The dust in outer space is known as cosmic dust. But cosmic dust is not like dust in your home. Cosmic dust consists of tiny particles of solid materials floating around in the space between stars. It is the material from which new stars and planets are formed.

Most cosmic dust absorbs and scatters visible light. The light is sent out again in a form of light we cannot see—mostly infrared radiation. Because the visible light is scattered, scientists had difficulty seeing into the far parts of the universe. Now they use instruments that detect the infrared light that we cannot see. Now scientists can look deep into space to learn more about many formerly unknown parts of the universe.

Model It

littleBits CHALLENGE

The technicians at a local laboratory have asked for your help. Astronomers have discovered a new object in space. They want to know whether the dust on Earth is similar to the cosmic dust in the object they have discovered. They would like you to develop a procedure for collecting dust on Earth to model how dust could be collected in space.

1. Brainstorm how many samples you will collect and where you will collect them. Record the information in the table.

2. What equipment will you use to collect the dust? Record the information in the table.

3. What procedure will you follow to collect the dust?

Samples I will collect:	Materials I will need:	Procedure I will follow:

4. **Distinguish** What are the differences between the contents of dust on a classroom floor and cosmic dust?

Lesson 2

Inner Solar System

I can...

Describe the inner planets of Mercury, Venus, Earth, and Mars.
Identify common characteristics of the inner planets.
Recognize the position of Earth within the solar system.

Literacy Skill
Use Text Features

Vocabulary
solar system
inner planets
orbit
moon

SC.5.E.5.2 Recognize the major common characteristics of all planets and compare/contrast the properties of inner and outer planets. **SC.5.E.5.3** Distinguish among the following objects of the Solar System—Sun, planets, moons, asteroids, comets—and identify Earth's position in it. (Also **SC.5.N.1.1**)

VIDEO

Watch a video about the inner planets of the solar system.

SPORTS Connection

The game of tetherball is a common playground game. To play the game, you tie a string to one end of a pole. Tie a ball to the other end of the string. Hold the ball and throw it. The ball will eventually move around the pole in a circle.

Tetherball is similar to a planet traveling around the sun. But with our solar system, a string does not hold the planets in their path. Gravity is the force that pulls the planet toward the sun. A planet is moving with great speed, which prevents gravity from pulling it into the sun. What would happen if the string in tetherball broke? The ball would go flying away. If the sun suddenly lost its gravitational pull on Earth, we would similarly go flying away into space!

Compare and Contrast How is the pull of the string in tetherball similar to the effect of gravity?

___

___

___

uInvestigate Lab

SC.5.E.5.3, SC.5.N.1.1

How does a planet's distance from the sun affect its path?

Like a tetherball that circles a pole, planets travel in a path around our sun. How does the distance from the sun affect the length of a planet's path?

Suggested Materials

- string
- pencil
- scissors
- tape
- stopwatch
- colored paper

Be careful using scissors.

Procedure

☐ **1.** Plan a model to show how a planet's distance from the sun affects its path. Choose materials for your model.

☐ **2.** Show your plan to your teacher before you begin. Record your observations.

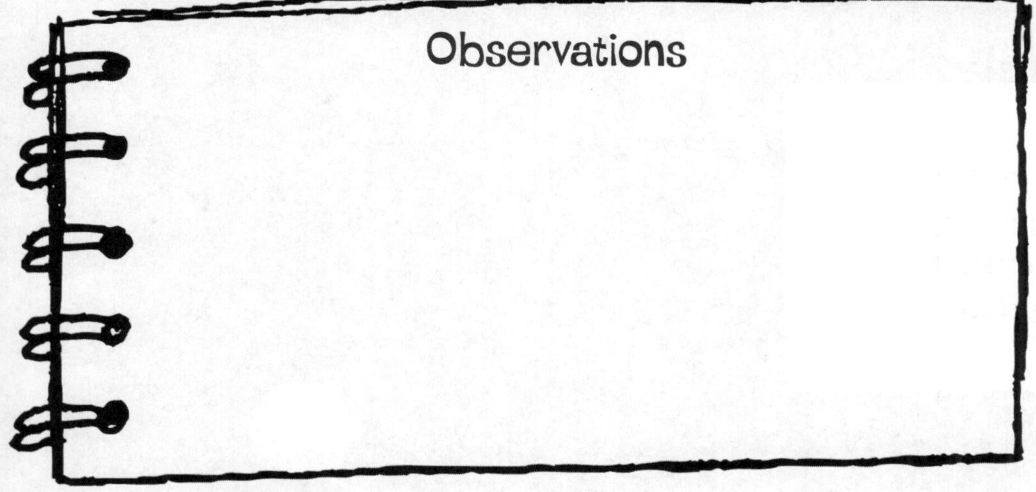

Science Practice

Scientists **use models** to support arguments.

Analyze and Interpret Data

3. Draw Conclusions How does distance from the sun affect the length of a planet's path around the sun?

____

4. Cite Evidence What evidence do you have from your investigation to support your answer?

____

____

Visual Literacy Connection

What is in our solar system?

Our **solar system** is a system of eight planets and the sun, along with moons, asteroids, and comets. Four of the eight planets are inner planets. Mercury, Venus, Earth, and Mars are called **inner planets** because they are closest to the sun.

Mars

- known as the red planet
- thin atmosphere
- iron-rich materials that form rust on the surface
- two moons

Venus

- hottest planet in the solar system
- thick, toxic atmosphere that traps heat
- surface covered with volcanoes and canyons
- no moon

INTERACTIVITY

Complete an activity on the inner solar system.

A planet is a large body of matter that travels around the sun.

Summarize what you have learned about the four inner planets.

____

____

____

____

____

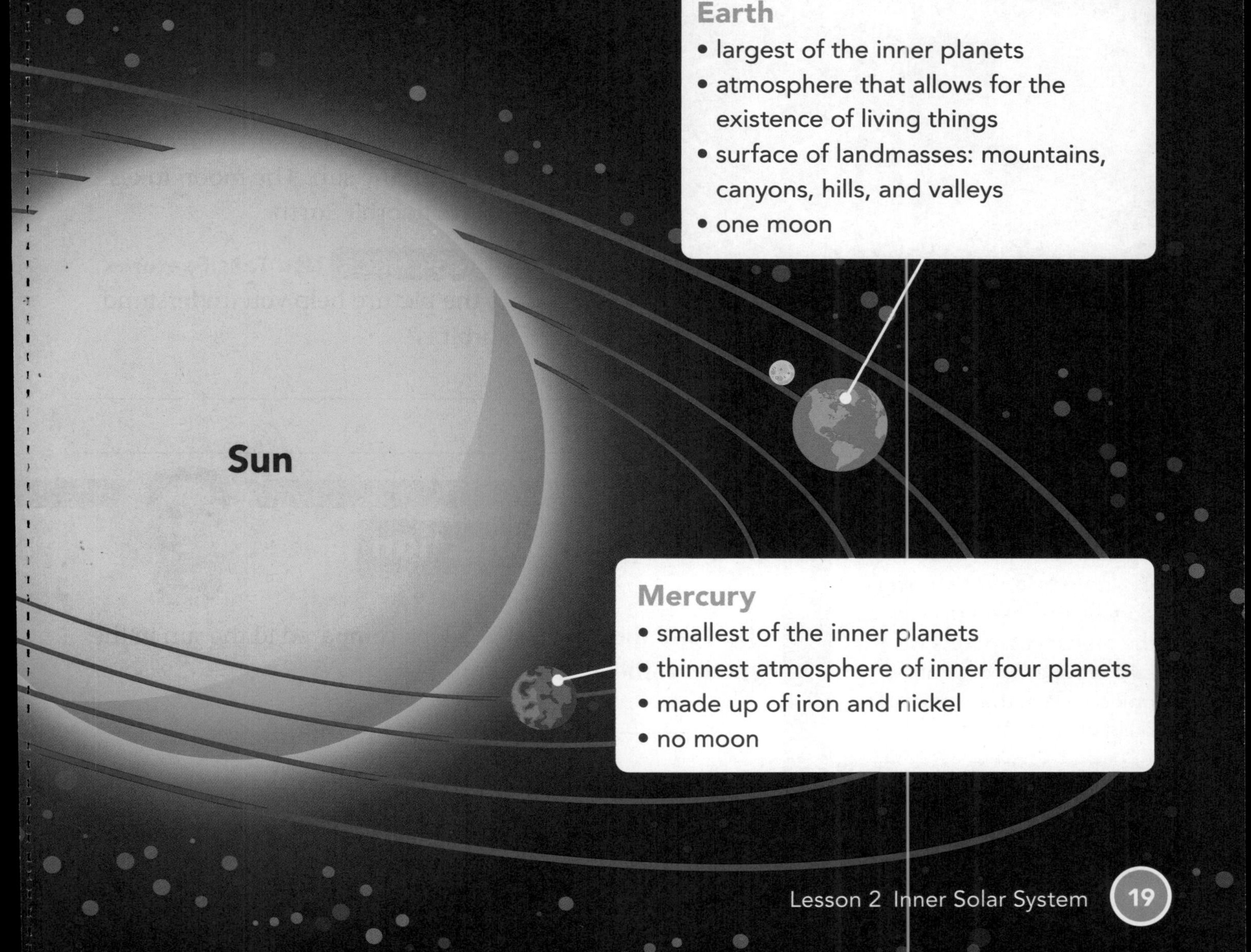

Earth

- largest of the inner planets
- atmosphere that allows for the existence of living things
- surface of landmasses: mountains, canyons, hills, and valleys
- one moon

Sun

Mercury

- smallest of the inner planets
- thinnest atmosphere of inner four planets
- made up of iron and nickel
- no moon

Question It!

Astronomers recently discovered a planet called Proxima b. This planet is orbiting the small star, Proxima Centauri. Astronomers predict that this planet might have similar qualities to Earth that could one day make it livable. If you could ask an astronomer two questions about this planet, what would you ask?

____

____

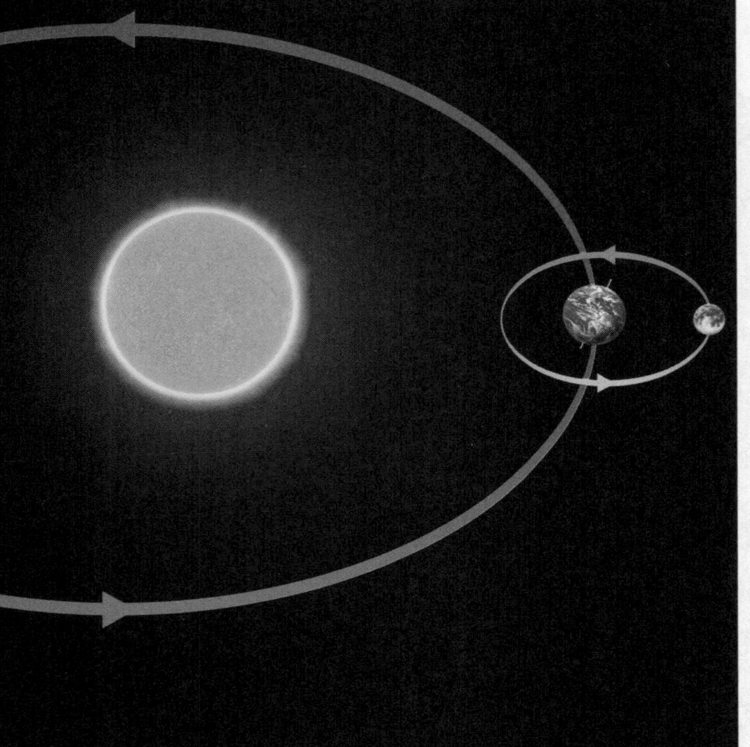

Planetary Orbit

The curved path of an object around a star, a planet, or a moon is called an **orbit**. Planets orbit the sun, and moons orbit planets. The amount of time each planet takes to orbit the sun is different because each planet is a different distance from the sun. The farther a planet is from the sun, the longer its orbit will be. Earth takes about 365 days to orbit the sun. The moon takes about 27 days to orbit Earth.

READING CHECK Use Text Features How does the picture help you understand what an orbit is?

____

____

Engineering Practice ▸ Toolbox

Evaluate Information Why do scientists need to know the orbits that rockets will take around Earth or other objects when the scientists are building them?

Quest Connection

How will the inner planets look compared to the sun in the model of the solar system?

____

____

Moons

A **moon** is a satellite made of rock and ice that orbits a planet. Two inner planets, Earth and Mars, have moons. Earth's moon has a very important impact on Earth. The moon's gravitational pull helps to stabilize Earth's wobbling motion as it rotates around its axis. The entire solar system relies on gravity, a force of attraction, to keep planets, moons, and other objects in orbit.

Write About It You are a new astronomer shadowing an experienced astronomer who is your mentor for the next week. You already know quite a lot about planet Earth, but you are interested in learning about the three other inner planets. In your science notebook, list five questions regarding the inner planets that you want to ask your mentor.

uBe a Scientist

Satellites in the Sky

The moon is a natural satellite that you can observe. You can also observe human-made satellites. Research when you will be able to see the International Space Station above Earth. Then on a clear night, go outside with an adult to find the space station.

Lesson 2 Check

SC.5.E.5.2

1. **Compare** What are two differences between Earth and Mars?

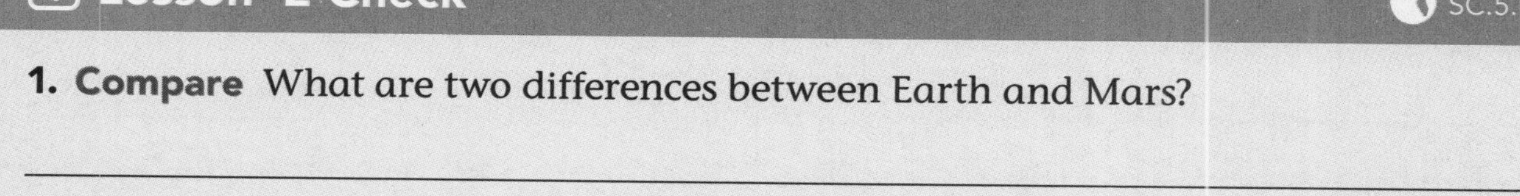

2. **Construct** Draw a model of an imaginary solar system that contains a star and three planets: Planet A (year = 300 days), Planet B (year = 100 days), and Planet C (year = 1,000 days).

Quest Check-In Lab

What's inside the solar system?

You are on a Quest to rebuild a model of the solar system for your school's lobby. In this activity, you will make models of the four inner planets.

Suggested Materials

- modeling clay
- clothespins
- string
- balls of various sizes

Science Practice

Scientists develop and use models to support arguments.

Procedure

☐ **1.** How will you determine how big to make each model planet?

____

____

____

☐ **2.** Using your knowledge of the four inner planets, sketch what each planet in your model will look like.

☐ **3.** Use the materials to make a model of the four inner planets. Also include Earth's moon.

☐ **4.** Show your models to your teacher. Then arrange the models with the backdrop you have completed in the Quest so far.

Analyze and Interpret Data

5. Draw Conclusions How does your model compare to the actual order and sizes of the inner planets?

____

____

____

____

____

____

____

6. Use Models Explain how your model shows planetary orbit. If it does not, how could you improve your model to show orbits?

____

____

____

____

____

____

Lesson 3

Outer Solar System

I can...

Describe the outer planets of Jupiter, Saturn, Uranus, and Neptune.
Identify common characteristics of the outer planets.
Recognize that there are moons, asteroids, and comets in our solar system.

Literacy Skill
Use Text Features

Vocabulary
outer planet
asteroid
comet

Academic Vocabulary
characteristics

VIDEO

Watch a video about the outer planets of the solar system.

SC.5.E.5.2 Recognize the major common characteristics of all planets and compare/contrast the properties of inner and outer planets. **SC.5.E.5.3** Distinguish among the following objects of the Solar System—Sun, planets, moons, asteroids, comets—and identify Earth's position in it. (Also **SC.5.N.1.1, MAFS.5.NBT.2.6**)

CURRICULUM Connection

All of the planets, except Earth, were named after Roman gods and goddesses. Jupiter and Saturn were given their names thousands of years ago. The ancient Romans could see them in the sky without a telescope. The other planets in our solar system were not discovered until telescopes were invented. Even then, the tradition of naming the planets after Roman gods and goddesses continued. Most of the moons are also named after the creatures, gods, and goddesses in Roman mythology.

Explain How did the planets get their names?

____

____

uInvestigate Lab

HANDS-ON LAB

SC.5.E.5.3, SC.5.N.1.1

How *hard* do space objects *hit* earth?

Scientists conduct research on space objects to determine the impact they have on Earth. What kind of impact do space objects have on Earth?

Materials
- blocks of various sizes and weights
- newspaper, various sizes, bunched up
- meterstick

Procedure

☐ **1.** Make a plan to model the impact of differently sized space objects when they hit Earth's surface.

☐ **2.** Show your plan to your teacher before you begin. Record your observations.

Science Practice
Scientists **use models** to support arguments.

Analyze and Interpret Data

3. Draw Conclusions Use your data collected to explain the relationship between a space object and its impact on Earth's surface.

____

____

____

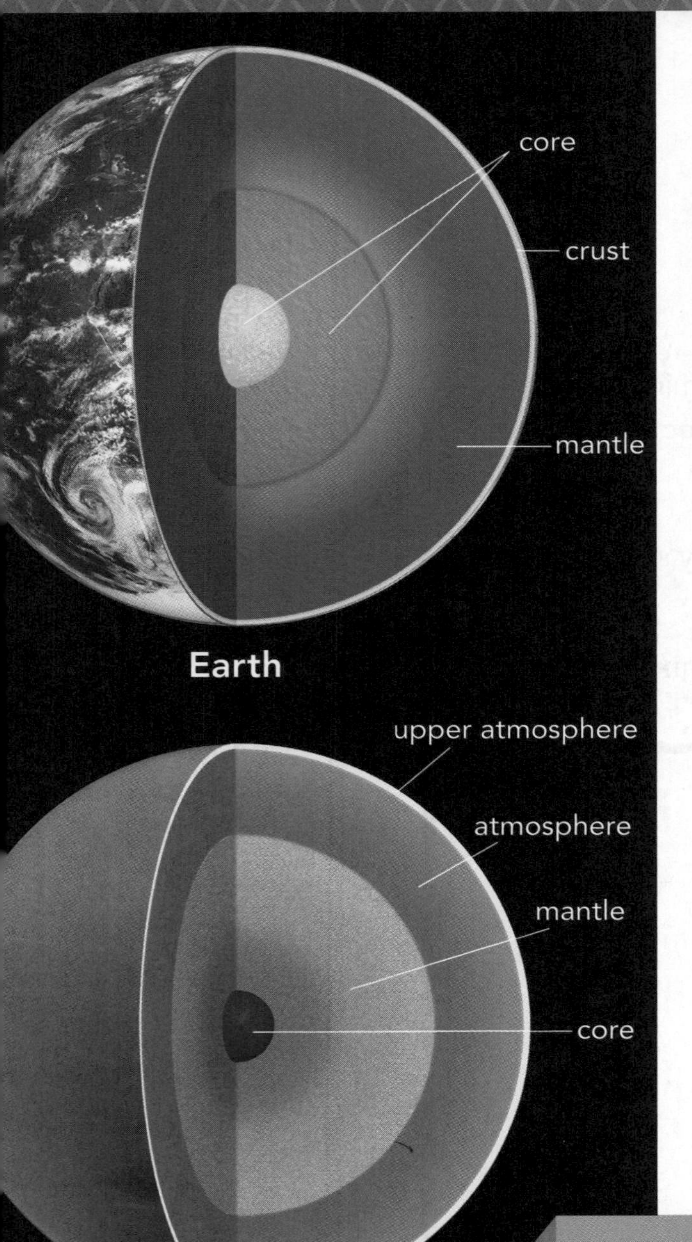

Earth

Neptune

Gas Giants

Beyond Mars are four more planets in our solar system—Jupiter, Saturn, Uranus, and Neptune. These four planets are called **outer planets** because they are farther from the sun than the inner planets. They are also significantly larger than the inner planets. You may recall that the inner planets have rocky, Earth-like surfaces. Some inner layers of the inner planets are solid. The outer planets do not have clearly defined surfaces. We see only the atmospheres of the outer planets. These thick atmospheres are made of gas. This is why the outer planets are often referred to as the gas giants. However, they also have large, liquid inner layers and solid cores. Each outer planet has rings of particles and many moons orbiting it.

Use Text Features These diagrams reveal the interior of Neptune, an outer planet, and the interior of Earth, an inner planet. How is the outer layer of Earth different from the outer layer of Neptune?

____

____

Quest Connection

Brainstorm what you might need to include in a model of the solar system. How would the outer planets compare to other objects in your model?

____

____

____

Jupiter: Gas Giant with Many Moons

Jupiter, a gas giant, is the fifth planet from the sun and the largest planet in the solar system. Jupiter's atmosphere is made up of hydrogen and helium, and it shows many bands of color. Jupiter is a large planet, but it has a low density, which means that its mass is not packed tightly together. The planet rotates much faster than Earth. In the time that Earth takes to complete one rotation, Jupiter completes more than two rotations. Jupiter also has many moons. In 1610, a scientist named Galileo was the first person to see the four largest moons of Jupiter. He saw them through his telescope.

Classify How is Jupiter's rotation different from Earth's rotation?

____

____

____

Saturn: A Planet with "Handles"

The sixth planet from the sun is Saturn. Jupiter and Saturn are very similar. Saturn is also a very large planet with a low density. Just like Jupiter, Saturn has an atmosphere that contains mostly hydrogen and helium. When Galileo looked at Saturn through his telescope, he saw what looked like a planet with handles. The "handles" are brilliant rings that orbit Saturn. The particles making up the rings are made up of ice, dust, and rock. They vary in size from tiny grains to boulders. The inner rings of Saturn revolve faster around the planet than the outer rings.

Relate What are two similarities and two differences between Saturn and Jupiter?

____

____

____

____

Science Practice ▸Toolbox

Engage in Argument from Evidence Each of the outer planets has many moons orbiting it. So far, scientists have found that Jupiter has 67 moons, Saturn has 62 moons, Uranus has 27 moons, and Neptune has 14 moons. Why do you think the outer planets have so many moons?

Visual Literacy Connection

How are the outer planets aligned?

The planets in the outer solar system are much larger than planets in the inner solar system. The outer planets also have different characteristics, or qualities, from the inner planets.

Neptune
- most distant from the sun
- coldest planet in the solar system
- 14 moons

Uranus
- orbits the sun on its side
- first planet discovered with use of a telescope
- 27 moons

Saturn
- known for its many rings
- atmosphere made up of hydrogen and helium
- 62 moons

INTERACTIVITY

Complete an activity on the outer solar system.

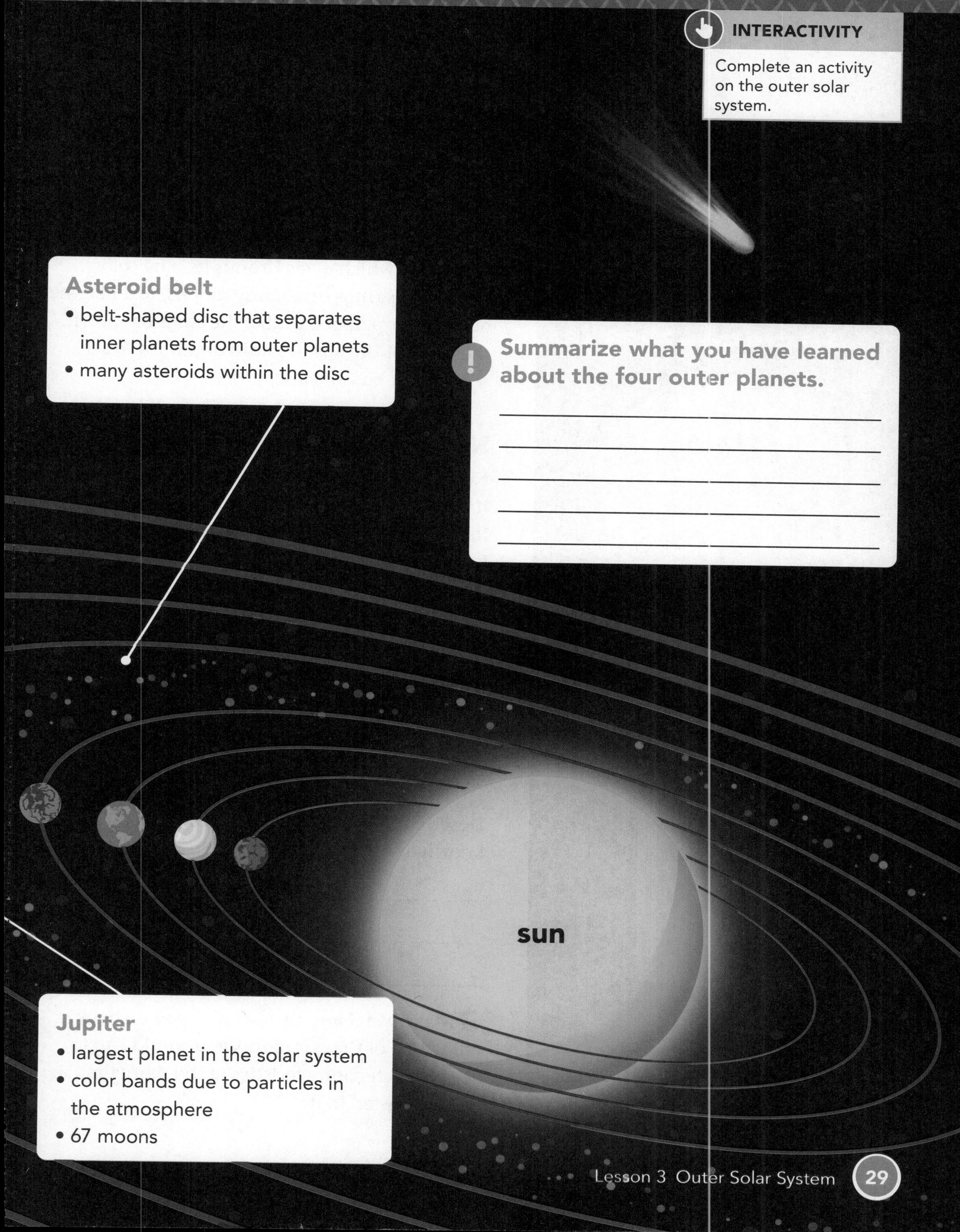

Asteroid belt
- belt-shaped disc that separates inner planets from outer planets
- many asteroids within the disc

Summarize what you have learned about the four outer planets.

____

____

____

____

____

sun

Jupiter
- largest planet in the solar system
- color bands due to particles in the atmosphere
- 67 moons

uBe a Scientist

Scale and Proportion

Find an object to represent Earth. If you were to model all the planets together, what objects would you use for the outer planets? Would your choice always be the same?

Uranus

Uranus is the seventh planet from the sun and the most distant planet visible without a telescope. Uranus's atmosphere contains hydrogen, helium, and methane. The planet is so cold that the methane in the atmosphere can freeze. Methane absorbs red light and reflects blue light, which gives Uranus its blue color. Uranus has rings and many moons, just like the other outer planets. Unlike the rings of Saturn, the rings of Uranus are dark and hard to see with Earth-based telescopes.

Neptune

Neptune is the farthest planet from the sun. It is too far away to see without a telescope. It takes more than one hundred Earth years for Neptune to orbit the sun. Neptune is the smallest of the outer planets. Even so, if Neptune were hollow, it could hold about 60 Earths. Neptune's atmosphere is like that of Uranus. Like Uranus, Neptune has a bluish color because of the methane in its atmosphere. Neptune also has bands of color like those of Jupiter. Of its 13 moons, the largest one is Triton.

Describe Why are the four outer planets also known as gas giants?

___

___

___

Make Meaning In your science notebook, tell which of the gas giants you would like to visit. Which characteristics of the planet make you interested in it?

Comets and Asteroids

Asteroids and comets are fragments left over from the giant cloud of gas and dust that formed the solar system more than 4.5 billion years ago. **Asteroids** are chunks of rock that measure in size from a meter to several kilometers in diameter. They orbit the sun. Objects smaller than asteroids are called meteoroids. Scientists have found more than 1,000,000 asteroids that lie in the asteroid belt between Mars and Jupiter. **Comets** are chunks of ice and dust or rock that have stretched-out orbits around the sun. As comets heat up, gas and dust are released and trail behind them. The sun illuminates the trail of gas and dust, which is why some comets are visible in the night sky.

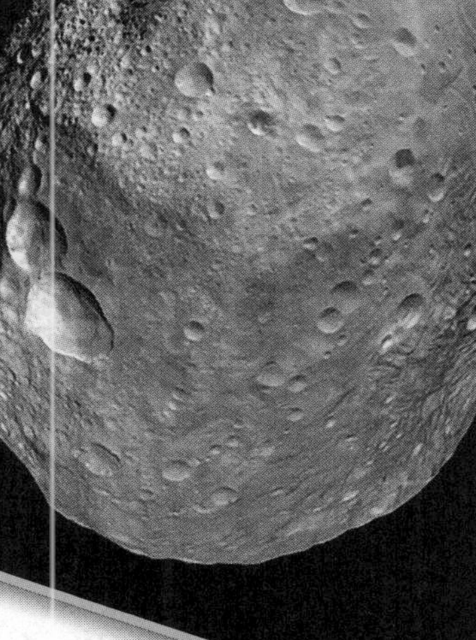

Infer Sometimes, comets have trails. Other times, they do not. What might cause a comet's trail to appear and disappear?

____

____

____

Lesson 3 Check

1. **Differentiate** Moons and comets travel through space and can be made of rock and ice. Evaluate how moons and comets are different.

____

2. **Compare** Choose two outer solar system planets. Compare the characteristics of each planet.

____

____

____

Quest Check-In Lab

HANDS-ON LAB

SC.5.E.5.2, SC.5.E.5.3

What planets are way out there?

As you have discovered in this lesson, the outer solar system contains four gas giants. In this lab, you will make a model of the outer planets. As you build your model, ask yourself this: How will my new model work with my model of the inner planets?

Suggested Materials

- modeling clay
- clothespins
- poster board
- coloring supplies
- balls of various sizes
- string
- tape
- ruler

Procedure

☐ **1.** How will you determine how big to make each of your model planets?

☐ **2.** Using your knowledge of the four outer planets, sketch what each planet in your model will look like.

☐ **3.** Use the materials to make a model that includes all four of the outer planets. Your model should also display the asteroid belt.

☐ **4.** Show your model to your teacher and arrange the model with the backdrop you have completed in the Quest so far.

Science Practice

Scientists **use models** to support their ideas.

Jupiter
Saturn
Uranus
Neptune

Analyze and Interpret Data

5. Compare and Contrast How does your model compare to the actual order and size of the outer planets?

6. Reflect What challenges did you encounter when planning and building your model?

MAFS.5.NBT.2.6

How many Earths can line up across the sun?

The size of the sun is much greater than that of the planets and Earth's moon. In this activity, you will calculate how many Earths you can line up straight across the diameter of the sun. Think about what tools will assist you in this activity.

Sun	diameter = 1,400,000 kilometers
Earth	diameter = 12,800 kilometers

Evaluate Your Model

1. **Predict** Make a prediction about how many Earths would be needed to line up straight across the diameter of the sun.

____

____

2. **Evaluate** Using the data in the table, divide the diameter of the sun by the diameter of Earth to calculate the number of Earths that can line up across the sun. Show your work in your science notebook.

3. Round your number to the nearest whole number.

____

4. **Evaluate** Earth is the largest of the four inner planets. Mars, another inner planet, has a diameter of 6,800 kilometers. Calculate how many Mars planets you could line up straight across Earth. Round to the nearest whole number.

____

____

5. **Reflect** Why is it not necessary for your numbers to be exact when doing your calculations?

____

____

Quest Findings

INTERACTIVITY

Organize data to support your Quest Findings.

Keeping the Planets in Order

How can you model your own solar system?

Meeting the Challenge

It is time to get the model ready for your school's lobby! Put the finishing touches on your model and the supporting backdrop. Write an information sheet that lists important characteristics of each planet. Compare and contrast the properties of the inner and outer planets. Describe whether your model is to scale. If you were not able to model the planets to scale with the materials you used, explain why.

Construct Explanations

Synthesize Another school is making a model of the solar system, and they left out the sun! Write a short letter to the students in charge of the solar system model at the other school explaining why they must include the sun in their model.

____

____

____

____

____

____

____

QUEST CHECK OFF

Career Connection

Astronomical Technicians

Astronomical technicians play a vital role in helping scientists perform successful research projects. They give astronomers the technical support that they need, from setting up telescopes in observatories to recording readings on instruments used to study space. Many of the technicians work in research laboratories, planetariums, observatories, or colleges and universities.

For those technicians that work at a college or university, they spend their days showing engineering, astronomy, and physical science students how astronomy instruments are used in laboratories, planetariums, and observatories. Technicians are also responsible for staying up-to-date on any changes, additions, or modifications to equipment, such as telescopes and refractors. These technicians are a great help to astronomers!

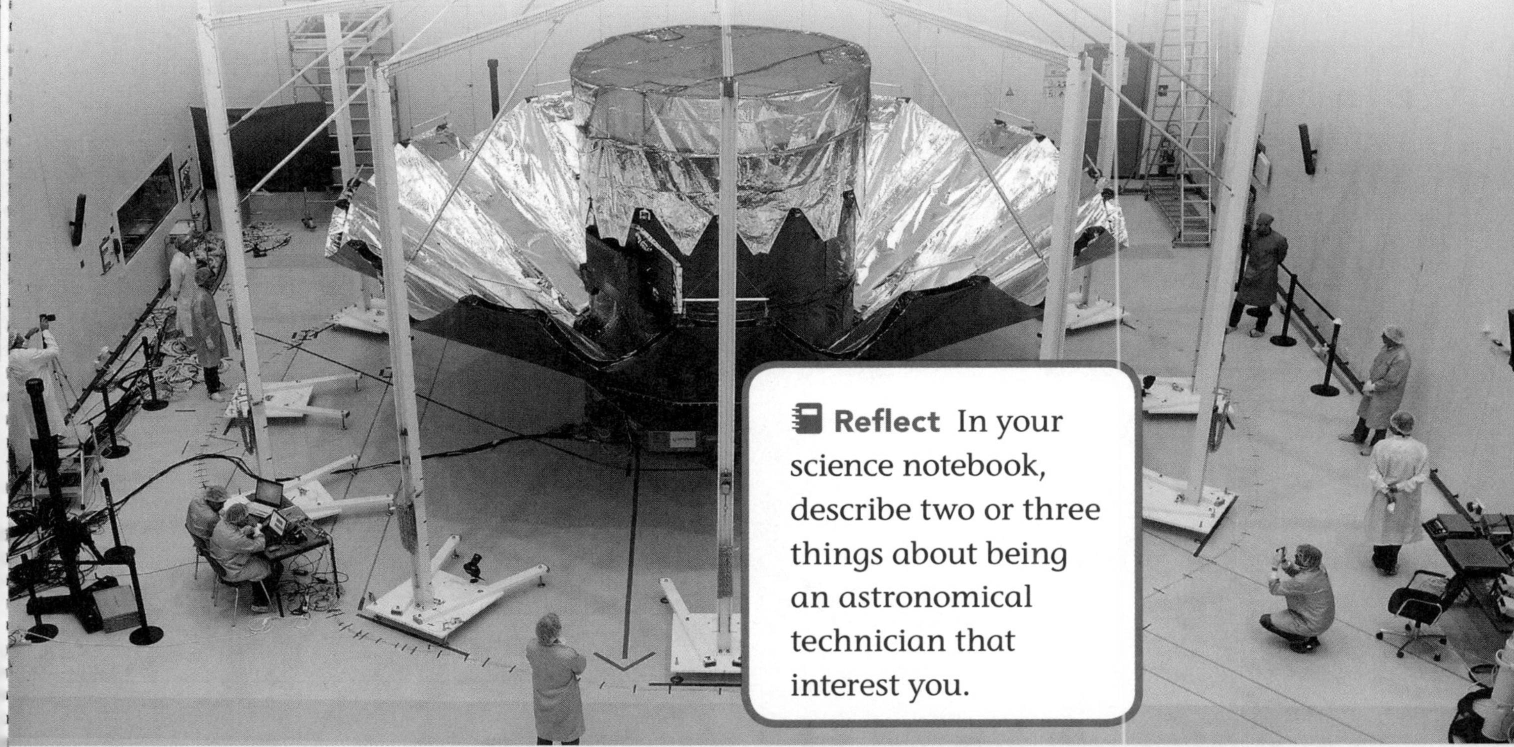

Reflect In your science notebook, describe two or three things about being an astronomical technician that interest you.

Assessment

Read each question and choose or write the best answer.

1. **Patterns** Scientists look for patterns to identify cause and effect relationships. For each characteristic of solar system objects, identify a related pattern.

Characteristic of solar system objects	Patterns that explains cause and effect
brightness	Example: Objects that are closer appear brighter.
year length	
size	
number of objects in orbit	
motion	

2. **Identify** Which planet is farthest from the sun?

   A. Neptune

   B. Venus

   C. Jupiter

   D. Mars

3. **Predict** Suppose a scientist identifies a rocky planet with a thin atmosphere in a different solar system. Based on the characteristics of planets in our solar system, what might the scientist predict?

   A. Like Neptune, the planet has a layer of methane gas.

   B. The planet is likely to have many moons.

   C. The planet is close to its sun the way Mercury is close to the sun in our solar system.

   D. A year on the planet is likely to be many times longer than a year on Earth.

4. **Summarize** What is a moon? How does Earth's moon affect our planet?

5. **Use Evidence** What evidence from the photo helps you conclude that the object is a comet and not a star?

A. Comets give off light energy, stars do not.

B. There is a streak of matter trailing behind the object. When comets heat up they release a trail of gas and dust.

C. The object is too large to be a star, so it must be a comet.

D. Stars are not as bright as the object shown in the photo.

6. **Infer** The sun is the smallest of all stars listed in the table. It also releases the least amount of energy. Why does the sun appear to be the brightest star in the sky?

Apparent Brightness of Stars

Name of star	Distance from Earth (light years)	Apparent brightness (rank; 1 = brightest, 4 = dimmest)
Sun	0	1
Hadar	320	2
Acrux	510	3
Adhara	570	4

The Essential Question *What is Earth's place in space?*

Show What You Learned

Earth is one of eight planets in our solar system. There are four inner planets and four outer planets. What makes Earth an inner solar system planet?

Science Practice Assessment

Read the scenario and answer questions 1–3.

Scientists use models to represent what they observe in nature.

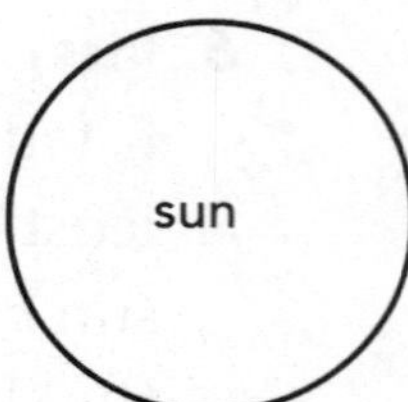

1 **Critique** This diagram model of our solar system has many constraints. Which feature is NOT a constraint of the model?

Ⓐ the relative size of the planets

Ⓑ the distances between space objects

Ⓒ the different types of objects that orbit the sun

Ⓓ the representation of planetary motion

2 **Create** Suppose you wanted to add moons to the model. How would you represent the moons of our solar system as accurately as possible?

Ⓕ I would place dots to represent moons only on the inner planets.

Ⓖ I would use large circles to represent moons and place an equal number of moons around each planet.

Ⓗ I would use large circles to represent moons and place them around the sun.

Ⓘ I would place dots around each planet to represent moons, using more dots around outer planets than inner planets.

3 **Construct** What labels could you add to the model to describe the composition of the different space objects shown?

Ⓐ Label each circle in the diagram with "made of rock and gases."

Ⓑ Label the sun with "very hot matter," the inner planets with "mostly rock," and the outer planets with "mostly gas with solid cores."

Ⓒ Label the sun with "mostly gases" and the planets as "mostly rock."

Ⓓ Label the sun and outer planets with "mostly gases," and the inner planets with "mostly rock."

Read the scenario and answer questions 4–5.

Sandeep is using a Venn diagram to compare and contrast comets and asteroids.

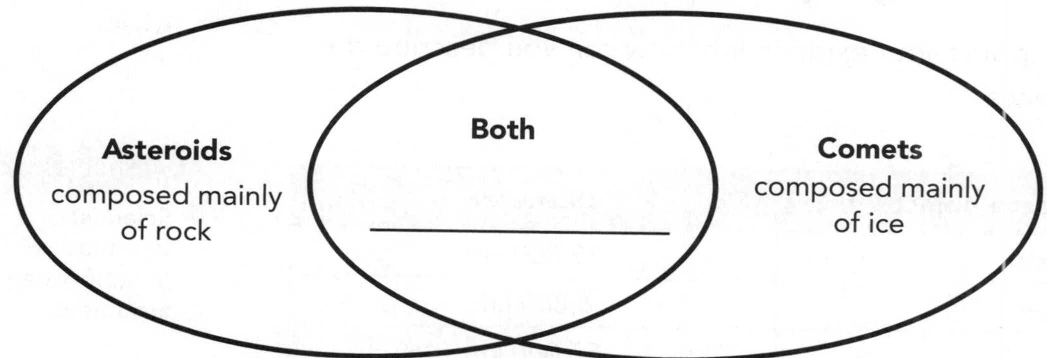

4 **Compare** What information should Sandeep include in the middle section of the Venn diagram?

Ⓕ as large as the moon

Ⓖ in orbit around the sun

Ⓗ found between Mars and Jupiter

Ⓘ traveling at the speed of light

5 **Draw Conclusions** Suppose Sandeep wanted to make another Venn diagram. Which pair of space objects would have many characteristics listed in the "Both" section of the diagram?

Ⓐ Venus and Neptune

Ⓑ sun and galaxy

Ⓒ Mars and Mercury

Ⓓ moon and asteroid

uDemonstrate Lab

How can you compare the sizes of objects in space?

Using a model to support your explanation, how can you describe the size of objects in space?

Materials
- classroom objects
- blocks
- balls

Science Practice
Scientists **use models** to support an argument.

Name of space object	Diameter
Earth	12,800 km
Mars	6,800 km
Uranus	57,000 km
Neptune	49,500 km
Earth's moon	3,500 km
Callisto (Jupiter's moon)	4800 km
Titan (Saturn's moon)	5200 km

Procedure

☐ **1.** Select a planet, a moon, and another object from the list. Circle your choices.

☐ **2.** Use the chart to help you make models of the objects you chose. How will this chart help you in your models?

☐ **3.** Develop your model. Write the steps you need to take to make your model accurate and useful.

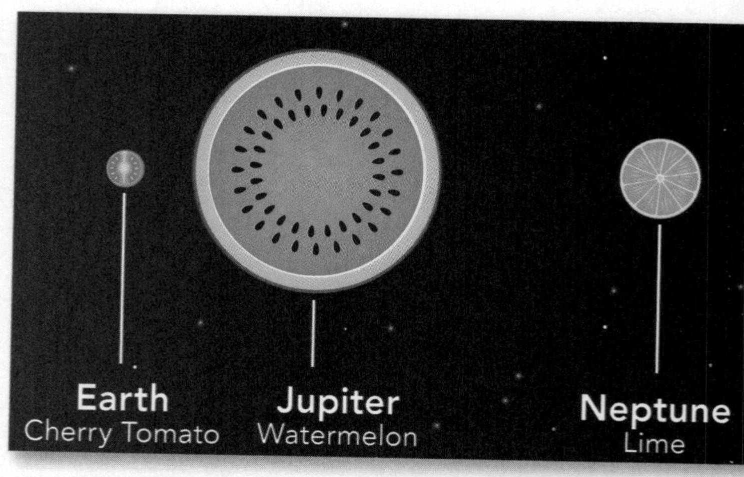

SC.5.E.5.3, SC.5.N.1.1

Step 1	Step 2	Step 3	Step 4	Step 5

☐ 4. With your teacher's permission, use your procedure and the materials to make your model.

Analyze and Interpret Data

5. **Explain** How did you decide what objects to use for your model? How were you able to correctly model the space objects?

____

____

____

____

6. **Evaluate** Why are some objects in space so much larger than others?

____

____

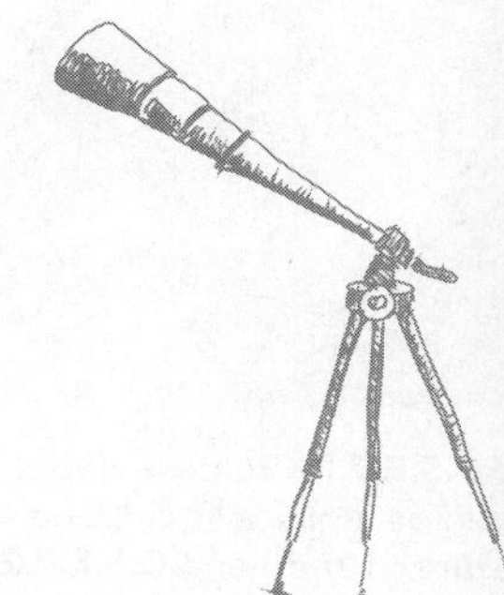

7. **Reflect** Suppose you are teaching your model to second graders. What would you tell them about the sizes of objects in space compared to the size of Earth?

____

____

____

Topic 2

Earth's Water

Lesson 1 Water Cycle
Lesson 2 Earth's Freshwater
Lesson 3 Earth's Ocean

SC.5.E.7.1 Create a model to explain the parts of the water cycle. Water can be a gas, a liquid, or a solid, and can go back and forth from one state to another. **SC.5.E.7.2** Recognize that the ocean is an integral part of the water cycle and is connected to all of Earth's water reservoirs via evaporation and precipitation processes. (Also **SC.5.N.1.1, MAFS.5.NBT.2, LAFS.5.RI.1.1**).

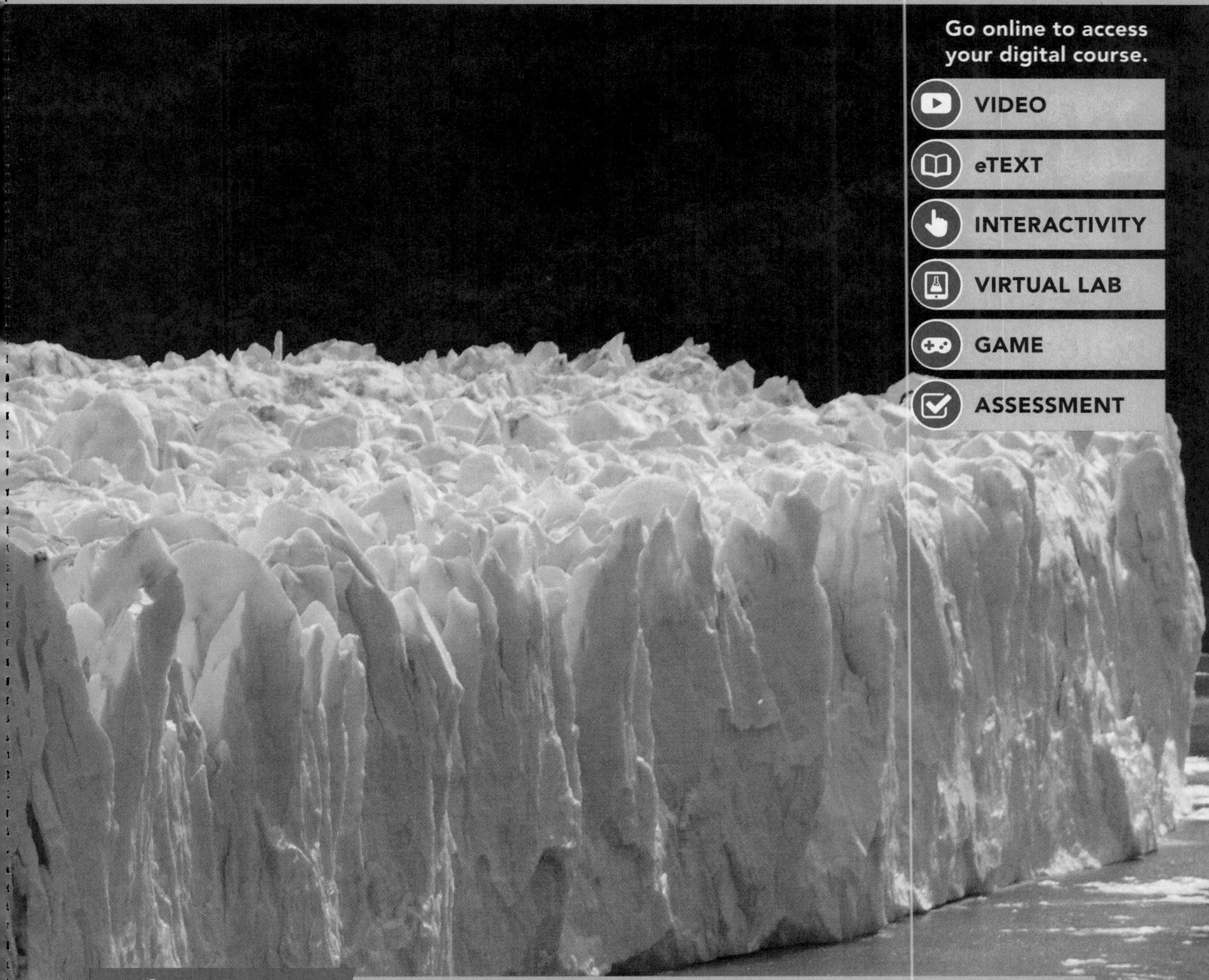

Go online to access your digital course.

- VIDEO
- eTEXT
- INTERACTIVITY
- VIRTUAL LAB
- GAME
- ASSESSMENT

The Essential Question

How much water can be found in different places on Earth?

Show What You Know

This ice is slowly melting. A piece breaks off and falls into the ocean. If many more of these very large chunks of ice melt, how might this change where water is found on Earth?

____

____

____

Quest Kickoff

Water, Water Everywhere!

How can you make undrinkable water drinkable?

Hello! I am Chris Walker, a water quality specialist. I have been hired to help several towns that do not have fresh drinking water. I would like your help with this task. In this problem-based learning activity, you will develop solutions to make unsafe water safe for the people who live in these towns.

Like a water quality specialist, you will develop technology to make unsafe water drinkable. You will evaluate the challenges of getting drinking water from different sources.

Follow this path to learn how you will complete the Quest. The Quest activities will help you complete the Quest successfully. Check off your progress on the path when you complete an activity with a QUEST CHECK OFF. Go online for more Quest activities.

Quest Check-In 1

Lesson 1

Learn how rainfall moves over land and enters the ground.

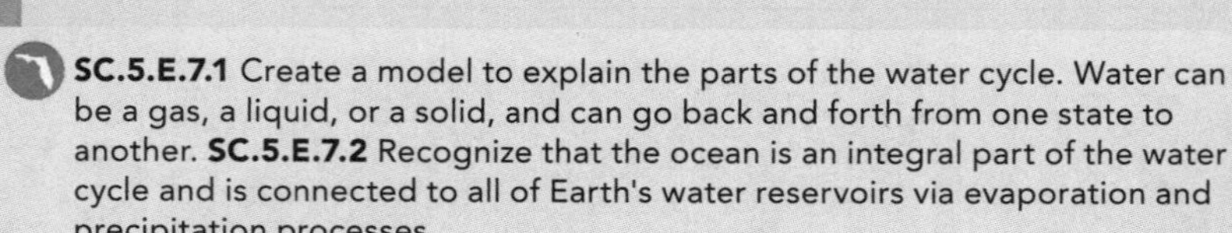

SC.5.E.7.1 Create a model to explain the parts of the water cycle. Water can be a gas, a liquid, or a solid, and can go back and forth from one state to another. **SC.5.E.7.2** Recognize that the ocean is an integral part of the water cycle and is connected to all of Earth's water reservoirs via evaporation and precipitation processes.

VIDEO
Watch a video about a water quality specialist.
Quest Check-In Lab 3
Lesson 3
Learn ways to turn salty ocean water into fresh, drinkable water.
Quest Check-In 2
Lesson 2
Apply what you learn about freshwater sources as you find ways to make water drinkable.
Quest Findings
Use what you know to help a community access fresh water, either filtering a polluted source or building a factory that removes salt from saltwater.

STEM uConnect Lab

HANDS-ON LAB

SC.5.E.7.1, SC.5.N.1.1

Where does water flow... and how fast?

Water quality specialists often must determine how quickly water moves from a reservoir to the user. How can you make water move faster?

Materials

- safety goggles
- apron
- funnel, wide stem
- bucket
- PVC pipe
- stopwatch
- graduated cylinder
- protractor

Wear safety goggles.

Wear safety apron.

Engineering Practice

Engineers **measure quantities** such as volume to answer questions.

Design a Solution

☐ **1.** Predict how the height from which water flows affects its speed.

___

___

☐ **2.** Make a plan to build a device to test your prediction on a measured amount of water. Show your plan to your teacher before you begin.

☐ **3.** Build your device and test your prediction. Record your results.

Analyze and Interpret Data

4. Calculate Based on the data you collected, how much faster were you able to move water with your device?

___

___

Draw Conclusions

LAFS.5.RI.1.1

GAME

Practice what you learn with the Mini Games.

When you read, you must figure out what information is in the text. Use these strategies to draw conclusions from text.

- Look for facts, such as dates, places, names, or other data.
- Ask yourself what the facts mean when you put them together.

Read these paragraphs. Look for clues that will help you draw conclusions from the text.

The Mystery of the Shrinking Lake

In the past, Utah's Great Salt Lake was the largest natural lake west of the Mississippi River. The lake is fed by several freshwater rivers. Today, the lake is drying up. Its water volume is about half of the normal volume. The lake's water level has dropped 3.4 meters when compared to its height in 1847.

Recently, Utah has recorded higher temperatures than normal and has experienced a long-term drought. The areas surrounding the lake have a shortage of freshwater. To overcome the lack of freshwater, local residents now get 40 percent of their freshwater from the rivers that supply water to the lake. The rivers were once full of water, but today their water barely trickles into the lake.

READING CHECK **Draw Conclusions** The pictures show the Great Salt Lake's Farmington Bay. Which picture is more recent? What makes you draw that conclusion?

Second picture because of the water cycle.

Lesson 1

Water Cycle

I can...

Explain the parts of the water cycle.
Recognize that the ocean is an important part of the water cycle.

Literacy Skill
Draw Conclusions

Vocabulary
water cycle
evaporation
condensation
precipitation

Academic Vocabulary
cycle

VIDEO
Watch a video about parts of the water cycle.

SC.5.E.7.1 Create a model to explain the parts of the water cycle. Water can be a gas, a liquid, or a solid, and can go back and forth from one state to another. **SC.5.E.7.2** Recognize that the ocean is an integral part of the water cycle and is connected to all of Earth's water reservoirs via evaporation and precipitation processes. (Also **SC.5.N.1.1, LAFS.5.RI.1.1**)

SPORTS Connection

The site for the Winter Olympic Games is chosen years in advance. Outdoor events, such as skiing and snowboarding, must take place in snow. How can these events occur in places that do not have enough snow? The solution is making snow by machine. A snow machine blows tiny droplets of water into air that is cold enough to freeze the droplets to form snow. At the Sochi Olympics in Russia, snow machines made enough snow to cover 500 football fields with about 60 centimeters of snow. However, making snow reduces local freshwater levels. It also increases soil erosion and is expensive. But no snow means no skiers. At one California ski area, 38 people work full-time to make snow.

Use Evidence from Text How did Sochi use technology to support skiing and snowboarding at the Olympics? What evidence supports your ideas?

____

____

____

____

uInvestigate Lab

HANDS-ON LAB

SC.5.E.7.1, SC.5.N.1.1

Where did that WATER come from?

A water quality specialist must understand the interactions of water with the environment. How can you investigate why water forms on the outside of a cup?

Suggested Materials

- 2 plastic cups
- water with ice cubes
- warm water

Procedure

☐ **1.** Write a hypothesis to answer the question: Will water form on the outside of a cup with warm water or with ice water?

☐ **2.** Write a procedure to test your hypothesis. Show your procedure to your teacher before you start. Record your observations.

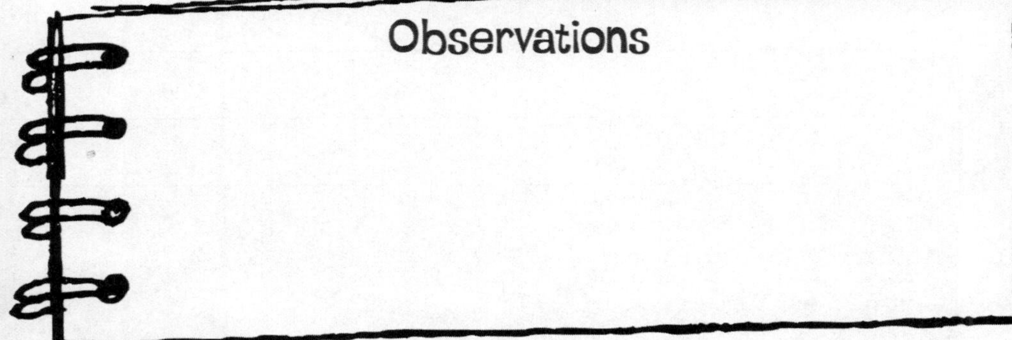

Science Practice

Scientists **use investigations** to find evidence that supports scientific ideas.

Analyze and Interpret Data

3. Draw Conclusions Was your hypothesis supported by evidence? What caused the difference between the cups?

Water on Earth

Earth is called the water planet because water is everywhere on the planet. It surrounds you all the time, not just when you are bathing or swimming. Water also always surrounds you in your classroom, in your home—even in the desert. Where is the water in these dry places?

Water is in the air and underground. Much of the water you cannot see is an invisible gas called water vapor. It is in the air that surrounds you. Air always has some water vapor. Water vapor in the air changes to liquid water when it cools.

It is important to understand that water vapor and steam are not the same thing. Water vapor is usually at the same temperature as the air around it. Steam, however, is above the air's temperature. It is created when water boils. What you see as steam is actually tiny water droplets formed when the hot water vapor meets the cool air in the room.

READING CHECK **Draw Conclusions** Early on a summer morning, the grass is wet. If it did not rain, where did the water come from? How did the grass get wet?

___

___

___

Connecting Concepts ▸ Toolbox

Energy and Matter What is another example that you observed of water changing to water vapor?

Movement of Earth's Water

The water vapor in the air is only a very small part of all the water on Earth. Most of Earth's water near the surface is in its ocean, but ocean water can become water vapor in the air around you. This happens when water particles that make up the ocean become water vapor that moves above Earth's surface.

Water on Earth constantly moves in a **cycle**, or a series of events or processes that repeat. As it moves, water can change into any of its forms—water vapor, liquid water, and ice. The **water cycle** is the continuous movement of water on Earth. Two of the processes of the water cycle are evaporation and condensation. Ocean water changes to water vapor when the water heats. **Evaporation** is the process of changing liquid water into water vapor. Heat causes air to rise, carrying water vapor as part of it. At higher altitudes, air temperatures are lower, and water vapor cools and changes to a liquid. This change from water vapor to liquid water is called **condensation**. Clouds are drops of liquid formed from cooled water vapor.

Write About It In your science notebook, write what you think would happen if water did not evaporate and condense.

uBe a Scientist

Solid, Liquid, Gas

Water changes state as it moves through the water cycle. At different times, water can be a gas, a liquid, or a solid. Make a model that helps you explain how water can change from one state to another and then back to the original state.

Visual Literacy Connection

How does water cycle on Earth?

The processes of the water cycle have no start or finish. They are affected by air temperature, air pressure, wind, and landforms. Water does not always flow in the same path through the water cycle. It can take many paths.

Precipitation

Precipitation is water that falls from clouds in the form of rain, sleet, snow, or hail.

Snow

Rain

Runoff

Runoff is water moving downhill. When precipitation falls, water runs off into streams and rivers. From there, water flows to lakes or the ocean.

River

Groundwater

Some precipitation soaks into the ground and becomes groundwater.

Do an activity about the water cycle and plants.

Condensation

In cold air, water vapor condenses into liquid water or ice crystals. Droplets of water combine with other droplets and may form a cloud.

Create a model to explain the parts of the water cycle. Draw a picture of the water cycle in your community. Show how water changes among the gas, solid, and liquid states.

Evaporation

As water evaporates, liquid water changes into water vapor.

River

Lake

Literacy ▸ Toolbox

Draw Conclusions When you draw conclusions, you examine facts to figure out what they mean. Use the information from this lesson to draw a conclusion about where the water you drink today will be in 100 years.

LAFS.5.RI.1.1

Energy and the Water Cycle

The sun provides the energy that makes the water cycle work. The sun's heat causes frozen water to melt and surface water to evaporate. Heat also causes winds to blow, and the wind moves clouds. Water in clouds falls as **precipitation**, which is water that falls as rain, snow, sleet, or hail, and the cycle continues. This cycle has been happening as long as Earth has had water—soon after its formation. The water that dinosaurs drank has been recycled millions of times through the processes of evaporation, condensation, and precipitation.

Quest Connection

How could you use the processes of the water cycle to make drinkable water?

___

___

Lesson 1 Check

1. **Explain Phenomena** Tran is conducting an investigation about weather. He uses a rain gauge to collect precipitation. On Monday, the gauge collects 15 mm of rain. He fails to record data the next few days. On Friday, he remembers, but the gauge now contains 12 mm of rain. Explain how his results relate to the water cycle.

___

___

2. **Recall** How is the ocean connected to the water cycle?

___

___

___

Quest Check-In

Follow the Flow

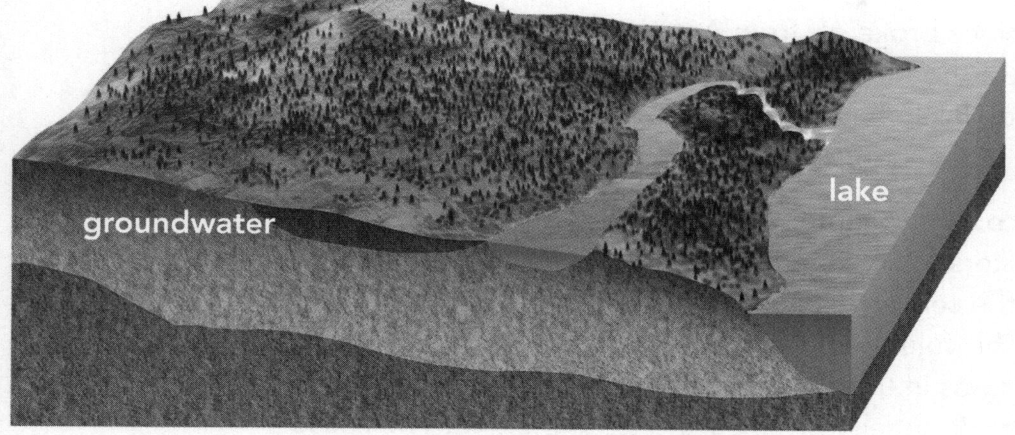

To advise a town on how to get clean drinking water, you should know what happens to water on Earth's surface. When precipitation falls on land, it soaks into the soil, sand, and rocks. Some of it is taken up by plants or is lost to evaporation. However, some of it eventually seeps down into cracks and crevices underground. Where does it go from there?

The diagram shows surface water and groundwater in an environment. Some parts are missing from the diagram.

1. Draw blue arrows to show how runoff will flow on this diagram.
2. Draw green arrows to show where precipitation enters the ground.
3. Place yellow arrows to show the flow of underground water to the lake.
4. **Describe** How might knowing how freshwater flows on and below Earth's surface help you provide clean drinking water to a community?

SC.5.N.1.1

VIDEO

Go online to learn about freshwater depletion.

It's Melting!

In 1992, a giant piece of ice broke off from Antarctica's ice shelves. It broke in two, and one of the pieces was about the size of Rhode Island—39 kilometers wide and 78 kilometers long. Since then, several large ice sheets in Antarctica have broken into smaller parts and floated out to sea.

The Arctic is also losing ice. Arctic winter temperatures normally freeze seawater that is 1 to 5 meters thick. Some of this sea ice forms and melts each year. Now, though, the sea ice is thinner, freezes later, and breaks up much earlier in the year. The volume of Arctic sea ice in the summers is now less than a third of what it was in the 1980s. Ice that took centuries to form can melt in just a few years. In other words, Earth's ice is melting! The cause is warmer global temperatures.

The melting ice can have major effects. Sea levels rise, and ocean currents change. Living things are affected too. Polar bears hunt seals on sea ice packs. When the ice melts early, polar bears cannot find enough food for themselves and their offspring.

Define It

Earth's temperatures have been getting warmer. Scientists are investigating to find out what is causing the climate to change. They think that the change can be slowed or possibly stopped. One way to do this is for people to reduce their carbon footprint. A carbon footprint is a measure of carbon dioxide that is produced by using fossil fuels. Increasing amounts of carbon dioxide cause Earth's atmosphere to become warmer.

Suppose you work for an organization that advises communities on how to reduce their carbon footprint. They want you to define the problem in your community.

- [ ] List five questions you would ask individuals and community leaders to help you define their carbon footprint.

1. ______
2. ______
3. ______
4. ______
5. ______

- [ ] What would you want individuals and communities to understand to help them avoid negatively affecting climate?

Lesson 2

Earth's Freshwater

I can...

Identify that most of Earth's freshwater is in glaciers, in ice caps, or underground.
Explain that some freshwater is found in lakes, rivers, wetlands, and the atmosphere.

Literacy Skill
Draw Conclusions

Vocabulary
glacier
aquifer
reservoir

Academic Vocabulary
distribute

VIDEO

Watch a video about Earth's freshwater.

SC.5.E.7.1 Create a model to explain the parts of the water cycle. Water can be a gas, a liquid, or a solid, and can go back and forth from one state to another. (Also **SC.5.N.1.1**)

LOCAL-TO-GLOBAL Connection

In the 1800s, Chicago's wastewater flowed through the Chicago River into Lake Michigan, which was the source of Chicago's drinking water. Over time, the river and the lake became polluted. To solve the problem, a canal called the Chicago Sanitary and Ship Canal opened in 1900. It changed the flow of the Chicago River so that it carried water away from Lake Michigan. Instead, the water flowed to the Mississippi river.

Chicago's problem was solved, but a new one developed. Today, invasive species, such as Asian carp, can be found in Lake Michigan. Some carp accessed Lake Michigan by swimming up the Mississippi River. The carp threaten the lake's fishing industry. People are now evaluating whether to close the canal.

READING CHECK **Draw Conclusions** Why was it a problem that the Chicago River flowed into Lake Michigan?

____

____

STEM uInvestigate Lab

HANDS-ON LAB

SC.5.N.1.1

How can you find water UNDERGROUND?

Water quality specialists must sometimes locate and test new sources of water. How can you use a model to find and test underground water?

Materials

- safety goggles
- baking pan
- sponge
- sand
- soil
- pebbles
- water

Suggested Materials

- string
- piece of drinking straw
- turkey baster
- tape
- cardboard

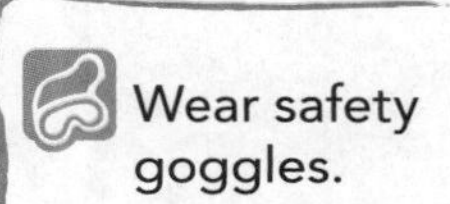
Wear safety goggles.

Design and Build

☐ **1.** Soak a sponge with water and then put it somewhere on the bottom of the baking pan. Cover the sponge with soil, rocks, and sand to make a landscape in the pan. Exchange landscapes with another group.

☐ **2.** Design a tool to find the water in the new landscape. Your tool should change the landscape as little as possible. What other criteria should you consider when designing the tool?

____

____

☐ **3.** Show your design to your teacher before you begin. Record your observations.

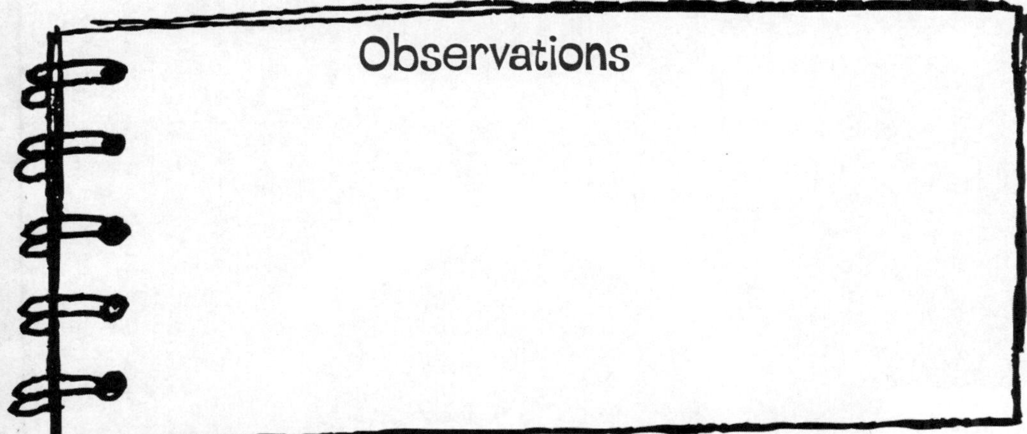

Engineering Practice

Engineers collect and interpret data to make conclusions.

Evaluate Your Design

4. Did your tool help you find water? How could you improve your tool?

____

____

Visual Literacy Connection

HOW IS freshwater distributed ACROSS EARTH?

Nearly three-fourths of Earth is covered by water. Only a very small amount of that water is freshwater. How is water distributed over Earth?

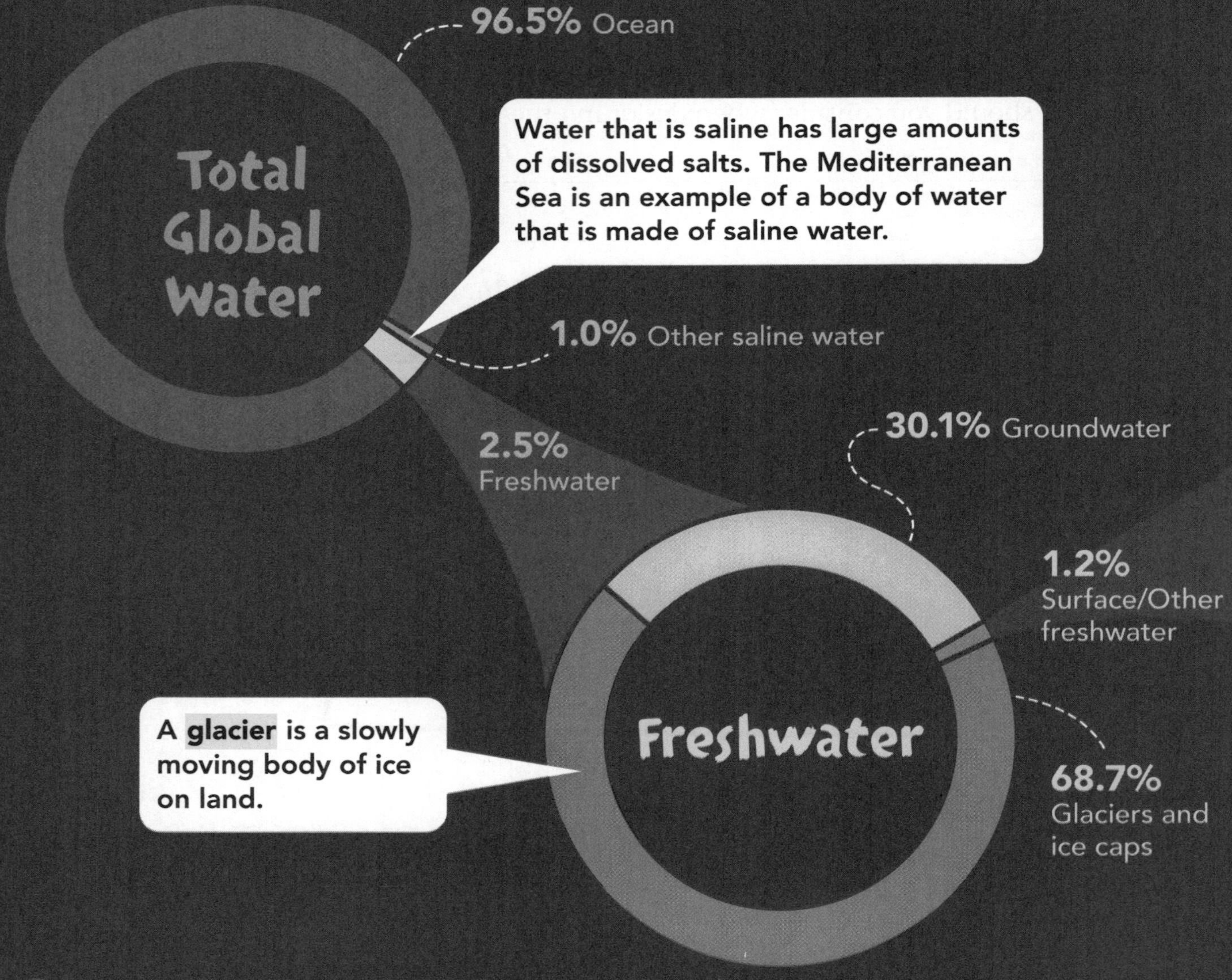

96.5% Ocean

Total Global Water

Water that is saline has large amounts of dissolved salts. The Mediterranean Sea is an example of a body of water that is made of saline water.

1.0% Other saline water

2.5% Freshwater

30.1% Groundwater

1.2% Surface/Other freshwater

Freshwater

A **glacier** is a slowly moving body of ice on land.

68.7% Glaciers and ice caps

List four freshwater sources that are included in surface water:

____

____

____

____

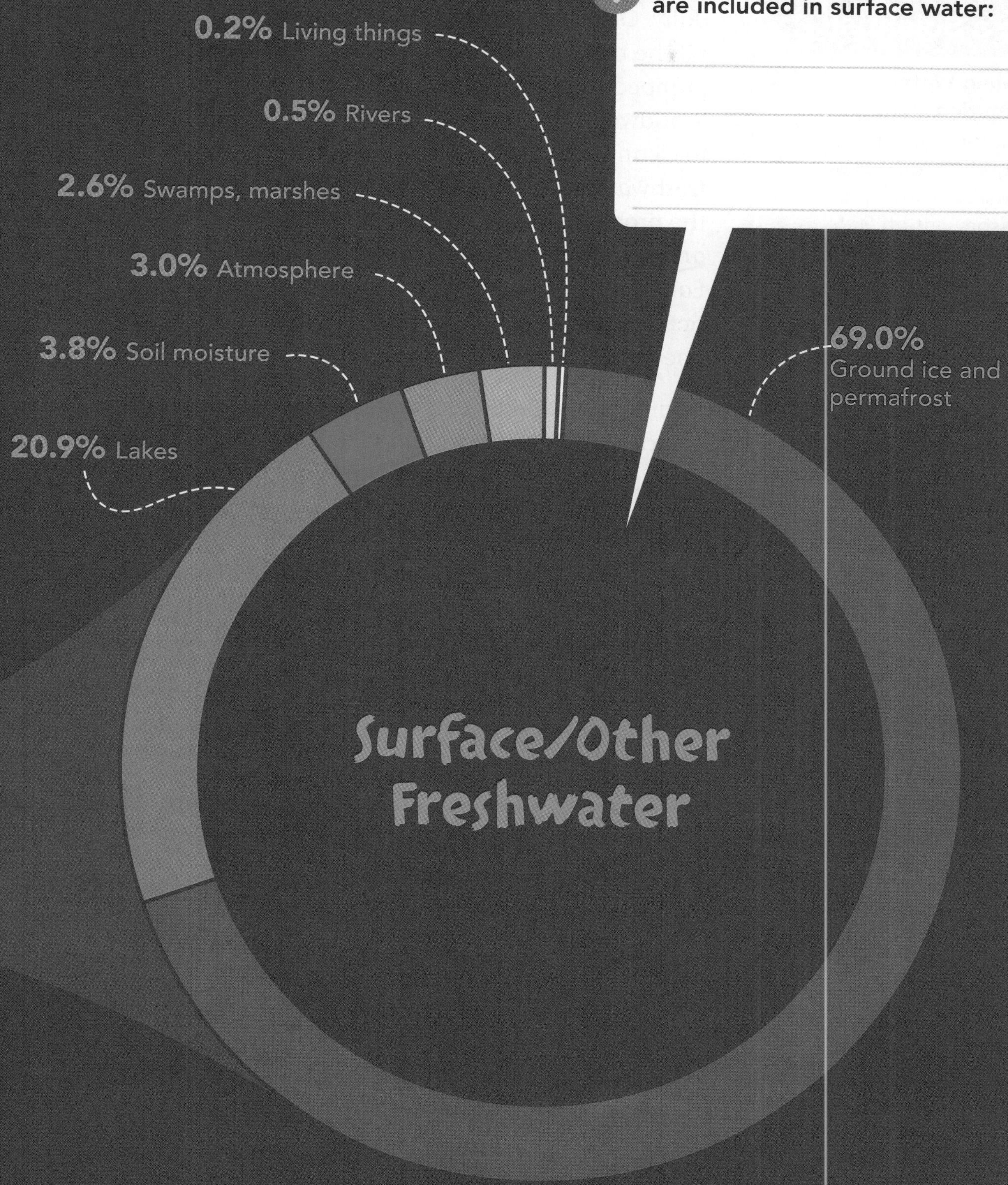

0.2% Living things

0.5% Rivers

2.6% Swamps, marshes

3.0% Atmosphere

3.8% Soil moisture

20.9% Lakes

69.0% Ground ice and permafrost

Surface/Other Freshwater

INTERACTIVITY

Complete an activity on conserving groundwater.

uBe a Scientist

Modeling Water Distribution

Using graph paper, mark off a grid 10 squares by 10 squares. With a pair of scissors, cut off 97.5 squares for the ocean and other saline water. You have 2.5 squares left. Cut off 1.75 squares of paper to represent water held in ice. The 100 original squares represent all of Earth's water near the surface. How much is left? That is the liquid freshwater for human use.

Freshwater Shortages

Earth's freshwater is not evenly **distributed**, or spread out. Some areas, such as Brazil's rainforests, get rain almost daily. Other areas, such as Chile's Atacama Desert, are dry all the time. In places like Nebraska, people rely on water pumped from **aquifers**, underground water supplies. Worldwide, about 1 billion people do not have access to clean water. Another 2.7 billion people do not have freshwater for at least one month a year. To help solve the problem, people build **reservoirs**, places to collect and store water. Scientists predict that about 75 percent of Earth's people will have water shortages by 2025 if we do not change the amount of water we use. Scenes such as the one in the photo will become more common.

Adding to the problem is water pollution and habitat destruction. More than half of the world's wetlands have disappeared. Wetlands are important ecosystems that can remove pollutants from the water. The Florida Everglades at one time covered 3 million acres, but in the last 100 years, people have dug canals and built dams there. They took water, built homes, and expanded agriculture. Today, the Everglades is less than half of its former size.

Reflect Why might someone who lives where freshwater is plentiful worry about water shortages elsewhere?

Quest Connection

Why is it important to find ways to make dirty, or polluted, water or saltwater drinkable in the future?

____

____

Model It!

You can use math to compare the volume of a lake to the volume of a glacier.

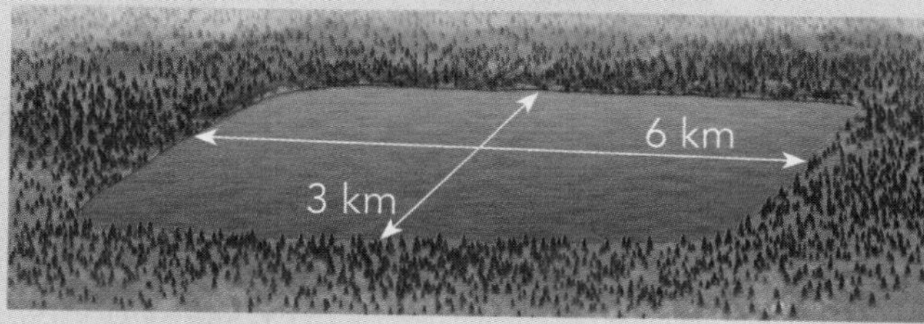

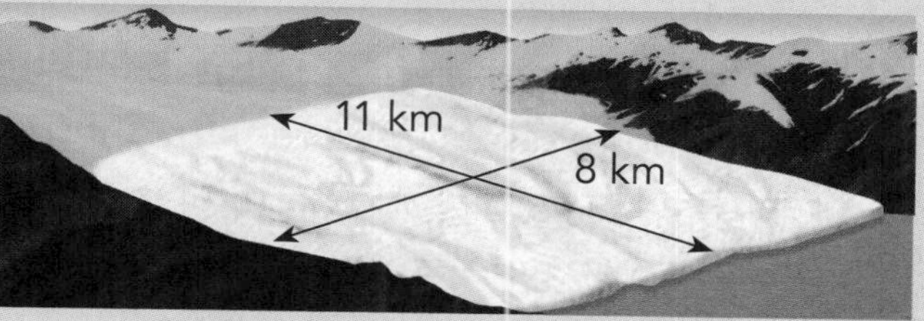

1. **Calculate** Find the surface area of the lake and the glacier using the formula. B (surface area) = $l \times w$

2. **Calculate** The depth of the lake is 0.1 km. The depth of the glacier is 0.2 km. Calculate the volume of each freshwater source using the formula. V (volume) = $l \times w \times h$

3. Round the volume of each up to the nearest round number. Estimate how many times more volume the glacier has compared to the lake.

Lesson 2 Check

SC.5.E.7.1

1. **Infer** If more than half of Earth is covered with water, why is freshwater so limited?

2. **Draw Conclusions** Evaluate the relationship between wetland desctruction and the availability of Earth's freshwater.

STEM Quest Check-In Lab

How do we filter water?

It's time to figure out a way to filter drinkable water from a freshwater source. Water straight from a lake or stream can have dirt and harmful materials that need to be removed before people drink it. How can you filter the water to make it cleaner?

Materials
- cup to hold filtered water
- cup of nonfiltered water
- white plastic lid or container
- safety goggles

Suggested Materials
- water bottle
- water bottle cap with hole in center
- coffee filter
- cotton balls
- eyedropper
- hand lens
- gauze square
- sand
- charcoal
- scissors

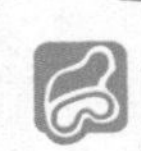
Wear safety goggles.

Handle scissors carefully.

Do not drink water used in the investigation.

Design Your Model

☐ **1.** List the criteria for your water filter.

___

___

___

☐ **2.** What materials will you use to filter the water?

___

___

☐ **3.** How will you test the water to see whether your filter is successful?

___

___

☐ **4.** Draw your filter design.

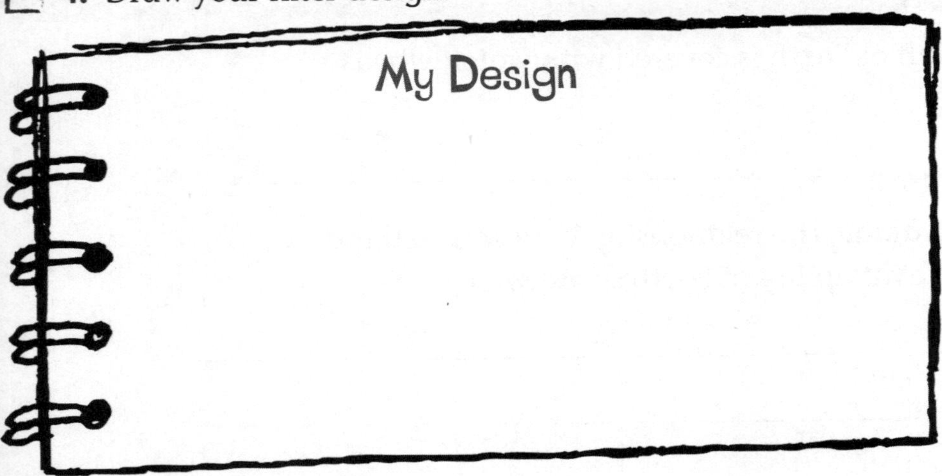

Engineering Practice

Engineers **develop and use models** to find solutions to problems.

☐ **5.** Develop a procedure, and show it to your teacher before you test your filter design. Record your observations.

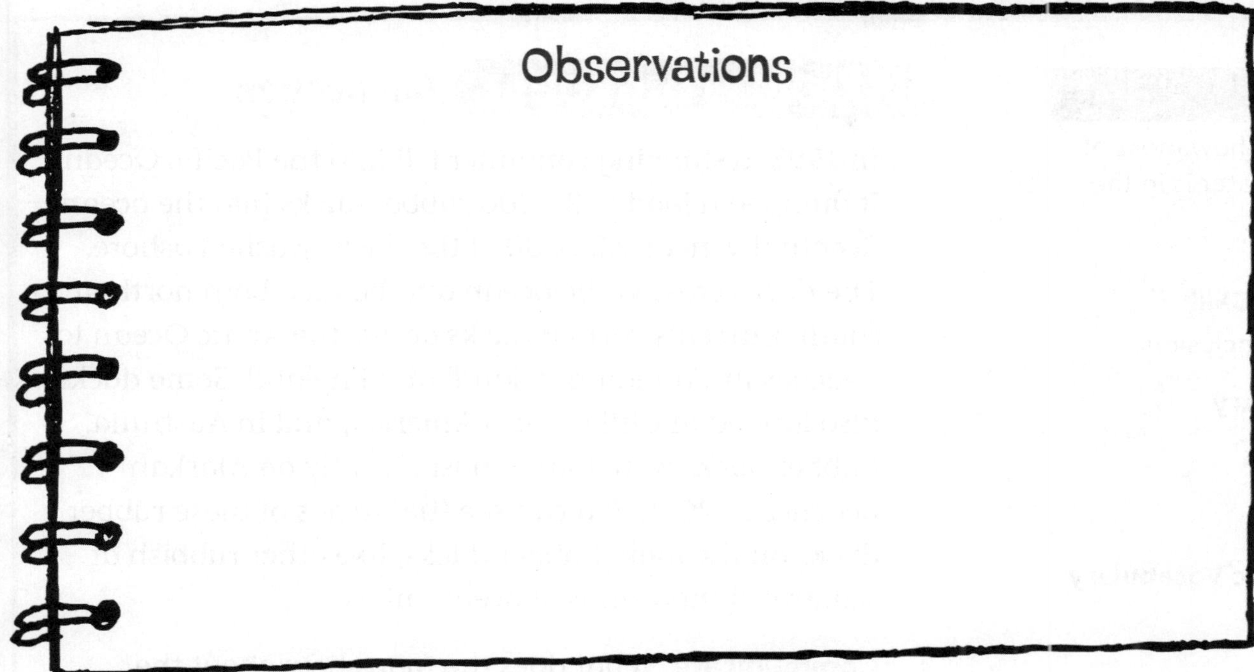

Evaluate Your Model

6. Evaluate Did the filter remove most of the particles from the water? How do you know?

____

____

____

____

7. Infer Is your water safe to drink now? Explain your answer.

____

____

____

____

____

Lesson 3

Earth's Ocean

I can...

Describe how most of Earth's water is in the ocean.

Literacy Skill
Draw Conclusions

Vocabulary
circulation
tides
salinity

Academic Vocabulary
primary

VIDEO

Watch a video about saltwater.

SC.5.E.7.2 Recognize that the ocean is an integral part of the water cycle and is connected to all of Earth's water reservoirs via evaporation and precipitation processes. (Also **SC.5.N.1.1**)

LOCAL-TO-GLOBAL Connection

In 1992, a shipping container fell into the Pacific Ocean. It dumped a load of 28,000 rubber ducks into the ocean. Eventually, nearly 26,000 of the ducks washed ashore. The ducks crossed the ocean and headed both north and south. Currents carried ducks across the Arctic Ocean to beaches in Canada, Scotland, and England. Some ducks also landed in Chile, South America, and in Australia. Rubber ducks were found most recently on Alaskan beaches in 2011. You can see the travels of these rubber ducks on the map. Rubber ducks, like other rubbish at sea, travel thousands of ocean miles.

Communicate What does the map show about the ocean? Explain.

____

____

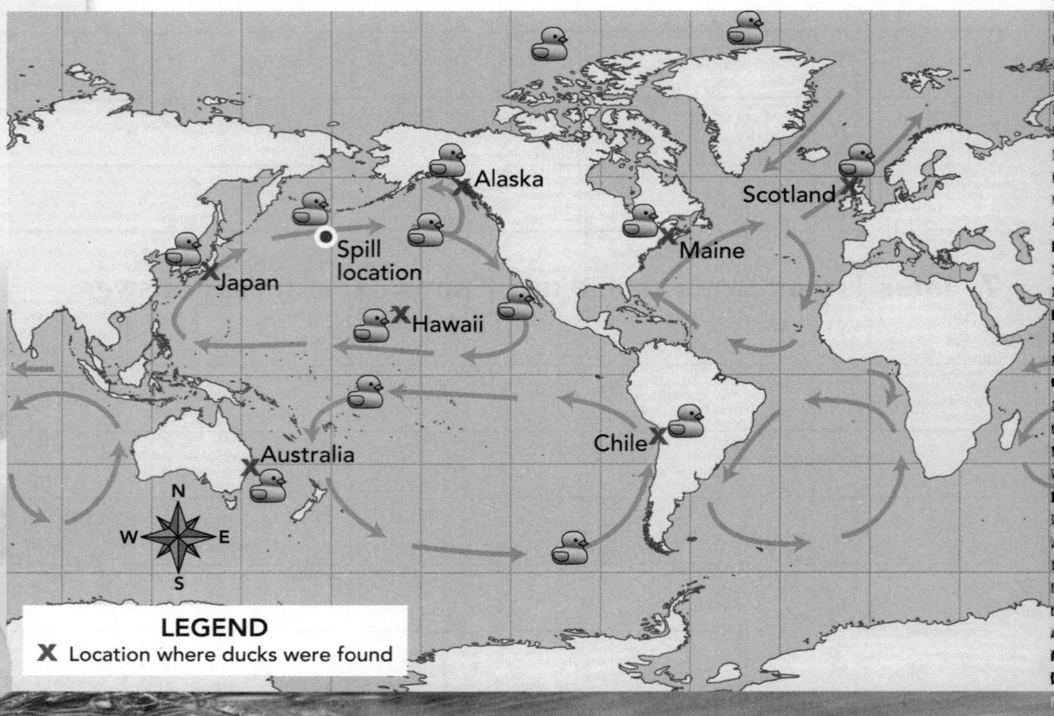

STEM · uInvestigate Lab

HANDS-ON LAB

SC.5.E.7.2, SC.5.N.1.1

How can you separate salt from water?

In places where water is scarce, engineers look for ways to get freshwater from saltwater. This process is called desalination. How can you get freshwater from saltwater?

Suggested Materials

- large bowl
- small plastic cup
- string
- cling wrap
- 2 stones
- saltwater
- beaker

Do not drink or taste anything in the lab.

Design and Build

☐ **1.** How can you use what you know about the water cycle to help separate the salt and the water in saltwater? Use the materials and what you know about the water cycle to make a plan to separate the salt and the water in saltwater. Include how you will know that the salt and water have been separated.

☐ **2.** Show your plan to your teacher before you begin. Record your observations.

Engineering Practice

Engineers develop practical solutions to common problems.

Observations

Evaluate Your Design

3. Apply How could the results of this investigation be applied to providing freshwater to a coastal city?

Where Is Water?

100%

0%

No matter where Earth's water is located, it is in a system called the hydrosphere. The hydrosphere can be divided into two main sections—saltwater and freshwater. Saltwater makes up about 97.5 percent of Earth's water. Many plants and animals, including humans, cannot use saltwater. The other 2.5 percent of water on Earth is found mostly in glaciers, ice caps, and groundwater.

Although different sections of the ocean have specific names, they are all connected. **Circulation**, or a swirling motion, moves ocean water around the globe. The ocean is Earth's main water storage and the **primary**, or most important, source for water in the water cycle. The water cycle links the ocean to all freshwater bodies.

Graph Data Fill in the bar chart with labels and the correct percentages of saltwater and freshwater.

Quest Connection

If Earth has so much water, why do people in some areas have none to drink? Explain.

Ocean Temperatures

The sun's heat warms Earth's ocean water. Water temperatures change with latitude because of the angle of Earth's axis and its relation to the sun. Sunlight at Earth's poles is spread out more than at the equator. Water temperatures near the equator are about 30°C (86°F). Polar ocean water can be as cold as –2°C (28°F). Surface water around the equator evaporates more quickly than at the poles.

Water temperature also changes with ocean depth. Deep ocean water receives less sunlight and is colder than surface water, even at the equator. Wind and waves stir up ocean water. Currents move water along the surface and beneath it. Ocean water is also moved by **tides**, or rising and falling patterns caused by the pull of gravity.

READING CHECK **Draw Conclusions** Using a ruler, make a dark line along the equator in the picture. Compare the temperature of the water north and south of the equator.

____

____

During which season in the north do you think this map was drawn? Why?

____

____

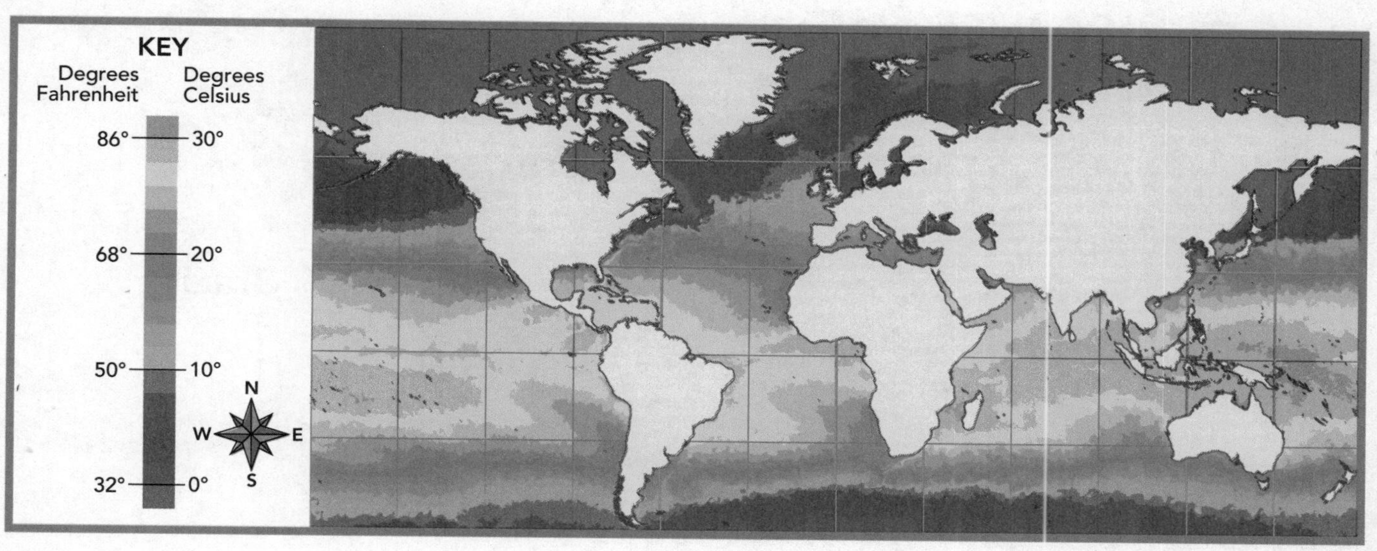

Visual Literacy Connection

What is the motion of the ocean?

The ocean's surface water moves in a consistent pattern in the form of currents. Surface currents are caused by wind. Scientists name currents to help identify their locations in the ocean. California, Peru, and East Australia are current names, for example.

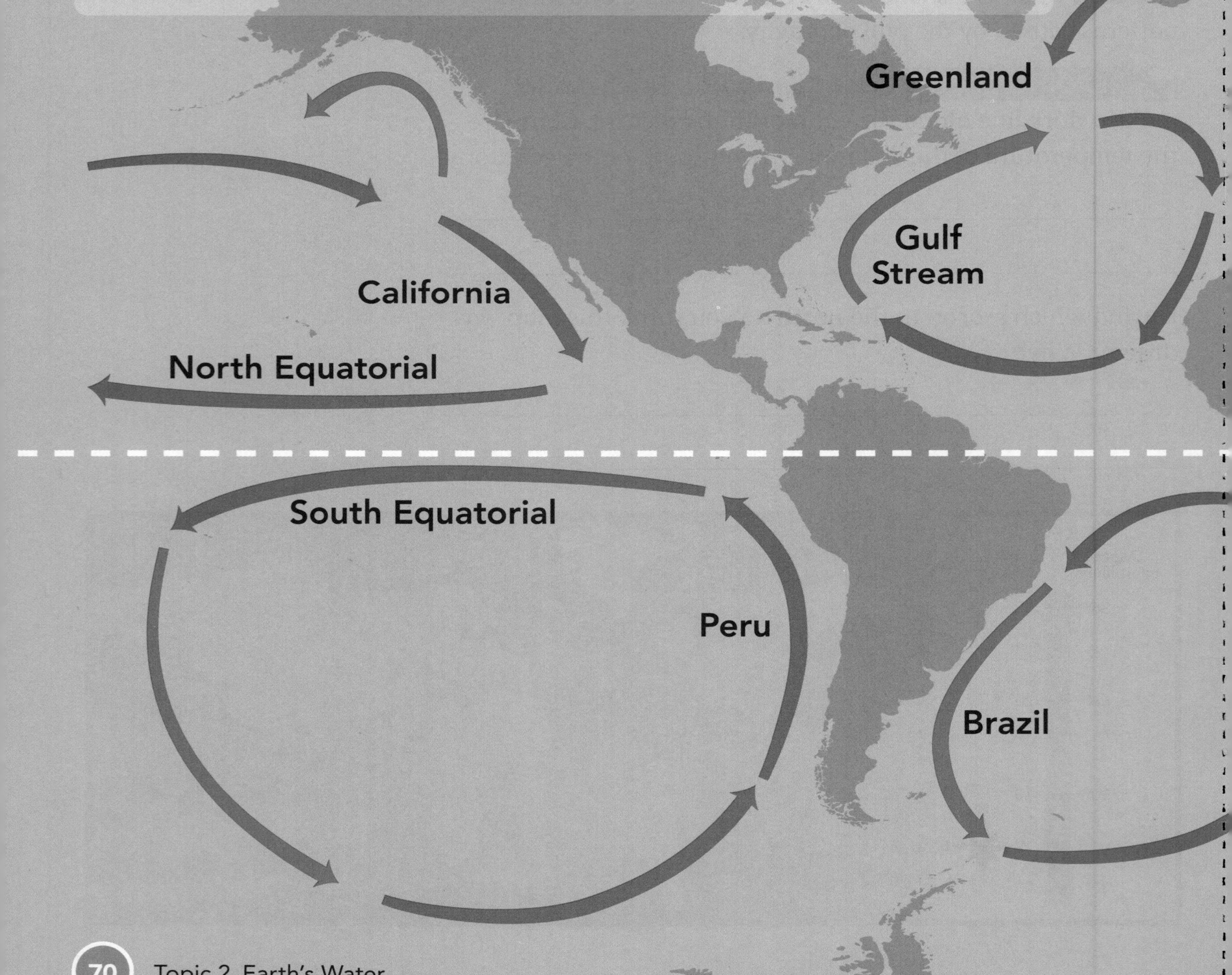

Complete an activity about water on Earth.

Describe a pattern of currents you observe on the map. Why do you think water circulates this way?

To model the movement of ocean water as a result of temperature differences, pour warm saltwater into a clear, 1-L container until the container is half full. Put 4 ice cubes that have been dyed with dark food coloring into the saltwater. Draw your observations.

2 minutes	4 minutes	6 minutes

Salt Levels

Ocean water is salty, but salinity varies in different ocean areas. **Salinity** is the amount of salt dissolved in water. It is measured in parts per thousand. The surface waters of the Atlantic Ocean have higher salinity than the surface waters of the Pacific Ocean. In places where rivers empty into the ocean, freshwater mixes with saltwater. Those areas have lower salinity.

Salinity	
Body of water	**Salinity (parts per thousand)**
Indian Ocean	32–37 ppt
Caribbean Sea	35 ppt
Arctic Ocean	30 ppt
Antarctic Ocean	34 ppt

Identify Circle the body of water with the lowest salinity. Underline the body of water that most likely has the highest salinity.

Threats to the Shoreline

People throughout the globe have challenges in saving ocean shorelines. Building along a coast can cause pollution. Erosion and rising sea levels cause beaches to shrink. Accidents from ocean oil drilling spill oil into the water. Birds, fish, marine mammals, and sea plants suffer when oil coats the water. Polluted water from rivers or garbage dumped into the ocean can spoil shorelines. Tides and currents leave garbage and waste on the sand.

READING CHECK **Draw Conclusions** Can oil spilled on land pollute the ocean? Explain your answer.

uBe a Scientist

Oil Spill in a Bottle

Fill a plastic water bottle 3/4 full of water. Add 6 drops blue or green food coloring. Swirl the water to mix the color. Add 1 cm of vegetable oil. Put the lid on tightly. Turn the bottle on its side and see how an oil slick spreads. Shake the bottle vigorously. Place the bottle on its side and wait a few minutes. What happens to the oil? Why can't the ocean get rid of an oil slick?

Lesson 3 Check

SC.5.E.7.2

1. **Identify** Through which processes in the water cycle is the ocean connected to all of Earth's water?

2. **Formulate** On Tuesday, the water temperature at Emerald Beach is 27°C. On Thursday, the water temperature is 30°C. Determine the factors that might have caused this temperature change.

Water Resources

Fill in the table based on what you have learned about water. Consider each source and its possibility of providing water for drinking. You need to consider the tasks you will complete as you get the water. You should also consider which tasks will cost money.

Glacier	Type of water: ________ Location: ________ Tasks involved: ________ ________ Factors affecting cost: ________
Groundwater	Type of water: ________ Location: ________ Tasks involved: ________ ________ Factors affecting costs: ________
Ocean	Type of water: ________ Location: ________ Tasks involved: ________ ________ Factors affecting costs: ________

Evaluate Which of these sources contains the greatest amount of water? What is one difficulty in making that water drinkable for humans?

____

____

____

____

____

____

 QUEST CHECK OFF

Can people live on Mars?

People may someday live on Mars. For humans to live on Mars, they will need a freshwater source. Recent studies by NASA show that Mars has plenty of water, but much of it is frozen. Water ice lies in an underground layer covering a large area of Mars. The water ice in this layer has about as much water as Lake Superior. Using radar, NASA looked at an area called Utopia Planitia. The water ice there covers more land than New Mexico. The water contains dust and rock. The chart shows a few other differences.

	Earth	Mars
Atmosphere	nitrogen, oxygen, argon, others	carbon dioxide, water vapor
Water content	97.5% saltwater, 2.5% freshwater	frozen, dirty freshwater, snowflakes of carbon dioxide
Climate	tropical, temperate, and polar regions	extreme cold to moderate, massive dust storms

Let's use what you know about finding and using water. Complete this claim: If people were to live on Mars, they would need food, water, and shelter. The water would come from

____

____

The process of obtaining water on Mars would be most like getting water from which sources on Earth?

____

____

The water could be made usable for humans by

____

____

Organize data to analyze your Quest Findings

Quest Findings

Water, Water Everywhere!

How can you make undrinkable water drinkable?

Apply what you learned to decide how to provide drinkable water to the two thirsty towns in the table.

Town	Nearest water source	Quality of water
Katherine, Australia	Katherine River	Little rain for many months of each year. Water contains soil particles from runoff.
Agadir, Morocco	Atlantic Ocean	Water source has salt content.

For each town, write a recommendation for how to solve its water problem. Do research to find additional information to support your recommendation. What challenges to success do you think might exist for each of the towns?

Katherine ______________________________

____

____

____

____

Agadir ______________________________

____

____

____

QUEST CHECK OFF

Career Connection

Water Quality Specialist

Water quality specialists understand how water conditions affect people. These scientists study ways people get water and ways human activity pollutes water. They have two water sources to check. The first is raw water, or water as it exists in nature. They check how this type of water changes because of runoff from land and roads. The other is treated water, the water you get when you turn on a faucet at home.

Water quality specialists need degrees in chemistry, earth science, or biology. They travel to water sources to take samples and investigate possible problems. Some work is done in labs and some in offices, but at least 40 percent of this job is done outdoors.

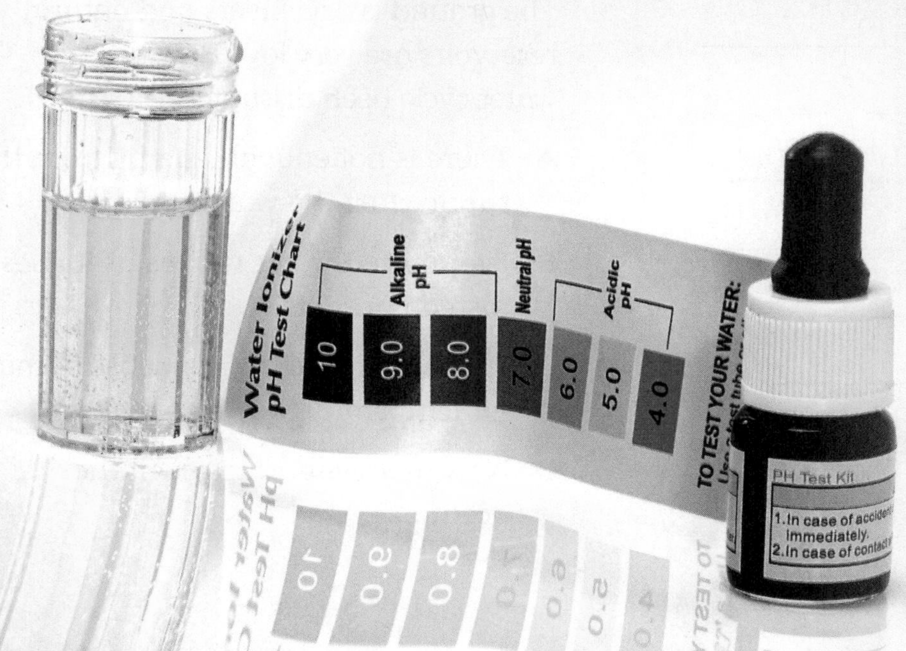

Reflect What are two or three things about being a water quality specialist that interest you?

Assessment

Read each question and choose or write the best answer.

1. **Identify** A city dams a river and makes a lake that stores its freshwater supply. This is an example of an artificial

_______________________.

2. **Design** Dean wants to use shallow pans, water, and adjustable lamps to make a model that compares how sunlight affects the ocean at Earth's equator and at its poles. How should he design his model?

____

____

____

____

____

____

____

____

____

____

____

____

____

____

Use the diagram to answer questions 3 and 4.

3. **Interpret Diagrams** Number 1 on the diagram represents which part of the water cycle?

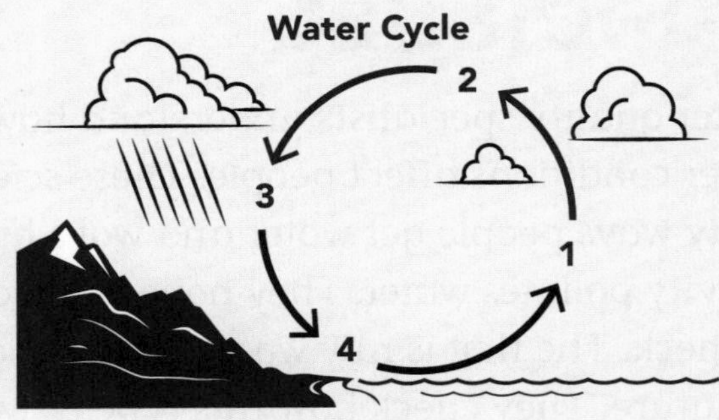

A. evaporation

B. precipitation

C. condensation

D. collection

4. **Explain Phenomena** A certain prolonged hot weather system causes a drought. The ground is dry. Rivers and natural reservoirs are very low. How has the water cycle been disrupted?

A. There is not enough energy from the sun to start the water cycle.

B. Evaporated water warms as it rises instead of cools.

C. Water vapor cannot condense because air temperatures are too high.

D. No water evaporates from the ocean.

Use the diagram to answer questions 5 and 6.

5. **Assess** Which of these would be an accurate title for the graph?

   A. Distribution of Earth's Water

   B. Earth's Saltwater Sources

   C. The Water Cycle

   D. Distribution of Earth's Freshwater

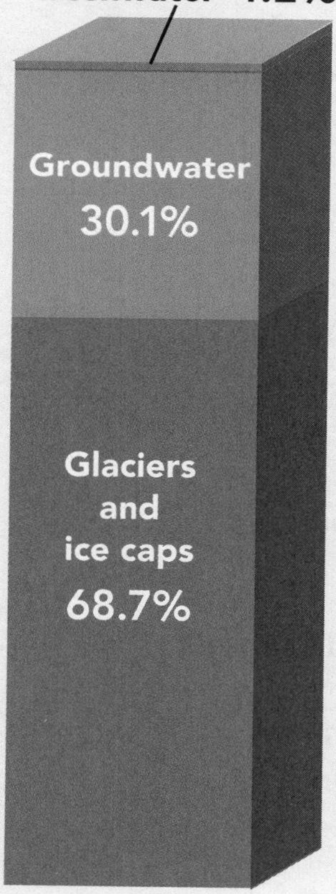

6. **Formulate** Suppose Earth's glaciers and ice caps melt. Evaluate the change that would be observed along the coast of Florida.

____

____

____

____

____

____

The Essential Question *How much water can be found in different places on Earth?*

Show What You Learned

You viewed several maps and graphs as you learned about Earth's water. Think about this evidence. What conclusions have you drawn about where saltwater and freshwater are found?

____

____

____

____

____

____

Science Assessment Practice

Read the scenario and answer questions 1–2.

Greg wants to make a terrarium to model Earth's water cycle. After he places the terrarium near a sunny window for three days, Greg draws a diagram to record his observations.

1 **Engage in Argument** Greg claims that the terrarium has a functioning water cycle. Based on evidence in the diagram, which statement **best** supports his claim?

Ⓐ There is no evidence of condensation in the container.

Ⓑ There is no evidence of precipitation in the container.

Ⓒ The water drops on the inside of the glass are evidence for condensation and precipitation.

Ⓓ The water drops are evidence of a water cycle, but the cycle will stop when energy trapped in the container is used up.

2 **Identify Effects** What would happen to the movement of water in the terrarium if it was placed in a dark closet?

Ⓕ The water cycle would continue to function in the same way.

Ⓖ There would be less energy for evaporation, so the cycle would stop functioning.

Ⓗ More evaporation would happen because less energy would be available.

Ⓘ Condensation would remain constant while evaporation decreased.

3 **Connect Ideas** A kettle boils and some liquid water converts into steam. Which natural phenomenon is this most like?

Ⓐ Hot lava causes evaporation when it contacts water.

Ⓑ Water vapor condenses and crystallizes at high elevations.

Ⓒ Warm areas have more precipitation than cold areas.

Ⓓ Areas by the ocean get more precipitation than inland areas.

Read the scenario and answer questions 4–5.

A group of environmental scientists wants to educate people about the importance of water conservation. They decide to develop a brochure claiming that drinking water is a limited resource. The scientists explain that people cannot drink saltwater, and frozen freshwater sources are too far from where most people live. They gather information about how much water is found in different types of water reservoirs to use as evidence in the brochure.

Water reservoir	Water volume on Earth (cubic km)	Percent of total water*
Ocean (saltwater)	1,338,000,000	96.53
Ice caps, glaciers, permanent snow	24,064,000	1.73
Fresh groundwater	10,530,000	0.76
Salty groundwater	12,870,000	0.93
Ground Ice and permafrost	300,000	0.02
Freshwater lakes	91,000	0.01
Saltwater lakes	85,400	0.01
Other freshwater reservoirs	34,305	0.01

*Percentages have been rounded.

4 **Evaluate Data** Which conclusion can you make using the data in the table?

Ⓕ Almost no water is stored on Earth as ice.

Ⓖ More freshwater is stored in freshwater lakes than underground.

Ⓗ Freshwater on Earth is evenly distributed.

Ⓘ Earth has several saltwater sources.

5 **Use Math** Given that people cannot drink saltwater and frozen water sources are difficult to access, what percentage of Earth's total water might be used as a source of drinking water?

Ⓐ less than 0.5 percent

Ⓑ less than 1 percent

Ⓒ less than 5 percent

Ⓓ less than 10 percent

STEM · uDemonstrate Lab

How can water move upward?

Water quality specialists need to pump water from underground to test it. How can you build a device to pump water upward?

Materials

- safety goggles
- squeezable plastic water bottle with a lid
- tape
- bucket
- water
- graduated beaker
- stopwatch

Wear safety goggles.

Engineering Practice

Engineers **measure quantities,** such as volume, to answer questions.

Design and Build

☐ **1.** Use the materials to design a device that will pump the greatest volume of water as quickly as possible.

☐ **2.** Draw a design for your device. Label the materials your device will use.

☐ **3.** How will you test your device?

____

____

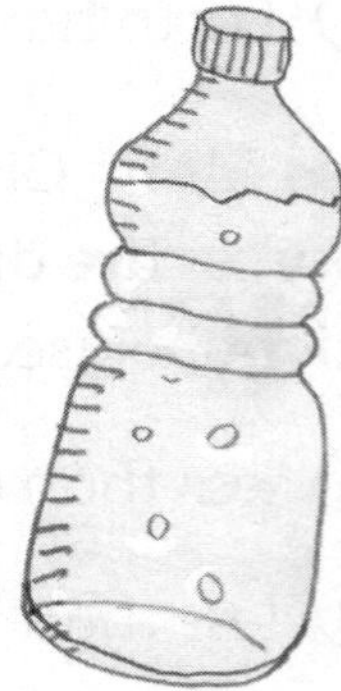

☐ **4.** Show your design and testing idea to your teacher before you begin. Record your observations.

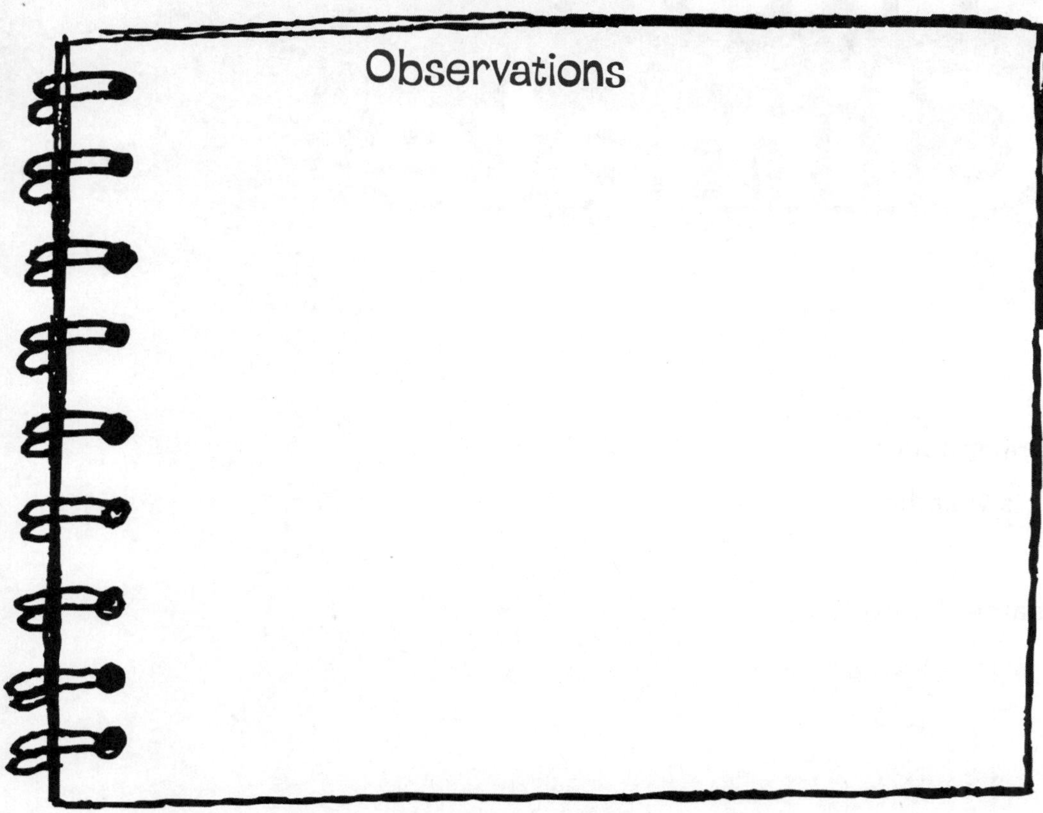

Analyze and Interpret Data

5. Compare and Contrast Compare your device with those of other students to identify the design that can pump the greatest volume of water in a specific time. What features do the most powerful devices share?

____

____

6. Infer How could you improve your model to make it more powerful?

____

____

____

____

Topic 3

Weather and Climate

Lesson 1 Weather
Lesson 2 Forms of Precipitation
Lesson 3 Land Affects Weather
Lesson 4 Climate
Lesson 5 Severe Weather Safety

SC.5.E.7.3 Recognize how air temperature, barometric pressure, humidity, wind speed and direction, and precipitation determine the weather in a particular place and time. **SC.5.E.7.4** Distinguish among the various forms of precipitation (rain, snow, sleet, and hail), making connections to the weather in a particular place and time. **SC.5.E.7.5** Recognize that some of the weather-related differences, such as temperature and humidity, are found among different environments, such as swamps, deserts, and mountains. **SC.5.E.7.6** Describe characteristics (temperature and precipitation) of different climate zones as they relate to latitude, elevation, and proximity to bodies of water. **SC.5.E.7.7** Design a family preparedness plan for natural disasters and identify the reasons for having such a plan. (Also: **SC.5.N.1.1, SC.5.N.1.3, SC.5.N.1.4, SC.5.N.2.1, MAFS.5.NF.2.7, LAFS.W.3.9, MAFS.5.G.1.1**)

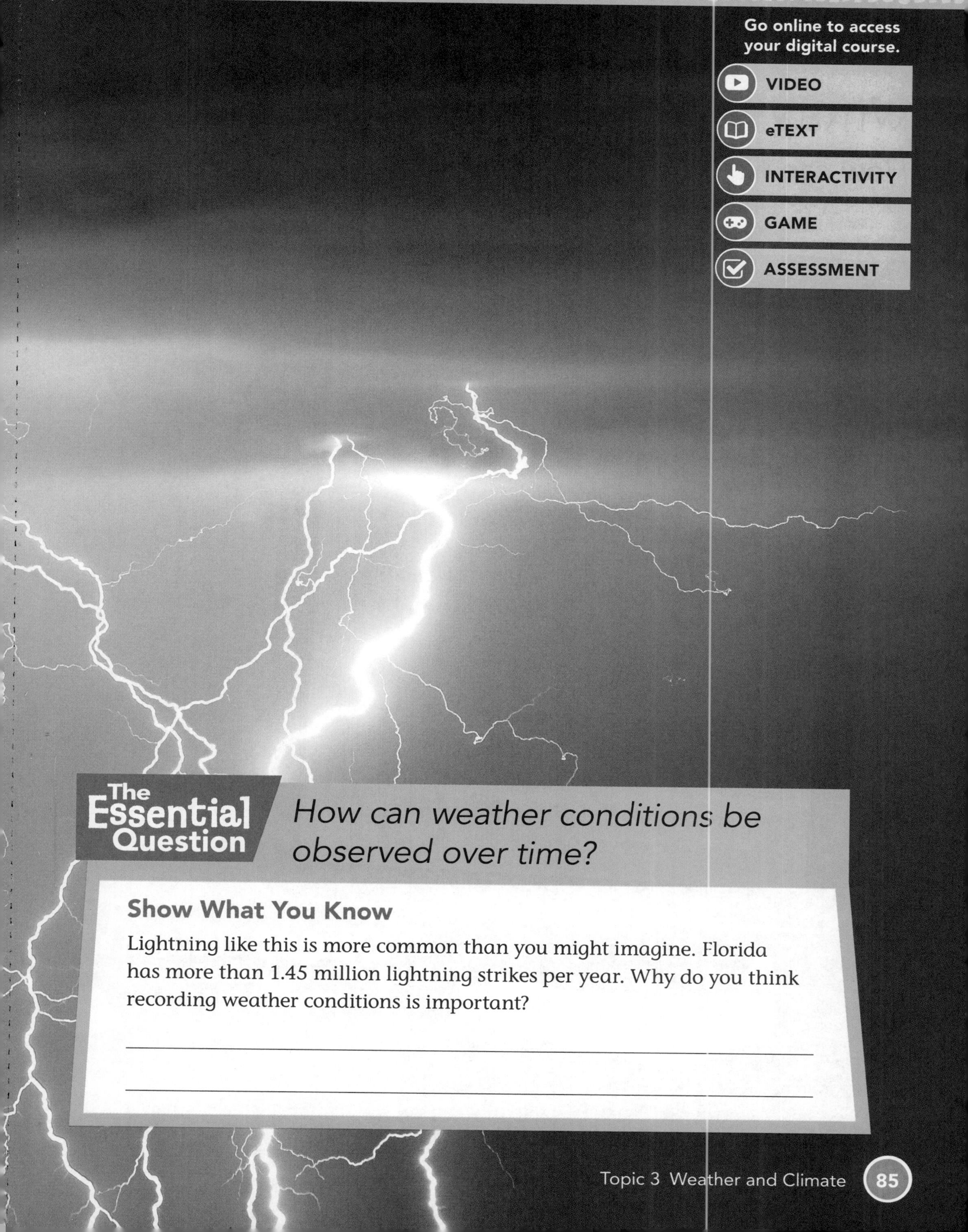

Go online to access your digital course.

- VIDEO
- eTEXT
- INTERACTIVITY
- GAME
- ASSESSMENT

The Essential Question

How can weather conditions be observed over time?

Show What You Know

Lightning like this is more common than you might imagine. Florida has more than 1.45 million lightning strikes per year. Why do you think recording weather conditions is important?

____

____

Quest Kickoff

Windy, Wet, Wild, or Wonderful?

How can we predict weather?

Hello, my name is Hassan Ali, and I'm a climatologist. I write a blog that suggests trips that cater to the weather interests of travelers. I need you to visit locations with different weather and write for my blog.

Like a climatologist, you will look at different weather patterns. You will help me inform travelers about the weather so they can enjoy the places they will visit. I'd like you to provide a creative evaluation of what it was like to visit different climates.

Follow the path to learn how you will complete your Quest. The Quest activities in the lessons will help you complete the Quest. Check off your progress every time you complete an activity with a QUEST CHECK OFF. Go online for more Quest activities.

Quest Check-In 1

Lesson 1

Learn about different types of weather. Use the information to find locations that might have the weather conditions that clients are looking for.

SC.5.E.7.3 Recognize how air temperature, barometric pressure, humidity, wind speed and direction, and precipitation determine the weather in a particular place and time. (Also **SC.5.E.7.4**, **SC.5.E.7.5**, and **SC.5.E.7.6**).

VIDEO

Watch a video about a climatologist.

Quest Check-In 3

Lesson 3

Use what you learn about how land affects weather to predict how certain environments affect the weather in those locations.

Quest Check-In Lab 4

Lesson 4

Analyze data and look for patterns to define a location's climate.

Quest Check-In 5

Lesson 5

Apply what you learn to advise travelers how to be prepared for severe weather.

Quest Check-In 2

Lesson 2

Find out about different forms of precipitation. Then research which locations have the best precipitation conditions for various travelers.

Quest Findings

Tell blog readers about the types of weather they are likely to experience at each location.

STEM uConnect Lab

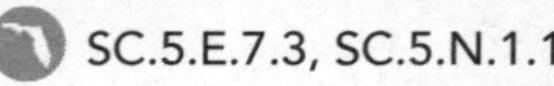

SC.5.E.7.3, SC.5.N.1.1

How can you measure rainfall?

Climatologists use tools to measure data about Earth's weather. How can you make a simple tool to measure rainfall?

Suggested Materials

- scissors
- plastic jar
- metric ruler
- permanent marker, fine tip
- clear plastic bottle
- clear plastic cup

Design and Build

☐ **1.** What criteria should your tool meet? Identify the data you need to collect. Identify the units you will measure.

____

____

Be careful when using scissors.

☐ **2.** Choose the materials you will use to meet your criteria. Draw your design.

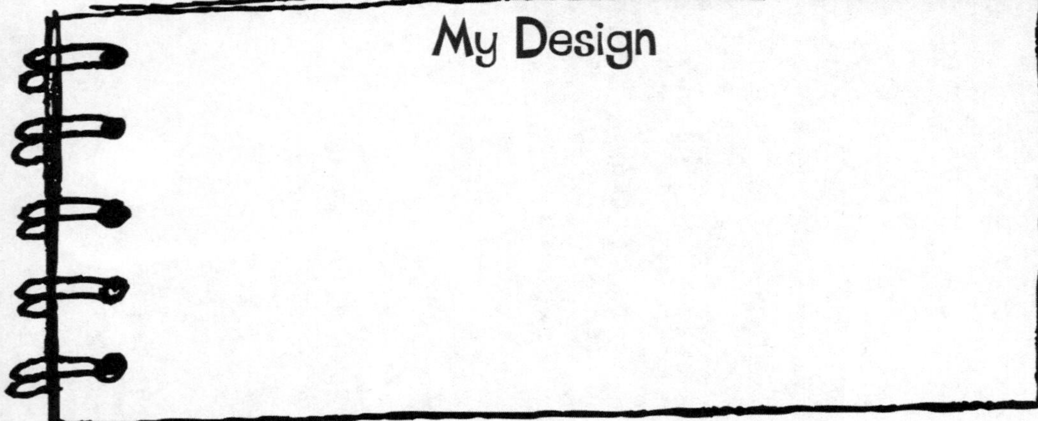

Engineering Practice

Engineers use tools to make measurements when gathering data.

☐ **3.** Show your design to your teacher before you start building it.

☐ **4.** Test your rain gauge and collect data.

Evaluate Your Design

5. Infer What can the data you collect with your tool tell you about the weather in an area?

____

____

____

Literacy Connection

Use Evidence from Text

LAFS.W.3.9

When you read carefully, you look for bits of information, or evidence, that support an idea. Use these strategies for finding evidence in text.

- Read through the text.
- Carefully reread the text and underline or note important facts.

Read the text to find out how weather changes in Tallahassee.

GAME

Practice what you learn with the Mini Games.

Tallahassee Season to Season

Welcome to Tallahassee! You can expect fairly predictable weather patterns here from season to season. In winter, expect daytime temperatures in the 13°C to 18°C range, but nights can get as cold as 0°C, and snow sometimes falls. Spring is mild and dry, with high temperatures between 23°C and 31°C in the daytime. Nights are cool with temperatures of about 8°C to 11°C. Summer is hot, around 33°C, with high humidity. Fall daylight temperatures are moderate, ranging from 32°C in September to 23°C in November.

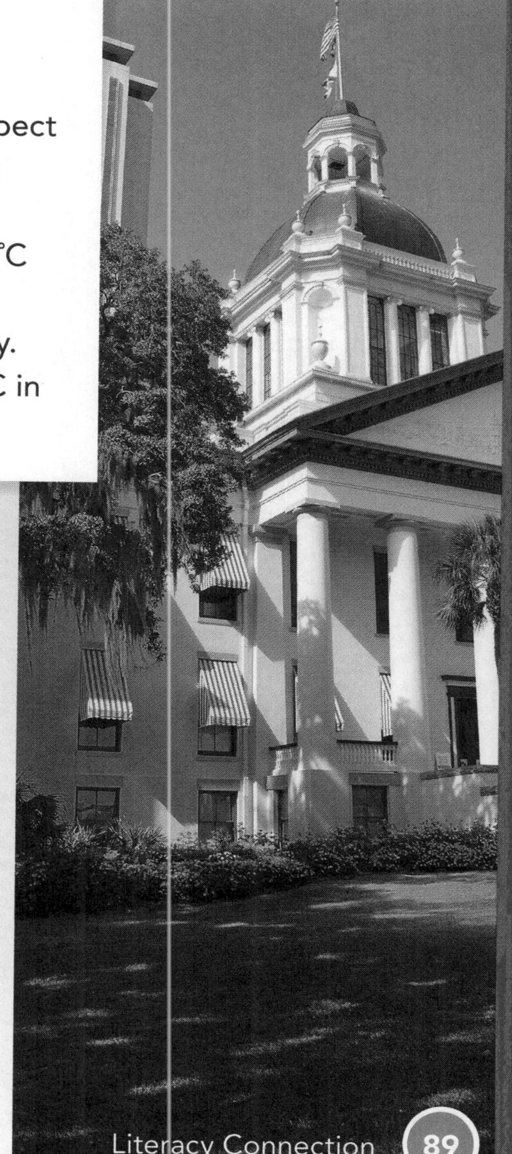

READING CHECK **Use Evidence from Text** What evidence did you find that changes occur from season to season in Tallahassee?

____

____

____

____

____

Lesson 1

Weather

I can...

Recognize factors that determine weather.

Literacy Skill
Use Evidence from Text

Vocabulary
weather
air pressure
humidity
circulation

Academic Vocabulary
determine

SC.5.E.7.3 Recognize how air temperature, barometric pressure, humidity, wind speed and direction, and precipitation determine the weather in a particular place and time. (Also **SC.5.N.1, MAFS.5.G.1.1**)

SPORTS Connection

It is a home run... Or is it? Two batters in Denver and Tampa Bay hit baseballs at the same angle with the same amount of force. You may think the baseballs will travel the same distance, but they do not. The hit in Denver turns out to be a home run. Uh-oh, the ball in Tampa Bay is caught in right field.

In Denver, the elevation is high and air pressure is low. Tampa Bay is at sea level. Air pressure there is higher. The greater air pressure in Tampa Bay will keep the ball from traveling as far as it would in Denver. Because air pressure changes as weather changes, the weather could be the reason a long hit lands inside or outside the stadium walls.

READING CHECK **Use Evidence from Text**
Underline the sentence that explains why the ball hit in Tampa Bay was caught in the outfield.

uInvestigate Lab

HANDS-ON LAB

SC.5.E.7.3, SC.5.N.2.1

What's with the weather?

Meteorologists study the weather and make predictions. How accurate are weather forecasts?

Materials

- local five-day weather forecast
- rain gauge
- thermometer

Procedure

☐ **1.** Look at a current five-day weather forecast. Record the predicted high temperatures and the amount of precipitation (rain, snow, sleet, or hail) for each day.

☐ **2.** Plan a prodecure to use the weather tools to evaluate the accuracy of the weather forecast.

☐ **3.** Show your plan to your teacher before you begin. Collect data and record it.

Science Practice

Scientists **use evidence** to make scientific explanations.

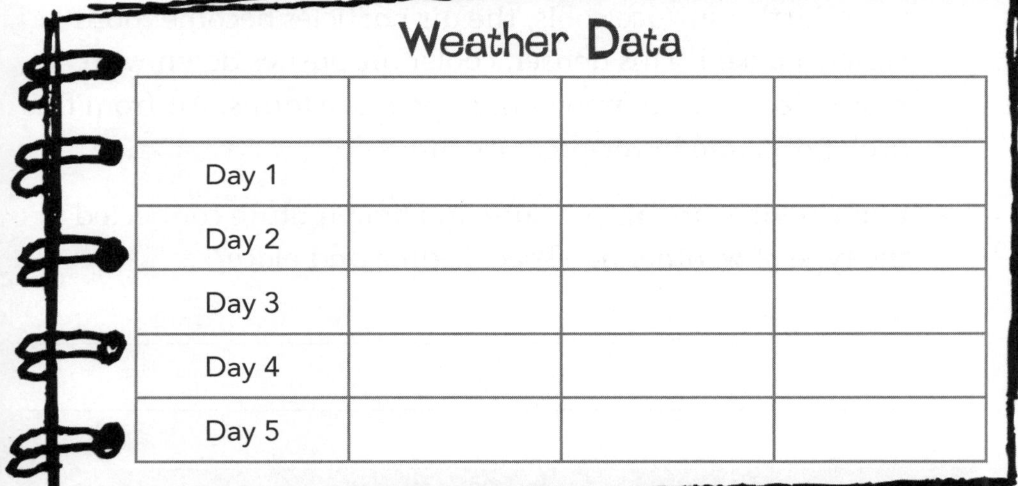

Weather Data

Day 1			
Day 2			
Day 3			
Day 4			
Day 5			

Analyze and Interpret Data

4. Use Evidence How accurate were the weather predictions? Explain.

Math ▸ Toolbox

Line Graphs On graph paper, label the days of the week on the x-axis and barometric pressure ranges on the y-axis. Record the daily barometric pressure for one week. Also record conditions such as sunny, rain, or snow. What pattern do you see?

 MAFS.5.G.1.1

Barometric Pressure and Temperature

You wake in the morning and wonder whether you will need a raincoat. The answer depends on the weather. **Weather** is the state of the atmosphere, including its temperature, wind speed and direction, air pressure, moisture, amount of rain or snow, and other factors.

Weather takes place in Earth's atmosphere, which is a mixture of invisible gases that surrounds the planet. Gravity pulls gases toward Earth's surface. The downward force of the gases is called **barometric pressure**. Air pressure changes with the weather. Low barometric pressure usually indicates rainy weather. High pressure usually indicates clear, sunny weather.

As the sun warms Earth's surface, air near the surface also warms. The warm air rises, and an area of low pressure forms. Air from higher-pressure areas rushes in. If the air near Earth's surface cools, the air particles become more closely packed. This denser, cooler air pushes down with more pressure. An area of high pressure forms. Air from this area flows into lower-pressure areas.

Explain How are air pressure and temperature connected to the type of weather in a specific time and place?

____

____

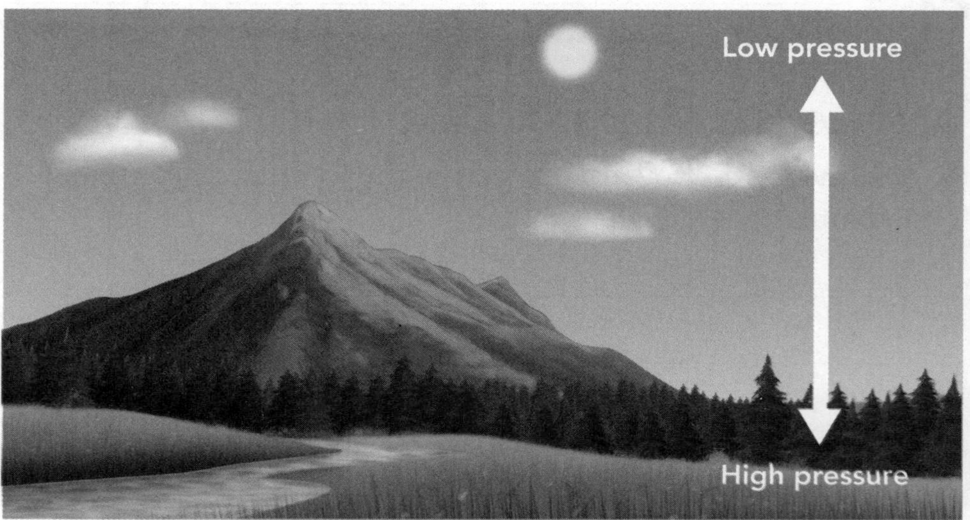

Winds

Wind is air movement caused by differences in pressure. In general, air moves from areas of high pressure to areas of low pressure. Wind speed and direction affect weather. Winds called jet streams can affect local weather. A jet stream is a narrow band of high-speed wind. The name of a wind is the direction from which it blows. For example, a north wind blows from the north toward the south.

This wind vane points toward the direction from which the wind blows.

Draw On the N-S-E-W line diagram, draw an arrow to represent a southeast wind. The arrow should show the direction the wind is moving.

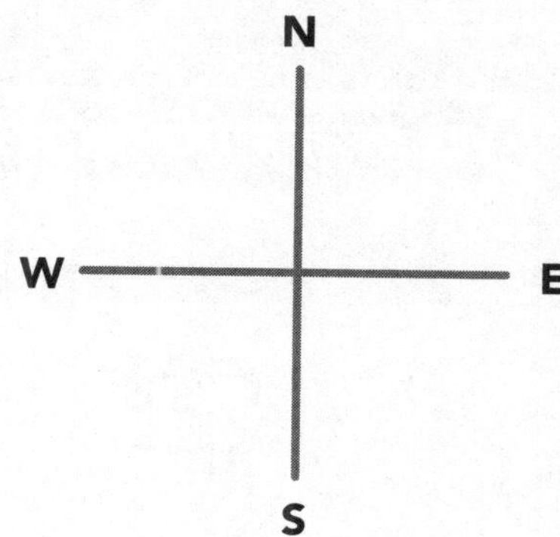

Humidity

Other factors for determining weather are humidity, clouds, and precipitation. **Humidity**, or the amount of water vapor in the air, makes air feel sticky. Water vapor is a gas. When conditions are right, water vapor can begin to condense to form small water droplets and ice crystals. These liquid water droplets and solid ice crystals reflect light from the sun. When that happens, we can see the water as a cloud.

Quest Connection

How might knowing whether a person prefers cool weather or warmer weather affect the place you suggest?

____

____

____

____

uBe a Scientist

Weather in a Bottle Work with an adult at home. Fill a plastic bottle with hot water. Wait 1 minute. Gently pour the water out of the bottle and immediately place the cap on the bottle. Now run cold water over the bottle. What happens? How could you reverse this process?

Visual Literacy Connection

Why do we use weather panels?

Scientists sometimes use weather panels to communicate current and predicted weather forecasts.

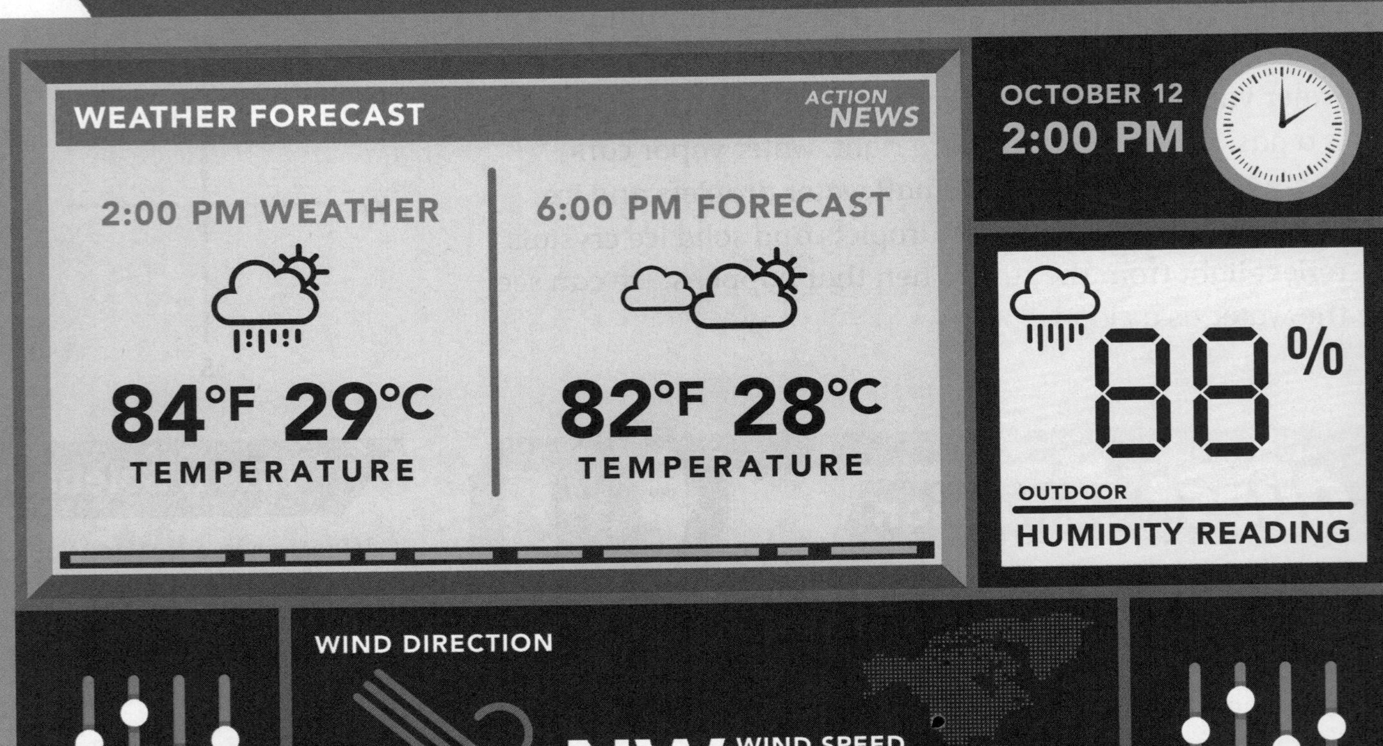

INTERACTIVITY

Do an activity about weather.

How do you know it is warm outside? **Circle** the evidence on the panel that supports your claim.

Predict what temperature you think it will be at 4 P.M. Fill in the thermometer to show this temperature.

°F: 120, 100, 80, 60, 40, 20, 0, -20, -40, -60

°C: 50, 40, 30, 20, 10, 0, -10, -20, -30, -40, -50

From what direction is the wind blowing?

____

Use the weather station information to write a weather report for the 2 o'clock news.

Literacy ▸ Toolbox

Use Evidence from Text, Scientists use facts and data to support their claims. Weather data might include air temperatures, wind speeds, or wind directions. Underline facts about air circulation in the text.

Air Circulation

The wind may blow from different directions, but winds do follow some large-scale patterns over continents and oceans. These patterns are **determined**, or controlled, by differences in temperature and pressure in different parts of the atmosphere. The large-scale movement of air that redistributes heat on Earth is called **circulation**.

For example, the trade winds are a persistent pattern of winds that blow near the equator. The warmest parts of our planet are near the equator. The air in this region becomes warm and rises, creating a low-pressure zone. High in the atmosphere, this warm air travels away from the equator, cools, and sinks. It then blows back toward the equator along Earth's surface, causing the trade winds.

Make Meaning In your science notebook, explain how you would observe different weather conditions based on what you have learned in this lesson.

Lesson 1 Check

Rosa is getting ready for school. It's sunny outside, but it is still winter. Rosa needs to get dressed in something appropriate for the weather.

1. **Identify** What does Rosa need to know about the weather to get dressed for school?

2. **Formulate** Miami and Boston are both coastal cities. Which one is likely to have a higher average humidity and why?

Ski, Swim, or Sail

You visited the three places below. You recorded weather data for each place. Tell your travel blog readers about each of these places. You want your readers to be ready for the weather they will experience.

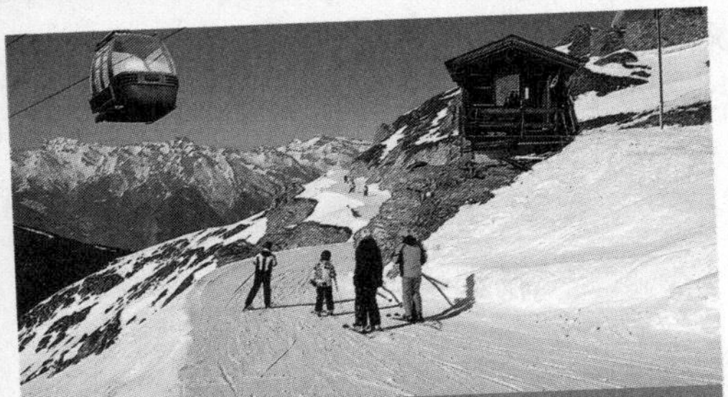

Thyon Region, Switzerland
Temperatures: High 2°C/Low -5°C
Wind: 6 mph NW
Cloudy

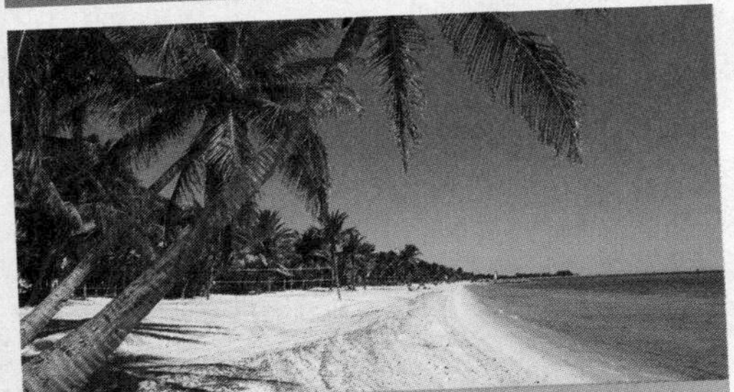

Key West, Florida
Temperatures: High 29°C/Low 27°C
Wind: 6 mph E
Sunny

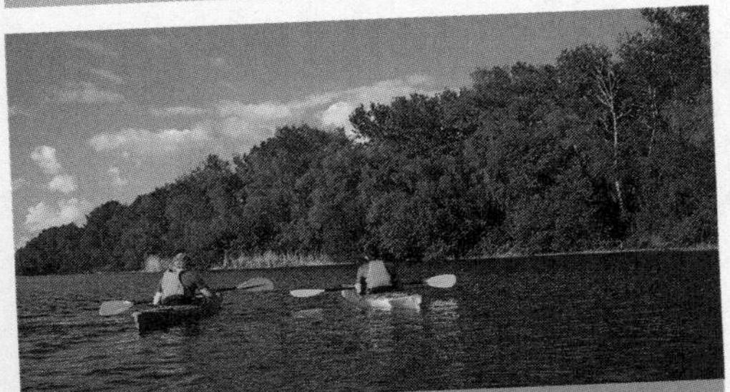

Crane Lake, Minnesota
Temperatures: High 25°C/Low 18°C
Wind: 2 mph NE
Partly cloudy

uEngineer It!  STEM

INTERACTIVITY

Go online to analyze how different homes are equipped for different kinds of weather.

The Goal Is Zero!

The energy bill just came, and it is very high. It is time to make some changes in how the family uses energy. The challenge is to reach the level of zero net energy. What is zero net energy? A zero net energy home is one that uses 60-70 percent less energy than the average home. The rest of its energy comes from renewable resources, such as wind. A family can help convert their home to a zero net energy home by reducing energy use. The family can also install extra insulation in walls and attics or hang awnings above windows to provide more shade. Making changes in habits results in reducing the amount of energy a family uses.

Insulate heating and air conditioning ducts.

Use fans to cool a home.

Improve It

littleBits CHALLENGE

Weather can have a big impact on a home's energy use—especially if you live where seasons are very hot or very cold. After all, everyone wants his or her home to be at a comfortable temperature. Keeping your home that way can use a lot of energy. How can you improve your home to use less energy while still keeping it comfortable?

- [ ] Choose a time of year that your family uses a lot of energy to heat or cool your home.
- [ ] Do a survey of your home to see where heat can be lost during cold weather or where heat can build up in hot weather. Write your findings in the first column of the chart.
- [ ] Then in the second column, write how you might improve your home to save energy. For example, how might you limit the flow of heat lost at a certain location.

Problem	How to improve my home
Cold air comes in through gaps around a door.	Put weather stripping in the gaps where cold air enters.

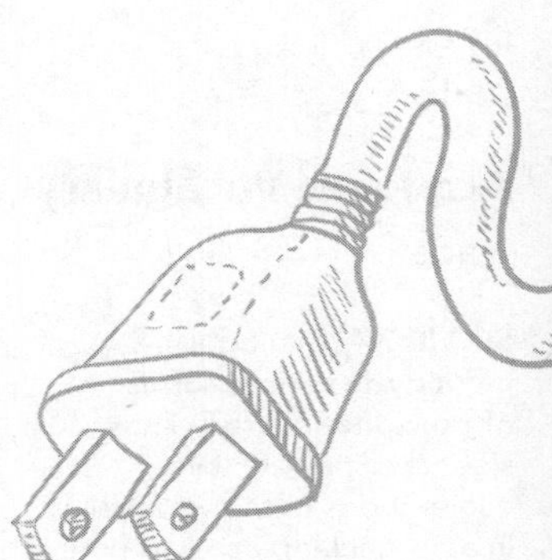

Lesson 2

Forms of Precipitation

I can...

Describe the different types of precipitation.
Connect types of precipitation with other weather conditions.

Literacy Skill

Use Evidence from Text

Vocabulary

precipitation
sleet
hail

Academic Vocabulary

trace

SC.5.E.7.4 Distinguish among the various forms of precipitation (rain, snow, sleet, and hail), making connections to the weather in a particular place and time. (Also **SC.5.E.7.3, SC.5.N.1.4, MAFS.5 NF.2.7**)

LOCAL-TO-GLOBAL Connection

Where you live has a big influence on the precipitation you experience. If you live in the Rocky Mountains of the United States or the Alps of Europe, you expect snow to fall from October to April. Vail, Colorado, received more than 510 cm of snow in 45 days in 2016. Albertville, France, received 662 cm of snow in 64 days in the same year.

Some locations have rainy seasons. Places in both the U.S. and India have rainy seasons with heavy winds and rain. Arizona's rainy season is in the summer and produces about 15 cm of rain out of a yearly 32 cm. India's rainy season produces about 89 cm of rain every year.

Infer What factors affecting weather do you think might be different between Arizona and India?

____

____

uInvestigate Lab

HANDS-ON LAB

SC.5.E.7.3, SC.5.N.1.4

How can you model how clouds form?

Climatologists must understand the conditions that cause clouds to form. How can you use a model to gather evidence about how clouds form?

Materials

- very warm water
- ice cubes
- 2 clear plastic bowls with lids

Be careful when handling the hot water!

Procedure

☐ **1.** Think about how you will use all of the materials to model how clouds are formed.

☐ **2.** Write a procedure to make and test the model. **Control variables** in your investigation. Show your procedure to your teacher before you begin.

☐ **3.** Record your observations.

Science Practice

Scientists **control variables** in an investigation.

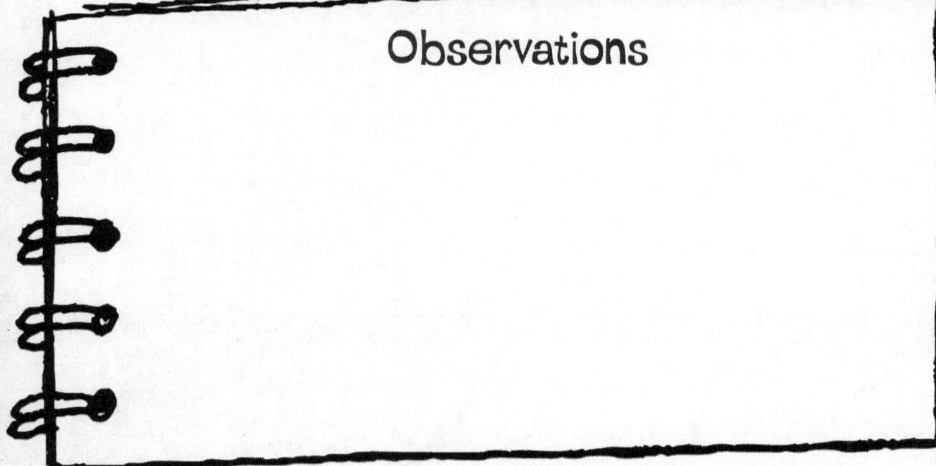

Analyze and Interpret Data

4. Communicate Explain how your investigation modeled cloud formation.

____

____

____

uBe a Scientist

Rainmaker Spray the inside of a pot lid with water. Keep spraying until droplets form. Use a toothpick to push the smaller drops together to form larger drops. Continue until the droplets run in a stream. Over a sink, turn the pot lid over. What happens?

Precipitation

Clouds form when water vapor changes into tiny water droplets or ice crystals. Whether a cloud is made of water droplets or ice crystals depends partly on air temperature. Air temperature in clouds is often much lower than air temperature near the ground. Even in summer, many clouds are made of ice crystals.

Ice crystals and water droplets in clouds can join to make larger particles. Particles increase in size until the gravity acting on their mass causes them to fall from the sky. This is how precipitation forms. **Precipitation** is water that falls to Earth as rain, sleet, snow, or hail. Even **trace**, or small, amounts of rain count toward overall rainfall levels.

Model It! Draw a sequence diagram that shows how precipitation forms.

Rain, Snow, Sleet, and Hail

Most rain in the United States starts as snow. High above Earth, air temperatures are often below 0°C. Ice crystals form in the cold air. The ice crystals grow larger and fall as snowflakes. If air temperatures between the cloud and the ground are below 0°C, the crystals will fall to the ground as snowflakes. Ice crystals may change as they fall through layers of air. If they fall into warmer air, they will melt and fall as rain. If ground-level air is very cold, the rain may freeze before it hits the ground. The frozen raindrops are **sleet**.

Sometimes, strong winds can blow upward through a thunderstorm cloud. These winds blow raindrops back up into the freezing air at the top of the cloud. This creates a small piece of ice. As the ice is blown through the cloud many times, layers of water freeze on it. Finally, it gets too heavy for the winds to carry it back up. This frozen precipitation that forms in layers is called **hail**. The hailstone falls to the ground. Most hailstones are about the size of a pea. Some can get bigger than a baseball.

READING CHECK **Use Evidence from Text** What type of precipitation would likely fall when water passes through freezing air at ground level? Underline evidence in the text that answers the question.

Math ▸ Toolbox

Calculate Rain is much denser than snow. On average, 10 cm of snow equals about 1 cm of rain. If Oakville gets 35 cm of snow, and Mapleton gets 3 cm of rain, how much liquid water precipitation does each city get?

MAFS.5.NF.2.7

Quest Connection

How might people predict whether hail or sleet are likely to happen in certain parts of the world?

Visual Literacy Connection

How does precipitation form?

Rain, freezing rain, sleet, and snow form when water vapor interacts with different conditions in the air.

Write about each kind of precipitation.

Rain

warm air.

Freezing rain

Freezing rain forms when rain makes contact with the ground that is 0°C.

INTERACTIVITY

Do an activity about forms of precipitation.

Most clouds are made of ice crystals and water droplets.

Warm Air

Cold Air

Sleet

Frozen rain.

Snow

It is saper cold

Precipitation and Weather Conditions

In Florida, precipitation in spring, summer, and autumn falls in the form of rain. Winter months can bring sleet, freezing rain, or snow, but only if the temperature drops below freezing. Hail is not seasonal like snow is. Hail is connected to thunderstorms, which can happen in any season.

Precipitation is sometimes connected to severe weather conditions. For example, cloudy conditions can worsen and produce thunderstorms. Thunder is the sound lightning causes as it passes through air. The air expands quickly, and a loud boom occurs. In certain situations, thunderstorms produce tornadoes, columns of air that whirl rapidly. Tornadoes spin at rates from 65 kilometers per hour (kph) up to more than 480 kph. The winds can lift material into their funnels. Like tornadoes, hurricanes are large spinning storms. Hurricanes, though, are much larger. Hurricane winds range from 120 kph to more than 260 kph. Hurricanes dump tremendous amounts of rainfall and cause storm surges that hit ocean coastlines.

Reflect In your science notebook, describe the different weather conditions when rain, snow, sleet, and hail fall in a city that experiences cold winters and hot summers.

Lesson 2 Check

SC.5.E.7.4

1. **Draw Conclusions** Suppose you know that the air temperature from the ground to a cloud is cold enough for water to freeze. What conclusion could you draw about the type of precipitation that would most likely fall?

If its cold sleet or s

2. **Summarize** How are rain and sleet alike?

They are both water.

Sunny, Cloudy, or Rainy

It's time to write your second blog. You want to tell your readers about precipitation at the places you visited. Use this weather data you gathered to explain why precipitation is important to include when describing the weather of a location.

Mojave, CA
Sunny
Rainfall this month: 0.2 cm

Orlando, FL
Cloudy
Rainfall this month: 55 cm

Seattle, WA
Rainy
Rainfall this month: 112 cm

Lesson 3

Land Affects Weather

I can...

Recognize different weather patterns in different environments.

Literacy Skill
Use Evidence from Text

Vocabulary
convection current

Academic Vocabulary
impact

VIDEO

Watch a video about convection currents.

SC.5.E.7.5 Recognize that some of the weather-related differences, such as temperature and humidity, are found among different environments, such as swamps, deserts, and mountains. (Also **SC.5.N.1.3**)

STEM Connection

Animals such as armadillos naturally live in the hot, dry desert. Tree frogs and the beautiful quetzal bird live in hot, wet rain forests. How can people who cannot go to a desert or rain forest experience the plants and animals that live in those places? Go to a zoo. Zoo engineers have designed specific habitats that mimic the natural habitats of each kind of animal.

To build each habitat, designers and engineers must consider each factor of the habitat. For example, to build a rain forest habitat, they might build a dome, similar to the one in the picture. A rain forest dome must keep the temperature between 34°C (93°F) and 20°C (68°F). Humidity must remain between 77 percent and 88 percent. Yearly artificial rain needs to be about 254 cm.

This desert dome works by keeping rain and snow out.

A zoo rain forest needs to control the warmth and moisture.

uInvestigate Lab

SC.5.E.7.5, SC.5.N.1.3

What can happen to warm air?

When zookeepers build habitats for their animals, they must consider many factors, including air temperature in all parts of the habitat from top to bottom. Why can the temperature at the top of a habitat be different from the temperature at the bottom?

Materials

- safety goggles
- bowl
- very warm water
- scissors
- thread
- tape
- Spiral Pattern sheet

Procedure

☐ **1.** Predict what you think happens to air as it warms.

____

____

☐ **2.** Write a procedure to test your prediction. Use all the materials. Remember to include more than one trial. Show your procedure to your teacher before you begin.

☐ **3.** Test your prediction, and record your observations.

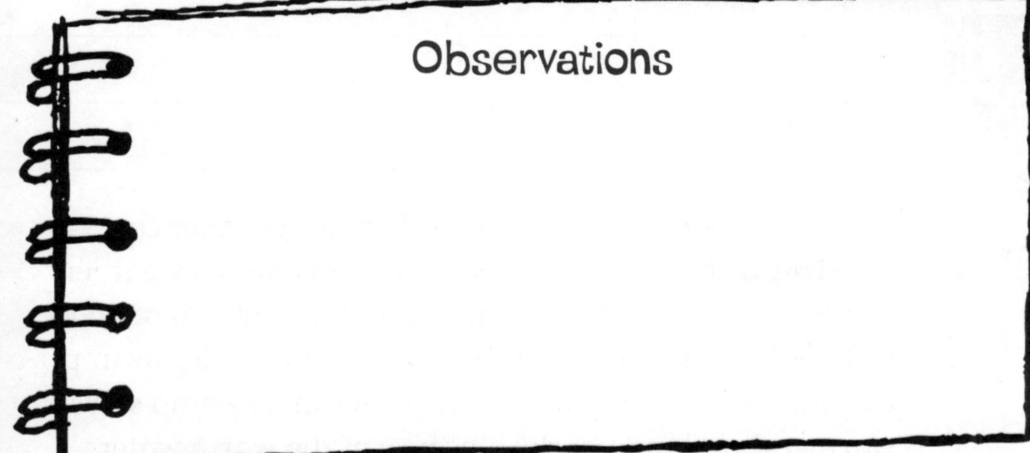

Be careful handling warm water.

Wear safety goggles.

Be careful using scissors.

Science Practice

Scientists **repeat investigations** to verify data.

Analyze and Interpret Data

4. Use Evidence What conclusion can you make about what happens to warm air? Use the data you gathered to support your conclusion.

____

____

Land Features and Weather

You can control climate indoors with special equipment. However, controlling climate outdoors is impossible because you cannot control various factors, such as landforms.

Have you ever wondered why a desert and a rain forest have different weather? One reason is the way the land in those places is shaped. The two places shown in the pictures have different weather.

Describe Write a caption to describe the shape of the land in each photo.

Swamps, deserts, mountains, and bodies of water can also **impact**, or influence, weather. This causes weather conditions, such as temperature and humidity, to often be different in different environments. For example, swamps are often warm and humid. The water in a swamp stays warmer than land nearby. Because of the warm water, nearby land is less likely to freeze. This is important when planting crops such as citrus trees, which can be damaged when they freeze.

READING CHECK **Use Evidence from Text** Underline an impact of swamps on land temperatures.

uBe a Scientist

Local Weather Is there a body of water in your area? How does that water affect temperatures, wind, and general weather there? How would you expect local weather in another place that is not near water, such as in the Great Plains or the Rocky Mountains, to change from day to night? Make a prediction and then investigate.

Connecting Concepts ▸ Toolbox

Patterns Knowing how the Rocky Mountains impact weather on both sides of the mountains helps people forecast weather around other mountain ranges. Suppose you know where a mountain range lies and the direction of winds in that area. Could you forecast expected weather patterns from this information?

Convection Currents

Have you ever walked fast over hot sand to get to the cool water of a lake or an ocean? Land heats more quickly in sunlight than water does. Land also cools more quickly than water at night. This uneven heating of Earth's surface causes air to be at different temperatures in different places. These temperature differences cause convection currents, like the one in the diagram, to form. A **convection current** is the rising and sinking of matter in a circular pattern due to differences in temperature. Temperature differences in air cause wind, storms, and all of the different types of weather.

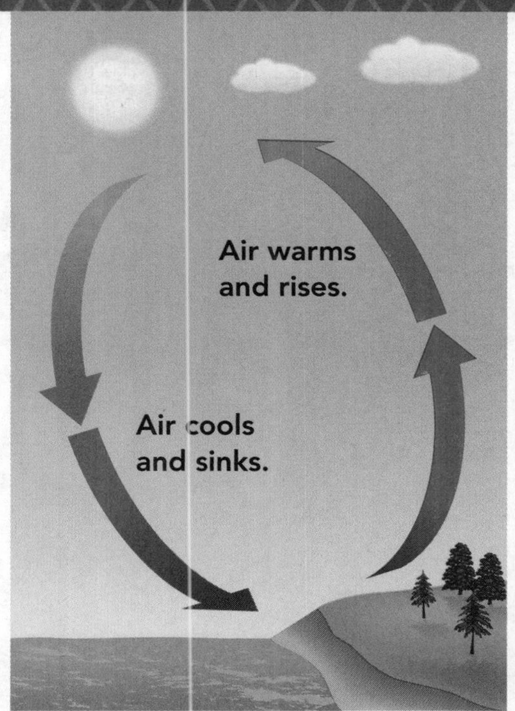

Explain Draw pictures of a lake and the land around it. Add arrows to show how the air moves as the time of day changes.

12:00 PM	9:00 PM

Quest Connection

Suppose that in your blog, you recommended that travelers visit an area with a large lake. You said that a lakeside location might have milder temperature changes, even in winter. Explain why this might be true.

____

____

____

Visual Literacy Connection

How does air flow?

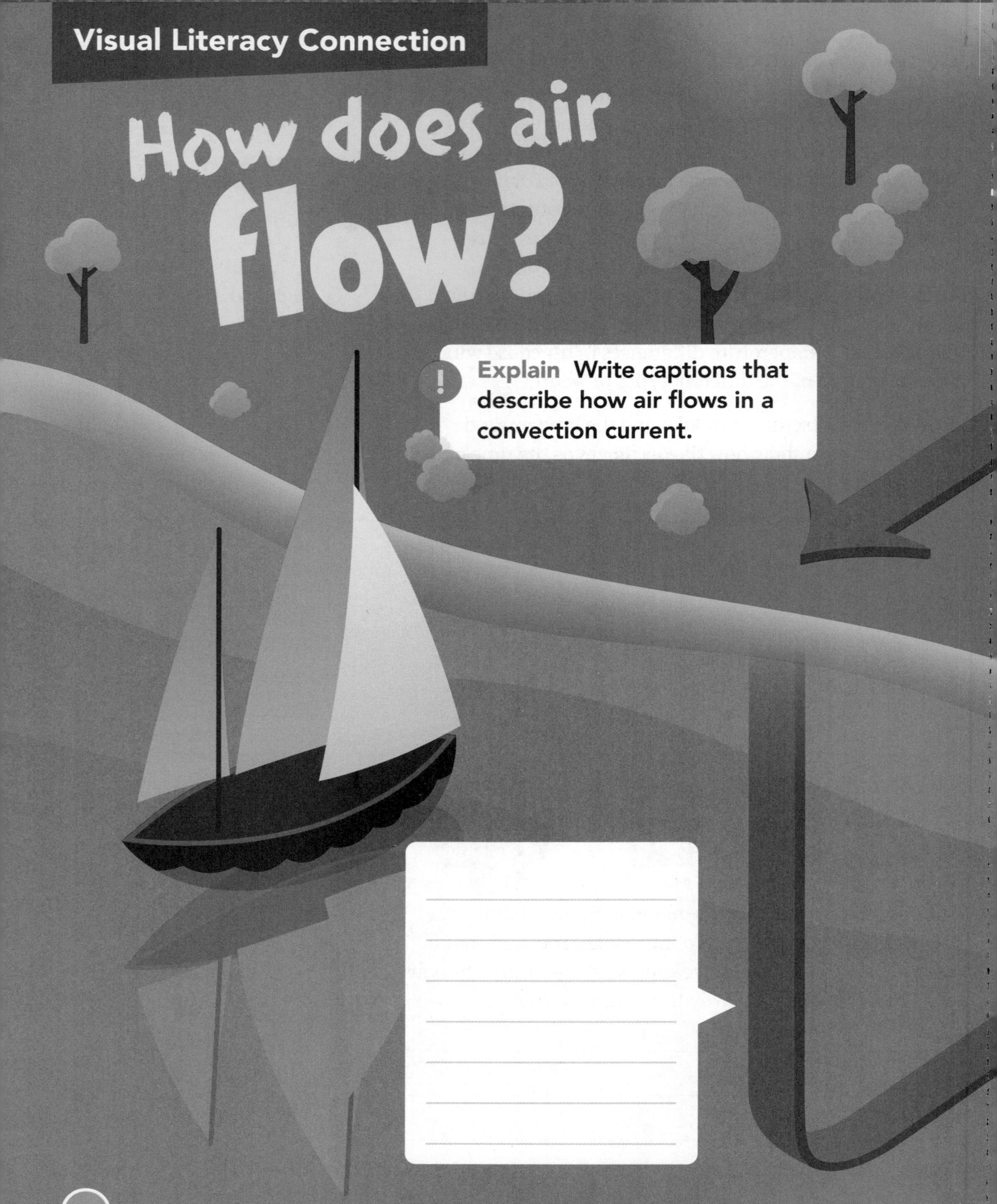

Explain Write captions that describe how air flows in a convection current.

INTERACTIVITY
Do an activity about weather and the environment.

Deserts

A desert gets very little precipitation. Therefore, the desert air is very dry. If the land heats during the day, it cools quickly at night. Because there is little water in the desert, clouds and precipitation do not form there often.

Mountains

When air flows up a mountainside, it cools. Clouds form, and precipitation may fall. Mountains can slow or block the flow of a storm system. Precipitation may occur on one side of the mountain but not on the other. The shape of a mountain affects an environment's weather conditions. One side of a mountain may be cool and humid while the other side is warm and dry.

Justify Look at both photos. The desert and mountains shown have no liquid water. Why is the mountain range not also considered desert?

____

____

____

Lesson 3 Check

SC.5.E.7.5

1. **Draw Conclusions** Why might a coastal region experience more clouds on a warm, sunny day than a desert region?

____

____

____

____

2. **Use Evidence from Text** What are two weather-related differences between environments such as swamps, mountains, and deserts?

____

Quest Check-In

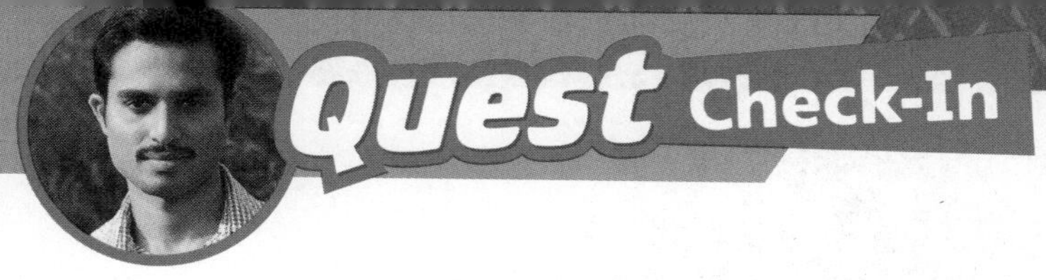

Mount Kilimanjaro

A traveler wants to experience warm, mild, and cold weather at a single location. In your blog, explain how Mount Kilimanjaro or similar mountains influence climate and provide variety in weather conditions. Explain how landforms add to a variety of weather.

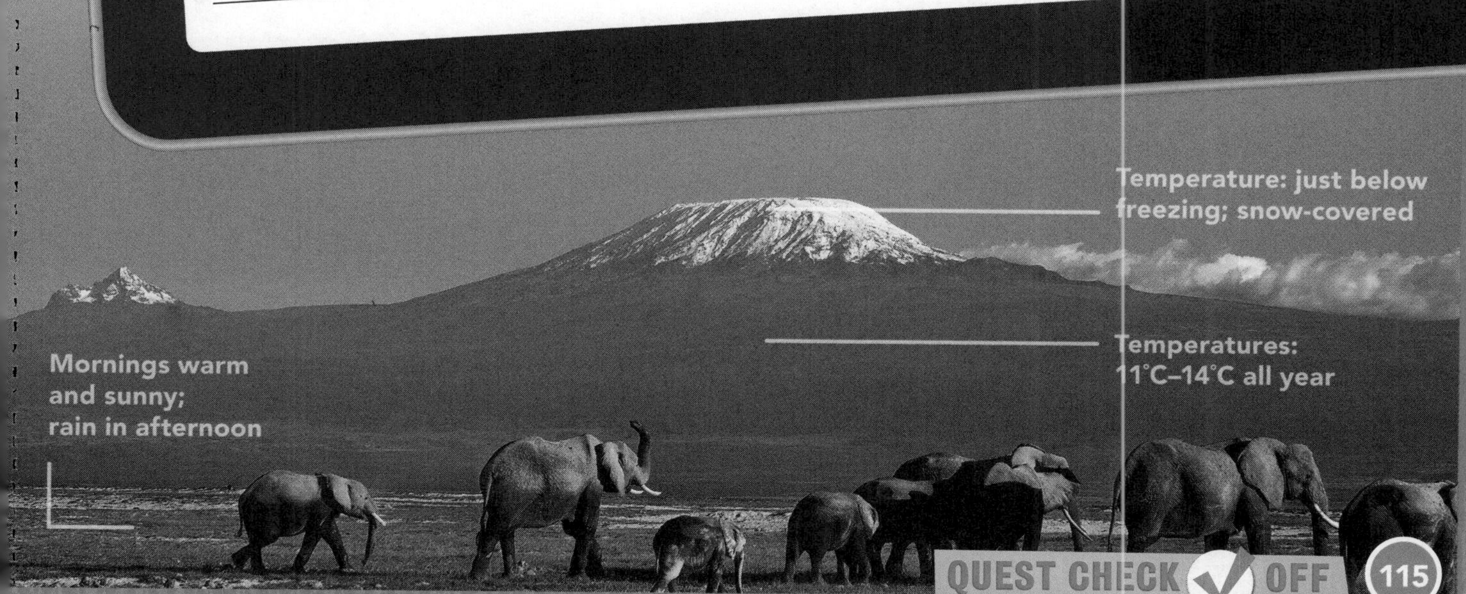
Temperature: just below freezing; snow-covered
Temperatures: 11°C–14°C all year
Mornings warm and sunny; rain in afternoon

QUEST CHECK OFF

Lesson 4

Climate

I can...

Describe characteristics of different climate zones.

Literacy Skill

Use Evidence from Text

Vocabulary

climate
latitude
elevation

Academic Vocabulary

pattern

SC.5.E.7.6 Describe characteristics (temperature and precipitation) of different climate zones as they relate to latitude, elevation, and proximity to bodies of water. (Also **SC.5.N.1.1**)

SPORTS Connection

The human body is an amazing machine. At higher elevations, where there is less oxygen, it produces extra red blood cells to carry more oxygen to all parts of the body. The body's cells use oxygen to help break down substances to release energy. The energy is needed to carry on the processes or actions of the body, such as running, jumping, breathing, and thinking.

Athletes who train at high altitude usually do so for a two-week period. Training for two weeks at high altitude is enough to increase red blood cell levels. Back at lower elevations, the extra red cells last from 10 to 20 days. The athlete performs at a higher level because more oxygen is available to power muscle movements and other processes.

Identify What are five other types of athletes or careers that might benefit from training at high altitudes.

___

___

___

uInvestigate Lab

HANDS-ON LAB

SC.5.N.11

How do bodies of water affect climate?

Climatologists use models to understand how different factors can affect the climate of an area. How can you use a model to make observations of one of these factors?

Materials

- cake pan
- cardboard, 15 cm x 15 cm
- warm water
- ice cubes
- goggles

Procedure

☐ **1.** Use the materials as a way to model how lake water temperatures can affect air temperatures.

☐ **2.** Show your plan to your teacher before you begin. Record your observations.

Science Practice

Scientists make observations and record data.

Analyze and Interpret Data

3. Infer Based on your observation, how do bodies of water affect the climate of an area?

____

____

____

____

____

____

____

____

____

____

____

Observations

Connecting Concepts ▸ Toolbox

Earth's Systems and Patterns Similar latitudes can have similar patterns. What are two places on the climate map that have climates similar to where you live? Mark the places on the map with Xs.

Climate

Weather and *climate* do not have the same definitions. *Weather* is "all the atmospheric conditions in one place at a single moment." **Climate** describes the weather conditions over a period of years. Climate includes average precipitation, average temperatures, and temperature highs and lows. Weather changes when atmospheric conditions change. Like weather, climate is always changing but over longer periods.

Climate around the world is divided into zones. A climate zone is a region where temperature ranges and climate conditions follow a similar pattern. A **pattern** is a design, characteristic, or series of events that repeats in a predictable way. Tropical zones are hot because they receive more direct sunlight than other zones. Brasília, Brazil, is in the tropical zone. Most of Greenland is in the polar zone. Polar zones receive less direct sunlight and are much colder. They also get less precipitation.

Latitude

One factor that affects the climate of a place is its latitude. **Latitude** is a measurement that tells how far a place is from the equator. Latitude is measured in degrees. Latitude increases from 0° at the equator to 90° at the North and South Poles. Areas near the equator are generally warm all year. Rainfall is often plentiful. They are in the warmest climate zone. In general, climate gets cooler and has less precipitation as you move away from the equator toward the poles.

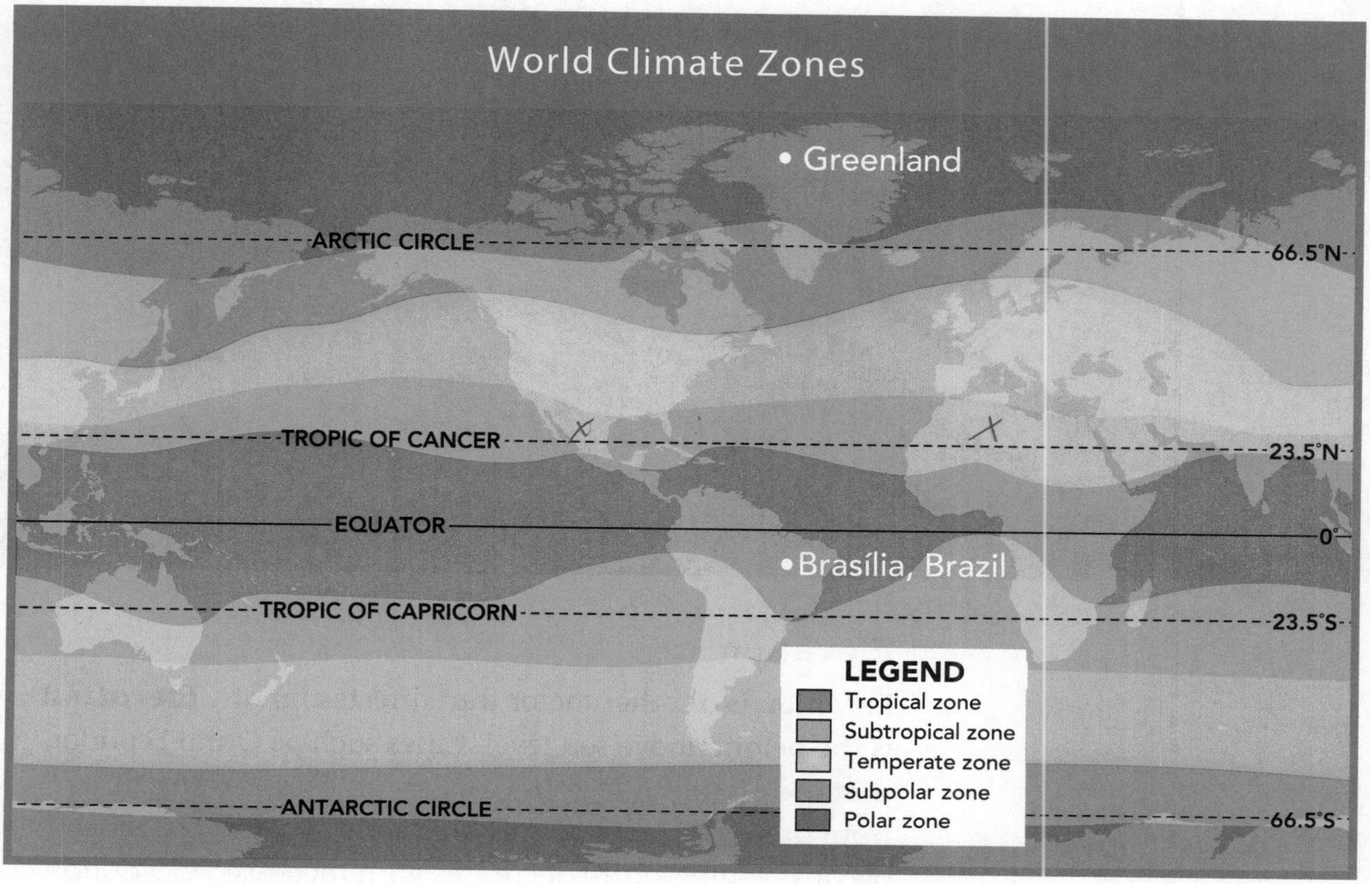

World Climate Zones

• Greenland

ARCTIC CIRCLE 66.5°N

TROPIC OF CANCER 23.5°N

EQUATOR 0°

• Brasília, Brazil

TROPIC OF CAPRICORN 23.5°S

ANTARCTIC CIRCLE 66.5°S

LEGEND
- Tropical zone
- Subtropical zone
- Temperate zone
- Subpolar zone
- Polar zone

Relate Find Brasília and Greenland on the map. How does latitude affect the temperature and rainfall of these two places?

Brazil is hot, greenland is cold.

Quest Connection

How can an understanding of climate zones help someone plan a trip?

To see if it's cold or hot.

Elevation

Elevation is another factor that affects climate. **Elevation** is the height above sea level. Cities such as Quito Ecuador, that are on mountains may have climates that are different from areas around them. Higher land is generally cooler because temperature decreases with increased elevation. This is what causes some mountaintops to have snow on them all year. However, there is not a consistent pattern of high precipitation at higher elevations. The amount of precipitation at each elevation varies. Sudden changes in elevation is the main elevation-related factor in precipitation amounts.

Other factors also cause climate differences around mountains. Areas on opposite sides of a mountain range can have very different climates. For example, look at the west side of the mountain in the diagram. It has a wet climate because, as the clouds rise and cool, precipitation forms. It may receive more than 2.5 m of precipitation each year. The other side of the mountains has a dry climate.

Explain Quito sits right on the equator among the Andes Mountains. Underline the text that explains why the climate of Quito is cooler than that of many other places near the equator.

Bodies of Water

Areas near large bodies of water often get more precipitation. Large bodies of water can affect a climate by slowing the rise and fall of the air temperature. Remember that bodies of water warm and cool more slowly than land. Because of this, the temperature of the air near water does not change as quickly as the temperature of the air inland. In the winter, large beaches often do not get as cold as areas just a few miles inland. In the summer, the air over beaches is often cooler than air over areas inland.

Describe The Galápagos Islands are west of Quito in the Pacific Ocean. How might this location influence the temperature and amount of precipitation in the Galápagos Islands?

It would be cold if it's far from the equater.

uBe a Scientist

Compare Climates Locate your city and its latitude on a map. Identify another city in a different part of the world at the same latitude. Would you expect this city to have the same climate as the one near you? What variables, or small changes, might make two cities at the same latitude and with the same climate have different weather? Share your research, claim, and evidence with your class.

Lesson 4 Check

1. **Describe** Describe the temperature and precipitation in a polar place that is inland, and has high elevation.

It would be cold and sleet or snow.

2. **Recall** Define latitude. Explain how latitude at the equator compares to latitude at the North and South Poles.

Equator latitude is hot but at North or south pole it would be cold

Quest Check-In Lab

How can you define the climate of a location?

You have collected much information for your blog. Now it is time to analyze the data, look for patterns, and develop a method to define the climate of a place, using only the information given.

Procedure

☐ **1.** Some of the data you have collected are summarized in the tables. They show some average climate conditions for the past 30 years in three locations. Analyze the data to look for patterns. Summarize what you find.

☐ **2.** Describe how you would define a location's climate using only the information in the tables.

Seasonal Average Precipitation (mm) over 30 years					
	Spring	Summer	Fall	Winter	Annual Total
Mojave, California	86 mm	11 mm	63 mm	194 mm	_______mm
Vail, Colorado	66 mm	88 mm	130 mm	82 mm	_______mm
Tallahassee, Florida	290 mm	330 mm	317 mm	565 mm	_______mm

High and Low Average Temperatures by Month (°C) (1985 – 2015)												
	Jan	Feb	Mar	Apr	May	Jun	Jul	Aug	Sep	Oct	Nov	Dec
Mojave	14°/ 1°	16°/ 2.8°	19°/ 5°	22°/ 7.8°	27°/ 13°	32°/ 17°	36°/ 20°	35.5/ 20°	32°/ 15.5°	21°/ 10°	18°/ 4°	14°/ 1°
Vail	-2°/ -15°	1°/ -13°	5°/ -9°	9°/ -5°	16°/ -0.3°	21°/ 2.6°	24°/ 6°	23°/ 5°	19°/ 2°	12°/ -4°	3°/ -9°	-3°/ -13°
Tallahassee	18°/ 4°	19°/ 6°	23°/ 8°	27°/ 11°	30°/ 17°	33°/ 21°	33°/ 22°	33°/ 22°	31°/ 20°	27°/ 14°	23°/ 8°	18°/ 5°

Analyze and Interpret Data

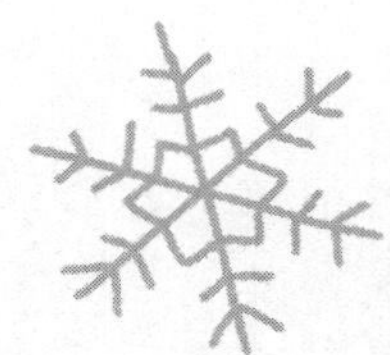

3. **Draw Conclusions** What conclusions can you draw from the data about the climate in these locations?

____

____

____

____

4. **Identify** The data in these tables are all long-term averages. What is another piece of climate data that would be useful to your readers?

____

____

QUEST CHECK OFF

Lesson 5

Severe Weather Safety

I can...

Make a plan for a natural weather disaster and know why I should have a plan.

Literacy Skill

Use Evidence from Text

Vocabulary

severe weather
natural disaster

Academic Vocabulary

strategy
organize

SC.5.E.7.7 Design a family preparedness plan for natural disasters and identify the reasons for having such a plan (Also **SC.5.N.1.1**).

CURRICULUM Connection

The year was 1926. Miami had a population of more than 100,000 people. Everywhere people looked were hotels, homes, and businesses. Ships at sea reported a hurricane on the way, but Miami's citizens were not warned. On September 18, the storm came ashore about 45 kilometers (km) south of downtown Miami. The category 4 hurricane struck Miami with winds up to 233 km per hour. Called the Great Miami Hurricane, the storm was nearly 525 km wide. Winds and flooding caused damage that in 2015 dollars would have been $190 billion. More than 370 people died, and thousands were left homeless.

Communicate How might damage and deaths have been different if citizens had been warned of the storm?

____

____

____

The hurricane that struck southern Florida on September 18, 1926, destroyed this post office and took between 325 and 650 lives.

STEM · uInvestigate Lab

HANDS-ON LAB

SC.5.E.7.7, SC.5.N.1.1

How can you stay safe during a storm?

Engineers plan ways to deal with major problems from storms, such as flooding. How can you build a structure that can withstand a flood?

Materials

- plastic container
- 2 cups sand or soil
- 1 cup gravel

Suggested Materials

- pitcher
- water
- scissors
- bamboo skewers
- craft sticks
- glue
- aluminum foil
- modeling clay
- sheet of craft foam
- duct tape
- clear plastic sheet

Design and Build

☐ **1.** Identify the criteria that you think are most important when designing a waterproof structure.

____

____

☐ **2.** Put the soil and gravel in the plastic container to model land. Choose materials to build a waterproof structure on the land.

☐ **3.** Test your structure. Slowly add water to your land model. Record your observations.

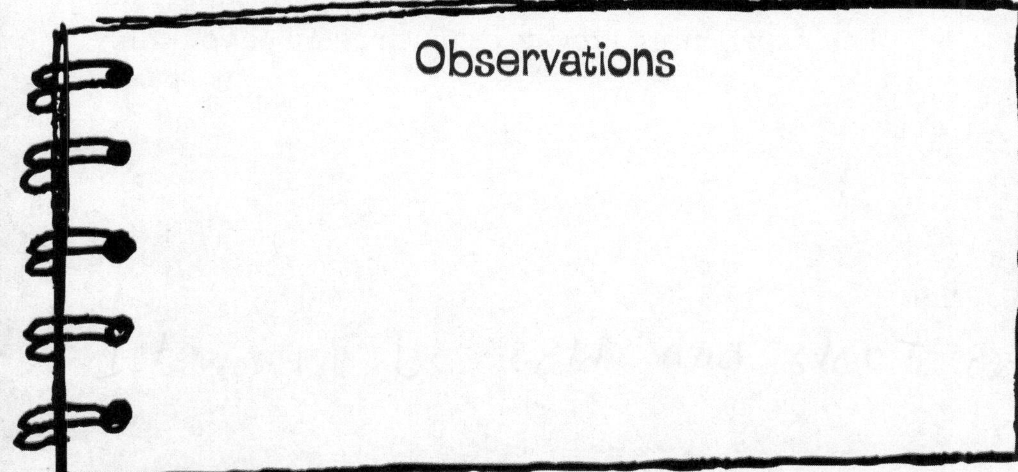

Be careful when handling sharp skewers or scissors.

Engineering Practice

Engineers **design solutions** to problems and test the solutions.

Evaluate Your Design

4. Use Evidence Was your structure floodproof? What could you have done to make your structure better? Explain your reasoning.

____

____

uBe a Scientist

Flash! Boom! Estimate your distance from a lightning strike. At the flash, start counting the seconds. Stop counting when you hear thunder. Divide the number of seconds by 5. This will give you the distance to the strike in miles. Divide the number by 3 and you get the distance in kilometers. You see a flash and hear the boom 15 seconds later. About how far away is the strike in miles? In kilometers?

Types of Severe Weather

Have you ever been startled by thunder or had to stay inside because the wind outside was too strong? Dangerous conditions of the atmosphere, such as tornadoes and hurricanes, are known as **severe weather**. Tornadoes can be hundreds of meters wide and travel great distances over minutes or hours. The winds in the tornado in the photo move at hundreds of kilometers per hour. Winds this fast can move cars and buildings around with ease. By contrast, the swirling winds of a hurricane are typically not as fast as a tornado's winds, but the winds of these ocean storms are more destructive. Why? First, hurricanes last for days, possibly hitting several locations. Second, a hurricane is hundreds of kilometers wide. Third, hurricanes can result in huge waves that cause severe damage and flood the coast. Heavy rains can also cause floods farther inland. Other forms of severe weather include thunderstorms and blizzards. Very high or low temperatures can be dangerous as well.

Write About It Write a description of your experience with hurricanes, or interview a parent or neighbor about their experiences. Provide as much detail as you can.

Staying Safe

A quick and destructive change in the environment that is not caused by people is called a **natural disaster**. Some examples of natural disasters include earthquakes, wildfires, floods, and severe weather. Some natural disasters, such as hurricanes and tornadoes, can be detected in time to warn the public. When a hurricane or a tornado is approaching, the National Weather Service issues watches and warnings on the radio and television, such as the one in the picture. Some towns alert people with a loud siren. Whether or not there is a warning, it is important to prepare for any emergency by having a safety **strategy**, or plan.

A natural disaster can make it impossible to drive to a store to buy food. Roads may get flooded and bridges may be damaged. Electricity is often interrupted, and the water supply may be contaminated. Keep on hand water and food that does not need to be refrigerated, as well as a first-aid kit, flashlights, and batteries. Also, keep tools such as hammers, nails, tape, screwdrivers, and screws in an emergency kit.

Identify In an emergency, it is a good idea to have important phone numbers handy and in one place. What important phone numbers should be included? Write them on the Contact Information card.

Contact Information

____

____

____

____

____

Visual Literacy Connection

How can you prepare for SEVERE WEATHER?

Describe Write one safety tip you would add to a safety plan for each type of severe weather.

Check out these safety tips!

Excessive Heat

____

____

Heavy Wind

____

____

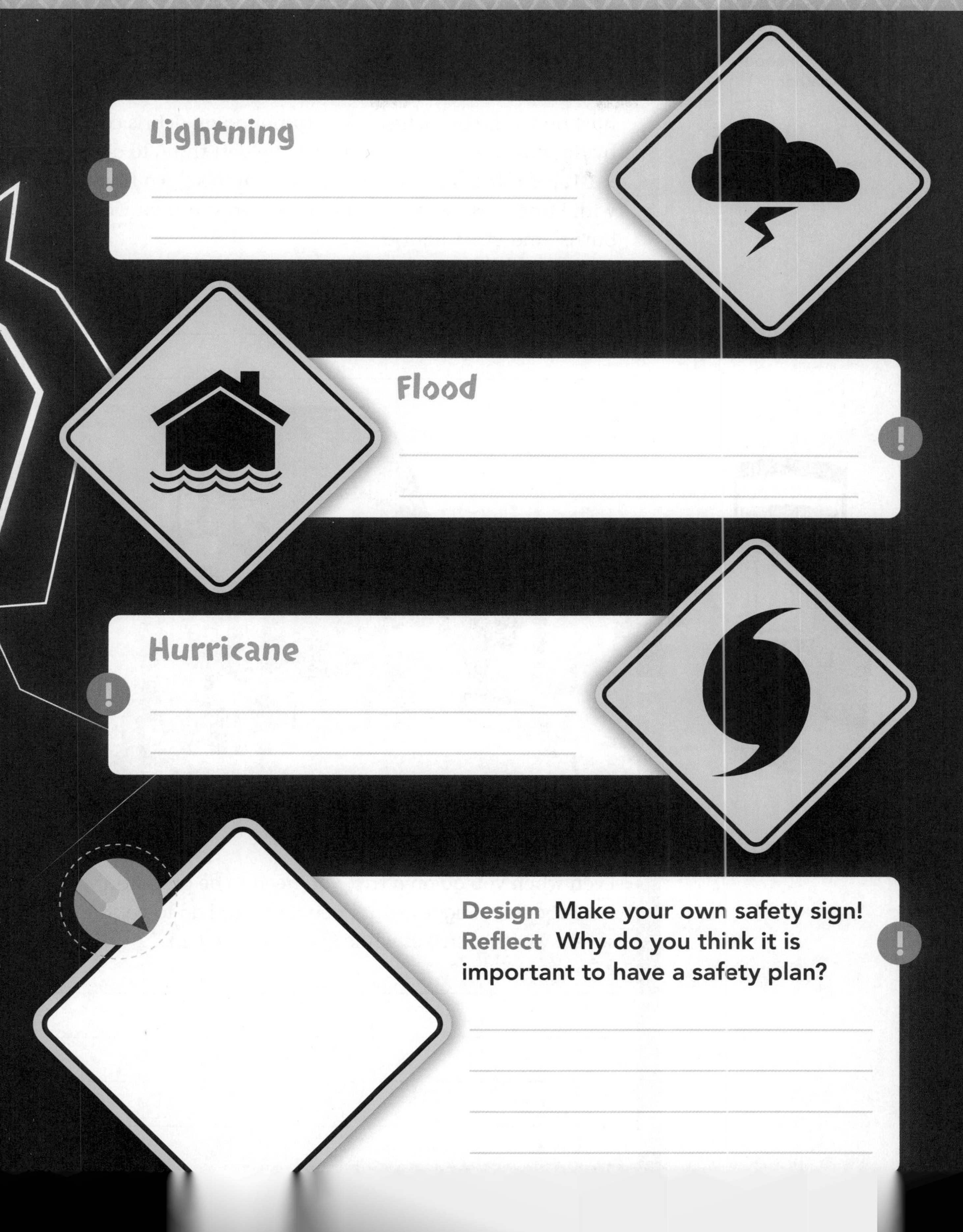

Design Make your own safety sign!
Reflect Why do you think it is important to have a safety plan?

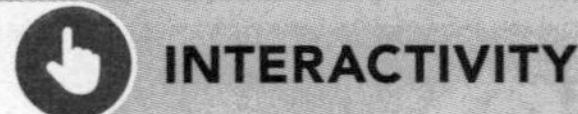

Do an activity about severe weather.

First Aid

Natural disasters can cause injuries. Sometimes people are hurt by falling branches or by stumbling on debris carried by floodwaters. In an emergency, the best thing to do is call 9-1-1. For minor injuries, it is important to keep a first-aid kit with bandages, tweezers, and other items to treat wounds, burns, and other injuries.

Apply What would you include in your family first-aid kit?

____

____

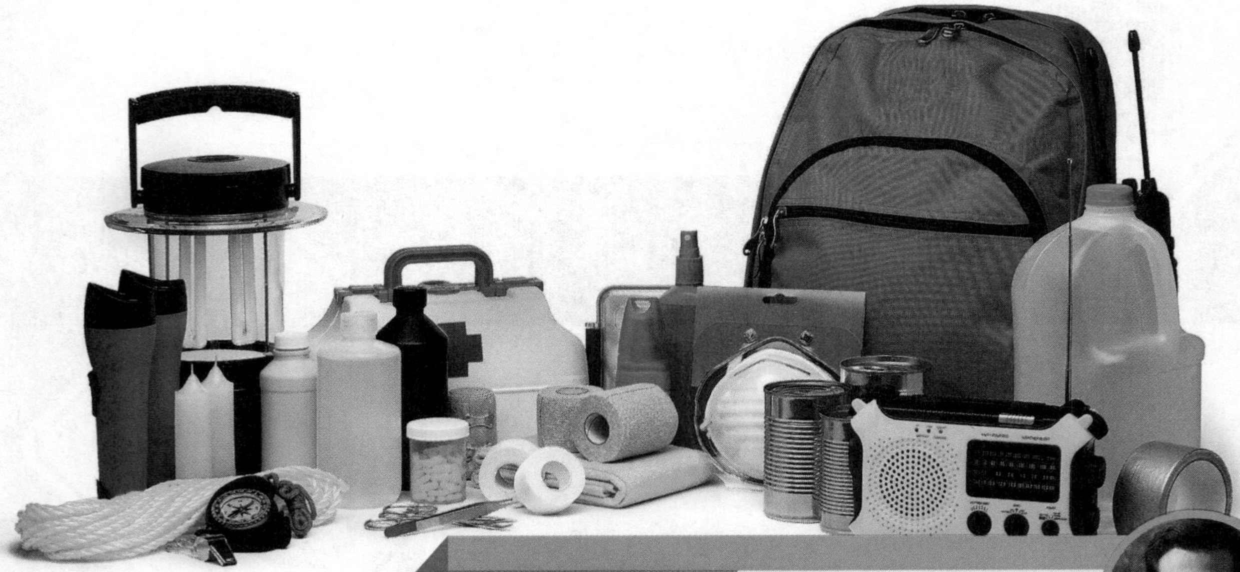

Quest Connection

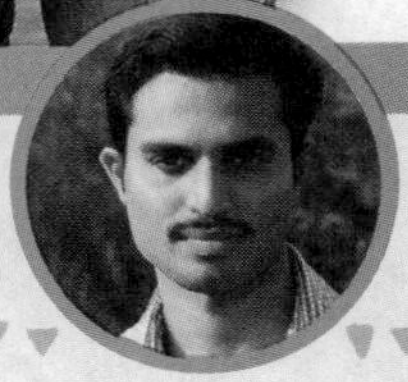

Even when you go on a trip, you need to be prepared with a safety plan. Suggest what people should do to be safe if severe weather strikes while they are on a trip.

____

____

____

____

Have a Plan

Sometimes it may be necessary to evacuate your home or school due to a natural disaster. In those cases, it is important to have a plan. You should know where you will meet with your family or classmates, and you should know at least two ways to get out of a room. Make sure you organize any supplies. When you **organize**, you put things in order or arrange them. If you have a plan and everyone in the family knows what to do, you will be safer.

Use what you have learned in this lesson to design a plan to prepare for when a natural disaster happens. Include contact information, what to include in a safety kit, and what actions to take.

Lesson 5 Check

1. **Summarize** Identify three ways you would prepare for a natural disaster.

____

____

2. **Critique** Your friend says there are no differences between tornadoes and hurricanes. How would you correct your friend's statement?

____

____

____

Quest Check-In

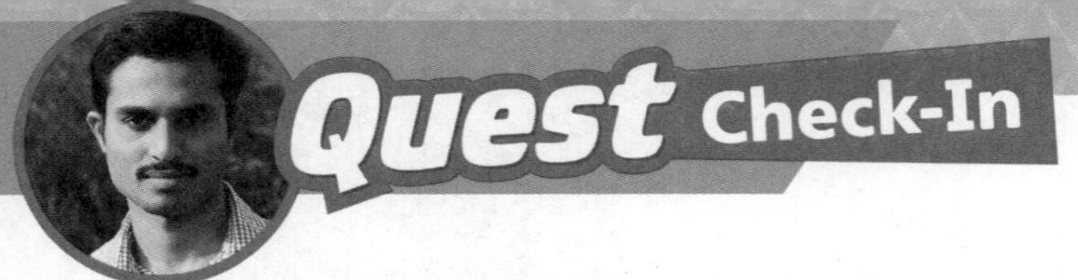

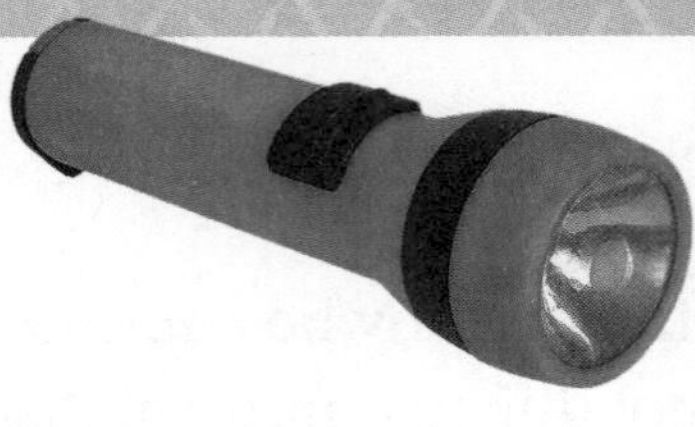

Safety While Traveling

You know some of your travelers might run into severe weather. In your blog, provide safety tips for possible severe weather issues in locations you wrote about in your brochure: Mojave, Vail, and Tallahassee.

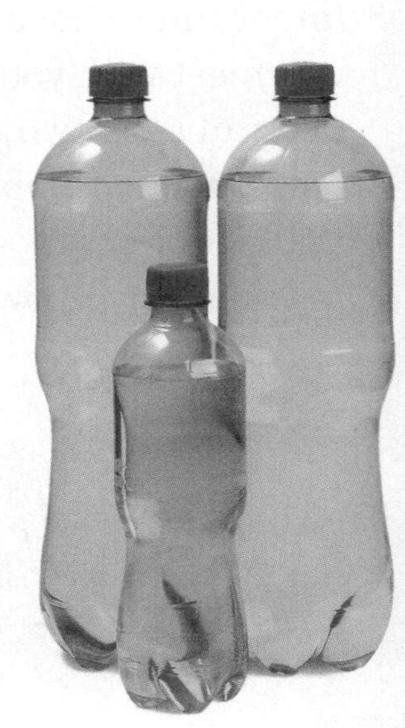

1. What should travelers know before they leave home for their destination?

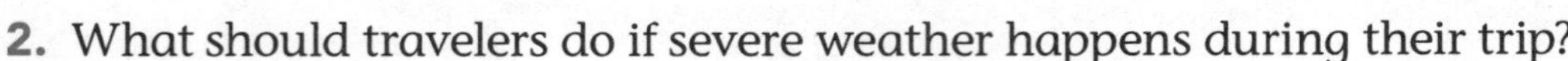

2. What should travelers do if severe weather happens during their trip?

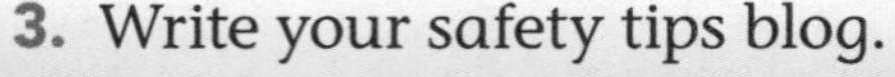

3. Write your safety tips blog.

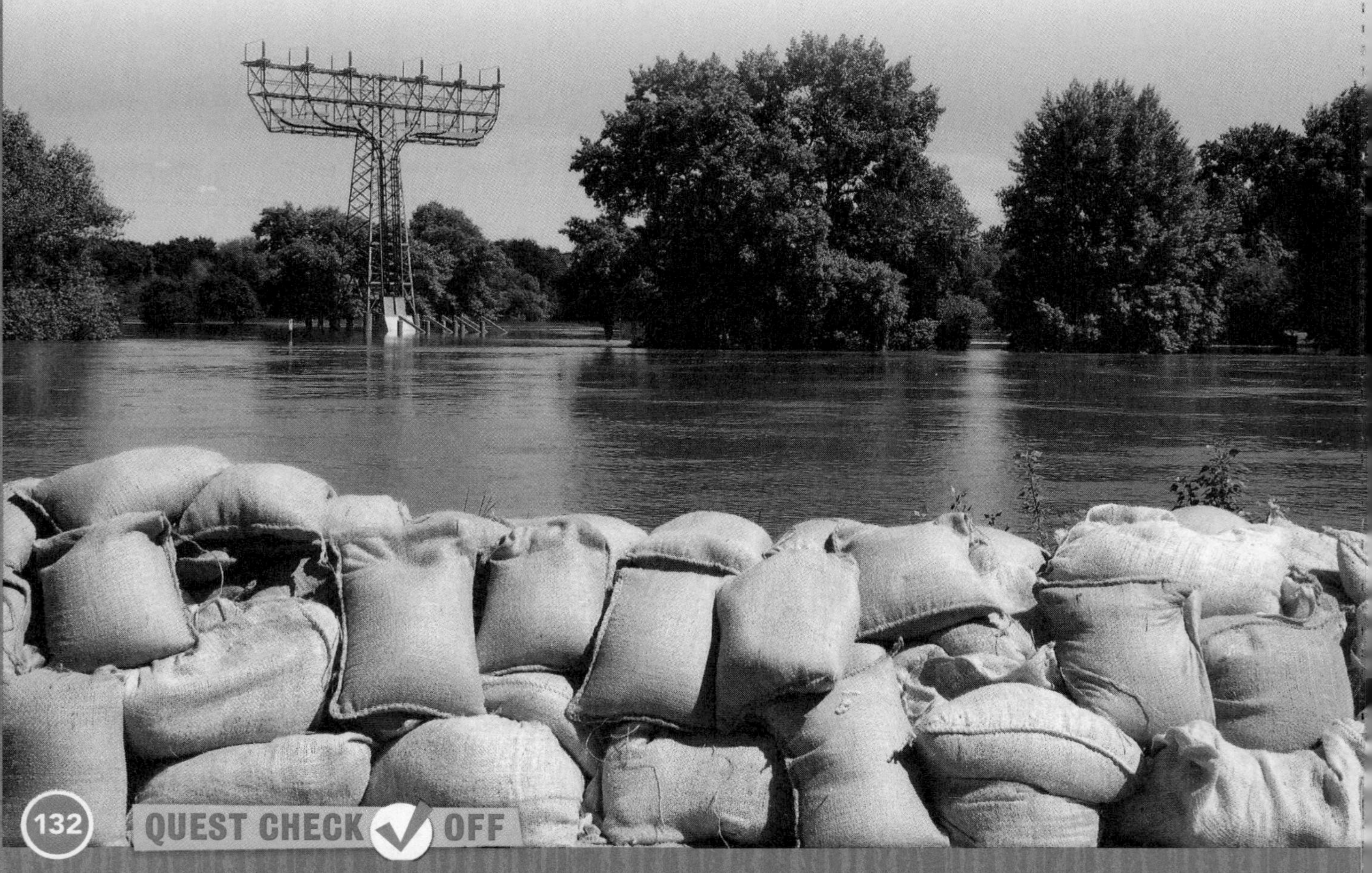

SOLVE it WITH Science

What if climate changed greatly?

Climate is always changing, but the changes take a long time. We are experiencing one of the most rapid periods of climate change ever recorded. Global temperature has increased more than 1°C over the past one hundred years. Suppose Earth's climate changed much more over the next ten years. How would that change daily weather?

The best way to answer this question is to consider the evidence you have for the climate change. Then ask reasonable questions. For example, if precipitation rates increased dramatically, you might compare daily rainfall rates for specific dates in the past. Just knowing the total precipitation might not be enough information, though. You might also need to know the types of precipitation that occurred. Did more or less snow fall than usual? How often did sleet occur? Are sea levels increasing or decreasing? Why? You might find there are new weather issues to deal with. Here are some questions to think about and answer:

What would happen if the average global temperature increased by 5°C?

____

____

____

How would the change affect more extreme climates?

____

____

How might seasons change?

____

____

Quest Findings

INTERACTIVITY

Organize data to support your Quest Findings.

Windy, Wet, Wild, or Wonderful?

How can we predict weather?

You've been writing your blog for a while. Now it is time to tell travelers about the different types of weather they are likely to experience at each location. This information will help travelers decide where to go on a trip. How will you present this information? That's up to you!

What data do you already have to share with your blog readers?

____

____

____

Brainstorm Information to Include

____

____

____

____

What other data could you collect in order to support your ideas?

____

____

What media could you use to present your facts?

____

____

Make your product and present it to the class.

Career Connection

Climatologist

A climatologist studies the long-term weather patterns of a particular area. They study different factors that might cause or influence weather. Climatologists might study ocean and air currents, and mountain formations. They might also fly into hurricanes or record tornado paths.

Climatologists may work outdoors, taking water samples or measuring wind patterns. They may also work in a lab or on a computer. Some work for the government, teach in colleges, or appear on radio or television.

Climatologists determine the causes of changing climates. Some causes are natural, such as changes in amounts of sunlight, changing ocean current patterns, or volcanic eruptions. Some causes are human made, such as the gases released from burning coal and gasoline.

Write About It In your science notebook, tell what kind of climatology work you would like to do. Tell why you chose this.

Assessment

Read each question and choose or write the best answer.

1. **Vocabulary** What is the state of the atmosphere at a given time and place called?

   A. climate

   B. weather

   C. circulation

   D. altitude

2. **Explain** How does barometric pressure affect weather?

____

____

____

____

____

Use the photo to answer questions 3 and 4.

3. **Summarize** Write three factors that determine the weather shown.

____

____

4. **Hypothesize** The border of this mountain range is next to a warmer, low elevation valley. What generalization can you make about the wind pattern along the border?

   A. Winds will blow from the valley up the mountains sides.

   B. Winds will blow up and down between the mountain sides and the valley.

   C. Winds will only blow through the valley.

   D. No wind will move air between the mountains and the valley.

5. **Analyze** Sean lives in an area that experiences hot, dry summers that change gradually to cold, snowy winters. If he wants to forecast the snowy days using only one measurement tool, should he use a weather vane, thermometer, or barometer? Use evidence to support your claim.

____

____

____

____

____

____

____

____

____

____

6. Use Evidence from Text Read the passage. What evidence explains how hail forms? Write the evidence in the table.

Hail forms when falling ice crystals get blown upward through a thunderstorm cloud by a strong wind. After the crystals begin to fall, the upward wind blows them through the cloud again. Hailstones gain more ice every time they pass through the clouds. Hail happens during thunderstorms.

Fact	
Fact	
Fact	

7. Explain Phenomena Air currents move objects in the air. Explain how a convection current might affect the flight of a hot air balloon.

____

____

____

____

____

____

The Essential Question

How can weather conditions be observed over time?

Show What You Learned

Explain how weather conditions can be observed over time. List some tools meteorologists use to study the weather.

____

____

____

____

____

____

____

____

Science Assessment Practice

Read the scenario and answer questions 1–2.

A river valley is an area of lower elevation between mountain ranges or hills that has a river running along the bottom. The Wei River Valley, which runs alongside the city of Xi'an, China, is characterized by hot, humid summers and cold, dry winters.

Climates in Two Cities			
City	**Average January high temp**	**Average July high temp**	**Average yearly precipitation**
Xi'an, China	-5° C	32° C	5 cm
Los Angeles, California	20° C	29° C	1 cm

1 **Explain Phenomena** Xi'an and Los Angeles are located at about the same latitude. What can explain the difference in the climate of each location?

Ⓐ Xi'an is located near the mountains in China so the climate is stable and mild.

Ⓑ Los Angeles is located near the ocean so the high and low temperatures are less extreme.

Ⓒ Xi'an is colder and drier because it is farther from the equator.

Ⓓ Los Angeles is experiencing drought conditions.

2 **Hypothesize** Why are summers hot and humid in the Wei River Valley near Xi'an?

Ⓕ Temperatures are higher in areas of decreased elevation.

Ⓖ Temperatures are lower in areas of decreased elevation.

Ⓗ The valley is near a mountain, which leads to higher amounts of precipitation.

Ⓘ The valley is near the equator.

Read the scenario and answer questions 3–5.

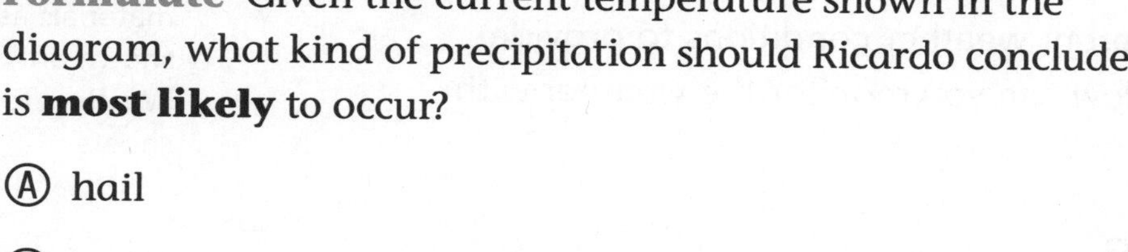

Ricardo looks at a thermometer each day to determine the outside temperature.

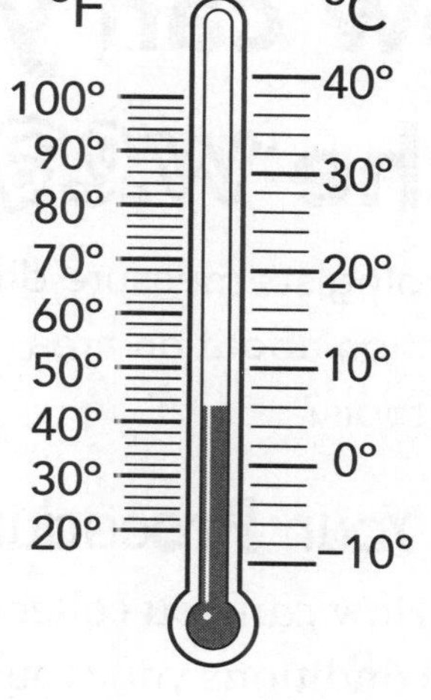

3 **Formulate** Given the current temperature shown in the diagram, what kind of precipitation should Ricardo conclude is **most likely** to occur?

Ⓐ hail

Ⓑ rain

Ⓒ snow

Ⓓ sleet

4 **Draw Conclusions** From April to November, Ricardo noted an average temperature of 25°C. From December to March, he noted an average temperature of 18°C. Using this information, what can you conclude about where Ricardo lives?

Ⓕ Ricardo lives in a city with cold temperatures during the winter months, such as Minneapolis or Chicago.

Ⓖ Ricardo lives in a city with a lot of precipitation during the summer months, such as New Orleans or Seattle.

Ⓗ Ricardo lives in a city with humid summers and cold winters, such as Boston or Baltimore.

Ⓘ Ricardo lives in a city with warm temperatures year-round, such as Atlanta or Dallas.

5 **Critique** Ricardo wants to prepare for any severe weather that may occur today. He is wearing a short sleeve shirt, shorts, and sandals. Propose a solution to help Ricardo plan for severe weather.

Ⓐ He should call 9-1-1.

Ⓑ He should have access to his family's emergency safety kit.

Ⓒ He should call his friends to inform them of today's temperature.

Ⓓ He and his family should go shopping for items they will need to include in their emergency safety kit.

STEM uDemonstrate Lab

How can you monitor the weather?

Meteorologists measure different weather conditions to provide information about an area. How can you monitor the weather with simple tools?

Materials

- Weather Tools sheets
- additional materials as shown on Weather Tools sheets

Wear safety goggles.

Do not taste any materials.

Wear a safety apron.

Plan Your Procedure

☐ **1.** How can you collect weather data? Choose three weather conditions you would like to monitor. Write what kind of tool you will need.

☐ **2.** Use the Weather Tools sheets to help you build your tools.

☐ **3.** Make a plan to collect weather data with your tools for one week. Show your plan to your teacher.

Science Practice

Scientists use tools to make measurements when gathering data.

My Plan

☐ **4.** Record your weather data for one week.

Weather Data

Evaluate Your Plan

5. Use Evidence How well did your tools measure weather conditions?

____

____

____

6. Interpret What does your data tell you about weather conditions in your area?

____

____

____

____

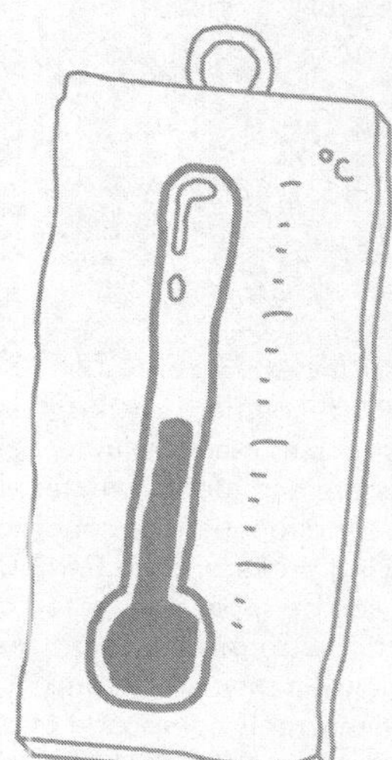

Topic 4

Properties of Matter

SC.5.P.8.1 Compare and contrast the basic properties of solids, liquids, and gases, such as mass, volume, color, texture, and temperature. **SC.5.P.8.2** Investigate and identify materials that will dissolve in water and those that will not and identify the conditions that will speed up or slow down the dissolving process. **SC.5.P.8.3** Demonstrate and explain that mixtures of solids can be separated based on observable properties of their parts such as particle size, shape, color, and magnetic attraction. **SC.5.P.8.4** Explore the scientific theory of atoms (also called atomic theory) by recognizing that all matter is composed of parts that are too small to be seen without magnification. **SC.5.P.9.1** Investigate and describe that many physical and chemical changes are affected by temperature. (Also **SC.5.N.1.1, SC.5.N.2.1, LAFS.5.W.3.9, MAFS.5.K12.MP.4.1**)

Go online to access your digital course.

- VIDEO
- eTEXT
- INTERACTIVITY
- VIRTUAL LAB
- GAME
- ASSESSMENT

The Essential Question

What evidence do we have that matter changes?

Show What You Know

At one time the exteriors of these boats looked very different. What do you think happened to cause their appearance to change?

___

___

___

Quest Kickoff

STEM Find the Right Mix—and Step on It!

How can we mix ingredients to make a model stepping stone?

Hi, I'm Alicia Gomez, a materials scientist! Suppose a school is setting up a prairie habitat. In this problem-based learning activity, you will build a model stepping stone for the habitat so that students can observe the habitat without damaging the plants.

Like a materials scientist, you will evaluate your design and learn how different combinations of materials can make your design solution more useful. And you can decorate your model stepping stones, too!

Follow the path to learn how you will complete the Quest. The Quest activities in the lessons will help you complete the Quest! Check off your progress on the path when you complete an activity with a QUEST CHECK OFF. Go online for more Quest activities.

Quest Check-In Lab 1

Lesson 1

Learn about the particles that make up matter as you explore materials you will use to develop your stepping stone.

 **SC.5.P.9.1** Investigate and describe that many physical and chemical changes are affected by temperature. (Also **SC.5.P.8.4**)

Watch a video about a materials scientist.

Quest Check-In 4

Lesson 4

Apply what you learn about physical changes in matter as you sketch a model for your stepping stone.

Quest Check-In Lab 5

Lesson 5

Find out about chemical changes and how they affect the model "concrete" you will make.

Quest Check-In 3

Lesson 3

Learn about the states of matter and their properties to help you develop a list of criteria and constraints to guide the development of your model stepping stone.

Quest Check-In Lab 6

Lesson 6

Use what you learn about mixtures and solutions as you revise your "concrete" formula to get the best product. Then build your model stepping stone.

Quest Check-In Lab 2

Lesson 2

Use what you learn about the properties of matter to compare materials you might use to build your stepping stone.

Quest Findings

Use your model to think about other important features of a concrete stepping stone. Suggest how you would change your model. Retest your model.

STEM uConnect Lab

HANDS-ON LAB

SC.5.P.8.3, SC.5.N.1.1

What happens to mass when objects are mixed?

Materials scientists investigate how substances can mix together by performing experiments and collecting data. How can you investigate the properties of a mixture of substances?

Materials

- 10 small beads
- 10 medium beads
- 10 large beads
- balance and gram cubes

Procedure

☐ **1.** What will happen to the mass of the three sets of beads when you mix them together? Write a prediction.

____

____

Science Practice

Scientists make measurements to produce data during investigations.

☐ **2.** Think of a procedure to test your prediction about mass. Use all of the listed materials. Share your procedure with your teacher before you begin.

☐ **3.** Make a bar graph to show your data. Label each bar on the x-axis. Label the units on the y-axis.

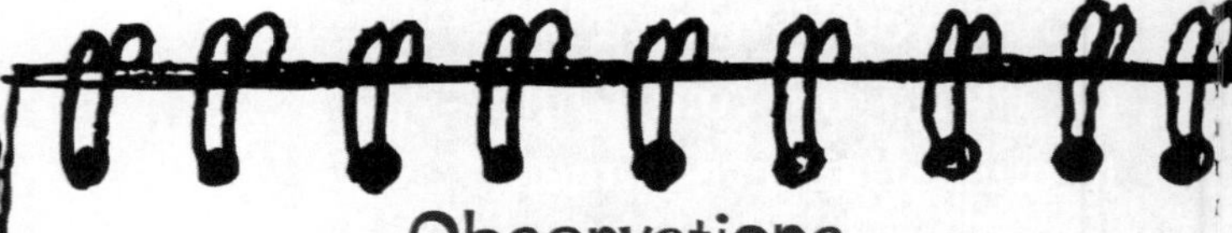

Observations

Bead	Small	Medium	Large	Mixture
Mass (g)				

Mass (g)

Bead size

Analyze and Interpret Data

4. Use Evidence What happens to the mass of objects when they are mixed?

____

____

____

____

____

____

Use Evidence from Text

LAFS.5.W.3.9

GAME

Practice what you learn with the Mini Games.

When you read carefully, you look for evidence. Use these strategies to help you look for evidence.

- Do a first read.
- Do a close read.
- Underline important facts.

Read the text to find out how materials scientists can help remove oil pollution from the environment.

Oil Spills and Aerogels

Small amounts of oil end up in streams and threaten the environment. One way to clean up this oil is with materials called aerogels. Aerogels are solids made from gels.

To make aerogels, materials scientists remove the liquid from the gel and replace it with gas. This process changes the physical properties of the gel. Aerogels are nicknamed "frozen smoke" because they are see-through and are the world's lightest solids. Some aerogels are very absorbent. Materials scientists tested the ability of these aerogels to clean up oil by mixing them with water and corn oil. In one investigation, the aerogel absorbed seven times its own weight in oil!

READING CHECK **Use Evidence from Text** Why do you think aerogels could be used to clean up oil spills in your community? Underline the important facts from the text that support your claim with evidence.

Lesson 1

Model Matter

I can...

Explain that matter is made of tiny particles too small to be seen.

Literacy Skill

Use Evidence from Text

Vocabulary

atom
atomic theory
compound
molecule

Academic Vocabulary

conclude

VIDEO

Watch a video about how to model matter.

SC.5.P.8.4 Explore the scientific theory of atoms (also called atomic theory) by recognizing that all matter is composed of parts that are too small to be seen without magnification. (Also **SC.5.N.2.1, LAFS.5.W.3.9**)

ENGINEERING Connection

Salt is a natural resource that people need in their diets. The salt that you use in your kitchen may come from a salt deposit. In these deposits, the salt is often a large, solid mass, like rock. People use tools to break it apart into smaller pieces. Even these small chunks are too big to use on your food. Sometimes the salt is crushed small enough to pour from a saltshaker. Another way to break the salt into smaller pieces is by using a salt grinder.

Predict What would happen if you could keep grinding the salt particles?

____

____

Divide Matter

When you grind salt, you divide chunks of salt into smaller pieces. These small pieces are still salt. The small grindings have a similar shape to the larger pieces. They taste the same on your food. You can crush them again with a spoon to make salt powder.

uInvestigate Lab

SC.5.P.8.4, SC.5.N.2.1

How can you detect matter without seeing it?

Materials scientists study all kinds of matter. How can you show evidence of matter that you cannot see?

Materials
- safety goggles
- 2 plastic syringes

Suggested Materials
- balloons
- rubber tubing
- cup of water
- plastic straw

Wear safety goggles.

Science Practice

Scientists use evidence to make an explanation.

Procedure

☐ 1. Pull the plunger to the last mark on the syringe. Observe the syringe. Write a description of what you think is in the syringe.

____

____

____

☐ 2. Choose materials from the list to test whether matter is in the syringe. Write a procedure test whether the syringe contains matter. Show your procedure to your teacher before you start.

☐ 3. Record your observations.

Observations

Analyze and Interpret Data

4. **Use Evidence** How did your data provide evidence that the syringe contained matter?

____

____

____

____

____

____

____

uBe a Scientist

Disappearance of Particles

Can you make matter disappear? Fill a clear glass with water. Then stir in a spoonful of salt. What do you think happened to the particles of salt? How can you explain your observations?

Atoms

From a distance, a sand castle on a beach looks like a solid object. If you look at it closely, you see that it is made of small particles of sand. The tiny sand grains combine to form the castle.

Explain What do you think is the smallest piece that you could break sand into? Why do you think so?

___

___

All matter is made of elements. An element is made up of only one kind of atom. The smallest part of an element that still has the properties of the element is called an **atom**. All substances are made of atoms. You cannot see atoms with a regular microscope because they are too small. However, special instruments can show how atoms are arranged in a particular substance.

The atoms of each element are different from the atoms of every other element. All the matter around you is made of atoms. The idea that everything is made of small particles is known as the **atomic theory**. The smallest piece of sand has many more atoms than the number of grains of sand in the whole sand castle.

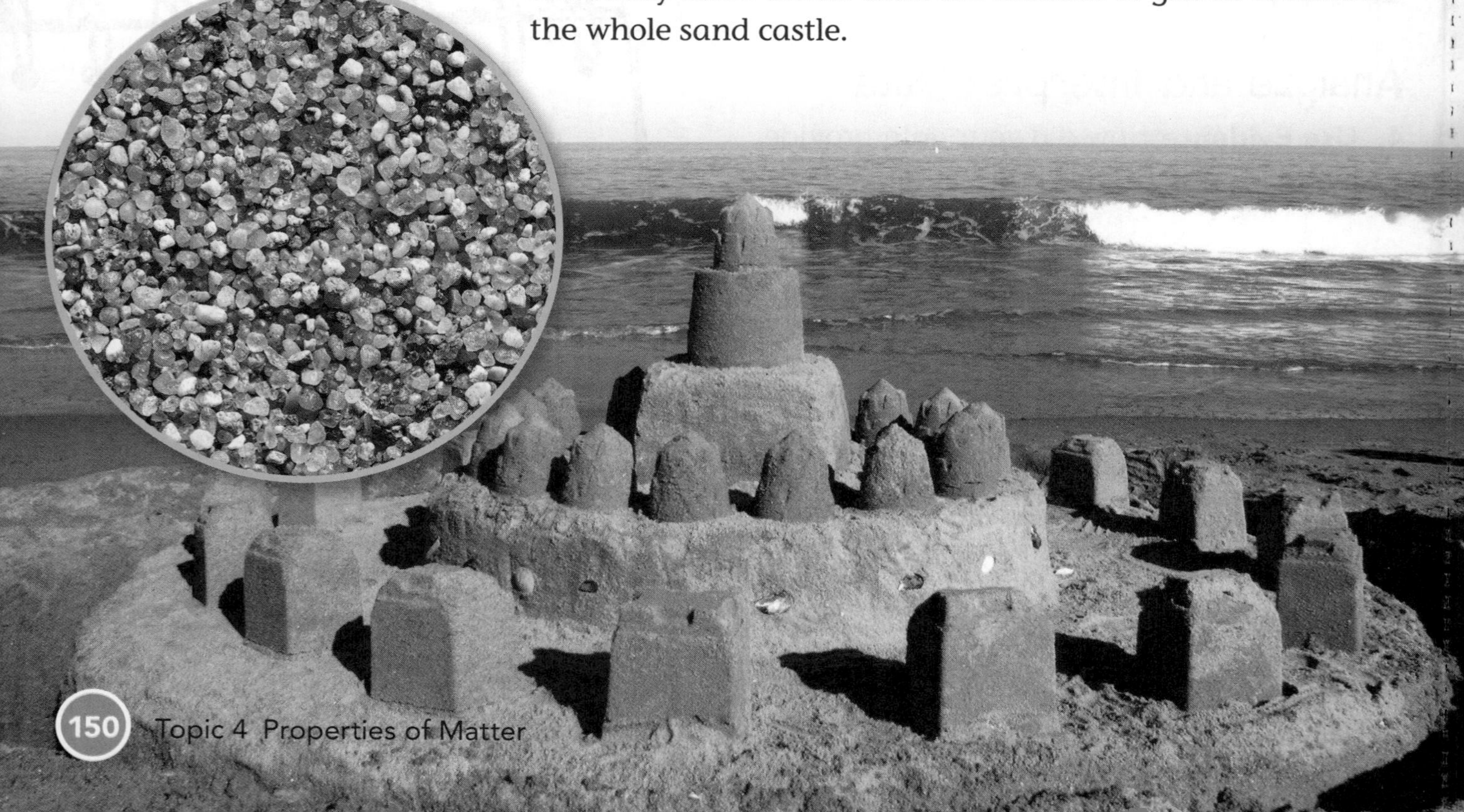

Molecules

Most things around you are **compounds**, which are matter made of two or more elements. The atoms of different elements are joined together in a particular way to form each compound. Table salt is a compound that is made up of the elements sodium and chlorine.

The smallest particle of a compound that still has the properties of that compound is called a **molecule**. For example, carbon dioxide is a molecule that has only three atoms. Molecules can be made of many atoms.

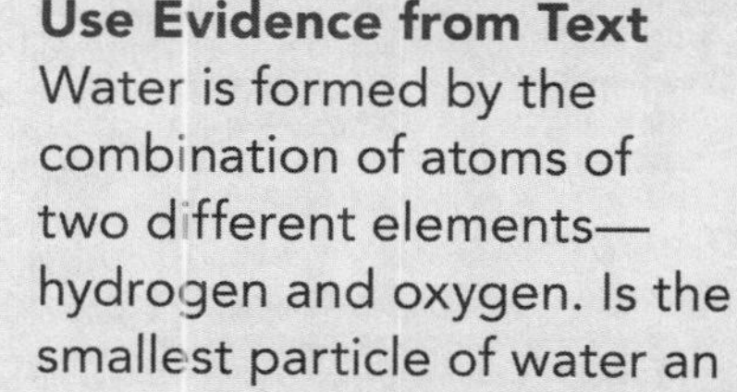

Use Evidence from Text Water is formed by the combination of atoms of two different elements—hydrogen and oxygen. Is the smallest particle of water an atom or a molecule? Why do you think so?

LAFS.5.W.3.9

Identify Circle the carbon dioxide molecule in the diagram.

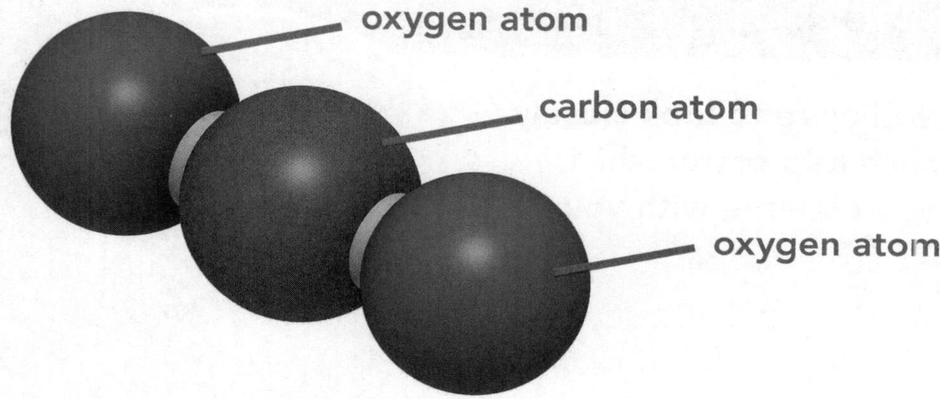

Quest Connection

Even when mixed, elements and molecules still keep their unique properties. Explain why.

Visual Literacy Connection

What is the matter?

All matter is made up of smaller particles. How can you observe the magnification of matter?

Describe If you were to look closely at a T-shirt, such as a cotton shirt, what might you observe with your unaided eye?

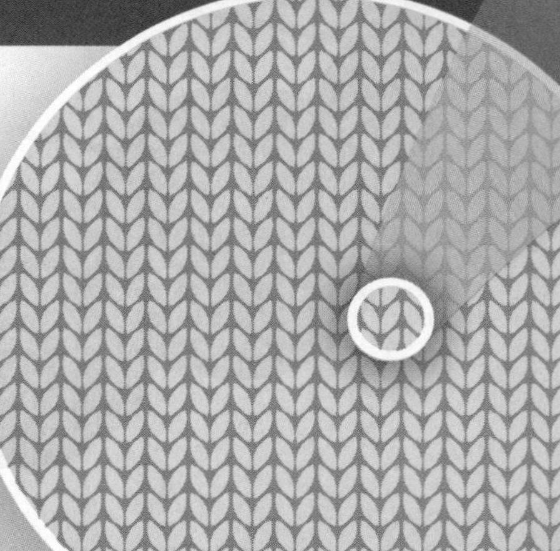

INTERACTIVITY

Complete an activity about matter.

Infer Why are you not able to see the loops holding the shirt together with just your eye?

Compare Scientists use magnification to help see fibers up close. How do the fibers in this image look different from the fibers without magnification?

Infer Draw what you think the atoms of the shirt might look like if you could actually see them. Why are you not able to see them?

Same Atoms, Different Matter

When the same kinds of atoms in a molecule combine in different amounts, different molecules form. For example, a water molecule has one atom of oxygen and two atoms of hydrogen. Another molecule is also made of hydrogen and oxygen atoms. However, it contains two hydrogen atoms and two oxygen atoms. Although this molecule also contains only hydrogen and oxygen, it is a substance different from water. It is hydrogen peroxide.

Changing the kinds of atoms in a molecule also results in a different molecule. Carbon dioxide is the gas you breathe out. Sulfur dioxide is a poisonous gas with an irritating smell. Because the properties of these two substances are different, you can conclude that their molecules are different. When you **conclude**, you use data and facts to make a statement.

Lesson 1 Check

1. **Conclude** Table salt is a compound made of sodium and chlorine atoms. From the table, what can you conclude about the properties of compounds and the elements they are made of?

Some Properties of Three Substances			
Property	**Chlorine**	**Sodium**	**Table salt**
State (at room temperature)	gas	solid	solid
Color	green	silver	white
Toxicity	poisonous	poisonous	not poisonous

2. READING CHECK **Use Evidence from Text** What makes up matter? Use the definition of *atomic theory* to answer.

STEM **Quest** Check-In Lab

SC.5.P.8.4, SC.5.N.2.1

How do you *know* that matter is still there?

When you mix two substances together, the appearance of the matter can change. Are the same atoms still there?

Materials

- safety goggles
- 3 beakers
- 3 small bowls
- 3 spoons
- salt
- sugar
- baking soda
- water
- wax marker

 Wear safety goggles.

 Do not taste.

Science Practice

Scientists **use evidence** to support their conclusions.

Procedure

☐ **1.** Label three beakers *Sugar, Salt,* and *Baking soda*. Pour the same amount of water into each beaker.

☐ **2.** Use a spoon to add some sugar into the beaker labeled *Sugar.* Stir until the sugar dissolves. Repeat with salt and baking soda. Use different spoons each time. Record your observations.

____

____

☐ **3.** How can you find out whether the original materials are still in each beaker? Write a procedure. Show your plan to your teacher before you begin. Record your observations.

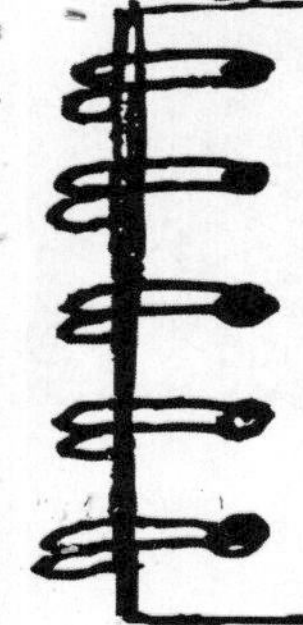

Observations

Evaluate Your Design

4. Synthesize Did your observations present any evidence that matter is made up of small particles? Explain how.

____

____

uEngineer It! Define STEM

INTERACTIVITY

Go online to evaluate and compare competing designs.

Foam Sweet Foam

Most surfboards are made of foam. Basic surfboards are often made of polyurethane foam, which floats easily in the water because it is very light. It is also strong. Other boards are often made of polystyrene foams. These foams are lighter than polyurethane foam, but they are not as strong. Besides, some polystyrene foams can sometimes absorb water. That, of course, is not a good quality for a product designed to float!

Recently, a group of chemists and engineers designed a new type of foam for surfboards. This new foam is not only lighter than any other surfboard foam. It also lasts longer and floats better.

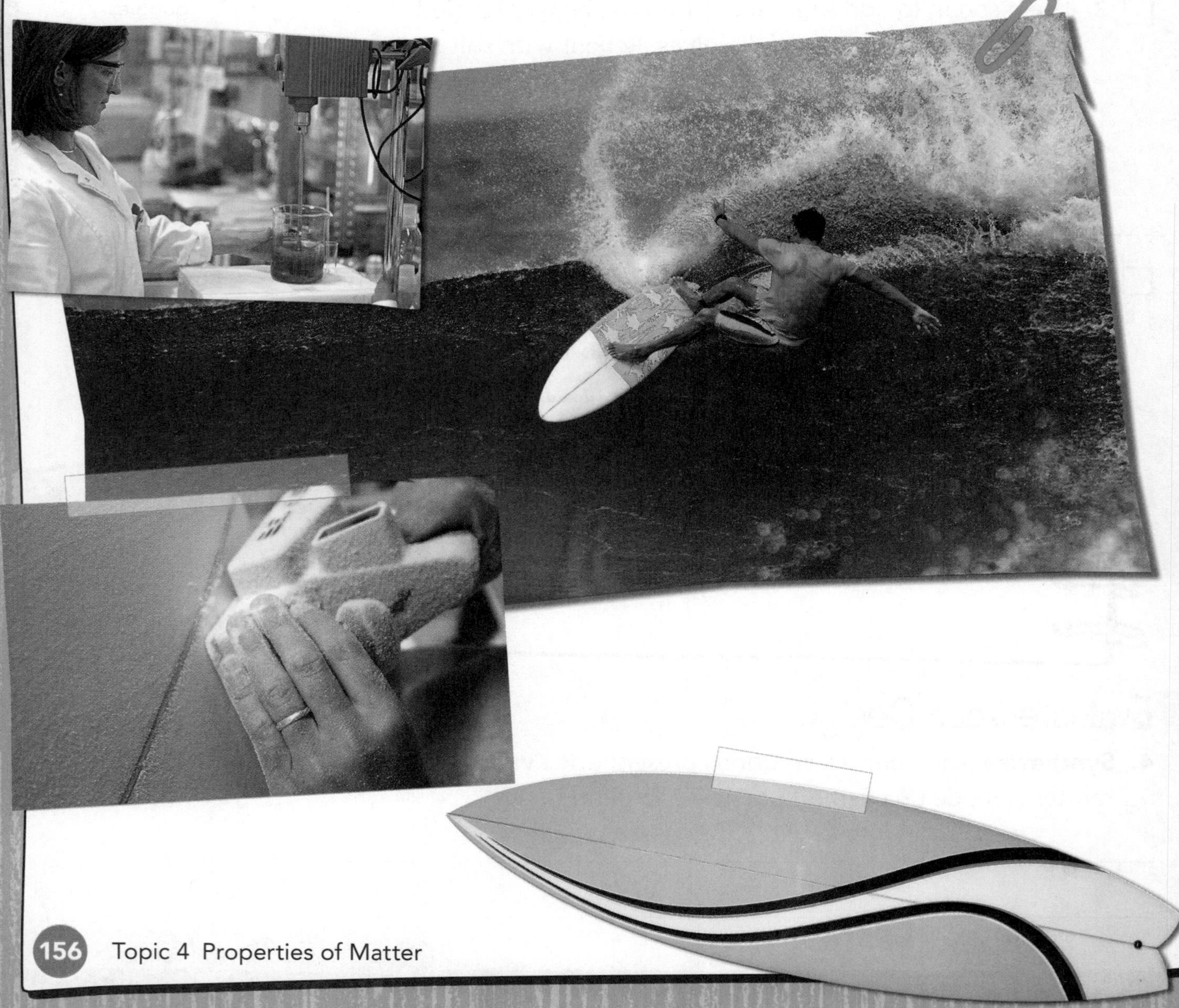

Define It

Foams are made using a series of chemical and physical changes. They are used in the design of many products, including automobiles, helmets, pillows, and food containers. There are many types of foam, and they each have different properties. Suppose you work for a company that builds playground equipment. The company wants to build a new piece of equipment for small children.

- [ ] Choose one piece of equipment that can be built using foam or that you think should include foam.

- [ ] Define the purpose of the foam in the product you choose.

- [ ] Brainstorm some **criteria** that could help you judge which foam is best for your product.

It should...	It should not...

- [ ] Draw your piece of equipment.

Lesson 2

Properties of Matter

I can...

Identify materials based on their properties.

Literacy Skill

Use Evidence from Text

Vocabulary

temperature
mass
volume

Academic Vocabulary

organize

VIDEO

Watch a video about properties of matter.

SC.5.P.8.1 Compare and contrast the basic properties of solids, liquids, and gases, such as mass, volume, color, texture, and temperature. (Also **SC.5.N.2.1**)

STEM Connection

Suppose that you are playing soccer on a winter evening. As it gets dark, you forget to take your ball inside. During the night, the air becomes very cold. In the morning, the ball seems different. It is not as round as it was. It feels soft and squishy. When you kick the ball, it does not go very far. It seems like some of the air is missing, but there is no leak. During the day, the ball gets warmer and goes back to the way it was yesterday.

The amount of air in the ball did not change during the night, but the volume of air did change. The air particles inside the ball put pressure on the inside of the ball. That is what causes the ball to inflate. As the air particles inside the ball cooled at night, the amount of pressure they put on the ball decreased. As a result, the ball shrank. When the particles warmed during the next day, they again put more pressure on the ball.

Reflect Did you ever play a sport on a cold day? What did you like the best about playing in the cold?

uInvestigate Lab

HANDS-ON LAB

SC.5.P.8.1, SC.5.N.2.1

How can you use properties to identify solids?

To identify an unknown substance, materials scientists compare its properties with the properties of known substances. How can you use properties to identify three substances?

Materials
- 3 substances labeled A, B, and C
- safety goggles
- 3 cups
- 3 spoons
- conductivity tester
- hand lens
- water
- wax marker

Procedure

☐ **1.** You have three substances labeled A, B, and C. Use the table to plan an experiment to identify the three unknown substances. Show your procedure to your teacher before you begin.

☐ **2.** Identify each unknown substance by writing its letter beneath the name of each substance in the table.

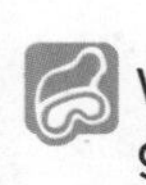

Wear safety goggles.

Do not taste.

Properties of Materials

Sugar	Salt	Cornstarch
white solid	white solid	white solid
irregular crystals	cube-shaped crystals	fine powder
dissolves in water	dissolves in water	does not dissolve in water
solution is not very conductive	solution is very conductive	does not form solution

Science Practice

Scientists **interpret data** when they analyze results of an investigation.

Analyze and Interpret Data

3. **Use Evidence** What evidence did you use to identify each unknown?

uBe a Scientist

Food Coloring in Water
With an adult, fill one bowl with hot water and one bowl with cold water. Put one drop of food coloring in each bowl. What differences do you observe? How can you explain your observations?

States of Matter

Scientists organize all matter according to its state. When you **organize** something, you sort it. The three main states of matter are solid, liquid, and gas. Water is a solid when it is ice. It is a liquid when you drink it. The gas form of water is called water vapor. The state of a material is due to the motion of its atoms or molecules. A material can change from one state to another as the motion of its particles changes. Water is a solid when it is very cold and its particles vibrate in place. It turns into a liquid when it is heated and its particles move more. Water becomes a gas when it is very hot and its particles move very fast.

Solid

The particles of a solid do not slide easily past each other. They vibrate, or move back and forth, in place.

Liquid

The particles of a liquid can move past each other.

Gas

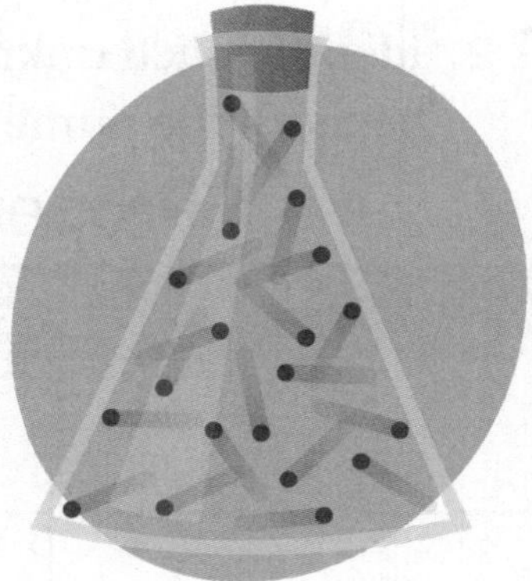

The particles of a gas move very fast and spread out evenly to fill available space.

Suppose that you are a particle. With your classmates, act out how particles behave in a solid, liquid, and gas. How did you show each state of matter?

____

____

____

Temperature

The **temperature** of an object is a measure of how fast its particles are moving. The higher the temperature, the faster the particles move. Different scales are used for measuring temperature. In science, you probably will find the temperature at which a substance melts given in degrees Celsius (°C). In a recipe, cooking temperature is most likely given in degrees Fahrenheit (°F). Both units are accurate measures of temperature.

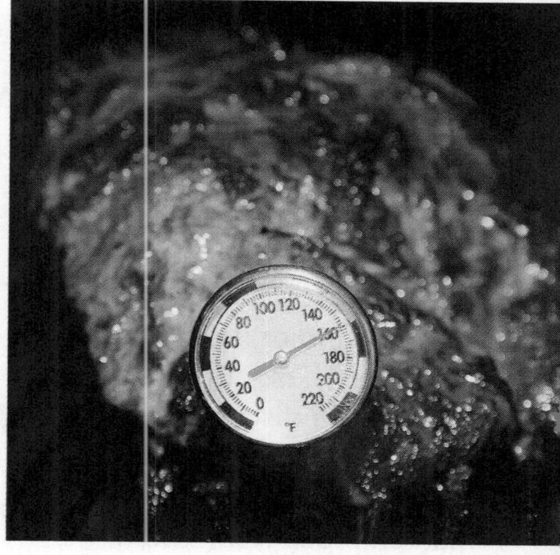

Collect Data This food thermometer shows the temperature of the meat. What is the temperature? Be sure to identify whether the temperature is given in Fahrenheit or Celsius.

____

____

Mass and Volume

The amount of matter in a substance is its **mass**. Scientists usually measure mass in units of grams (g) or kilograms (kg). To find the mass of an object, you can compare it to other objects that have a known mass. On a balance, the sides will be uneven, like those in the photo, when the masses are different.

The amount of space an object takes up is its **volume**. Volume can be measured in milliliters (mL). Solid and liquid materials have a definite volume. They take up a certain amount of space. Gases also have volume. The volume of a gas will change to fill all of the space available.

Infer Describe the relationship between mass and volume.

____

____

____

____

____

____

____

INTERACTIVITY

Complete an activity about physical properties.

Connecting Concepts ▸ Toolbox

Stability and Change
One main goal of science is understanding how things change. Think about the properties discussed on these pages. How easily do you think these properties can change? Rank them from most changeable to least changeable.

Color

The physical properties of a material can be observed, measured, and described without changing the material. Color is a physical property of matter. Color is an easy property for identification because you can determine the color of something just by looking at it. You can often organize various types of matter based on similarities and differences in color.

Apply Give an example when using color to identify a substance would be important.

____

____

____

Quest Connection

Do you think that color and texture are important properties of a stepping stone? Explain your answer.

____

____

____

Texture and Hardness

When you touch a solid object, you can feel whether it is smooth, lumpy, grooved, spongy, or rough. This surface structure that you can feel by touching a material is its texture. Hardness is another property of a solid that you can feel. If something is hard, it tends to keep its shape when you push it or strike it. If it is soft, it tends to bend.

READING CHECK Use Evidence from Text What is texture? Describe the texture of the brick and copper.

____

____

____

____

____

____

____

____

brick

copper

Lesson 2 Check

SC.5.P.8.1

1. **Analyze** A heavy brick weighs more than a fluffy cushion, but the cushion takes up more space. Which object has more matter? How do you know?

____

____

2. **Explain** Why does a solid fill only part of a closed jar while the same mass of a gas fills the whole jar?

____

____

Quest Check-In Lab

How can you compare the properties of matter?

The work of materials scientists involves understanding how the properties of materials vary. How can you learn about the properties of familiar materials?

Suggested Materials

- cups
- water
- hand lens
- wooden block
- metal coin
- sugar
- salt
- flour
- baking soda
- white sand
- paper
- spoon

Do not taste.

Science Practice

Scientists compare observations to find similarities and differences.

Procedure

☐ **1.** Choose four objects from the list of materials. Record which objects you have chosen in the first column of the table.

☐ **2.** Choose three different physical properties of the objects that you will test. Record the properties that you will test in the top row of the table.

☐ **3.** Plan how you will test the properties. Write your plan and have your teacher approve it.

SC.5.P.8.1, SC.5.N.1.1

☐ 4. Test the three properties. Record your data and observations in the table.

Properties of Materials

Material ______	Property 1 ______	Property 2 ______	Property 3 ______
1			
2			
3			
4			

Analyze and Interpret Data

5. **Evaluate** Suppose you had an unknown sample and knew that it was one of the four materials you tested. How could you identify which material you had based on the properties you tested?

____

____

____

____

6. **Evaluate** What is another property that you could use to tell which of the four substances you have? Explain your answer.

____

____

____

Lesson 3

States of Matter

I Can...

Identify the differences among the three states of matter.

Literacy Skill
Use Evidence from Text

Vocabulary
solid
liquid
gas

Academic Vocabulary
differentiate

VIDEO

Watch a video about states of matter.

SC.5.P.8.1 Compare and contrast the basic properties of solids, liquids, and gases, such as mass, volume, color, texture, and temperature. Also **SC.5.P.9.1** Investigate and describe that many physical and chemical changes are affected by temperature. (Also **SC.5.N.2.1**)

LOCAL-TO-GLOBAL Connection

Think about the clothing that you wear when you go outside on a warm day. It is made of fairly thin fabric that protects you from too much sunlight or from biting bugs. If you were at the South Pole, though, you would dress very differently. There are no warm days at the South Pole. The temperature is always so cold that all of the water there is frozen. Vast plains of ice, or solid water, surround the pole. Explorers and researchers who travel near the South Pole need clothing that holds in warmth.

Relate Explain why it is necessary for travelers to the South Pole to wear clothing that protects them from the cold.

____

____

____

uInvestigate Lab

HANDS-ON LAB

SC.5.P.8.1, SC.5.N.2.1

Is goop solid or liquid?

Most of the materials around you are clearly solid, liquid, or gas. Could there be substances that are hard to classify?

Materials
- water
- cornstarch
- spoon
- bowl
- safety goggles
- measuring cup
- graduated cylinder, 50mL

Suggested Materials
- food coloring

 Wear safety goggles.

 Do not taste.

Science Practice

Scientists use evidence to make explanations.

Procedure

☐ **1.** In the bowl, add one cup of cornstarch to 100 mL of water. Mix the substances with your hands or with the wooden spoon. If the mixture stirs easily, add a bit more cornstarch. If some of the cornstarch stays powdery, add a bit more water. You can also add a drop or two of food coloring.

☐ **2.** When the cornstarch and water are thoroughly mixed, stir it slowly with the spoon. Then stir it very quickly. Record your observations.

☐ **3.** Pick up some of the mixture in your hand. Try to roll it into a ball. Keep pushing on the mixture while rolling it. Then stop pushing on the mixture while you hold it over the bowl. Record your observations.

☐ **4.** What are some other investigations that you can do with the mixture?

____

____

____

Observations

Analyze and Interpret Data

5. Classify Can you classify the mixture as a liquid or a solid? Explain your answer.

____

____

____

Visual Literacy Connection

What states of matter do you see?

You are surrounded by different states of matter: solids, liquids, and gases. Study the different states of matter you see in this picture. Identify as many different types of states of matter as you can find.

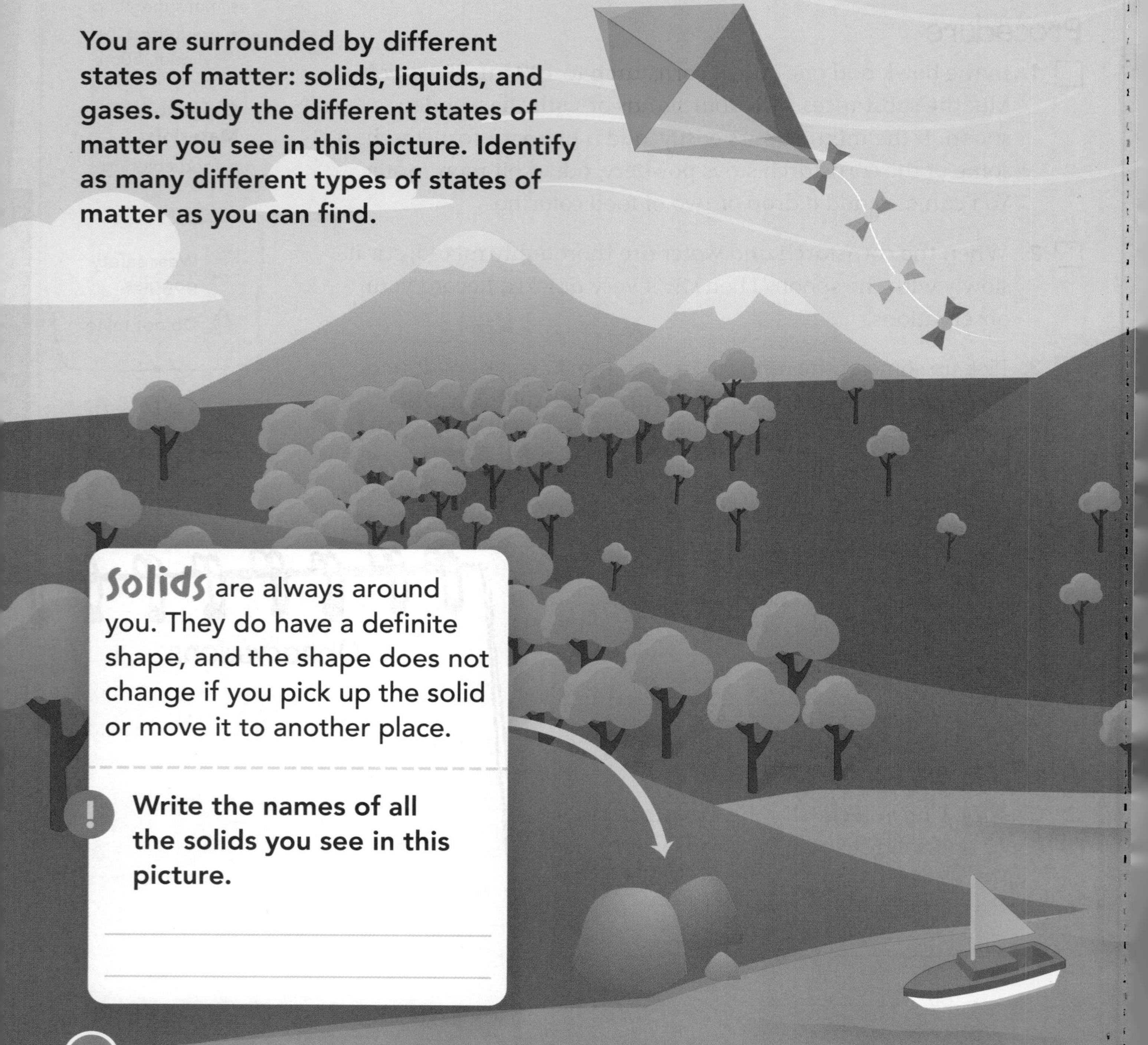

Solids are always around you. They do have a definite shape, and the shape does not change if you pick up the solid or move it to another place.

Write the names of all the solids you see in this picture.

Gases are always there but usually not visible. Gases do not have a definite shape, and they move everywhere.

Write the names of all the gases you see in this picture.

Liquids are often nearby. They do not have a definite shape and can change shape easily.

Write the names of all the liquids you see in this picture.

uBe a Scientist

Solid + Liquid = Gas?

Baking soda is a solid, and vinegar is a liquid. You may know already that those two substances react when they are mixed. In a large resealable plastic bag, mix one teaspoon of baking soda with four tablespoons of vinegar. Seal the bag right away. What did you observe about the bag? How can you explain this observation?

Solids

Solid, liquid, and gas are the three states of matter. Most substances can exist in any of these states, depending on temperature. A **solid** can be identified because it has a definite shape. When you place a solid object such as an ice cube in a cup, it does not spread to cover the bottom of the cup. An ice cube is solid and keeps its shape in the cup. As it becomes warmer, the ice cube may melt. Then it is no longer a solid.

READING CHECK **Use Evidence from Text** Ice is a solid that can come in many different shapes, such as crushed, cubed, or shaved. Explain how this can be. Support your answer with evidence from the text.

____

____

____

____

Liquids

When an ice cube melts, it forms water, which is a liquid. A **liquid** is a substance that has a definite volume but does not have a definite shape. If you pour liquid from a shallow, round bowl into a tall glass, its shape changes a lot. The new shape matches that of the inside of the glass, while the volume of the liquid in the bowl and in the glass are the same.

Liquids flow from one place to another unless something holds them in place. For example, the water in the waterfall rushes downward because nothing is stopping it.

Reflect What did you learn in this lesson that helped you understand something you observed in the past but could not explain? Write your thoughts in your science notebook.

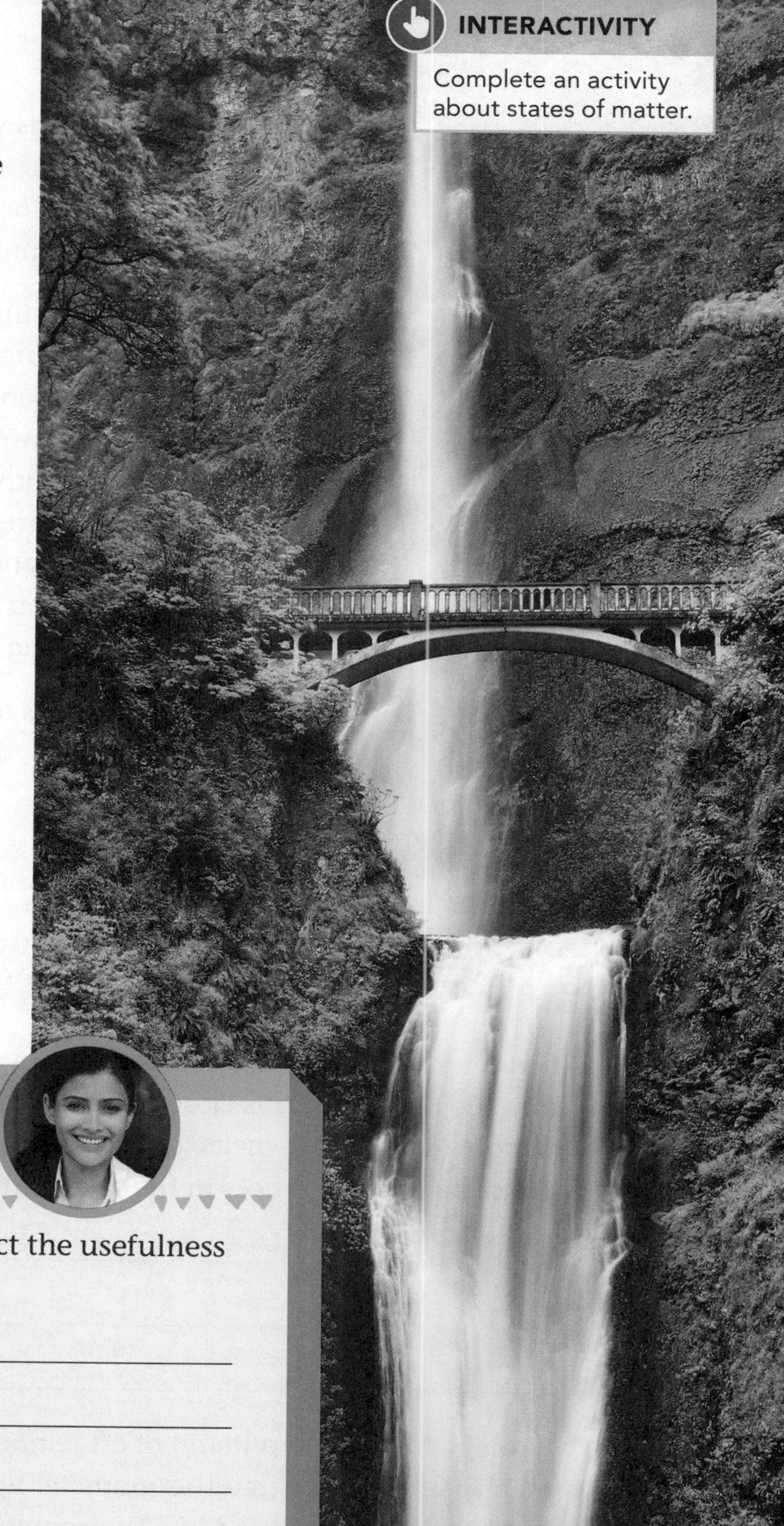

INTERACTIVITY

Complete an activity about states of matter.

Quest Connection

Describe how the state of matter will affect the usefulness of materials used in a stepping stone.

____

____

____

____

____

Science Practice ▸Toolbox

Designing Solutions
Engineers design solutions to problems by applying scientific knowledge. Suppose you must move a toy boat across a pond. How can you use your knowledge of gases to move the boat?

Gas

Matter surrounds you all of the time. The air that you breathe is matter in the form of gas. If you move your hand back and forth quickly, you can feel the matter even though you cannot see it.

Gas is a form of matter that does not have a definite shape or a definite volume. You can **differentiate**, or tell the difference between, a gas, a liquid, and a solid because gases in a container always fill the entire volume of the container. Although some gases have color that you can see, most common gases are colorless. You can detect them by their effects on other objects. If you blow through a straw into a glass of water, you will see bubbles of gas coming up through the water. Moving air causes a wind turbine to turn.

Classify What is a characteristic of a gas?

____

____

____

Lesson 3 Check

SC.5.P.8.1

1. **Compare and Contrast** A few pieces of shaved ice is placed in a large jar. The lid of the jar is closed tightly, and the jar is left on a sunny window sill. The ice melts, and all of the liquid water becomes a gas. Describe the differences in the three states of matter.

____

____

____

2. **Explain** Mercury is a liquid at all temperatures. What properties allow mercury to be used in a thermometer while other metals, such as gold or silver, cannot be used in a thermometer?

____

____

It's a Matter of Materials

Some types of matter may be useful for making a stepping stone. Other types of matter will not work as well. Answer the questions below to help decide some of the properties that materials for your stepping stone will need.

1. For your stepping stone project, describe the things that the stone must be able to do. List some of the criteria that will help you figure out what kind of design would work.

____

____

____

2. Identify the state of matter that is most likely to meet your criteria. Will all materials in the state of matter that you identified meet the criteria for your design problem? Explain your answer.

____

____

____

____

3. What other characteristics are important in the materials you will use?

____

____

____

QUEST CHECK OFF

Lesson 4

Physical Changes

I can...

Use evidence to show that matter is conserved during a physical change.
Explain how temperature can affect a physical change.

Literacy Skill
Use Evidence from Text

Vocabulary
physical change

Academic Vocabulary
establish

VIDEO
Watch a video about physical changes.

SC.5.P.9.1 Investigate and describe that many physical and chemical changes are affected by temperature. (Also **SC.5.N.1.1**)

STEM Connection

When a building is constructed, engineers and builders use different materials to put it together. Modern buildings over a few stories tall are often built using steel beams and concrete. These materials are strong and durable. Even if the materials are strong, people may want to remove a building. It may not be designed for modern uses. A taller or more modern building design may use the land better. When a building is knocked down using heavy equipment, the material it is made of does not change. The concrete is still concrete even though it is broken into small pieces. The beams are still made of steel even if they are bent and crumpled. The materials do not change, but their shape changes.

Infer How could you show that the building materials do not change when the building is knocked down?

___

___

___

uInvestigate Lab

HANDS-ON LAB

SC.5.P.9.1, SC.5.N.1.1

Which properties are affected by temperature?

When materials scientists develop new materials, they must consider how temperature affects the properties of a material. Which properties are affected by temperature?

Materials

- aluminum foil
- piece of thin rubber
- sugar cubes
- safety goggles
- water
- plastic cups
- spoon
- large dish of ice water
- large dish of warm water

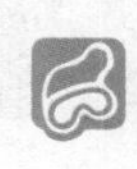
Wear safety goggles.

Do not taste.

Procedure

☐ **1.** Use all the materials. Think of a way to test how temperature affects solubility and flexibility, and how shiny a material appears. In the table, identify which substance you will use to test each property.

☐ **2.** Write a procedure to test each property. Show your plan to your teacher before you start. Record your observations.

Observations

	Sugar	Aluminum foil	Rubber
Property tested			
Observations			

Science Practice

Scientists **make observations** to reach conclusions.

Analyze and Interpret Data

3. Compare Which physical changes were affected by the temperature difference and which were not affected by the temperature difference?

____

____

____

____

Changes in Shape

Matter often changes size and shape. A **physical change** is a change in some properties of matter that does not form a different kind of matter. A melted juice pop, torn paper, and broken glass are all examples of physical changes.

Some physical changes give matter a different shape. If you drop a cell phone, the glass screen might shatter. The glass has undergone a physical change. Some of its properties have changed, but the properties that make it glass are still there. It is still hard and clear. It still does not react with most substances. Cutting paper and stretching a rubber band are also physical changes. After breaking glass or stretching a rubber band, you still end up with glass or rubber. The mass of the parts of the broken phone screen is exactly the same as the mass of the unbroken screen.

Explain How can you tell that a physical change does not make a new substance?

____

____

Quest Connection

Why would you want to use a material that is not likely to undergo a physical change for your stepping stone?

____

____

____

____

____

Changes in Temperature

The temperature of an object or material is one of its physical properties. A change in temperature is a physical change. A cold object feels different from how the same object feels when it is warm. When the temperature of an object changes, other physical properties might change at the same time. You can **establish**, or demonstrate, this concept with a balloon. If you put one of these inflated balloons in the freezer, it will shrink. That is because the volume of air will change when the air temperature changes. After you take the balloon out of the freezer, it will become warmer. It will then return to its original size.

The railroad tracks in the photograph appear to be warped and bent. That change in shape happened when the tracks became hot. The metal expanded. Sections of track could not stretch longer because they pushed against other sections. That caused the tracks to bend. In very hot climates, people must inspect the tracks often to keep them safe.

Cause and Effect Metal railroad tracks shrink when they get colder. Why do you think shrinking does not cause the tracks to warp?

____

____

____

INTERACTIVITY

Complete an activity about physical changes in food.

Science Practice ▸ Toolbox

Construct Explanations Water freezes at 0°C/32°F. At a higher temperature, water will be a liquid. How can you use this information to predict the precipitation that will fall on a given day?

A Change of Physical State

Another physical change of a substance is a change of its physical state. As liquids get colder, their particles slow down. When the temperature gets cold enough, the particles can only vibrate in place. They cannot slide past each other, so the liquid becomes a solid. This change is called freezing. The opposite change can occur when a solid is heated. As its particles gain energy, they again move past one another. The solid melts to form a liquid.

Freezing and melting occur at the same temperature. When a liquid turns into a solid, this temperature is called the freezing point. It is called the melting point when a solid turns into a liquid. Each substance has its own melting point. The melting point can be used to help identify a material.

The melting point of water is 0°C. Below that temperature, water is solid ice. Above the melting point, water is a liquid.

Apply Concepts Label the liquid, solid, and gas in the photos. Predict the temperature for each state.

____

____

____

Particle Changes

Evaporation takes place when particles leave a liquid and become a gas. Particles evaporate from a liquid when they are at the surface of the liquid and are moving upward with enough speed. This is how rain puddles and wet clothes become dry.

If the temperature of a liquid is high enough, particles will change to a gas not only at the surface but also throughout the liquid. As gas particles move quickly upward through a liquid, bubbles of gas form under the surface of the liquid. The boiling point of a liquid is the temperature at which this occurs. As with the melting point, each substance has its own boiling point. The boiling point can be used to help identify a substance. The boiling point of water is 100°C.

READING CHECK **Use Evidence from Text** How can you use the melting point or boiling point to help identify a substance?

uBe a Scientist

Saltwater Ice Cubes
With an adult, fill an ice cube tray with water. In half of the spaces, use salt water. Use fresh water in the others. Make sure to keep track of which are which. Put the ice cube tray in a freezer. Check your tray one hour later. What can you infer from your observations about the properties of water and salt water?

Lesson 4 Check

1. **Infer** Melting is a physical change. How does the mass of a melted ice cube compare to the mass of the solid ice cube?

2. **Cite Evidence** Identify three different physical changes you have observed in the world around you.

Stepping Stone Properties

For your stepping stone, you might want to use a material that does not change easily. Draw a model of what your stepping stone will look like. Apply what you have learned about physical changes as you sketch your model stone. Consider the size, shape, and physical state of the stone. Label some of the physical properties of the stepping stone.

Design

QUEST CHECK OFF

Look Out for Flying Rocks!

Meteorites are small chunks of rock and metal that have traveled through space and fallen to Earth. In many ways, a meteorite is like other rocks on Earth. Still, finding a piece of matter that has traveled through space can be exciting. More than 50,000 meteorites have been found on Earth. Perhaps one is waiting for discovery in your backyard!

You can use the physical properties of a rock to figure out whether it is a meteorite. Almost all meteorites are made mostly of iron and nickel, so many times a magnet will stick to them. You can also look at the shape. If the rock is round like a smooth pebble, it is not a meteorite. Most often, as the meteorite falls through space, different parts of it melt or evaporate. This causes most meteorites to be unevenly shaped. They may even look like they have been burned. Meteorites are also much heavier than other rocks that are the same size. If your rock passes all these tests, it might be a meteorite. However, the only way to be sure is to have a lab test its true properties.

Connect What makes this meteorite different from the rocks that originated on Earth?

____

____

Lesson 5

Chemical Changes

I can...

Use evidence to show that matter is conserved during a chemical change.

Literacy Skill
Use Evidence from Text

Vocabulary
chemical change
conservation of matter
chemical reaction

Academic Vocabulary
support

VIDEO
Watch a video about chemical changes

SC.5.P.9.1 Investigate and describe that many physical and chemical changes are affected by temperature. (Also **SC.5.P.9.2, SC.5.P.9.3, SC.5.N.1.1, LAFS.5.W.3.9, MAFS.K12.MP.4.1**)

STEM Connection

Charcoal can be made from materials such as scraps and grass clippings. Materials scientists can determine how much of each material to use. Manufacturing engineers change this matter into charcoal, water and other liquids, and gases. They put the matter into a large metal container and heat it. After about 2–3 hours, charcoal is formed.

Describe Explain how matter is changed when engineers make charcoal.

____

____

New Substances

If you take a piece of charcoal and break it into pieces, the smaller pieces will still be charcoal. However, something different happens when you burn charcoal. Burning is an example of a chemical change. A **chemical change** is a change that produces one or more new substances. When charcoal burns, a chemical change occurs in which charcoal and oxygen form new substances. These new substances are ashes and gases that you cannot see.

uInvestigate Lab

HANDS-ON LAB

SC.5.P.9.1, SC.5.N.1.1

How can you identify chemical changes?

Materials scientists conduct investigations to provide evidence that their product does what it is supposed to do. What evidence can you look for to show that a chemical change has occurred when substances are mixed?

Materials
- safety goggles
- plastic cups
- spoons
- graduated cylinder, 50 mL

Suggested Materials

Dry materials
- sugar
- baking soda
- salt

Wet materials
- vinegar
- water
- lemon juice

Wear safety goggles.

Do not taste.

Procedure

☐ **1.** Write a hypothesis about chemical change when substances are mixed.

____

____

☐ **2.** Choose at least one liquid and one dry material. Write a procedure to test your hypothesis about chemical change. Remember to think about your variables. Show your procedure to your teacher before you start.

☐ **3.** Record your observations.

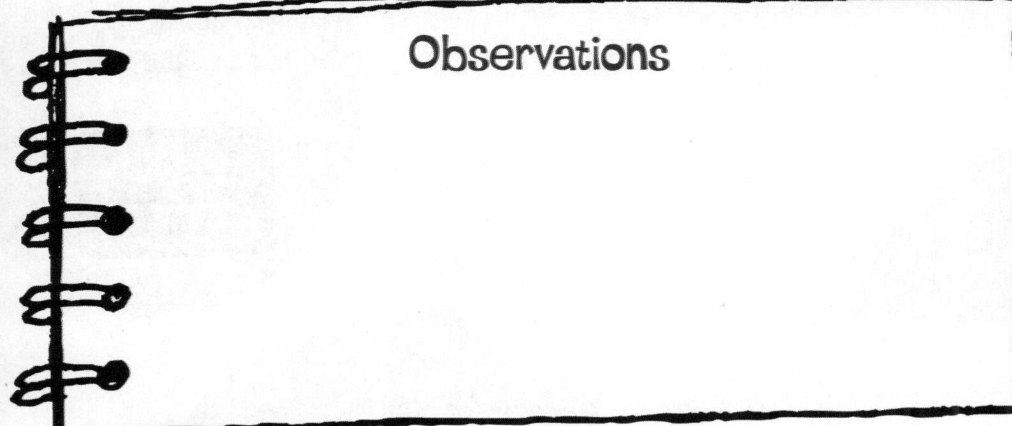

Science Practice

Scientists collect data when they investigate a scientific question.

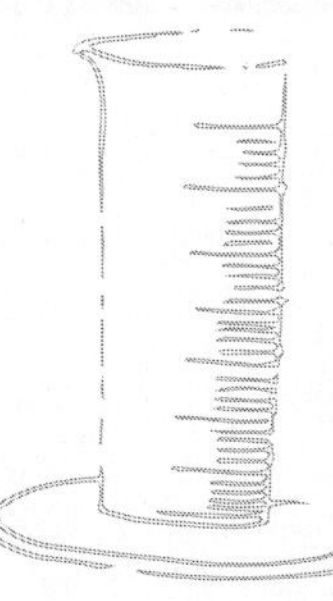

Analyze and Interpret Data

4. Use Evidence How does your data support your hypothesis?

____

____

Let's look at the changes that take place in another familiar example—baking a cake.

READING CHECK **Use Evidence from Text** Circle the evidence that baking a cake involves a chemical change.

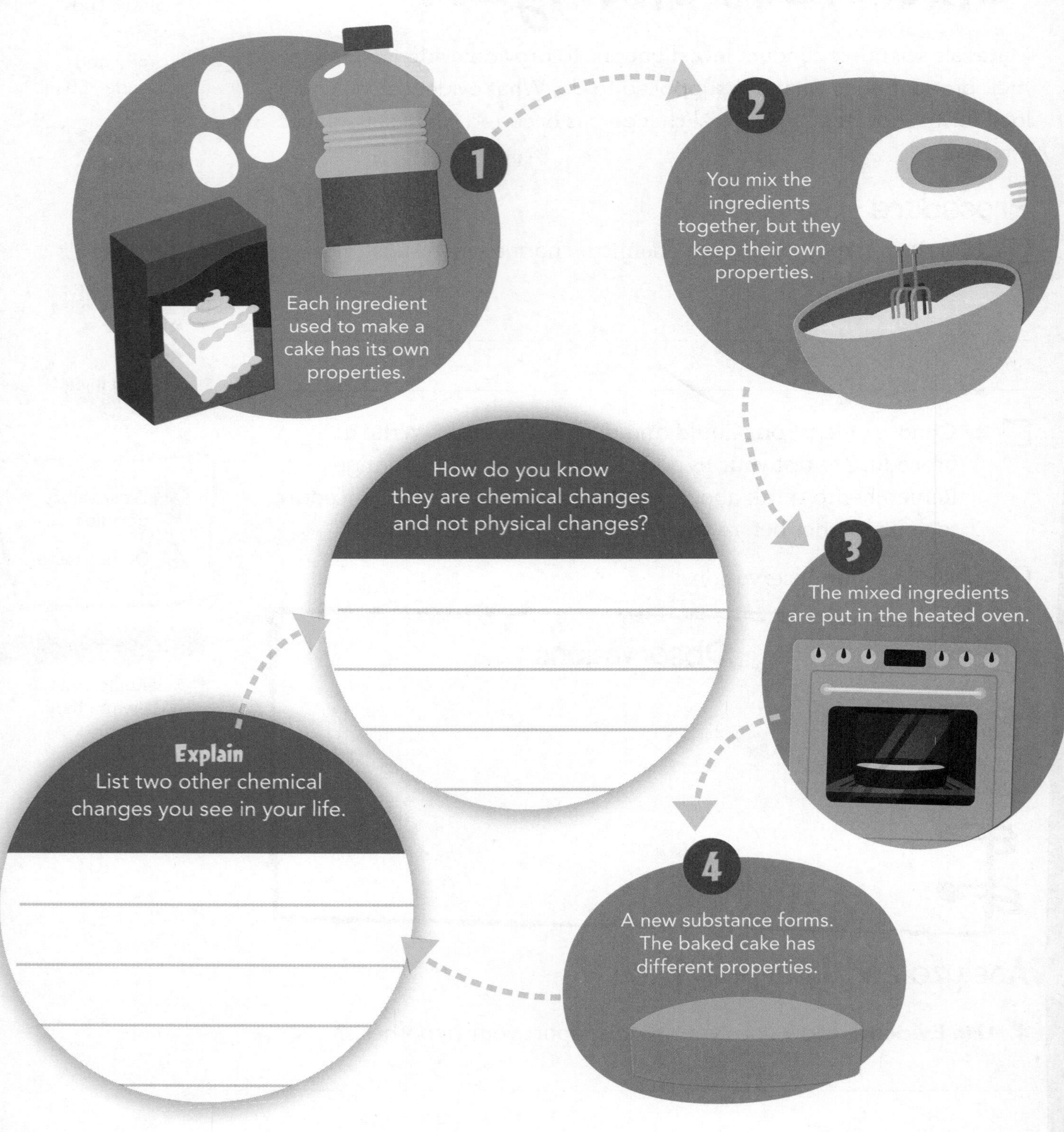

Particles and Chemical Changes

When a chemical change occurs, the particles that make up the original substances rearrange to form new substances. It is not always easy to tell whether a substance has changed chemically. Evidence of chemical change may include the release of heat or light, a change in color, a new smell, gas bubbles, or the formation of a solid.

You can use building blocks to model a chemical change. In the picture, the blocks represent particles of matter. They are connected to form two substances. You can connect them in other ways to form different substances.

Math ▸ Toolbox

Use Models Models can help you represent thoughts or ideas. How can you use the blocks in the image below to explain the idea that particles rearrange when they form new substances?

MAFS.K12.MP.4.1

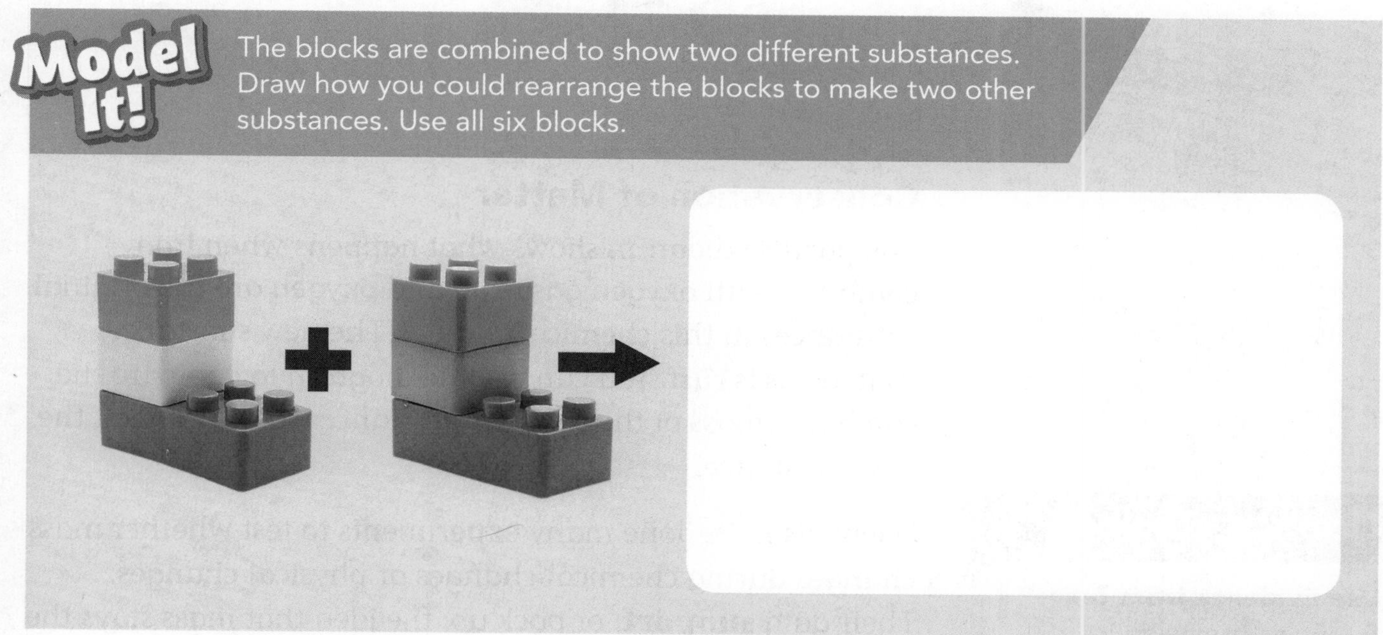

Like the building blocks, the particles that make up matter rearrange during a chemical change. In the example below, the balls each represent a different kind of particle in the two substances. After a chemical change happens, the same particles are in the two new substances, but they are arranged differently.

original substances **new substances**

Model It! In this diagram, each orange particle has a mass of 4 units, and each red particle has a mass of 1 unit. Write the combined mass of the particles in each space below the word equation.

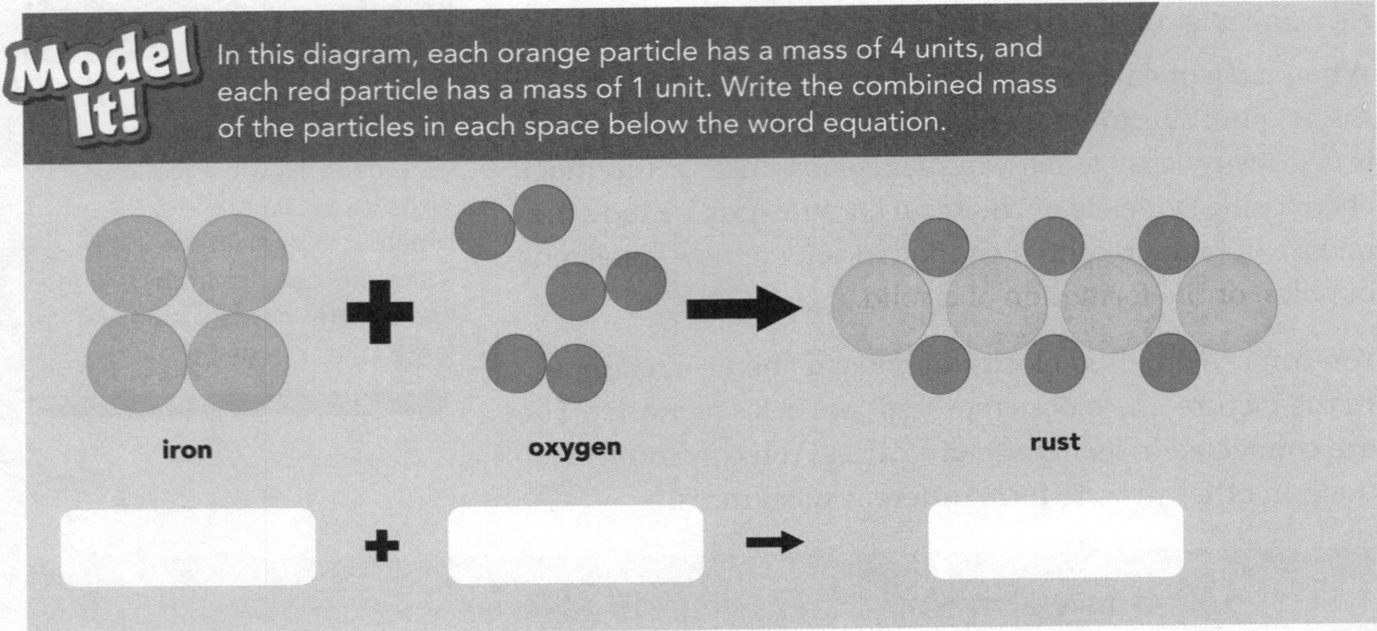

Conservation of Matter

The particle diagram shows what happens when iron combines with oxygen gas. Iron and oxygen are the original substances in this chemical change. The new substance that forms is rust. You can use the diagram to compare the combined mass of the original substances to the mass of the new substance.

Scientists have done many experiments to test whether mass changes during chemical changes or physical changes. Their data **support**, or back up, the idea that mass stays the same before and after any change—no matter what. From this evidence, scientists developed the law of **conservation of matter**. The law states that in any chemical change or physical change, the total mass of the matter does not change.

In a chemical change, all the particles that make up the original substances end up in the new substances. So, the combined mass of the substances before a chemical change is the same as the combined mass of the substances after the chemical change.

Literacy ▸ Toolbox

Use Evidence from Text
Scientists use evidence to support a claim. You can observe rust on a nail. The new substance, rust, is evidence of a chemical change. Read about the law of conservation of matter on these pages. Find and use evidence to support the claims of this law.

LAFS.5.W.3.9

Complete an activity about chemical changes.

Look at the nails. The shiny new nails are made of iron. Over time, the nails can rust. Rusting is a chemical change. The change occurs when the iron on the surface of a nail combines with oxygen gas in the air to form rust.

When you observe one or more substances change into one or more new substances, you observe a **chemical reaction**.The nails rust as a result of a chemical reaction. The iron in the nails and oxygen gas from the air react to form rust.

READING CHECK **Use Evidence from Text** If you measure the mass of nails before and after they rust, will the masses be the same? Explain your reasoning.

____

____

____

____

____

____

Quest Connection

Use the law of conservation of matter to explain what you think will happen to the substances you will mix to make modeling dough.

____

____

____

____

____

Visual Literacy Connection

Is matter conserved?

Read the information for each step to see what happens during the chemical reaction. Write a math equation to model how the masses of the original substances and the new substances compare.

1

108 g

Mass of substance A

90 g

Mass of substance B

Each flask holds a different substance. Read the mass on each scale. The mass seen on each scale is the mass of the substance. The mass of the flask has been subtracted.

Two new substances

The color of the liquid substance is different from the colors of substances A and B. A new solid substance is visible, too. These observations provide evidence of a chemical change.

?

3

Write the total mass of the two new substances. (Ignore the mass of the beaker.) Hint: Use the information in step 1.

____

2

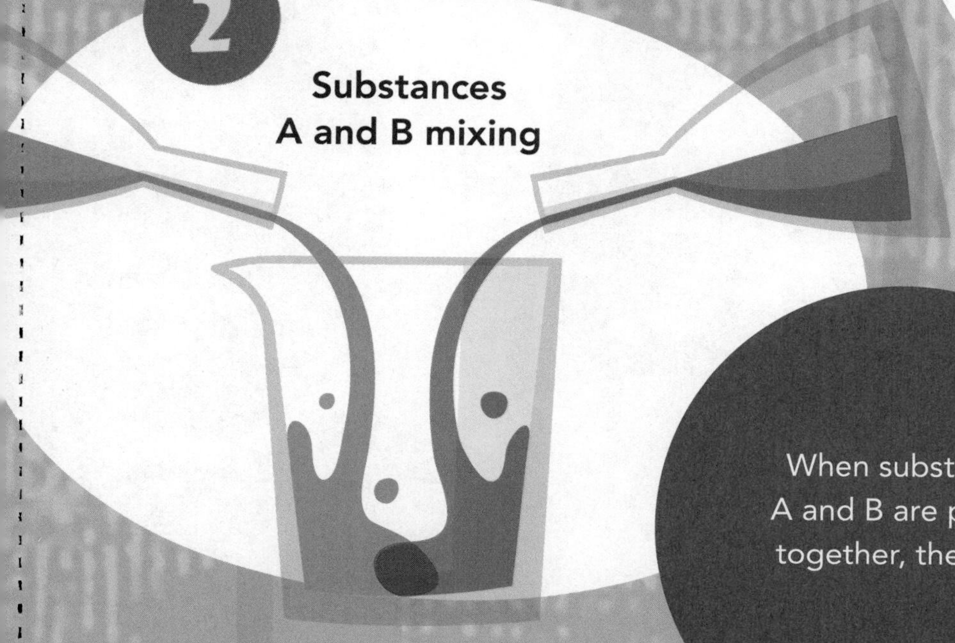

Substances A and B mixing

When substances A and B are poured together, they mix.

uBe a Scientist

Mass and Plant Growth

Chemical changes happen in living things, too. Try this! Put a wet paper towel in a sealable bag. Put a seed in the paper towel and seal the bag. Find the mass of the prepared bag. Wait until the seedling grows and has a few leaves. Find the mass again. You will see that the masses are the same. The plant's mass increases as it grows because it uses matter from the water and the trapped air. The water and air decrease in mass as the plant grows.

Examples of Chemical Changes

Chemical changes happen in the kitchen all the time. A chemical change occurs when a chef makes fresh cheese. To make fresh cheese, the chef adds lemon juice to whole milk. Once the two liquid ingredients are mixed, solid pieces start to form. The solid pieces, called curds, are chunks of the fresh cheese. They form as a result of a chemical change. To prepare the cheese to eat, the chef separates the curd from the liquid.

Different kinds of cheeses are produced by further processing the curds. For example, to make soft, stringy cheese like mozzarella, the curds are kneaded. Many cheeses are "aged." During aging—which can take months—bacteria in the cheese chemically change the cheese. Gouda is an example of an aged cheese.

Write About It Do a close read on the paragraph above. Identify the main idea. In your science notebook, explain how the author uses key details to help support the main idea.

You may have noticed another chemical change. Over time, some pennies change color from copper to green. This color change happens because of a chemical change. The copper metal that makes up a penny combines with oxygen in the air to form a green substance. The green substance is copper oxide.

Identify What two substances is copper oxide made of?

_______________ + _______________ → **copper oxide**

Explain Do you think the old penny will have the same mass as the new penny? Explain your reasoning.

____

____

____

____

Lesson 5 Check

Kolab recorded the properties of two liquid substances, A and B. He then mixed them together in a beaker, and the liquid changed colors. He recorded the properties of the mixed substances.

Substance	Color	Odor	Mass
A	colorless	none	3.6 grams
B	colorless	foul	2.1 grams
A + B	yellow	none	?

1. READING CHECK **Use Evidence from Text** Is this a chemical change? How do you know?

____

____

2. **Analyze** Write the mass of the mixture of substances A and B. How can this mass be used as evidence of the conservation of matter?

____

____

STEM Quest Check-In Lab

How can you make modeling dough?

It's time to make the dough you will use to build your model stepping stone. Look at the list of suggested materials and decide which materials to use and the quantities of each. How will using different quantities of materials affect the dough?

Materials
- bowl
- sealable bags
- balance and weights
- spoon
- plastic gloves

Suggested Materials
- water
- flour
- cooking oil
- salt
- sand
- glitter
- food coloring

Do not taste.

Wear plastic gloves.

Engineering Practice

Engineers **develop models** to test that a design meets specific conditions.

Design Your Model

☐ **1.** Make a list of criteria your stepping stone needs to meet.

___

___

___

My Formula

___

___

___

___

___

___

___

SC.5.P.9.1, SC.5.N.2.1

- [ ] **2.** Choose your materials and list them on the formula card.
- [ ] **3.** Make two different formulas by changing the quantities of materials.
- [ ] **4.** Measure each material and record the amount on the card.
- [ ] **5.** Share your formula card with your teacher before you start.
- [ ] **6.** Make your different formulas.
- [ ] **7.** How can you test which formula will best meet your criteria?

Evaluate Your Model

8. Use Evidence Do your results show whether a chemical change occurred? Provide evidence to support your answer.

9. Evaluate Which formula met your criteria for a model stepping stone? Provide evidence to support your answer.

10. Use Models How does your modeling dough compare to concrete that is used to make stepping stones?

Lesson 6

Mixtures and Solutions

I can...

Explain what happens when different substances are mixed.
Explain how to slow down or speed up the dissolving process when mixing materials in water.
Demonstrate that mixtures of solids can be separated.

Literacy Skill
Use Evidence from Text

Vocabulary
mixture
solution

Academic Vocabulary
component

VIDEO
Watch a video about mixtures and solutions.

SC.5.P.8.2 Investigate and identify materials that will dissolve in water and those that will not and identify the conditions that will speed up or slow down the dissolving process. **SC.5.P.8.3** Demonstrate and explain that mixtures of solids can be separated based on observable properties of their parts such as particle size, shape, color, and magnetic attraction. (Also **SC.5.N.1.1**)

CURRICULUM Connection

When you look at an oil painting from a distance, it might seem to have large areas of a single color. For most paintings, a closer look tells a different story. There are many different colors side by side, often in very small patches of color. How do artists have so many colors to work with? Do they have to buy hundreds of different colors and shades so that they can always have the one they need? No, artists start with a few basic colors of paint. Then they mix them together to get just the right color for a particular place on the canvas. By combining these basic colors in different groupings and amounts, the artist can make any color that you can imagine.

Apply Most packages of food coloring have only four bottles of food dye. How could you make different colors of icing for a cake?

____

____

uInvestigate Lab

HANDS-ON LAB

SC.5.P.8.3, SC.5.N1.1

How can you s p r t a mixture?

Knowing physical properties of matter can help scientists separate individual substances from a material. How can you use physical properties to separate the parts of the mystery mixture?

Materials
- mixture
- plastic cups
- water
- sieve
- magnet inside a plastic sealable bag
- safety goggles
- spoon

Wear safety goggles.

Do not taste.

Science Practice

Scientists **define a problem** so that they can develop a solution.

Procedure

☐ **1.** Observe the mixture. What parts of the mixture can you identify?

____

____

____

☐ **2.** Plan a way to separate the components from one another. Use all of the materials. Show your procedure to your teacher before you start.

☐ **3.** Separate the components of the mixture and record your observations.

Observations

Analyze and Interpret Data

4. Use Tools How did the magnet help you separate the components of the mixture?

____

____

____

____

____

____

____

Model It!

Look at the objects in the pictures. For each mixture, draw the materials that go into making the mixture.

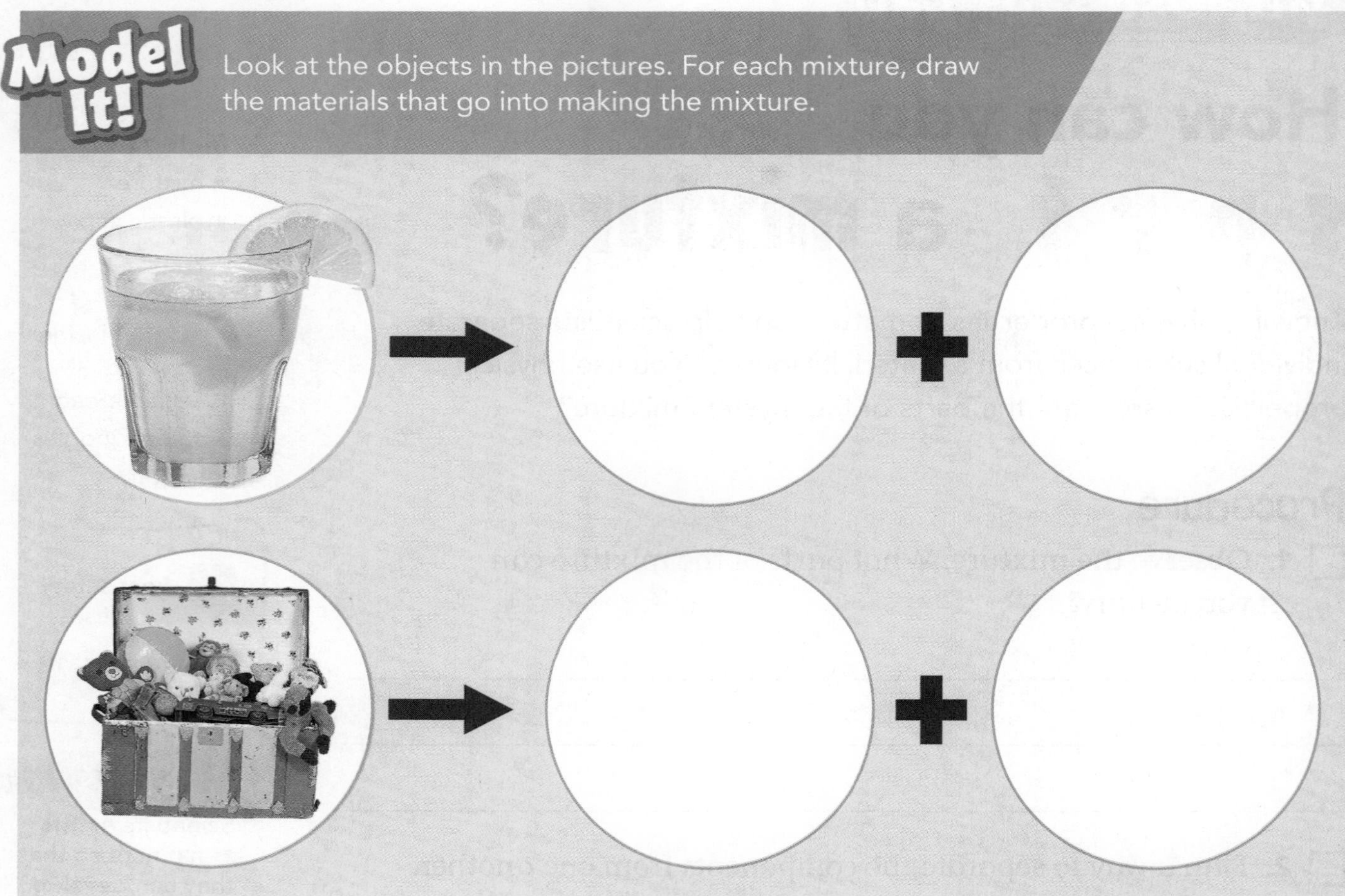

Mixtures

If you mix peanuts and raisins, each of the substances keeps its own properties. In a **mixture**, different materials are placed together, but each material in the mixture keeps its own properties. In the nut and raisin mixture, you can easily separate the nuts from the raisins. Different parts of a mixture can be separated from the rest of the mixture. When sand and blocks are mixed, you could separate the blocks from the mixture by picking them out. You could also use a strainer to separate the parts.

Some mixtures cannot be separated as easily as the nuts and raisins. For example, iron ore is a rock that is a mixture of different substances. One of these substances is iron. Large factories separate the iron from the other **components**, or parts, of the mixture. To do this, they use a lot of energy to make the iron liquid and separate it from the other components.

Solutions

If you place salt in water, the salt and water form a mixture. But the salt seems to disappear. That is because the salt water is a solution. A **solution** is a mixture in which substances are spread out evenly and do not settle to the bottom of the container. The substance that is dissolved in a solution is called the solute. The substance in which the solute is being dissolved is called the solvent. When the salt dissolves in the water, individual salt particles separate from the solid and spread evenly throughout the water. Ocean water is a familiar example of a salt and water solution. The water has a salty taste because salt is dissolved in the water. You can make solids dissolve in a liquid faster by stirring or heating the solution. Grinding a solid into smaller pieces will also help it dissolve faster.

Not all solutions are made by dissolving a solid in a liquid. Two liquids can make a solution. For example, vegetable oils used in cooking might be a solution of soybean oil and sunflower oil. A gas can also dissolve in a liquid. For example, water can contain dissolved oxygen and carbon dioxide gases.

READING CHECK **Cite Evidence from Text** Circle the words or phrases on this page that support the explanation of how to change the speed of the dissolving process.

Engineering Practice ▸ Toolbox

Construct Explanations Although it is not always an easy process, the components of a mixture can be separated, and they keep their properties. How can you know that something is a mixture?

Quest Connection

When you make your stepping stone, you may want to include pebbles or coarse sand as a component. How could you tell if these are part of a mixture or a solution?

____

____

____

Visual Literacy Connection

When is a mixture also a solution?

Some mixtures have parts that can be easily separated.

Draw the parts that make up the mixture.

INTERACTIVITY

Complete an activity about mixtures and solutions.

In a solution, the parts mix evenly and cannot be easily separated.

Draw the parts that make up the solution.

Separating Solutions

The components of a solution keep their own properties, but they usually cannot be separated as easily as other mixtures. That is because the components of a solution are evenly mixed. You cannot pick out chunks of one material from the mixture. You cannot remove a solid component with a filter paper. Its particles are spread out and become part of the liquid. However, the parts of a solution can be separated. To separate the parts of the solution, you use physical properties of the substances in the solution.

Plan It! How can you separate the salt and the water in a saltwater solution? Identify the properties you can use. Then write a plan to separate the materials.

Mixtures and Solutions

Remember that all solutions are mixtures, but not all mixtures are solutions. You can tell the difference by observing the mixture closely. A solution is the same in all parts. For example, clear apple juice is a solution. Any samples of the juice are just alike, and there are no separate particles in the mixture. Fresh squeezed orange juice is not a solution. You can see chunks of orange in the mixture. If you let the orange juice pass through a filter paper into a glass, it will separate. The glass will contain a clear liquid, and the filter paper will have solid orange pulp. You cannot separate a solution by filtering it. To separate a solution, you have to cause a physical change to one or more of its components.

Infer If you separate orange juice by filtering it, is the liquid in the glass a solution? Why or why not?

____

____

Make Meaning Mixtures and solutions are important to people in their everyday lives. In your science notebook, identify mixtures or solutions that you use every day. Why are they important to you?

Be a Scientist

Kitchen Science

Mix common kitchen substances, such as salt, pepper, sugar, and cinnamon with water. Observe the mixtures to determine which substances form solutions and which do not form solutions.

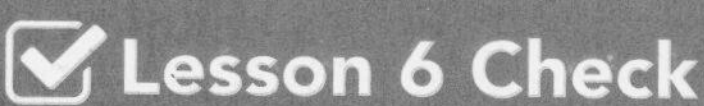

Lesson 6 Check

SC.5.P.8.2

1. READING CHECK **Use Evidence from Text** Sugar consists of fine white crystals. Salt also consists of fine white crystals. If salt and sugar are stirred together, is the result a solution?

____

____

2. **Summarize** Explain how a solution can consist of more than two components.

____

____

Quest Check-In Lab

How can you make a new and improved formula?

Consider how well your stepping stone model met the criteria and constraints of your engineering problem. How will using different materials or quantities of materials affect the model?

Materials

- bowl
- sealable bags
- balance and weights
- spoon
- plastic gloves

Suggested Materials

- water
- flour
- cooking oil
- salt
- sand
- glitter
- food coloring
- pebbles
- copper wire

Do not taste.

Wear plastic gloves.

Engineering Practice

Engineers **redesign a solution** after testing to find a solution meets specific conditions.

Design Your Model

☐ **1.** Write any criteria that your model did not address well.

____

____

☐ **2.** Choose your materials and list them on the formula card.

My New Formula

____

____

____

____

____

____

- [ ] **3.** Write a new formula by changing the materials or quantities that you use in the model. Measure each material and record the amount on the card.
- [ ] **4.** Share your formula card with your teacher before you start.
- [ ] **5.** Make your new formula.

Evaluate Your Model

6. Test Decide how to test your new model in order to determine whether it meets the criteria and constraints better. Write down your test.

7. Evaluate Did the new formula improve the model? Provide evidence to support your answer.

8. Use Models How does your new model compare to concrete that is used to make stepping stones?

Quest Findings

INTERACTIVITY

Organize data to support your Quest Findings.

STEM

Find the Right Mix—and Step on It!

How can we mix ingredients to make a model stepping stone?

Identify Factors and Retest

When you made the dough, you provided criteria. With a group, discuss if your model stepping stone met the criteria you set.

Discuss how you would change your model to improve it. Write a procedure for testing your improved model. Retest your model.

Procedure to Retest

____

____

____

____

____

Construct Explanations

Did the change to your model improve it? How do you know?

____

____

____

Do you think the same change to the concrete stepping stone would result in a better product? Why or why not?

____

____

Career Connection

Materials Scientist

Materials scientists develop many of the products we use. These individuals develop new kinds of materials and find ways to improve existing materials. They consider ways that products can be made better, lighter, or stronger. For example, a materials scientist might develop a helmet that is lighter and that can hold up under greater forces. Many of the materials used to build bikes and skateboards were developed by a materials scientist to improve their ability to move fast and to withstand the rigors of their tasks.

Materials scientists usually work in labs. They identify needs or problems and think of possible solutions. They design products, test prototypes, and identify improvements that need to be made. They also communicate with other scientists as they work.

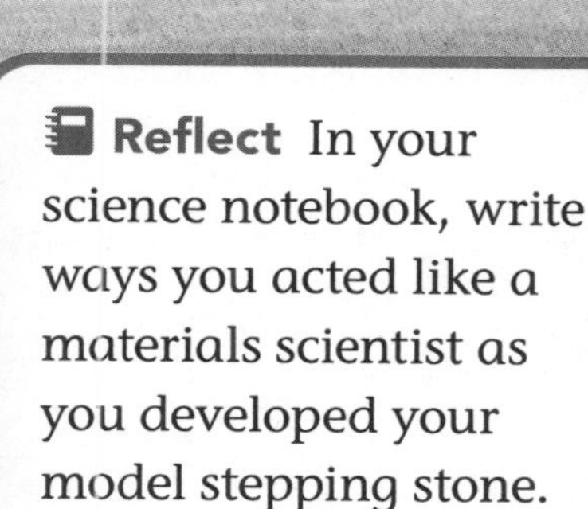

Reflect In your science notebook, write ways you acted like a materials scientist as you developed your model stepping stone.

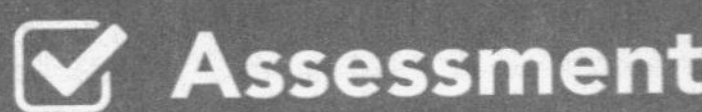

Assessment

Read each question and choose or write the best answer.

1. **Use Diagrams** Marisol wants to model the arrangement of the particles that make up an ice cube and the particles that make up liquid water. She finds the diagrams below in a library book. What is the **best** way for her to use these diagrams to model the particles of an ice cube and water?

States of a Substance

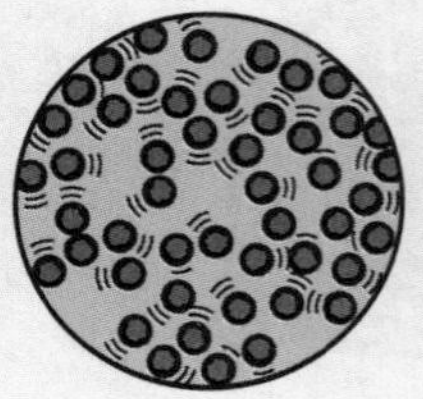

Diagram A

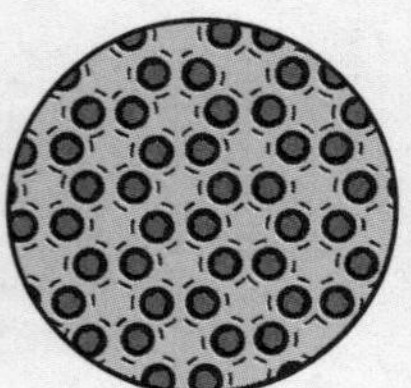

Diagram B

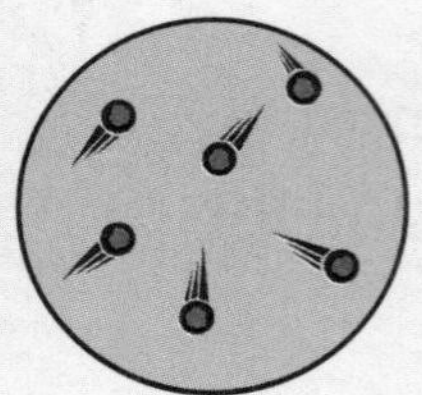

Diagram C

A. Use diagram A to model the ice cube and diagram B to model the water.

B. Use diagram A to model the ice cube and diagram C to model the water.

C. Use diagram B to model the ice cube and diagram A to model the water.

D. Use diagram B to model the ice cube and diagram C to model the water.

2. **Develop a Logical Argument** Tiffany leaves several balloons filled with helium gas inside her car on a sunny day. When she returns to her car, some of the balloons are much larger and a few have popped. Explain what happened.

3. **Connect** Suppose you needed to teach a younger student about mixtures and solutions. Use evidence from your life to list examples of mixtures and examples of solutions.

4. Interpret Which picture shows evidence of both a chemical change and a physical change?

A.

B.

C.

D.

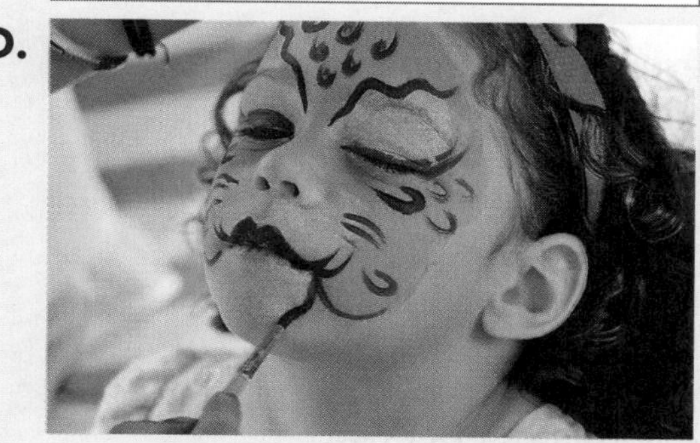

5. Vocabulary Which process is an example of a chemical change?

A. Bread is toasted.

B. Oil soaks through a shirt.

C. A girl forms a soap bubble.

D. Red food coloring spreads out in water.

6. Summarize What happens to the particles of substances when a chemical change occurs?

____

____

____

The Essential Question *What evidence do we have that matter changes?*

Show What You Learned

Several changes occurred when you mixed the ingredients to make modeling dough. Based on the evidence you saw, what kind of changes took place?

____

____

____

____

____

____

Read the scenario and answer questions 1–2.

A scientist in a lab was given a white substance to identify. The substance was known to be one of four possible substances. The chart shows some properties of the four substances.

Properties of Substances				
Property	**calcium carbonate**	**calcium sulfate**	**sodium bicarbonate**	**fructose**
Solubility in water	not soluble	not soluble	soluble	soluble
Color	white	white	white	white
Particle appearance	powder	crystals	powder	crystals
Makes bubbles in vinegar	yes	no	yes	no

1 **Analyze** Which two properties should the scientist use to identify the unknown chemical?

Ⓐ color and particle apperance

Ⓑ color and reaction with vinegar

Ⓒ solubility in water and particle appearance

Ⓓ particle appearance and reaction with vinegar

2 **Explain Phenomena** Which statement **best** describes what happens when calcium carbonate mixes with vinegar?

Ⓕ The calcium carbonate molecules spread out evenly in the vinegar.

Ⓖ The calcium carbonate remains suspended in the vinegar but then settles to the bottom of the container.

Ⓗ The calcium carbonate molecules break apart while the vinegar remains unchanged.

Ⓘ The atoms in calcium carbonate and vinegar rearrange to form new substances.

Read the scenario and answer questions 3–4.

Physical properties can be used to separate the components of many mixtures. For example, some materials are different colors and shapes, and others respond to a magnet.

salt and sugar

large and small iron pieces

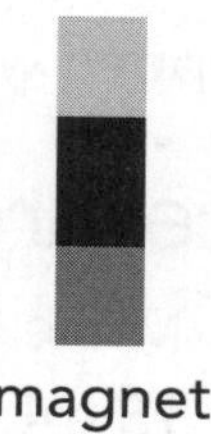
magnet

rocks and iron filings

sand and salt

3 **Investigate** Which of the mixtures shown in the picture would you be able to easily separate using a magnet?

Ⓐ The mixture of salt and sugar particles.

Ⓑ The mixture of large and small iron pieces.

Ⓒ The mixture of rock pieces and iron filings.

Ⓓ The mixture of sand and salt particles.

4 **Formulate** Suppose the mixture of salt and sugar is poured into a glass of warm water. Which of the following processes will happen?

Ⓕ The salt and sugar will dissolve in warm water.

Ⓖ The salt and sugar will form a solid.

Ⓗ The salt will dissolve and the sugar will float.

Ⓘ The sugar will dissolve and the salt will float.

uDemonstrate Lab

How does mass change when you make glop?

When materials scientists mix ingredients, they produce data that shows what happens to mass. They make observations about any changes that occur when ingredients are mixed. What do you think will happen when you mix glue, water, and borax solution?

Materials

- 3 measuring cups
- white glue
- balance
- gram cubes
- food coloring
- water
- borax solution
- spoon
- safety goggles

Wear safety goggles.

Do not taste.

Wash your hands when finished.

Procedure

☐ **1.** Make glop using 30 mL of glue, 15 mL of colored water, and 15 mL of borax solution. What will happen to the mass of the ingredients after they become glop? Write a hypothesis.

____

____

____

____

____

☐ **2.** Write a procedure to test your hypothesis about mass. Use all of the listed materials. Show your procedure to your teacher before you begin.

____

____

____

____

____

____

____

Science Practice

Scientists **make measurements** to produce data during investigations.

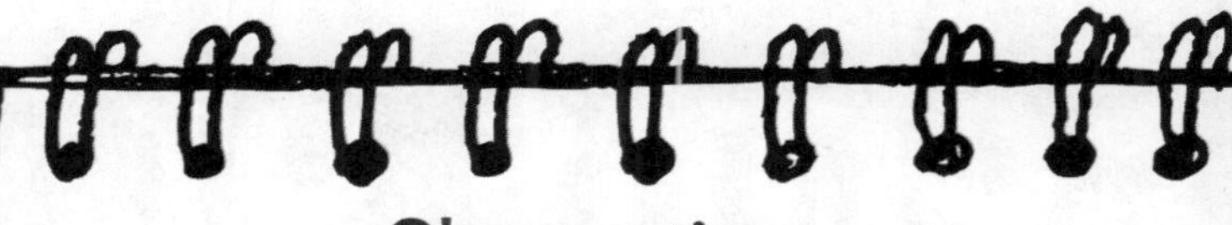

SC.5.P.8.3, SC.5.N.1.1

☐ **3.** Make a table to show your data. Your table should display evidence that relates to your hypothesis.

Observations

Substance	Mass of substance and cup (g)	Mass of substance (g)
Glue		
Colored water		
Borax solution		
Glop		

Analyze and Interpret Data

4. Calculate Add together the masses of the glue, water, and borax solution. How does this combined mass compare to the mass of the glop?

5. Use Evidence Did a chemical reaction occur? Provide evidence to support your answer.

6. Draw Conclusions Is your hypothesis supported by your data? Explain.

Topic 5

Forms of Energy

Lesson 1 Different Forms of Energy
Lesson 2 Electrical Energy
Lesson 3 Electric Circuits

SC.5.P.10.1 Investigate and describe some basic forms of energy, including light, heat, sound, electrical, chemical, and mechanical. **SC.5.P.10.2** Investigate and explain that energy has the ability to cause motion or create change. **SC.5.P.10.3** Investigate and explain that an electrically-charged object can attract an uncharged object and can either attract or repel another charged object without any contact between the objects. **SC.5.P.10.4** Investigate and explain that electrical energy can be transformed into heat, light, and sound energy, as well as the energy of motion. **SC.5.P.11.1** Investigate and illustrate the fact that the flow of electricity requires a closed circuit (a complete loop). **SC.5.P.11.2** Identify and classify materials that conduct electricity and materials that do not. (Also **SC.5.N.1.1, SC.5.N.2.2, LAFS.5.RI.1.3, MAFS.5.NBT.2.7**)

The Essential Question *How is energy transformed and transferred?*

Show What You Know

This roller coaster uses energy to move the cars on the track. What is one form of energy that the roller coaster uses?

____

____

Quest Kickoff

STEM Fun and Flashy

How can you use electrical energy to make a toy?

Hi, I'm Layla Hammond, a toy designer. Suppose a company has asked you to design a toy. In this problem-based learning activity, you will design, build, and test a new kind of toy that uses electrical energy.

Like a toy designer, you will decide what the toy should do. Then you will make a model, test it, and evaluate your design. Your toy will change energy from one form to another. You will use electricity to produce sound, light, or motion. The toy must also be safe for children ages 5 to 9.

Follow the path to learn how you will complete the Quest. The Quest activities in the lessons will help you complete the Quest! Check off your progress on the path when you complete an activity with a QUEST CHECK OFF. Go online for more Quest activities.

Quest Check-In 1

Lesson 1

Identify the types of energy used and produced by familiar toys.

SC.5.P.10.4 Investigate and explain that electrical energy can be transformed into heat, light, and sound energy, as well as the energy of motion.

VIDEO

Watch a video about a toy designer.

Quest Check-In Lab 3

Lesson 3

Build a prototype and evaluate whether it meets the criteria of the engineering problem.

Quest Check-In 2

Lesson 2

Design your toy and select the materials you will use to build it.

Quest Findings

Have classmates test your toy and give recommendations for ways to make your toy more fun.

HANDS-ON LAB

SC.5.P.10.2, SC.5.N.1.1

Where does the energy go?

Toy designers look for ways to use energy to make toys fun. How is energy used in different toys?

Suggested Materials
- wind-up toys
- toy cars
- ramp
- glow sticks
- toy musical instruments
- yo-yos

Procedure

☐ **1.** Choose three toys from the list. Play with each toy. Observe what it does. Record any changes in the toy you observe.

Analyze and Interpret Data

Science Practice
Scientists **interpret data** that they record during an investigation.

2. Cause and Effect What kind of change occurs when each toy is used? What caused each of the changes to occur?

____

____

____

3. Draw Conclusions Based on your observations, what can you conclude about how the toys used energy?

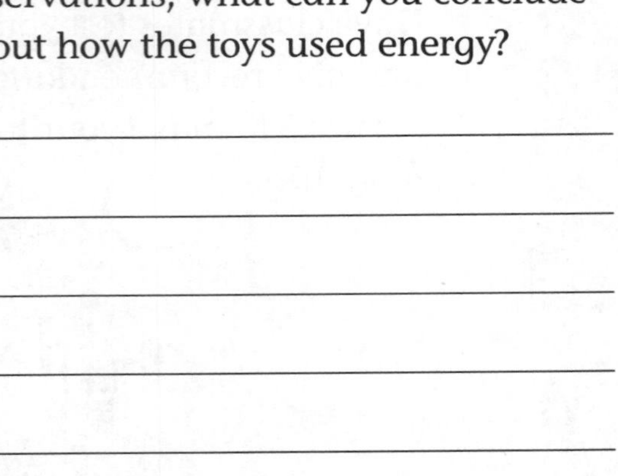

Observations

Toy	Change observed

Sequence

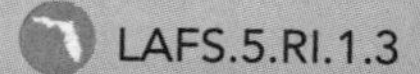

Many events are made up of a series of smaller events. Often these smaller events happen in a particular order. This ordered arrangement of events is called a sequence. You can identify the parts of a sequence as you read.

- Read the text. Identify all of the events that are part of the sequence.
- Look for clue words, such as *before, after,* and *then.*
- Make a list of the events in order.

Read the text describing what happens when you make a cell phone call.

GAME

Practice what you learn with the Mini Games.

Long-Distance Communication

Suppose that you are on vacation far from home. You want to share with your best friend what you are doing. How can you do that? If your cell phone is charged, you can call your friend and talk all about it.

First, you dial your friend's number. Then, a connection forms between the two of you. As you talk, an electronic signal travels from your phone to a cell tower nearby. Then the tower sends the signal to a tower close to your friend. After that tower receives the signal, the signal goes to your friend's phone. Your phone has taken sound energy and changed it to electrical energy. Your friend's phone then takes the electrical signal and changes it into a sound signal—just like your voice.

READING CHECK Sequence The steps of a phone call have to happen in the right order. Number the steps of a phone call in the text.

Lesson 1

Different Forms of Energy

I can...

Identify and describe the basic forms of energy.
Describe how energy has the ability to cause motion and change.

Literacy Skill
Sequence

Vocabulary
energy
kinetic energy
potential energy
sound energy

Academic Vocabulary
differentiate

VIDEO
Watch a video about forms of energy.

SC.5.P.10.1 Investigate and describe some basic forms of energy, including light, heat, sound, electrical, chemical, and mechanical. **SC.5.P.10.2** Investigate and explain that energy has the ability to cause motion or create change. (Also **SC.5.N.1.1, LAFS.5.RI.1.3**)

SPORTS Connection

A basketball player launches a jump shot at the basket. He uses his muscles to transfer energy to the ball. This energy causes the ball to move upward and toward the basket. It is not the only energy that affects the ball, though. As the ball moves, a gravitational force pulls the ball down. Swish! The ball passes through the basket, and the player's team scores two points. The moving ball has energy that comes from the player.

You can watch the game because of the light energy coming from the sun. In an indoor court, the lights get energy from electricity.

Predict The ball moves when the player takes a shot. Draw a line to show how the ball moves from the player through the basket. Where does the ball get the energy to move toward the net?

___

___

uInvestigate Lab

SC.5.P.10.2, SC.5.N.1.1

How does *energy* move?

Toy makers must understand how energy works so that they can make toys that operate correctly. What observations can you make about energy?

Materials
- dominoes
- balance and gram cubes
- toilet paper tube
- scissors

Be careful using scissors.

Science Practice

Scientists plan and carry out investigations to obtain evidence to support explanations.

Procedure

☐ **1.** Use the materials. Predict whether an object with more mass or less mass will move the dominoes.

____

____

☐ **2.** Make a plan to test your predictions. Think of a way you can measure mass.

☐ **3.** Show your plan to your teacher before you start. Record your observations.

Analyze and Interpret Data

4. Explain Tell how your observations did or did not support your prediction.

____

____

____

____

5. Explain How did energy change during your investigation?

____

____

____

Observations

Visual Literacy Connection

WHAT ARE SOME forms of energy?

In science, **energy** is the ability to do work or cause a change. You can find different forms of energy anywhere you go.

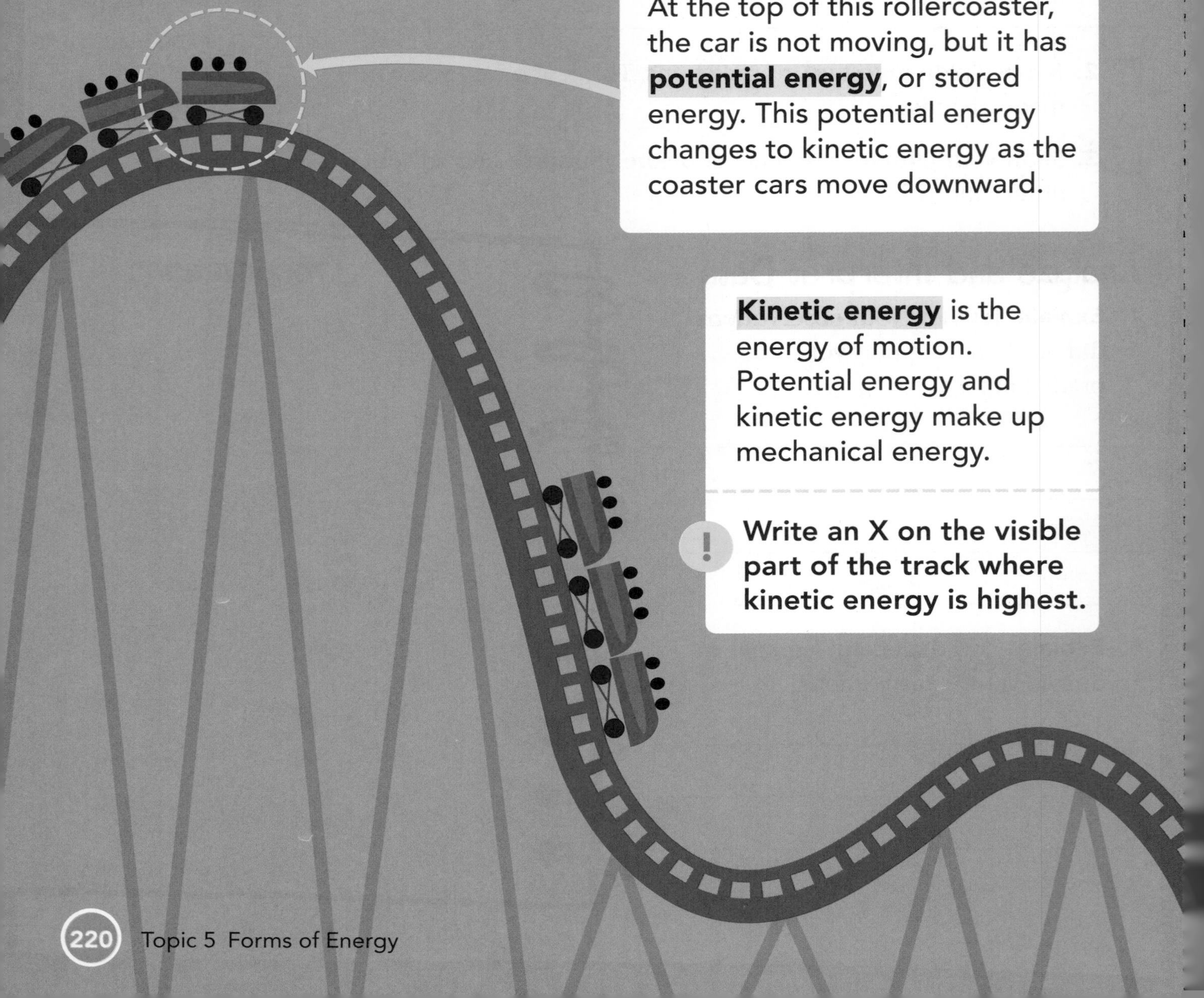

At the top of this rollercoaster, the car is not moving, but it has **potential energy**, or stored energy. This potential energy changes to kinetic energy as the coaster cars move downward.

Kinetic energy is the energy of motion. Potential energy and kinetic energy make up mechanical energy.

! **Write an X on the visible part of the track where kinetic energy is highest.**

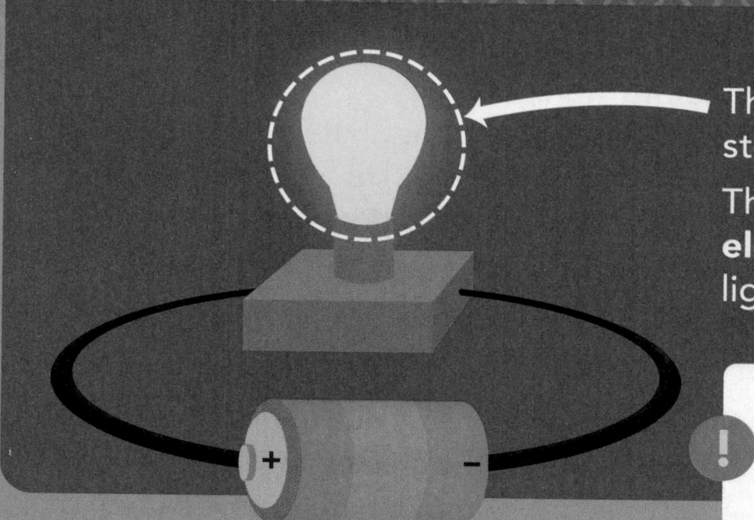

The battery in this electric circuit stores **chemical energy**.

The chemical energy changes to **electrical energy** that causes the light to come on.

Circle the parts of the circuit that carry electrical energy.

Sound energy travels though matter as particles move outward from the source of the sound.

Draw an arrow showing the direction of the sound energy the trumpet produces.

Light energy travels from a light source to an object and then to your eye.

Heat is a transfer of energy that raises the temperature of an object.

Draw arrows to show the direction of energy.

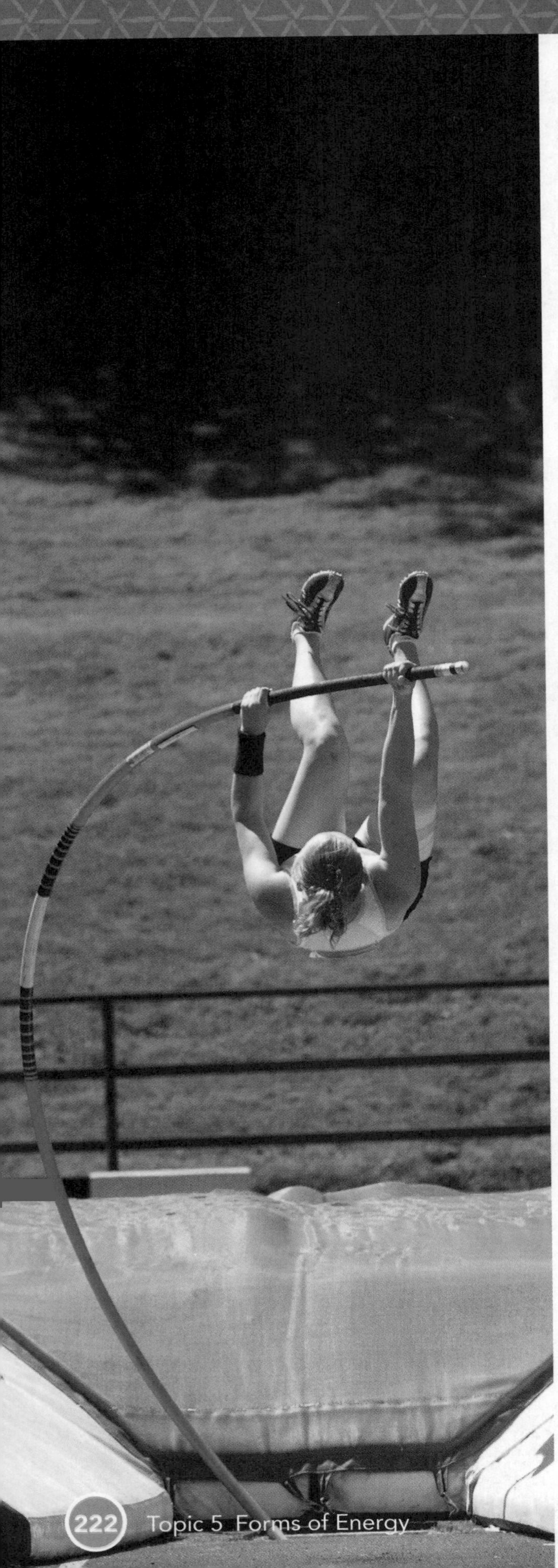

Mechanical Energy

In science, energy is the ability to do work or cause a change. Energy can change an object's motion, color, shape, temperature, or other characteristics. Energy cannot be made or destroyed, but it can change form. It can also move from one object to another.

Kinetic energy is energy due to motion. The faster an object moves, the greater its kinetic energy is. A slow-moving hammer barely moves a nail that it hits. The same hammer moving very fast can push a nail farther into the wood. The hammer has more kinetic energy when it moves faster.

An object does not need to be moving to have energy. Potential energy is energy an object has that is not causing any changes now but could cause changes in the future. One kind of potential energy is gravitational potential energy. An object above the ground has stored energy. Potential energy and kinetic energy together make up mechanical energy.

As the pole-vaulter reaches the top of her jump, she gains potential energy relative to the ground. The higher she goes, the more potential energy she has. She loses potential energy as she falls. The potential energy changes form. As the vaulter falls, more potential energy becomes kinetic energy, and she falls faster and faster.

Infer What clue from this picture tells you that the pole-vaulter has potential energy?

____

____

Make Meaning Recall where you have been throughout one day. In your science notebook, write when your potential energy was greatest.

Elastic Energy and Chemical Energy

Gravity is not the only source of potential energy. Elastic potential energy is the energy of a stretched rubber band or a compressed spring. This type of potential energy is present when objects are bent or stretched. When the vaulting pole bends, elastic potential energy increases. The more a rubber band is stretched, the more elastic potential energy it has. Elastic potential energy can cause the motion of objects to change.

Where does the pole-vaulter get the energy to start a jump? That energy is stored in her body as chemical potential energy. We get chemical energy from food. Some foods, such as those rich in sugars, contain more chemical energy than others.

Fireworks and gasoline also have chemical energy. When fireworks explode, their energy becomes light, sound, and heat. When gasoline burns in the engine of a car, its chemical energy becomes kinetic energy and heat.

Literacy ▸ Toolbox

Sequence When you sequence events, you tell the order in which they happened. Think about a person pole-vaulting in a competition. Many energy changes occur, starting with food. Write a sequence about all the energy changes you can identify during the vault.

MAFS.5.OA.1

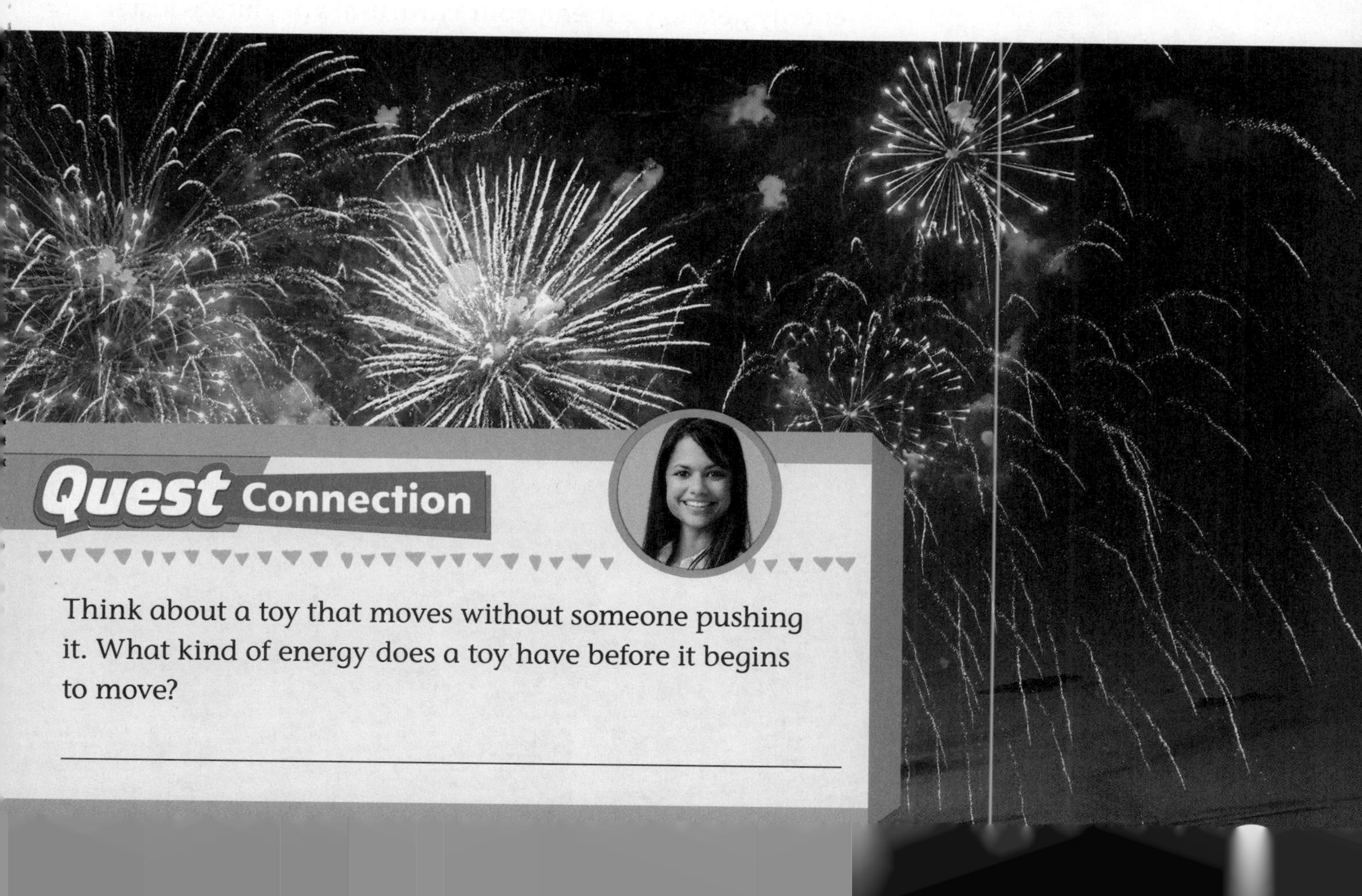

Quest Connection

Think about a toy that moves without someone pushing it. What kind of energy does a toy have before it begins to move?

____

uBe a Scientist

Observe Sound Travel Sound travels better through some materials than others. How can you test whether sound travels better through wood, metal, or air?

Sound

Sound is a form of energy made up of vibrations that spread from a source. A vibration is the back-and-forth motion of an object. Sound energy travels through a material, such as air, water, or wood. Sound energy causes the particles in the material to vibrate in a regular pattern. The particles bump into each other and pass the pattern of vibration to other particles.

One property of sound is pitch. Pitch tells how high or low a sound is. A flute is an instrument that has a high pitch. A tuba has a low pitch. In between is a wide range of different pitches. When you listen to a band play, you can **differentiate**, or tell the difference between, pitches as the music plays.

Why are some sounds louder than others? The property of loudness of sound is called its volume. A loud sound has more volume than a soft sound. The louder sounds have more energy when they get to your ear. When the higher energy gets to your ear, your eardrum will vibrate faster than if the sound were softer.

Compare and Contrast The hummingbird and the airplane both make sounds when they fly. Compare the volume of the two sounds.

___

___

Light

Light energy is present almost everywhere you go. It might come from the sun, lamps, or cell-phone screens. Light normally travels in a straight line from a source to the observer. Sometimes objects or materials make light change direction.

All light can travel through empty space, but not all light is exactly the same. The kind we can see is called visible light. The way visible light interacts with matter depends on the kind of matter. You may have observed that light can pass through some materials and not others. Transparent materials like clear glass let nearly all light pass through them. Translucent materials let some but not all light pass through. Waxed paper and most lampshades are translucent. An opaque material does not let any light pass through it. Light that hits an opaque object either bounces off the object, or it is taken in by the object. Wood, stone, and metals are opaque materials.

INTERACTIVITY

Complete an activity about the forms of energy.

Math ▸ Toolbox

Calculate Distance Light travels so fast that you can see light given off by a faraway object almost immediately. Sound travels through air at about 330 meters per second at 0°C. You see a fireworks explosion and hear the bang 2 seconds later. How far away from you was the explosion?

MAFS.5.OA.1

Compare and Contrast How is light energy different from sound energy?

____

____

____

Identify Draw a line from each label to a section of a marble that it describes.

transparent

opaque

translucent

Reflection and Refraction

Light moves in a straight line. When light hits an object, some light can be bounced off the object. Reflection happens when light bounces off an object. The light still moves in a straight line but goes in a different direction. Mirrors reflect light very well. Shiny objects reflect some or almost all of the light that hits them.

Light bends whenever it enters a new material. Look at the spoon in the photo. It appears bent because light bends when it goes from water to air. This bending is called refraction.

A lens is a polished piece of glass that makes things look larger or smaller when you look through the lens. Lenses do this by refracting the light. Microscopes, cameras, and prescription glasses have lenses.

Apply Find at least three objects that either reflect or refract light. Discuss the path of light as it hits each object.

Lesson 1 Check

SC.5.P.10.1, SC.5.P.10.2

1. **Compare** How does the mechanical energy of a ball that is starting to fall compare to its total energy just before it hits the floor?

2. **Identify** When you stand in sunlight, what form of energy is emitted by the sun?

3. **Evaluate** An eye doctor wants to design reading glasses that also function as sunglasses. Should the eye doctor use a reflective-transparent material or a reflective-opaque material for the lenses? Support your claim.

Playing with Energy

You know that energy is the ability to cause something to change. If you want to make a toy that children will enjoy, you want the toy to do something interesting. That means a change should happen when someone plays with it. Now that you have learned about many kinds of energy, you can figure out what makes a toy work.

Look at each toy. Think about the kind of energy the toy uses and the kind of energy that it produces when someone plays with it. Under each toy, describe the way that it transforms energy.

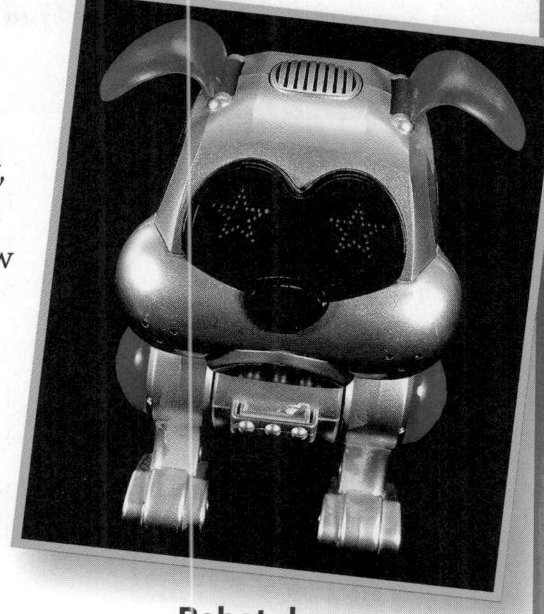

Robot dog

Uses ____________________

Produces ________________

Spring toy

Uses ____________________
____
____

Produces ________________

Glow rings

Uses ____________________

Produces ________________

Lesson 2

Electrical Energy

I can...

Show that a charged object can repel or attract other objects without touching them. Explain that electrical energy can be transformed into other forms of energy.

Literacy Skill
Sequence

Vocabulary
electric charge
electric current

Academic Vocabulary
evident

SC.5.P.10.3 Investigate and explain that an electrically-charged object can attract an uncharged object and can either attract or repel another charged object without any contact between the objects. (Also **SC.5.N.1.1, LAFS.5.RI.1.3**)

CURRICULUM Connection

Before the invention of the electric light bulb, people relied on candles, gaslights, or fires for light at nighttime. These sources of light were inefficient and sometimes dangerous.

The invention of the light bulb allowed people to extend their day and continue many activities that had not been possible at night. Businesses extended the workday, allowing owners to make more money. The increased profits enabled them to invest in more generators and wires. This led to more electricity becoming available.

In the home, the availability of electricity meant that more people could use more appliances. Life became easier for many. The invention of the light bulb helped society in many ways.

Relate Describe another way that inexpensive and safe lighting changed people's lives. Give a specific example.

____

____

____

uInvestigate Lab

SC.5.P.10.3, SC.5.N.1.1

How can a balloon help you understand charge?

Materials
- balloon
- wool cloth

Scientists and engineers study electric charge to find new ways to use energy. How can you observe electric charge in a balloon?

Science Practice

Scientists draw conclusions based on evidence from investigations.

Procedure

- [ ] 1. Think of ways to use the materials together to make the balloon stick to a wall. Make a plan. Show your plan to your teacher before you begin. Record your observations.
- [ ] 2. Observe what happens when the balloon interacts with other objects around your classroom. Record your observations.

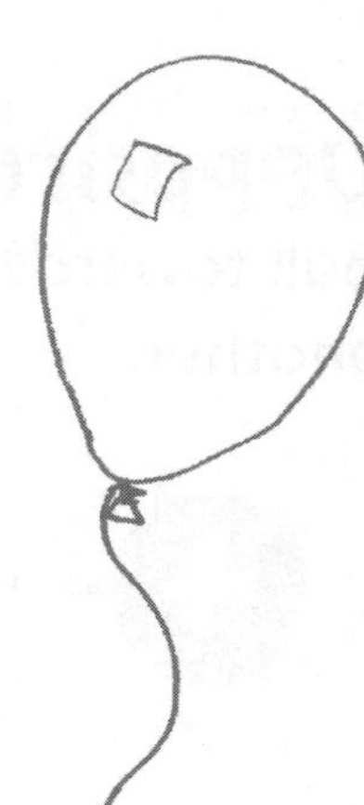

Analyze and Interpret Data

3. **Draw Conclusions** What do you think happened to the balloon? Why did it interact with different objects in ways that it did?

Visual Literacy Connection

HOW DO electric charges interact?

Atoms are the building blocks of everything. The atoms themselves are made of smaller particles. Some of these particles attract each other or push away each other. This happens because the particles have electric charge. **Electric charge** can be positive or negative.

Alike charges push away from one another.

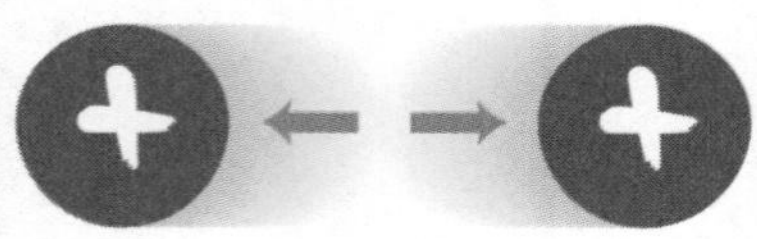

Opposite charges pull towards one another.

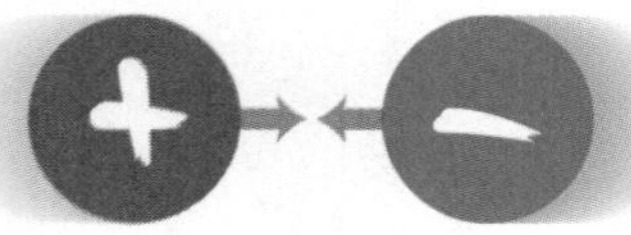

Use arrows to show how the electrically charged balloons will move.

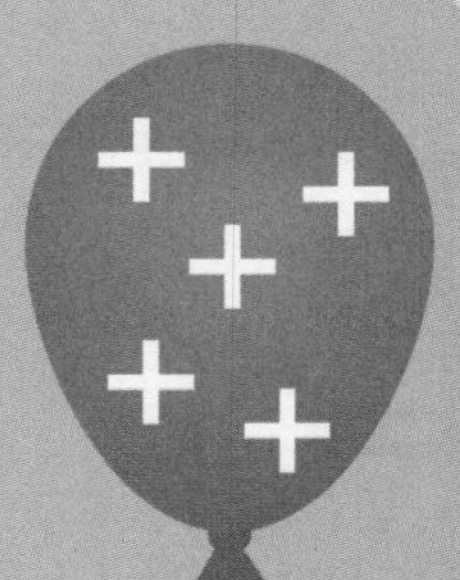

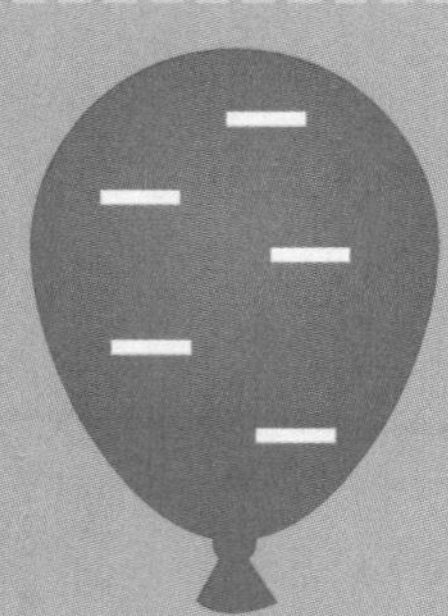

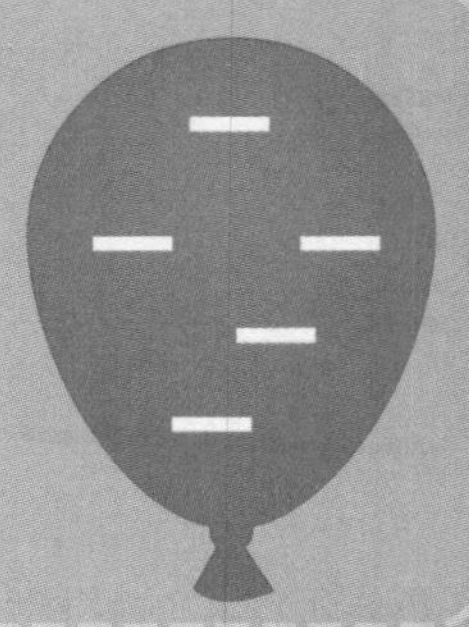

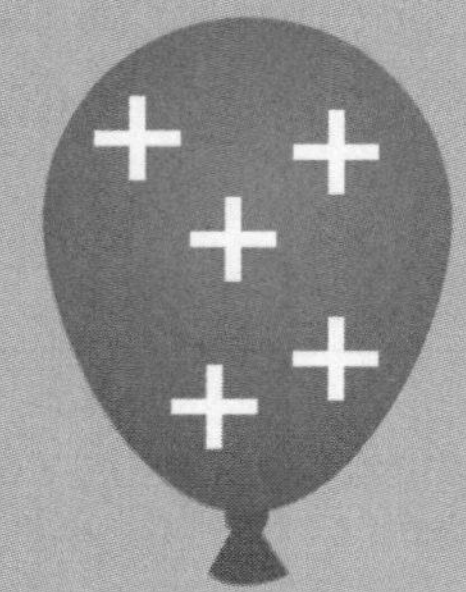

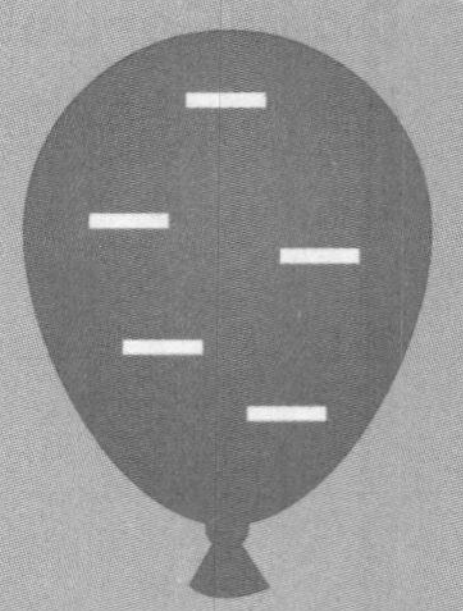

When you use a battery, negatively charged particles move from the negative end of the battery towards the positive end of the battery. The particles need a path to follow.

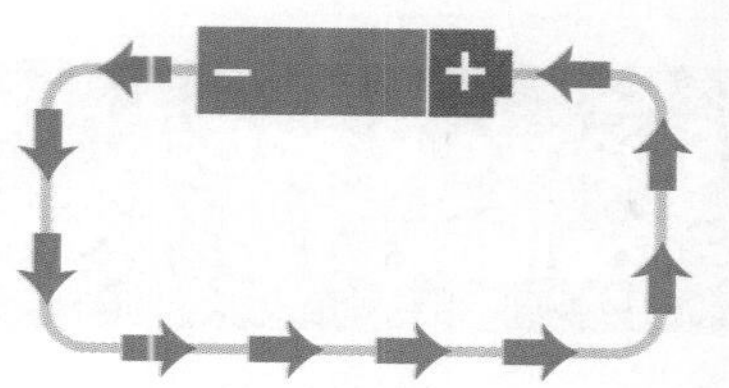

Circle the diagram that you think allows the electric charges to move and follow a path.

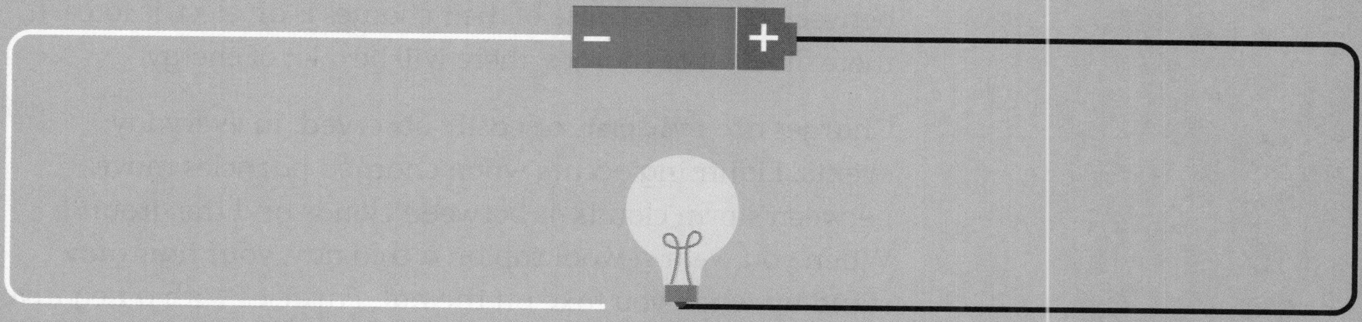

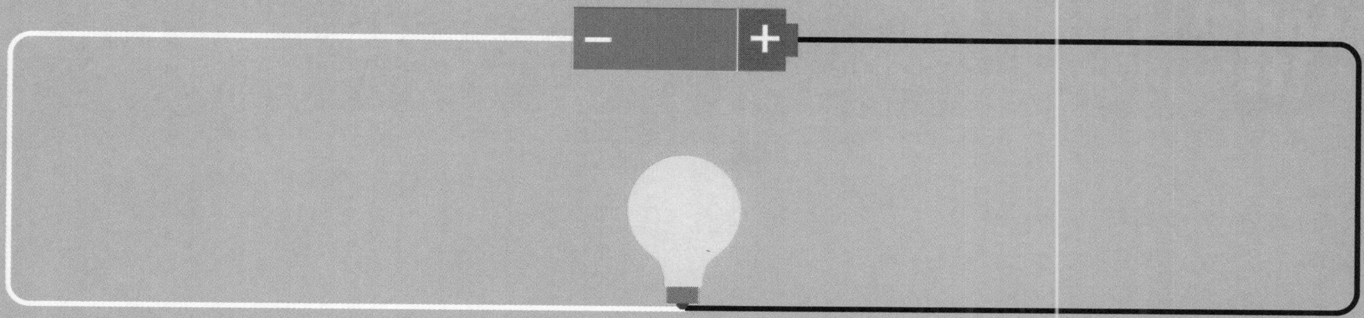

INTERACTIVITY

Complete an activity about electrical energy.

Science Practice ▸ Toolbox

Plan an Investigation How could you test objects to see whether they had no charge, a positive charge, or a negative charge?

Electric Charges

All matter is made up of atoms. The atoms are made of smaller particles. Some of these particles attract each other or push away each other. Within an atom, the number of positive and negative charges are the same. So, the positive and negative charges in the object are balanced. The object is neutral.

Sometimes objects have opposite charges—one is positive and the other is negative. Then the objects will attract, or pull toward, each other. If the objects have the same type of charge, they will repel, or push away from, each other. This happens without the objects touching each other. The push or pull between objects because of their charges is an electric force. If there are a lot of charges, there will be a lot of energy.

Charges are **evident**, or easily observed, in everyday events. Lightning occurs when charged particles move between storm clouds or between clouds and the ground. When you wear a wool cap on a cold day, your hair may stand up when you take off the hat. Particles with a negative charge move from your hair to the cap. Each hair strand is left with a positive charge. The hairs repel each other.

READING CHECK **Sequence** After you take off a wool cap, your hair stands up. What events happen to cause this? List them in order.

____

____

Model It! Make a diagram that models what happens to your hair when you rub a balloon on your head and the hairs spread out. Draw + and - to show how the charges are related to what happens.

Electric Energy

An **electric current** is the flow of charged particles. As the current flows through a device, the device gets energy from the particles that flow through it. Many devices transform, or change, electrical energy into other kinds of energy. For example, when you read at night, you use light energy that is transformed from electrical energy. Some of the electrical energy is also transformed into heat energy. That is why a light bulb becomes hot. Another example is when the electricity that flows into an electric guitar is changed into sound energy—and heat energy.

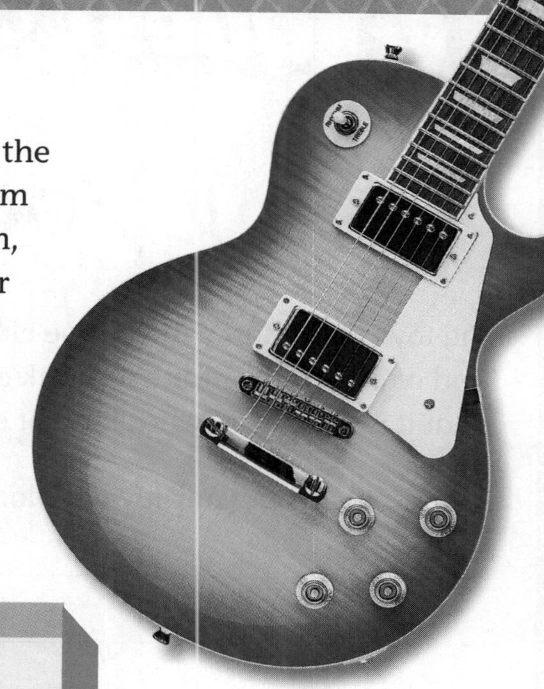

Quest Connection

How does a battery provide energy to a toy car?

____

____

____

Relate In your science notebook, list all the electrical devices you use in one day and the kind of energy each produces. Give specific examples.

Lesson 2 Check

SC.5.P.10.3

1. **Plan an Investigation** How could you show that a charged object could repel or attract another object without touching it?

____

____

2. **Infer** An object becomes electrically charged when negative charges move into it from a second object. Does the second object also become electrically charged? Explain your answer.

____

____

Charge Your Toy

The toy you design will change electrical energy into some other kind of energy. It is time to think about how the toy will work, what it will do, and what kind of energy needs to be produced.

1. Describe what your toy will do.

____

____

2. List of materials you will need to build a model of your toy.

____

____

____

3. Make a sketch of your toy showing its parts.

My Toy

STEM Math Connection

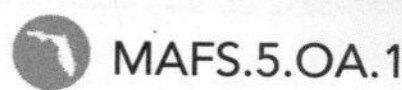

Calculate

Scientists use data to make calculations. Read the paragraph. Then use the data in the paragraph to answer the question.

Energy from Sunlight

Solar energy panels change light energy from the sun into electric current. A home has solar energy panels to provide electrical energy. The solar energy system receives 15 hours of sunlight during a particular day. That system produces 30,000 watt-hours. A watt-hour is the amount of electrical energy that a device uses or produces in one hour. A lamp has a light bulb that uses 100 W to stay lit.

How many hours can a 100 W light bulb stay lit with the watt-hours the solar energy system produces in a day? Follow these steps to answer the question. Be sure to show your work.

- Record all of the data that you have.
- Pay attention to units in each number.
- Determine how you can get the desired information.
- Set up an equation and calculate.

uEngineer It! Improve STEM

VIDEO

Watch a video about electricity.

Heat of the Action

Computers use a lot of energy when they process data. The largest supercomputers can fill gigantic rooms and process amazing amounts of data. Electrical currents flow constantly inside the computer chips that process the data. These supercomputers use millions of dollars' worth of electric power every year. Most of that energy is used for air-conditioning. Even with the best conductors, flowing electric currents change some of the electrical energy to heat. With millions of chips close together, the heat adds up very quickly. Remember, heat is the flow of energy that goes into raising the temperature of an object. When computers get too hot, they do not work very well. They may even stop working completely. That is why supercomputers need so much air-conditioning.

Heat is a problem even for small computers. Think about what happens to your phone or tablet when you download a big file. It gets warm.

Improve It

littleBits CHALLENGE

Like supercomputers, a desktop computer converts a lot of electrical energy into heat energy. The electronic parts of a computer are inside a box. The box causes the heat energy to get trapped, so the box and processor get hotter. As the processor gets hotter, it becomes less efficient. Computers are designed to shut down if they get too hot. This action protects the processor from damage.

Suppose that you are an engineer working for a company that manufactures computers. You want to design a system to prevent the inside of a computer from getting too hot.

- [ ] State the improvement that you need to make. This is your engineering problem.

- [ ] Identify some criteria and constraints for your problem. Remember that they must apply to a product, so cost could be a constraint.

Criteria	Constraints
The solution needs to....	The solution cannot...

- [ ] Propose one or more solutions that could be tested to improve the computer.

Lesson 3

Electric Circuits

I can...

Show that electricity needs a closed circuit in order to flow. Identify conductors and insulators.

Literacy Skill
Sequence

Vocabulary
conductor
insulator
series circuit
parallel circuit

Academic Vocabulary
illustrate

SC.5.P.11.1 Investigate and illustrate the fact that the flow of electricity requires a closed circuit (a complete loop). (Also **SC.5.P.11.2, SC.5.N.1.1, SC.5.N.2.2**)

LOCAL-TO-GLOBAL Connection

Electricity is the most common form of power used in the world. In order to provide electrical energy to users, power companies build power plants. Electrical energy is usually generated by a spinning magnet called a turbine. The turbine is moved by wind, water, burning fuel, or some other energy source. This energy then travels through power lines to homes, schools, and businesses. The United States has about 7,700 power plants. Throughout the world, there are approximately 62,500 power plants.

Another way to produce electrical energy is to use a solar panel. Solar panels use light energy from the sun to produce an electric current. This energy source can work on a small scale, such as producing energy to power a single street light. It can also work on a very large scale. A large solar powered facility uses thousands of large panels to produce enough energy for a small city.

READING CHECK **Sequence** Number the order of events involved in producing electric energy and supplying it to a home.

STEM · uInvestigate Lab

SC.5.P.11.1, SC.5.N.2.2

How can you turn the bulb on and off?

Electrical engineers use their understanding of electricity to design systems. How can you design an electric lighting system?

Materials

- D-cell battery in holder
- miniature light bulb
- switch
- lengths of insulated copper wire

Engineering Practice

Engineers **design solutions** to problems when they develop systems.

Design

☐ **1.** Make a plan to build a circuit that can turn a light bulb on and off. Use the materials to make the circuit. Draw the circuit you will make. Show your drawing to your teacher before you build it.

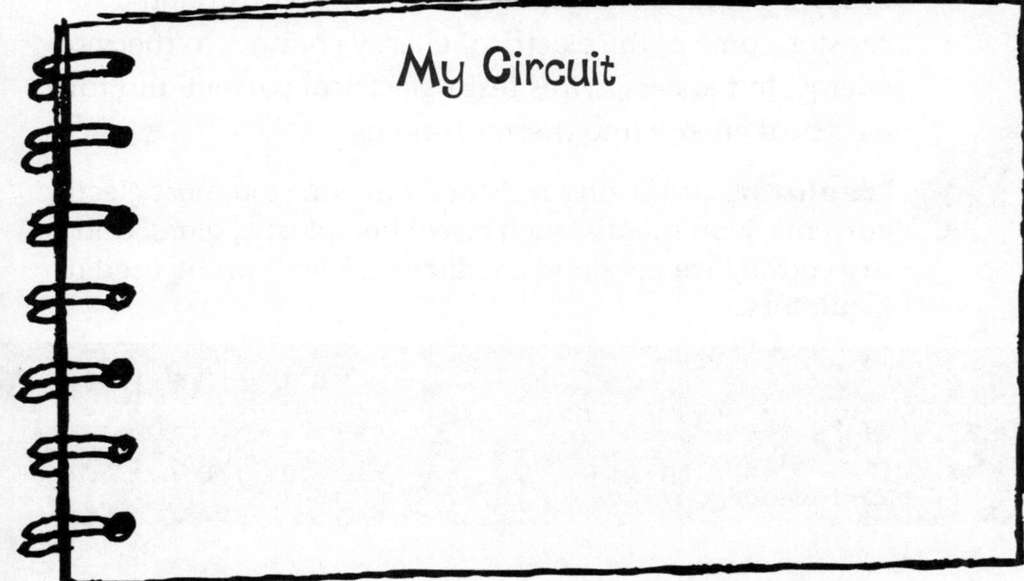

☐ **2.** Add arrows to your drawing to show how energy flows. Label the parts of your circuit.

Communicate Your Solution

3. Conclude Were you successful in getting your light bulb to turn on and off? What can you conclude about lighting a bulb?

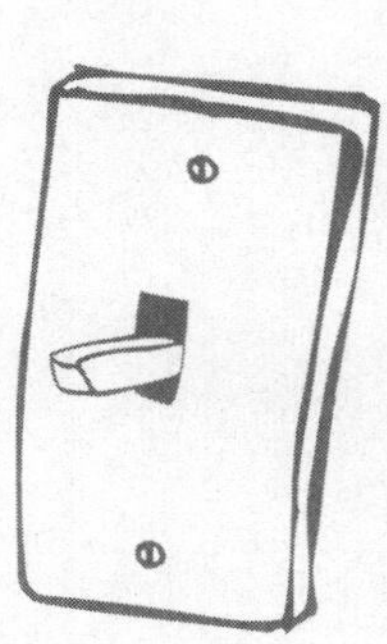

Insulators and Conductors

A material through which an electric charge can move easily is called a **conductor**. Some materials are better conductors than others. Metals, such as copper, gold, silver, and aluminum, are usually good conductors. Electric wires are often made from copper and aluminum. Your body is also a conductor. Sixty percent of the body is water, which is a good conductor of electricity. As a result, the body easily conducts electricity. That is why you should not touch a power line that has been knocked to the ground. Electricity always takes the shortest route when it flows. In this case, that would be right through your body!

A material through which an electric charge cannot move easily is called a resistor. As current moves through a resistor, some of the electrical energy changes to thermal energy. In toasters, wires resist electrical current and turn electrical energy into thermal energy.

Insulators are strong resistors that can stop most electric currents. Non metals, such as rubber, plastic, glass, and dry cotton, are not good conductors. They can be used as insulators.

Plan It! Suppose you need to design a product in which you must use an insulator in part of the product. You are considering four different materials for use in the product. Sketch or write the steps you would use to find out which of the four materials is the best insulator.

Energy Flow in a Circuit

An electric current is the flow of electrical charges through a material. An electric circuit is a loop through which an electric current can flow. Electricity can flow only in a closed circuit like the one in the photo. A circuit is closed if it has no gaps that can stop the flow of electricity. If the circuit has gaps, it is an open circuit, and electricity cannot flow.

Circuits are a way to provide electricity to devices that can change electric energy into other forms of energy. A circuit needs a source of energy. In some circuits, this source is a battery. In others, it is an electrical outlet or a solar cell. The devices connected to the circuit determine the type of energy that will be produced. For example, in a computer, the electric energy is changed into light, sound, and heat. A fan turns electric energy into kinetic energy as the blades turn. In every circuit, some energy is lost as heat.

Explain Often a switch such as the one in the picture is added to an electric circuit so that the flow of electric current can be turned off and on. How would the switch control whether electricity flows?

____

____

Engineering Practice ▸ Toolbox

Use a Model Engineers model an electric circuit using a circuit diagram. Find out what symbols engineers use in the diagrams. Draw a diagram for a simple electric circuit with a battery, a buzzer, and a switch.

Quest Connection

Your toy will use a battery for power. Why will you need to use an electric circuit to make the toy work?

____

____

____

INTERACTIVITY

Complete an activity about electric circuits.

uBe a Scientist

Plan a Circuit

Draw a circuit that you could use to light four different parts of a room.

Series Circuits

An electric circuit can be made in two ways. A **series circuit** is an electric circuit in which all of the elements are connected in a single loop. In the pictures of series circuits, you can see that electric current must travel through both bulbs to complete a circuit. To **illustrate**, or explain with an example, look at the two light bulbs connected by a series circuit in the picture on the left. Now look at the circuit on the right. In that circuit, the bulbs are no longer lit.

Conclude Why are the light bulbs no longer lit in the right picture? How could you fix the problem?

____

____

____

____

____

____

____

Parallel Circuit

If you have several electrical devices in your room, you probably do not want to have to turn them all on or off at the same time. You can use a parallel circuit. In a **parallel circuit,** devices are connected by more than one loop. Find the two loops in the diagram. The electric current has different paths that it can follow. In a parallel circuit, one device can break its circuit, but other devices are still part of a complete circuit.

Draw In your science notebook, make a sketch of a toy that has a buzzer and a light powered by the same battery. Show how the buzzer can make sound while the light is off.

Lesson 3 Check

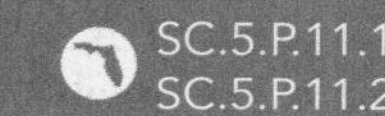

Julia made an electric circuit using one battery, one light, one motor, and one switch. She connected all of the parts and then observed what happened when she turned the switch on and off.

Switch	Light	Motor
Closed	On	On
Open	Off	Off
Closed	Broken	Off
Open	Broken	Off

1. **Use Evidence** Based on Julia's observations, did she make a series circuit or a parallel circuit? How do you know?

____

____

2. **Classify** Why are electric wires covered with a material such as plastic?.

____

____

STEM Quest Check-In Lab

How can you use energy in a toy?

It's time to build a prototype, or model, of your toy! Your toy must meet two criteria. First, it must transform electrical energy into two of these three types of energy: motion, light, or sound. Second, the toy must be safe and fun for children ages 5 to 9.

Materials

- 2 D-cell batteries in holders
- lengths of insulated copper wire
- switches
- safety goggles

Suggested Materials

- lights
- buzzers
- electric motors
- toy tires
- aluminum foil

Wear safety goggles.

Engineering Practice

Engineers **design a solution** to an engineering problem.

Design and Build

☐ **1.** Decide what you want your toy to do. Write a short description of its purpose.

☐ **2.** Choose the materials that you will use to build your toy.

SC.5.P.10.4, SC.5.P.11.1, SC.5.N.1.1

- [ ] **3.** Make a diagram that shows how you will arrange the materials. Label the components. Show your diagram to your teacher before you begin.

- [ ] **4.** Build your device. If the device does not work, revise your drawing and rebuild the device.

Evaluate Your Model

5. Use Evidence Does your toy meet the first criterion of transferring electrical energy into two of these three types of energy: motion, light, sound? Provide evidence to support your answer.

____

____

____

____

6. Evaluate How could you test your device to find out whether it meets the second criterion of being fun for a child age 5 to 9?

____

____

____

____

Quest Findings

INTERACTIVITY

Organize information to support your Quest findings.

STEM

Fun and Flashy

How can you use electrical energy to make a toy?

Identify Factors and Revise

Before you built your toy, you identified criteria. With a group, discuss whether the toy meets the criteria. If you can have younger children play with the toy, have them tell you whether it is fun to play with. If you cannot have younger children play with the toy, have some classmates play the role of toy tester. They can play with the toy and give you feedback. Have your toy testers recommend ways to make the toy more fun. Write their recommendations on the card.

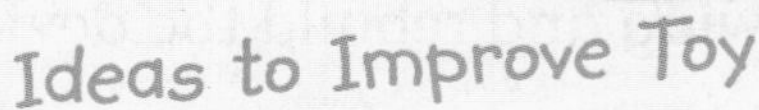

____

____

____

____

____

Cause and Effect

How did your toy change energy when it was used?

____

____

____

What are some ways to make the toy better?

____

____

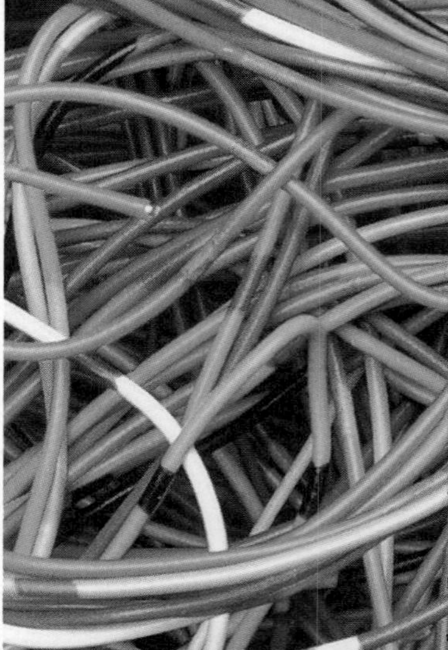

Career Connection

Toy Designer

Toy designers come up with the ideas for all of the fun things that end up in toy stores. They work with their minds and their hands. They have to imagine what a new toy will look like and how it will be used. They use science and engineering to design the toy so that it will work correctly. And they use their hands to build prototypes. Some toy designers work for big companies. Others work for themselves and sell their ideas to toymakers. Designing toys is a great job for someone who likes to think and play.

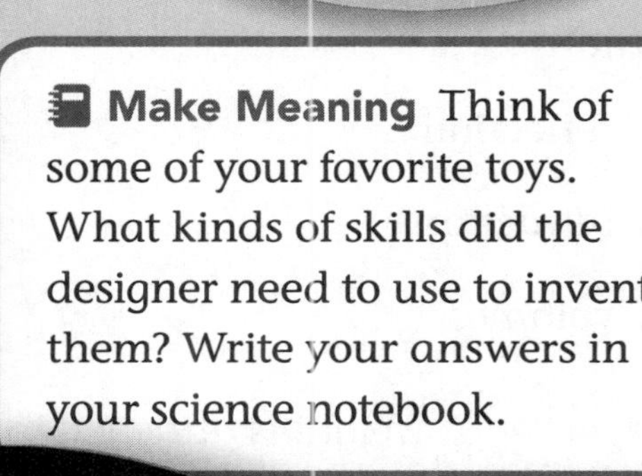

Make Meaning Think of some of your favorite toys. What kinds of skills did the designer need to use to invent them? Write your answers in your science notebook.

Assessment

Read each question and choose or write the best answer.

1. **Vocabulary** When Micah looked through a glass ball, things looked strange. What property of light caused the strange appearance of the view?

A. pitch

B. reflection

C. refraction

D. volume

2. **Interpret** A weight is attached to a spring. The weight drops and stretches the spring. Then, the spring pulls the weight upward. What energy change occurs after the spring is stretched as far as it will go?

A. kinetic energy to elastic potential energy

B. elastic potential energy to kinetic energy

C. gravitational potential energy to elastic energy

D. gravitational potential energy to kinetic energy

3. **Evaluate** An orchestra conductor instructs drummers to start playing. Describe the energy transformations that occur.

4. **Explain** If you rub a piece of glass tubing with a silk cloth, the glass gets a positive charge. Which statement explains what happens to the silk cloth?

A. The cloth gets a positive charge because it touched the positively charged glass.

B. The cloth gets a negative charge because it received charged particles from the glass.

C. The cloth does not get an electric charge because charges can move in only one direction.

D. The cloth does not get an electric charge because only hard, solid objects can become charged.

5. Use Tables Lee made a hypothesis that electrical conductors are always made of metal. He built a circuit using a battery, a light bulb, and wires. He arranged the wires so that the material he was testing was part of the circuit. He recorded his observations on the table.

Material	Is it a metal?	Did the light turn on?
Copper	Yes	Yes
Graphite	No	Yes
Glass	No	No
Aluminum	Yes	Yes
Distilled water	No	No
Salt water	No	Yes

Did the results support Lee's hypothesis?

A. no, because some metals do not conduct electric current

B. no, because some materials that are not metal do conduct electric current

C. yes, because copper and aluminum are both electrical conductors

D. yes, because glass and water are electrical insulators

6. Use Evidence A parking lot is lit by a long cable with many light bulbs. As a car drives past the lights, the tire causes a stone to hit one of the lights. The light bulb breaks and goes out. The rest of the lights stay lit. Use evidence to draw a conclusion about the type of circuit used in the string of lights.

____

____

____

____

____

____

The Essential Question

How is energy transformed and transferred?

Show What You Learned

You used electricity to make your toy work. Based on the evidence you saw, what are some energy transformations that can occur in an electrical device?

____

____

____

____

Science Assessment Practice

Read the scenario and answer questions 1–2.

Jayla carries a bowling ball under one arm and climbs a ladder. She holds the ball above the ground next to the eighth rung while she checks that no one is near the ladder. When Jayla sees that no one is nearby, she releases the ball and it falls to the ground. She hears a loud sound when the ball hits the ground.

1. **Apply Concepts** When will the falling bowling ball have an equal amount of potential energy and kinetic energy?

   Ⓐ just before Jayla drops it

   Ⓑ just before it strikes the ground

   Ⓒ when it passes rung 6 on the ladder

   Ⓓ when it passes rung 4 on the ladder

2. **Use Reasoning** Jayla places a mattress below the ladder and drops the ball a second time. This time the bowling ball lands on the mattress, and it makes a softer sound than before. Which energy transfer is responsible for the change in the loudness of the sound?

   Ⓕ potential energy of the ball to kinetic energy of the ball

   Ⓖ potential energy of the ball to sound energy in the air

   Ⓗ kinetic energy of the ball to elastic potential energy of the mattress

   Ⓘ mechanical energy of the mattress to sound energy in the air

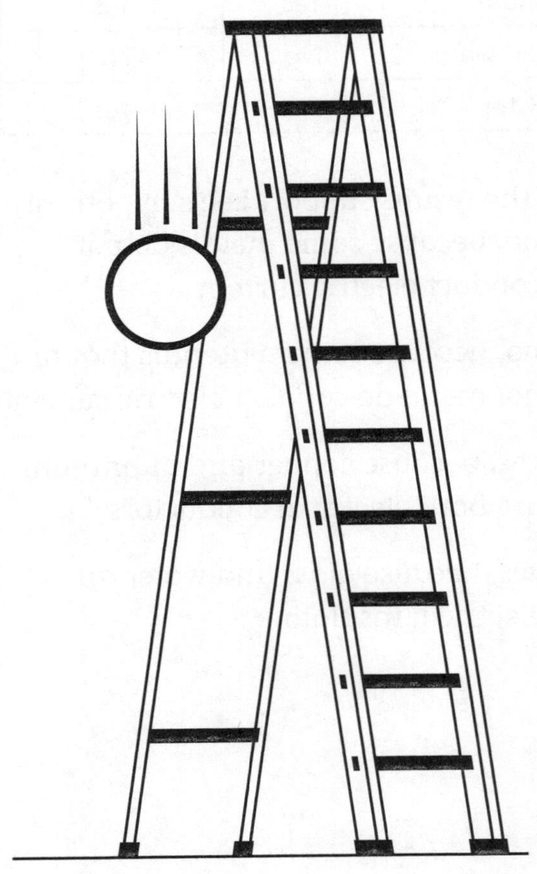

SC.5.P.10.1, SC.5.P.10.2, SC.5.P.10.3, SC.5.P.11.2

Read the scenario and answer questions 3–4.

Frank built a circuit using one battery, one switch, and two light bulbs. He connected all the parts. Then he observed what happened when he turned the switch on and off. He recorded his observations in a table.

Switch	Bulb A	Bulb B
closed	on	on
open	off	on
closed	on	broken

3 **Use Evidence** What evidence shows that the battery and the switch are connected in parallel, not in series?

Ⓐ All lights go on when the switch is closed.

Ⓑ The broken bulb causes Bulb A to turn off.

Ⓒ Bulb B remains on when the switch is open.

Ⓓ Bulb A turns off when the switch is open.

4 **Explain** Why does bulb A go out when the switch is left open?

Ⓕ Bulb B is on a separate branch from bulb A.

Ⓖ Bulb A is on the same branch as the switch.

Ⓗ The battery is on its own branch.

Ⓘ The open switch has no effect on Bulb A.

5 **Formulate** Carlos walked across a wool carpet. He then touched a doorknob and received a shock. Which of these choices **best** describes the energy source for the shock?

Ⓐ The metal doorknob handle is a conductor, so it produces charged particles.

Ⓑ Kinetic energy was transformed into electrical energy as Carlos walked.

Ⓒ Charged particles were transferred from Carlos to the carpet as he walked.

Ⓓ Electrical energy in between Carlos's hand and the doorknob caused the shock.

uDemonstrate Lab

Where did the energy go?

Engineers know ways that energy transforms from one type to another. They use that knowledge when designing new products. How do toys use energy transformations?

Suggested Materials

- wind-up toys
- toy cars and ramp
- glow sticks
- toy musical instruments
- yo-yos

Procedure

☐ **1.** Choose three toys from the list.

____

____

____

☐ **2.** Make a plan to investigate how toys use energy. Show your plan to your teacher before you begin. Make a table to record your observations.

Science Practice

Scientists **interpret data** that they record during an investigation.

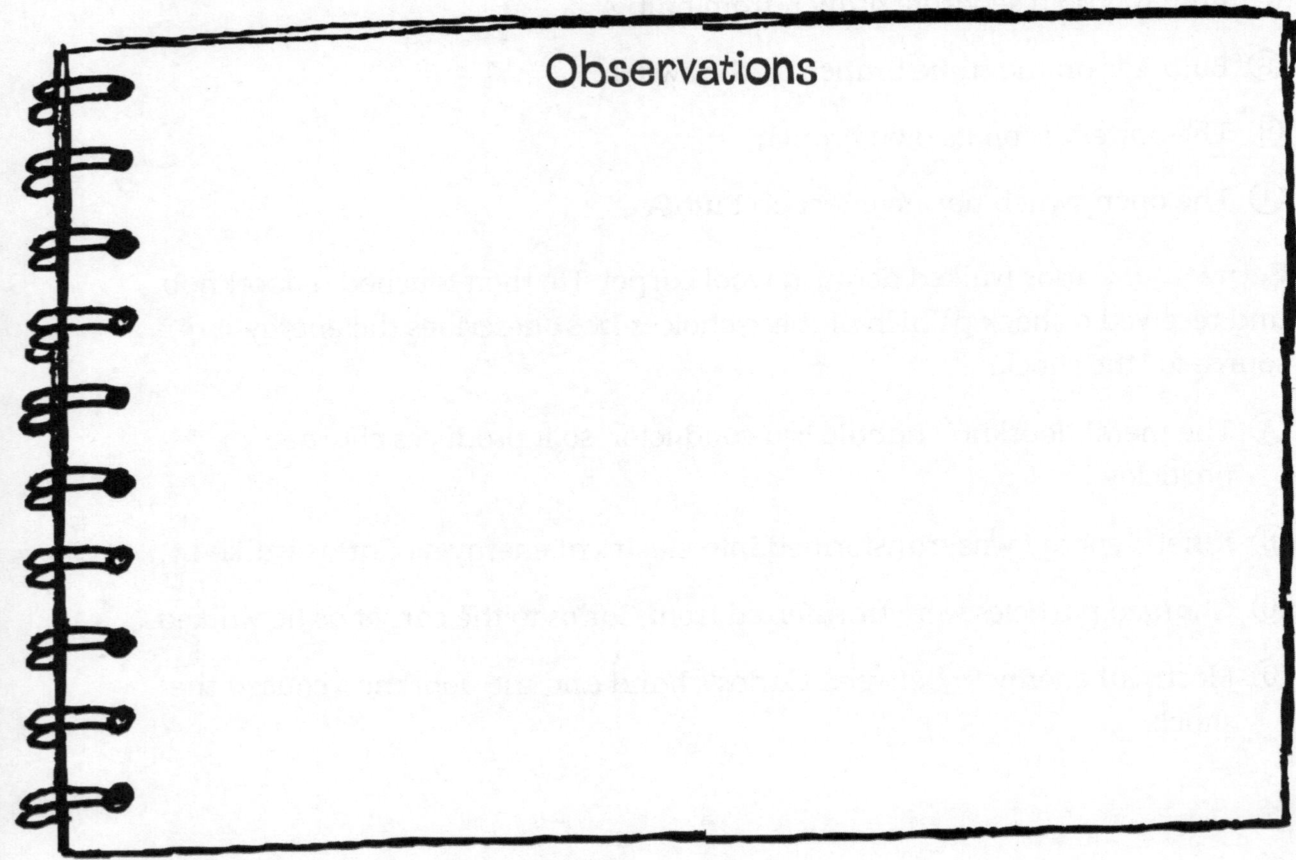

SC.5.P.10.1, SC.5.P.10.2, SC.5.N.1.1

Analyze and Interpret Data

3. **Cause and Effect** Look over your observations. Complete the table and identify the starting energy and the energy produced in each toy.

Toy	Starting	Energy produced

4. **Interpet Data** What can you infer from your data about energy transformations?

____

____

____

____

____

5. **Evaluate** How can you increase the amount of energy that a toy produces by energy transformations?

____

____

____

____

____

____

Topic 6

Forces and Changes in Motion

SC.5.P.13.1 Identify familiar forces that cause objects to move, such as pushes or pulls, including gravity acting on falling objects. **SC.5.P.13.2** Investigate and describe that the greater the force applied to it, the greater the change in motion of a given object. **SC.5.P.13.3** Investigate and describe that the more mass an object has, the less effect a given force will have on the object's motion. **SC.5.P.13.4** Investigate and explain that when a force is applied to an object but it does not move, it is because another opposing force is being applied by something in the environment so that the forces are balanced. (Also **SC.5.N.1.1, SC.5.N.1.4, LAFS.5.RI.1.3, MAFS.5.MD.1.1**)

Go online to access your digital course.

- VIDEO
- eTEXT
- INTERACTIVITY
- VIRTUAL LAB
- GAME
- ASSESSMENT

The Essential Question

What affects the motion of objects?

Show What You Know

During a rally, a skateboarder moves in ways that seem impossible. Identify some ways to control motion.

____

____

____

Quest Kickoff

STEM

Forces in Outer Space Game

How can you apply forces in a space-based video game?

Hi, I'm Mike Spense, a video game designer working with NASA's Kennedy Space Center. NASA uses video games to train astronauts in how to operate spacecraft and other equipment. These simulations help trainees experience the reaction to forces in a space environment. Besides that, they are fun and exciting!

In this problem-based learning activity, you will design a video game that demonstrates how forces work. Like a video game designer, you will think about ways to make the game fun. Other students will judge your design and make suggestions for improvement.

Follow the path to learn how you will complete the Quest. The Quest activities in the lessons will help you complete the Quest! Check off your progress on the path when you complete an activity with a QUEST CHECK OFF. Go online for more Quest activities.

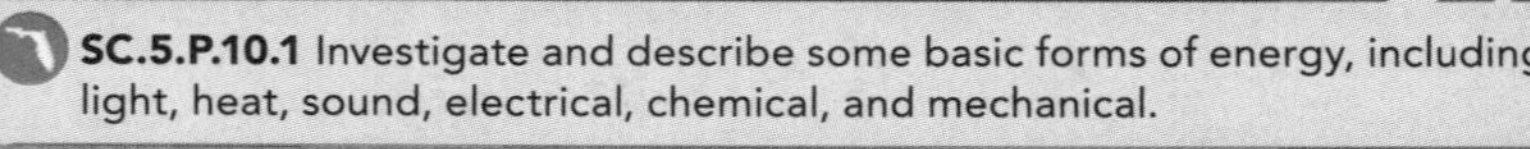

SC.5.P.10.1 Investigate and describe some basic forms of energy, including light, heat, sound, electrical, chemical, and mechanical.

VIDEO

Watch a video about a video game designer.

Quest Check-In Lab 1

Lesson 1

Gravity is a force that affects objects all the time. Consider how your video game will use gravity or fight against gravity.

Quest Check-In 2

Lesson 2

Forces change the motion of an object. Consider how you can use force as the player works through the challenges of the video game.

Quest Check-In 3

Lesson 3

Some forces are balanced and some are unbalanced. How will you use balanced and unbalanced forces to control the motion of game objects?

Quest Findings

Present your video game design as a slide presentation to the class. Your audience will judge whether it is fun and whether it follows the laws of force and motion.

STEM uConnect Lab

HANDS-ON LAB

SC.5.P.13.1, SC.5.N.1.1

How do things move?

When you drop something, you expect that it will fall. How can you change the way a toy falls when you drop it?

Materials
- sheets of paper
- scissors
- glue
- tape
- string
- small toy

Design a Solution

☐ **1.** Crumple one sheet of paper into a ball and leave a second sheet flat. Predict how the two sheets of paper will fall if you drop them from above your head.

____

____

Engineering Practice

Engineers **investigate** to identify cause and effect relationships.

☐ **2.** Design a device to slow the fall of a toy. Use the materials. Draw your design. Show it to your teacher before you begin.

☐ **3.** Build the device and then test it. Record your observations.

Be careful when using scissors.

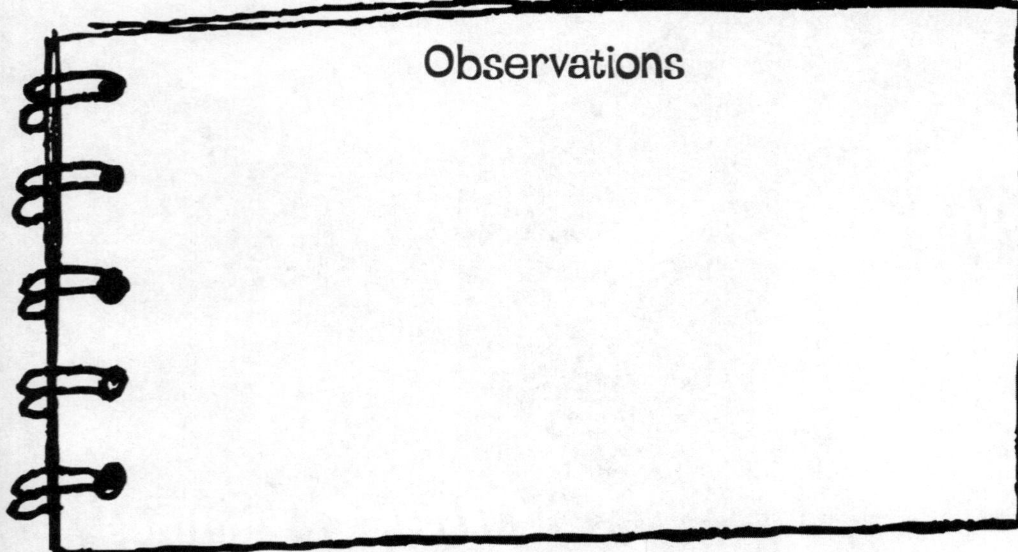

Communicate Your Solution

4. Evaluate Compare your results with those of other students. Which design caused the toy to move slowest? Why do you think that is so?

____

____

Cause and Effect

LAFS.5.RI.1.3

GAME

Practice what you learn with the Mini Games.

Cause and effect relationships show how two events are related. Causes are reasons. Effects are results.

Use these strategies to help you identify causes and effects when reading informational texts.

- Ask yourself questions like, "What happened?" or "How did it change?" to identify an effect.
- Ask yourself, "Why?" to identify the cause.
- Look for clue words such as *because* and *so*. They can signal cause and effect.

Read the passage about an avalanche. Then answer the question that asks you to identify the cause and effect.

Avalanche!

As snow accumulates on the side of a mountain, forces from various factors can cause snow to rush down the mountainside. These factors include wind, ice, human activity, rainfall, sleet, or debris. The snow rushing down the mountain can travel at speeds up to 130 kilometers (80 miles) per hour. When this occurs, the event is considered an avalanche.

In 2002, a giant mass of ice, snow, and rock broke off of Mount Kazbek in North Ossetia, Russia. Ice, snow, and rock thundered down the Karmadon Gorge. As a result, the avalanche displaced 20 million tons of snow.

READING CHECK **Cause and Effect** Underline the cause and effect of the avalanche in North Ossetia, Russia.

Lesson 1

Forces and Motion

I can...

Identify some forces that cause objects to move.

Literacy Skill
Cause and Effect

Vocabulary
force
noncontact force
gravity
contact force
friction

Academic Vocabulary
deduce

SC.5.P.13.1 Identify familiar forces that cause objects to move, such as pushes or pulls, including gravity acting on falling objects. **SC.5.P.13.2** Investigate and describe that the greater the force applied to it, the greater the change in motion of a given object. Also **SC.5.N.1.1, SC.5.N.1.4, LAFS.5.RI.1.3**

SPORTS Connection

A long jumper approaches the jump with a fast run. The force of each step of the running approach increases the forward speed. The runner carefully places her foot on the last step to get as much force as possible for the jump. Her leg muscles push hard as she takes off. She rises into the air and right away starts to get into position for the landing. As the jumper sails through the air, another force works to bring the jump to an end. Gravity pulls the jumper's body downward. After the jumper lands in the sandpit, judges make measurements to find the length of this jump. The world record long jump is just less than 9 meters (30 ft). That is a long jump!

Infer No matter how far the jumper goes, she eventually returns to the ground. What can you infer about the direction of the force acting on the jumper?

____

____

____

uInvestigate Lab

HANDS-ON LAB

SC.5.P.13.1, SC.5.N.1.1

What makes it *move*?

If you set a ball on a flat tabletop or floor, it does not move. What are some ways to cause a ball to move?

Materials
- small steel ball

Suggested Materials
- magnet
- ruler

Procedure

☐ **1.** Think of three ways you can make the steel ball move. Make a plan to test whether each idea makes the ball move. Show your plan to your teacher before you begin.

☐ **2.** In the table, record the ways you will make the ball move. Then test your ideas. Record your observations.

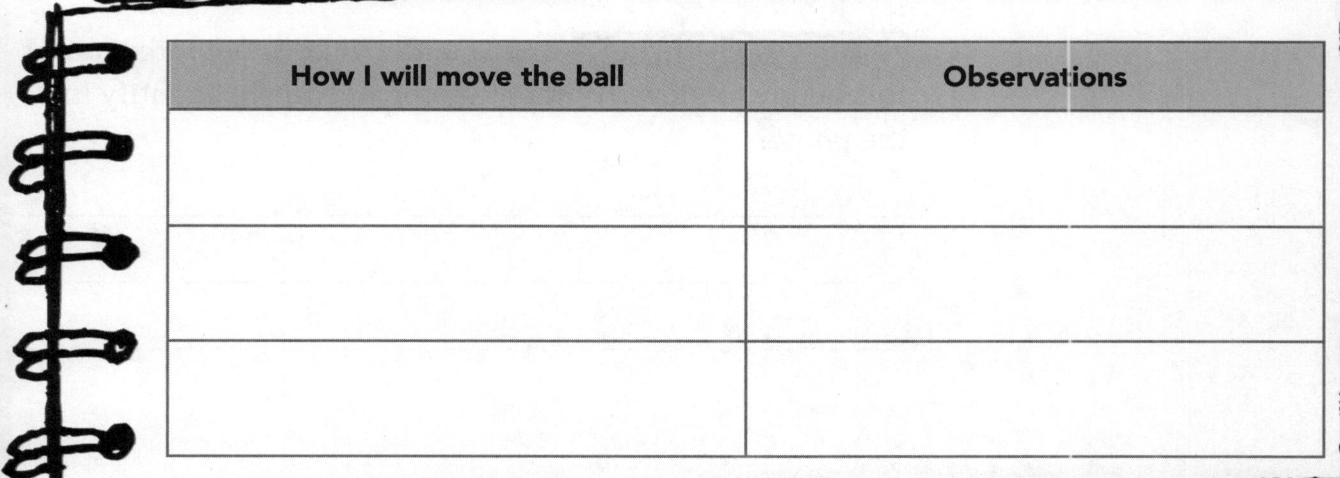

How I will move the ball	Observations

Science Practice

Scientists **observe** details during an investigation.

Analyze and Interpret Data

3. Infer What caused the ball to move in different ways?

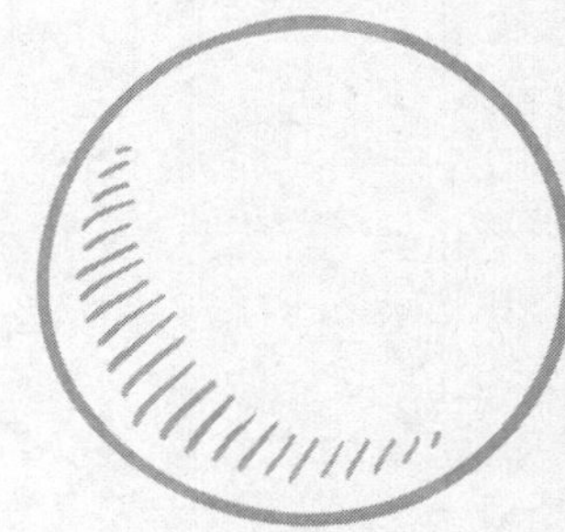

Literacy Toolbox

Cause and Effect A cause is a reason why something happens. An effect is the result. Underline one example of a cause and effect that you read.

 LAFS.5.RI.1.3

Forces

As your plane begins to move on the runway, you can feel your seat pushing you forward. As the plane moves toward takeoff, the force on your body increases. A **force** is a push or pull that acts on an object. Some forces are easy to observe. If you push a younger child on a swing, you exert a force. It causes the child to move away from you. You can feel the force in your hands and arms as you apply your push. You can see the result of the push when the child and swing move forward. Each push causes the child to go higher.

Any time that a change in an object's motion happens, you can deduce that a force acted on the object. To **deduce** means to come to a conclusion based on evidence. A change in motion is evidence of a force. Forces do not always change motion, though. If you push very hard on a brick wall, you can feel that you are pushing. Yet the wall does not move. Other forces acting on the wall keep it from moving.

READING CHECK **Cause and Effect** What force causes this buggy to move? What other forces can you identify in the photo?

____

____

____

Properties of Forces

Every force has a strength, or magnitude. This magnitude is measured in units called newtons (N). A force also has a direction. The direction of a force can be described by telling which way the force is pushing or pulling an object.

Forces can change the way objects move. When an object begins to move, it is because a force has acted on it. When an object is already moving, forces can make it speed up, slow down, or change direction.

Identify Draw an arrow on the photo to show the direction of the force on the object.

Question It! What questions would you ask if you wanted to identify how forces were acting on a bouncing ball?

____

____

____

____

____

____

Visual Literacy Connection

What are noncontact forces?

Some forces can cause a push or a pull on an object without touching it. Forces that can act at a distance are called **noncontact forces**. Three types of noncontact forces are gravity, electricity, and magnetism.

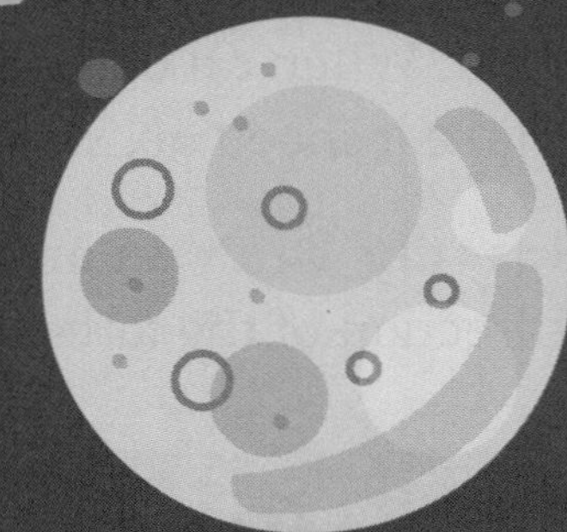

Gravity

Gravity is a **force** that acts between any two objects that pulls them toward one another. Draw arrows to show the direction of the gravitational forces between the following:

- Earth and the satellite
- Earth and the moon

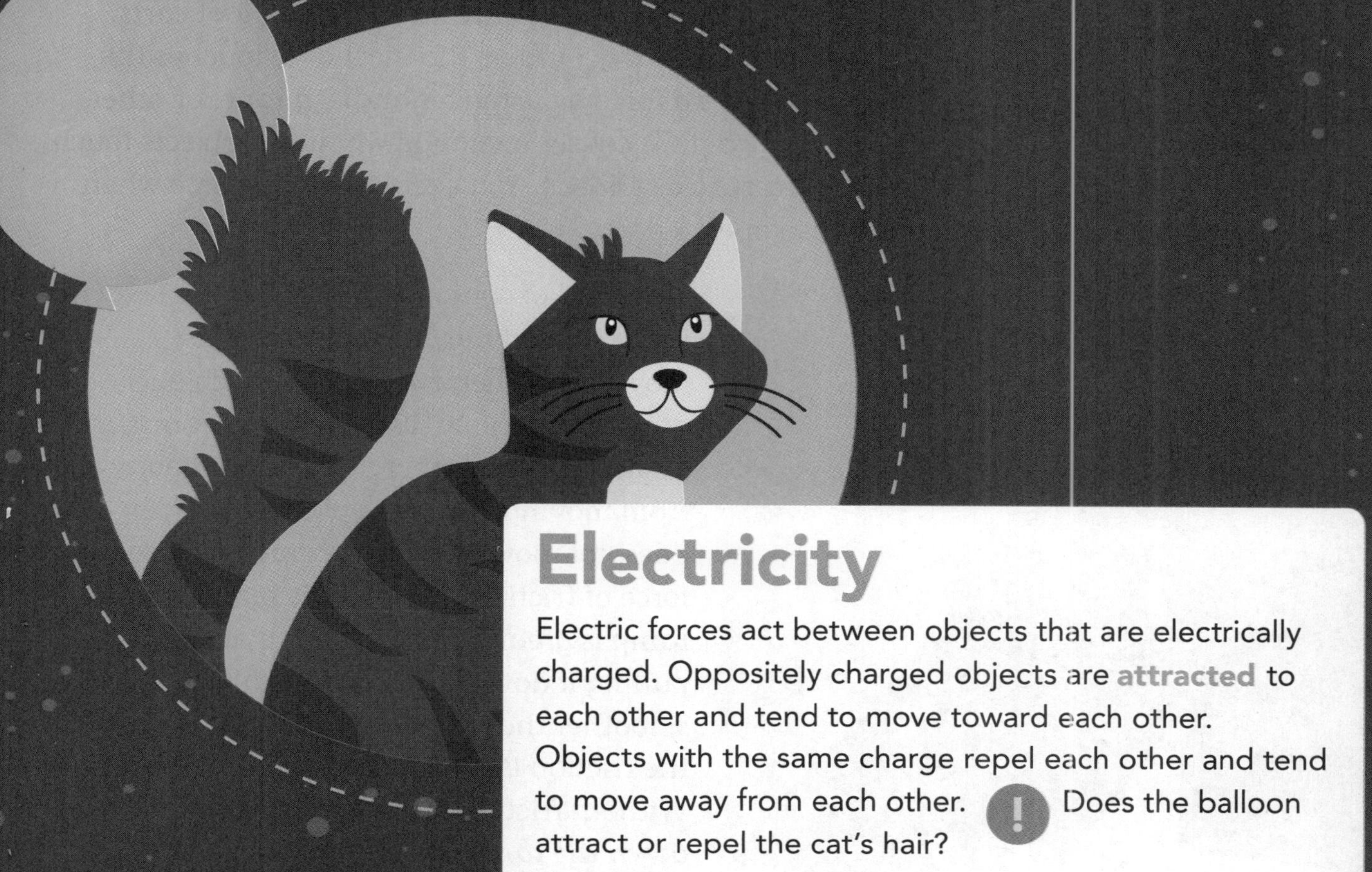

Electricity

Electric forces act between objects that are electrically charged. Oppositely charged objects are **attracted** to each other and tend to move toward each other. Objects with the same charge repel each other and tend to move away from each other. ! Does the balloon attract or repel the cat's hair?

____

Magnetism

Magnetic force is a noncontact force that can **exert a pull** on magnetic objects, such as iron. Magnets can either attract or repel other magnets. Draw an arrow to show the direction of the force that the magnet is exerting.

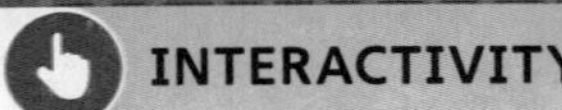

INTERACTIVITY

Complete an activity about forces in games.

Contact Forces

Car mechanics use forces to lift tires and pull tool carts. These forces cannot act unless the mechanic touches the tires or applies a force by using a handle, a rope, or other object. A force that causes a change when two objects touch is called a **contact force**. You exert a contact force when you push open a door.

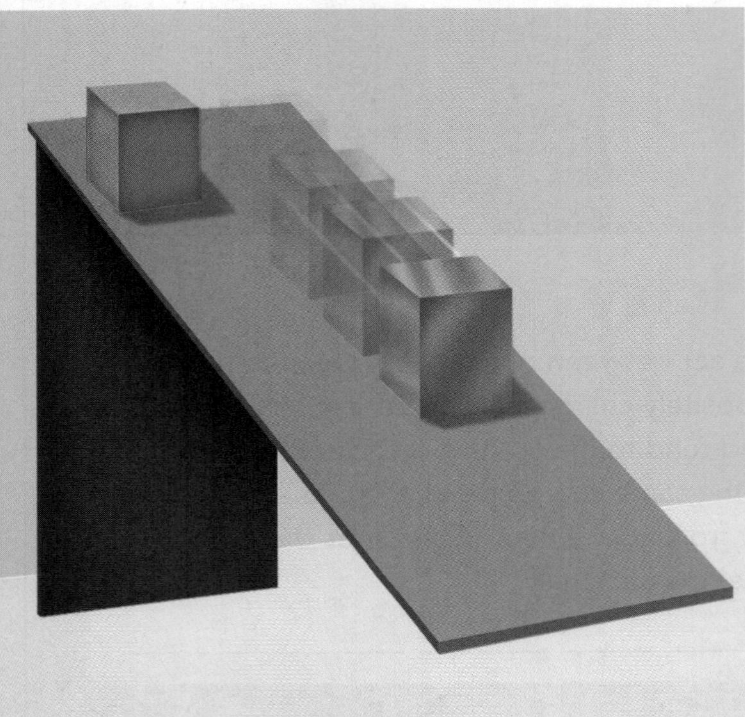

One kind of contact force is friction. **Friction** is the contact force that acts against movement when two objects touch each other. Friction makes it harder for one surface to move past another. It also keeps objects from moving. For example, the wooden block does not move down the ramp because the force of friction between the block and the ramp is greater than the force of gravity pulling it downward. The metal block is smoother than the wooden block, and so the friction is less. It slides down the ramp. Without friction, both blocks would slide down the ramp without any force acting against their motion. The amount of friction between two objects may depend on their texture, shape, and speed.

Write About It In your science notebook, write what you think would happen if fiction did not act between you and the floor.

Quest Connection

Your video game will involve moving objects. How could you include contact forces in the game design?

____

____

Solids are not the only materials that can cause friction. Air and water also resist motion when they touch an object. Air resistance is a type of friction that occurs when particles of air contact a surface. If you ride a bike very fast, you can feel the air pushing against your face. Friction between the air and you (or the bike) slows the movement of the bike. Water causes a similar type of friction. When you swim, you must use force to overcome the friction between your body and the water. In swimming competitions, swimmers often wear suits that are designed to reduce friction. This helps them swim faster.

Wind pushes a sailboat forward, but some of the wind's force must overcome friction between the boat and the water.

Apply Describe an example of when you experienced friction between you and the air or water.

___

___

Lesson 1 Check

SC.5.P.13.1

1. READING CHECK **Cause and Effect** A soccer player kicks a ball into the air. The ball hits the ground and rolls to a stop. What are three forces that affect the ball's motion?

___

___

___

2. **Use Evidence** Gigi stops a rolling ping pong ball by blowing air through a straw. Jared claims that the force that stops the ball is a noncontact force. Is he correct?

___

___

Quest Check-In Lab

How fast does it fall?

Gravity makes objects move toward the ground or floor. How can you test the effect of gravity on an object's movement? How can you use what you learn as you design your game?

Materials

- rubber ball or large marble
- boards
- blocks
- meterstick
- stopwatch

Science Practice

Scientists use a **control** when doing experiments.

Procedure

☐ **1.** Think of a way to test the effect of gravity on an object's motion. Write your plan. Show it to your teacher before you begin. Be sure to consider which variables you must control.

____

____

____

____

____

____

☐ **2.** Predict how the results will change when you change a variable during your test. State what you will change and predict the effect of the change.

____

____

____

____

____

____

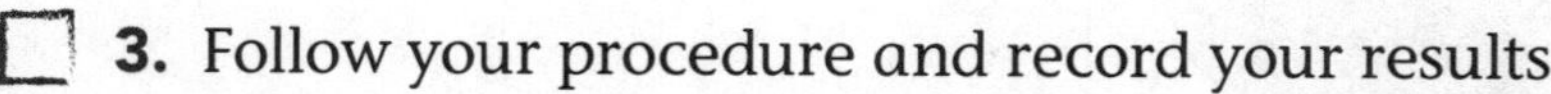

☐ **3.** Follow your procedure and record your results.

SC.5.P.13.2, SC.5.N.1.4

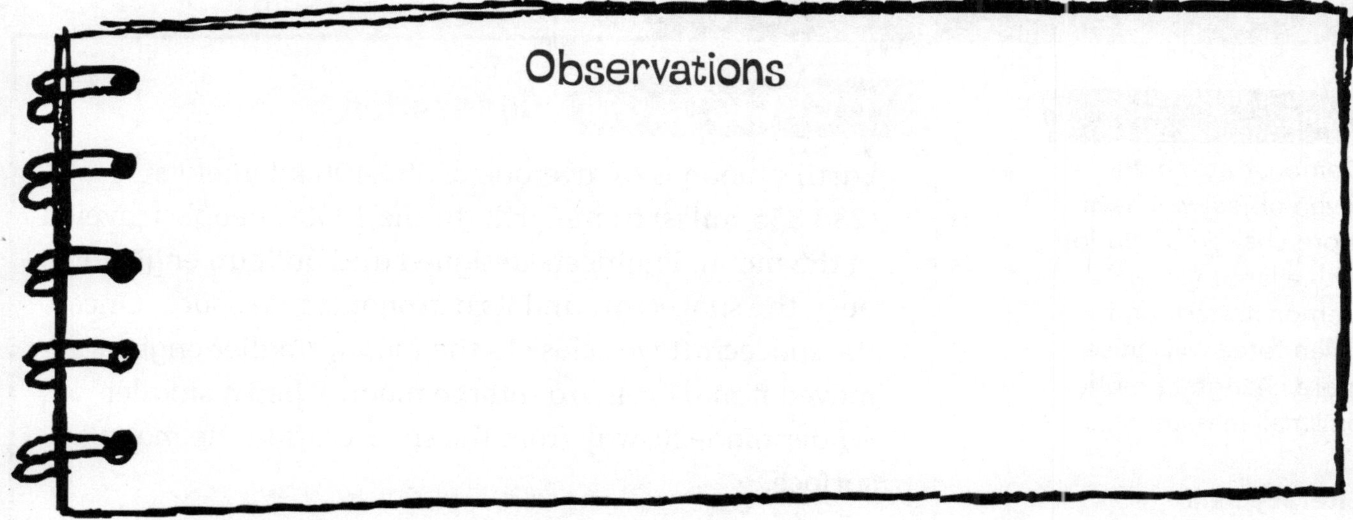

Analyze and Interpret Data

4. Evaluate Based on your observations, what effect does gravity have on rolling objects?

5. Patterns How did changing a variable of the test affect the results? Explain your answer.

6. Cause and Effect How could you use what you learned in this lab to design your game?

Lesson 2

Newton's Laws

I can...

Demonstrate that a given object will have more change of motion with a large force. Demonstrate that a given force will cause more change of motion on small masses.

Literacy Skill
Cause and Effect

Vocabulary
acceleration
inertia

Academic Vocabulary
formula

SC.5.P.13.2 Investigate and describe that the greater the force applied to it, the greater the change in motion of a given object. **SC.5.P.13.3** Investigate and describe that the more mass an object has, the less effect a given force will have on the object's motion. (Also **SC.5.N.2.2, SC.35.CS-CS.2.2**)

VIDEO

Watch a video about forces and motion.

CURRICULUM Connection

Earth's moon is an average of 384,400 kilometers (238,855 miles) from Earth. In the 1960s, people traveled to the moon. Engineers designed and built an engine to push the spacecraft and its astronauts into space. Once the spacecraft was close to the moon, smaller engines moved it into orbit around the moon. Then a smaller lander made its way from the spacecraft to the moon's surface.

How could scientists, engineers, mathematicians, and other experts get to an exact location so far away? They used some basic laws of science, called Newton's laws of motion. The laws describe how forces and motion are related. The scientists used the laws and a lot of math to move the spacecraft to the moon. Just the right amount of fuel in the engine gave the spacecraft exactly the right push. As it approached the moon, gravity gave it a pull.

Infer How do you know that a force was exerted when engines fired on the ship as it approached the moon?

___

___

uInvestigate Lab

HANDS-ON LAB

SC.5.P.13.2, SC.5.N.2.2

How does force change motion?

Materials

- large toy car
- spring scale

If you apply a force to an object, its motion will change. How will the motion of an object change if a constant force acts on it?

Science Practice

Scientists **compare data** to see whether results can be replicated.

Procedure

☐ **1.** Attach the toy car to the spring scale. Pull on the spring scale while holding the car in place. Observe and record what happens to the spring scale as you use more force.

☐ **2.** Make a plan to test how different amounts of force change the motion of an object. Show your plan to your teacher before you begin. Record your observations.

Observations

Analyze and Interpret Data

3. Use Evidence What can you conclude about the relationship between force and changes in motion based on your observations?

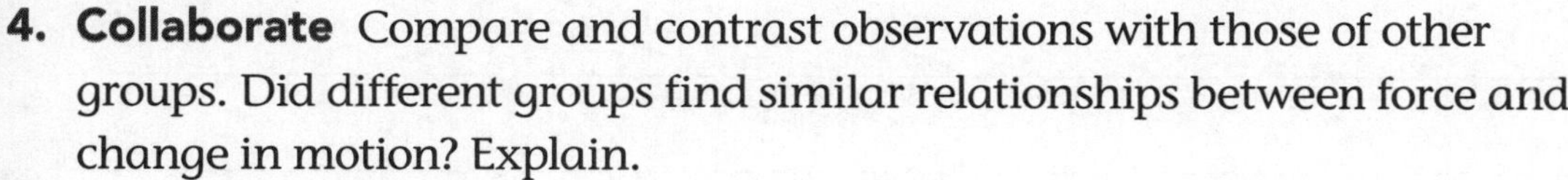

4. Collaborate Compare and contrast observations with those of other groups. Did different groups find similar relationships between force and change in motion? Explain.

Changes in Motion

As a car approaches a red light, the driver pushes the brake pedal. The speed of the car drops to zero. When the light turns green, the driver pushes the gas pedal. The speed of the car climbs from zero as the car starts moving. At a corner, the driver turns the steering wheel, and the car changes direction. When an object speeds up, slows down, or changes direction, its motion changes. The rate at which the speed or the direction of motion of an object changes over time is its **acceleration**.

Analyze Look at the two photos of people in the sky. Ask a question about acceleration related to the photographs.

___

___

In science, the word *acceleration* means "any change in speed or direction." Consider a Ferris wheel. Even when the wheel turns with constant speed, the riders change direction all of the time. They go up, then forward, then down, and then backward. They are constantly accelerating.

An object moving in a straight line at constant speed does not have any acceleration. Neither does an object that is not moving at all. A train traveling at a steady speed on a straight track is not accelerating. A book sitting on a table is not accelerating. Its speed is zero.

Plan It! If you are running a short race, it is important to start with as much speed as possible. Suppose you are in a sprint. Plan how you will use force to get a fast start. Write the steps of your plan.

___

___

___

___

___

Newton's First Law

Newton's first law of motion states that an object's motion will not change unless a force acts on the object. Without a force acting on it, an object at rest will stay at rest and a moving object will move with the same speed and in the same direction. For example, a marble will not move on a floor unless you push it. If the marble is already moving, it will continue to move at a constant speed in a straight line until a force acts on it.

READING CHECK **Cause and Effect** If you roll a marble on the floor, it will eventually stop rolling. Do you think a force has acted on the marble? Explain your answer.

____

____

____

The tendency of an object to resist any change in motion is known as **inertia**. Inertia is what causes your body to be pushed against the side of a car when the car turns. Inertia causes your body to keep moving in a straight line when the car changes direction. Moving objects eventually stop moving because other forces are acting on them. Friction and air resistance will slow a marble until it stops. However, even without fuel, this space probe keeps moving through space because friction is not acting on it. It only needs fuel to change direction or to slow.

An object's inertia depends on its mass. Less force is needed to make a small rock start moving than to make a heavy rock move. The small rock has less inertia. If you push harder on the small rock, it will move faster.

Engineering Practice ▸ Toolbox

Design Solutions Traffic engineers can design ways to make a highway safer. One solution is to get drivers to travel slower. Some solutions, such as speed bumps, change the motion of the car. Other solutions, such as warning signs, warn drivers so that they will change their motion. Design a way to slow traffic, and explain how the solution affects the car or the driver.

Visual Literacy Connection

WHAT IS NEWTON'S 2ND LAW?

Newton's second law of motion describes how acceleration, mass, and force are related. Force is the product of mass and acceleration.

The **mass is small** so the **acceleration is large**. The ball moves fast.

$$F = m\mathbf{a}$$

The **mass is large** so the **acceleration is small**. The ball moves slowly.

$$F = \mathbf{m}a$$

This relationship can be shown by the formula: $F = ma$. A **formula** is an equation that describes the relationship between variables. The variables in this formula are force, mass, and acceleration.

force → $F = ma$ ← acceleration (m: mass)

The **force is large** so the **acceleration is large**. The ball moves fast.

The **force is small** so the **acceleration is small**. The ball moves slowly.

$F = ma$

The wooden bat hits with more force than the plastic bat. Draw a line to connect the bat and ball combination that will result in the greatest change in motion.

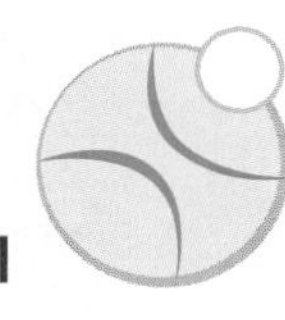

baseball

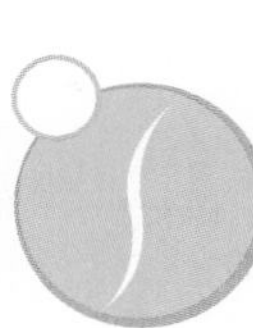

tennis ball

INTERACTIVITY

Complete an activity about forces and motion.

Newton's Third Law

Newton's third law of motion states that when one object exerts a force on a second object, the second object exerts a force on the first. These forces are equal in strength and opposite in direction.

It is impossible to have one force without an equal and opposite force. For example, if you have ever ridden bumper cars, you know that when a moving car collides with a stationary car, both drivers feel the force of the collision. The driver of the stationary car feels a force and starts to move. The driver of the moving car feels an opposite force that slows the moving car.

Quest Connection

Your video game might involve collisions. How would you use Newton's second and third laws to show what would happen when a large object bumps into a small object?

___

___

___

Lesson 2 Check

SC.5.P.13.2

1. **Use Context Clues** A cat jumps from a bed to the floor. What are two forces that occur when the cat lands on the floor?

___

___

2. **Explain** Why is it easier to push an empty shopping cart than one that is full of groceries?

___

___

Motion Follows Laws

The effects of a force on an object's motion depend on the object's mass and speed. Answer the questions below to help decide some of the effects of forces that you will include in your video game.

1. Your video game should use motion in a way that makes sense to the player. That means it must follow the laws of motion. How can you use forces to affect different objects in the game based on their masses?

2. How will you use Newton's third law of motion to make your game realistic?

3. Think about what your video game will do. Write a short description that includes the basic idea of the game and the types of forces that will be in your game.

QUEST CHECK OFF

uEngineer It! Design STEM

SC.35.CS-CS.2.2

VIDEO

Watch a video about safety devices in automobiles.

Ready, Set, Action

Video games use computer codes to create the images and actions that occur on-screen. Computer programmers and engineers write thousands of instructions for the computer to make the action feel real. The first step in designing a computer code is to write what should happen. A flow chart is one way to organize the information. Other ways are to write an outline or a list of steps.

The designer also describes the images that will appear on-screen. Then, the computer programmer produces characters and objects to make the images move.

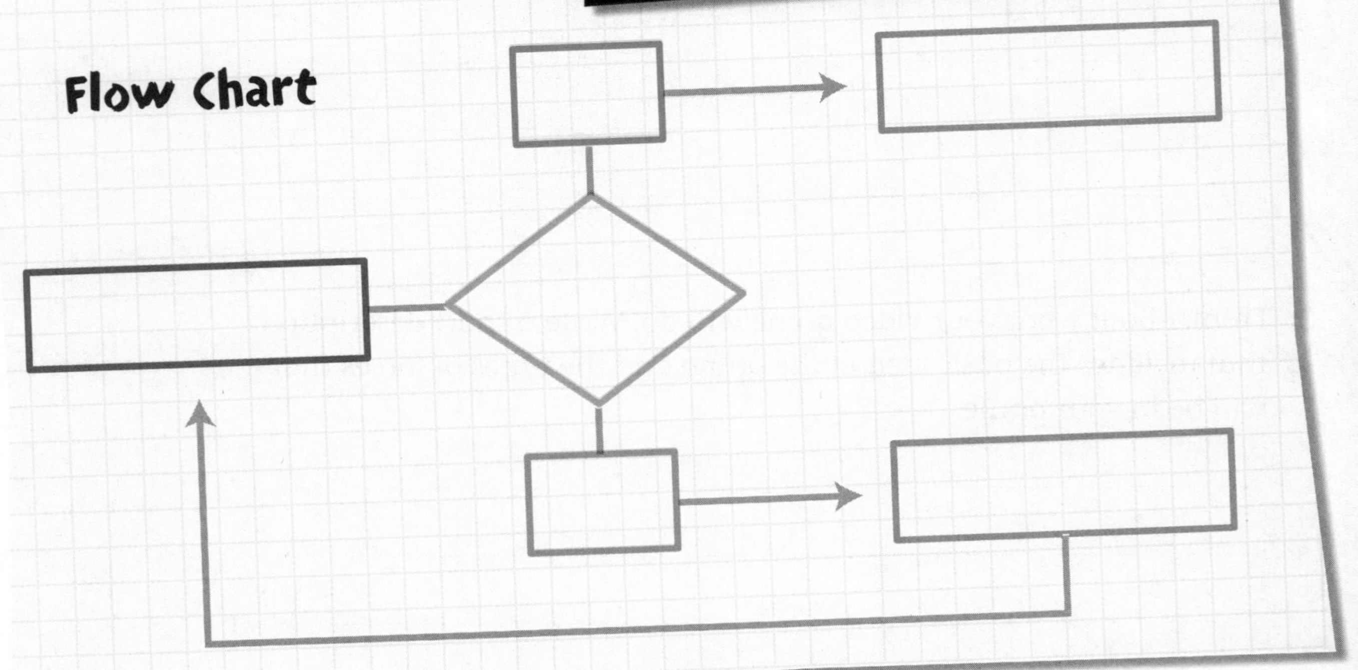

littleBits
CHALLENGE

Design It

For your video game, you will need to design a series of actions that will occur on the screen.

- [ ] Choose a series of actions that can be written in steps. Write what will happen and what forces cause a change.

- [ ] Write your code as a series of steps that occur in order. You can use an outline or a flow chart.

- [ ] Select one of your steps in the code, and make a sketch of what will appear in the video game.

Lesson 3

Combined Forces

I can...

Demonstrate that an object will not start moving if the forces acting on it are balanced.

Literacy Skill
Cause and Effect

Vocabulary
balanced

Academic Vocabulary
compute

SC.5.P.13.4 Investigate and explain that when a force is applied to an object but it does not move, it is because another opposing force is being applied by something in the environment so that the forces are balanced. (Also **SC.5.N.1.1, MAFS.5.MD.1.1**)

ENGINEERING Connection

In a large concert hall, different types of performances often need different instruments. The concert hall staff must be ready to set up for each performance. One big challenge is moving a concert piano. The instrument is much too large and heavy for one person to move. Sometimes, several people work together to move the piano, each adding their own force to the move. One person might push the piano on a cart, while another person pulls the cart. Their forces combine to move the heavy load. If the piano must be raised high on the stage, the people moving it may use a block and tackle system. This system involves one person using force by pulling on a rope to raise the load, while other people push or pull it into place. This is just one example of how people have to combine forces to complete a task.

Write About It Describe a time when you moved a heavy object. What tools did you use, and what forces did you need?

uInvestigate Lab

HANDS-ON LAB

SC.5.P.13.4, SC.5.N.1.1

How do forces combine?

Scientists look at ways that forces interact with objects. How can you use more than one force to keep a paper clip in the air?

Materials

- string
- paper clip
- magnet
- tape
- plastic ruler

Procedure

☐ 1. Use the materials. Make a plan that combines two or more forces to keep a paper clip in the air.

Science Practice

Scientists analyze information to draw conclusions.

☐ 2. Show your plan to your teacher before you begin. Record your observations.

Observations

Analyze and Interpret Data

3. **Identify** What forces did you use?

4. **Analyze** How did combining forces affect the paper clip? Why do you think this happened?

Visual Literacy Connection

How do forces combine?

You can show a force using an arrow. The direction of the arrow indicates the direction of the push or pull. The size of the arrow shows the relative size of the force.

A longer arrow is a stronger force.

⟶

Two arrows pointing in the same direction can be added together.

→ + → = ⟶

If the arrows point in exactly the opposite direction, one force is subtracted from the other force.

⟶ + ← = →

If two identical forces point in opposite directions, then the total force is zero. Motion does not change.

⟶ + ⟵ = 0

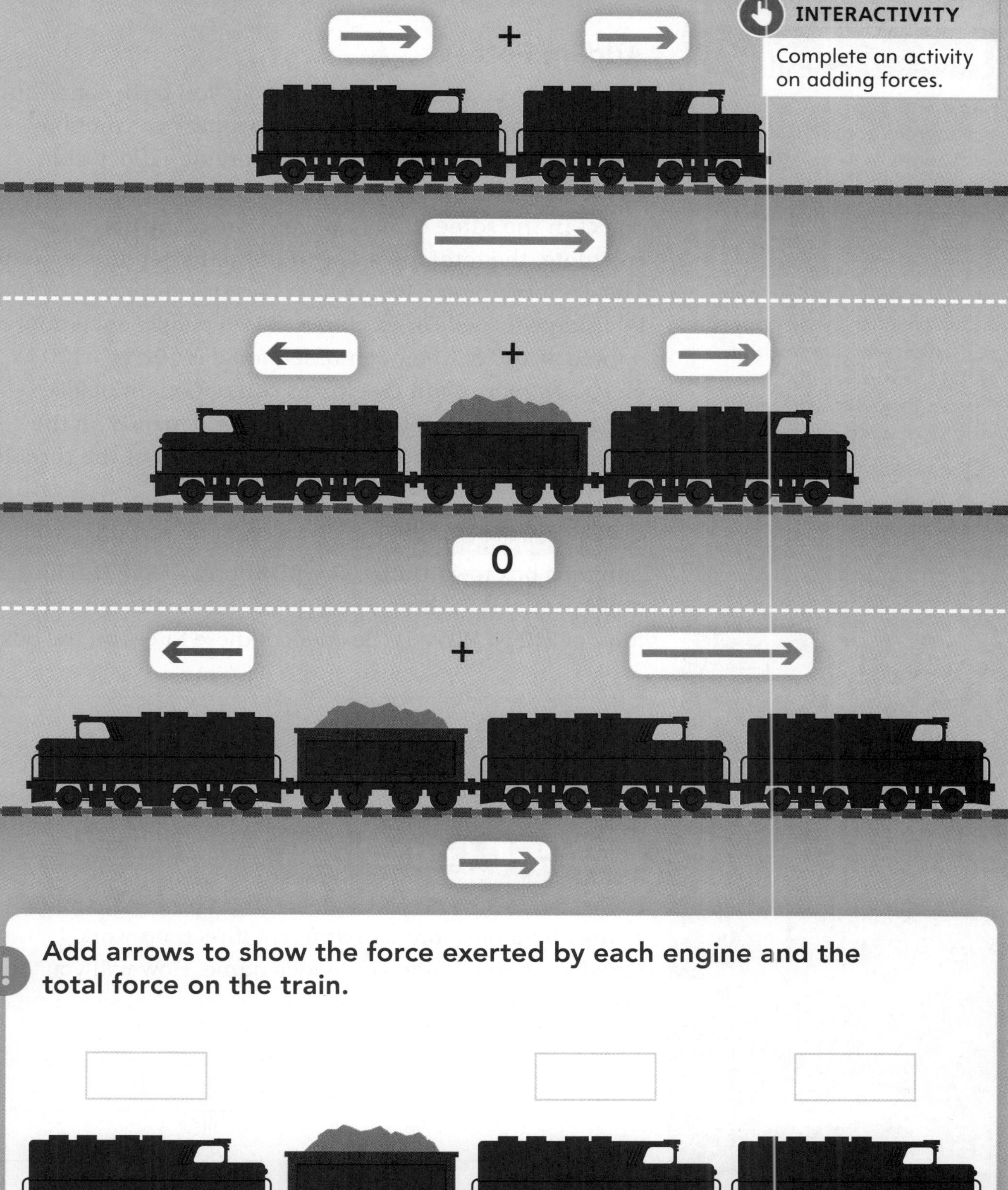

INTERACTIVITY

Complete an activity on adding forces.

Add arrows to show the force exerted by each engine and the total force on the train.

Math ▸ Toolbox

Add and Subtract When two forces act in opposite directions, one direction has a positive force, and the other direction has a negative force. Suppose a push in one direction exerts a force of 10 N. An identical push in the opposite direction exerts a force of –10 N. If you add the two forces together, you will find the total force on the object.

MAFS.5.MD.1.1

Adding Forces

Have you ever asked a friend to help you push something heavy? By pushing together, two people can combine their forces into a force that has a greater effect than either single force. When two forces act on the same object in the same direction, you can **compute**, or calculate, the total force. Just add their strengths together. The combined force will act in the same direction as the two single forces. For example, if two people each apply a force of 100 N, their combined force is 100 N + 100 N or 200 N. More than two forces can act on an object. For example, the motion of the spider depends on the downward pull of gravity, the upward pull of the thread, and the force of moving air around it.

READING CHECK **Cause and Effect** One person is pulling a box toward the left with a force of 350 N. The other person is pushing on the same box to the left with a force of 210 N. What is the effect of these forces on the box?

___

___

Quest Connection

Think about how forces in different directions work together as you design your video game. How will you use these forces?

___

___

___

___

uBe a Scientist

Balancing Act Hang a 1 m long piece of string over a doorknob. Get two objects that are identical, and tie one to each end of the string. Raise or lower one end. Observe what happens to the other end. Explain what takes place when you stop moving one end and why this might be.

Balanced Forces

When you hold a book in your hand, your hand is pushing upward on the book. Earth's gravity is pulling downward on it. The two forces are of equal strength but opposite in direction, so the book does not move. Two forces of equal strength that combine to act on the same object but in opposite directions are **balanced**. Balanced forces do not change the object's motion. Several forces can be balanced at the same time. For example, several ropes pull on the camping tent without causing a change in motion.

Lesson 3 Check

SC.5.P.13.4

1. **Explain** Jake pushes a heavy box across a carpeted floor. Name three forces that act on the box, and explain how you know the forces are unbalanced.

____

____

____

2. **Analyze** A car is traveling in a straight line at a constant speed. The car's engine is exerting a constant force on the car. Explain why the car is not accelerating.

____

____

____

Too Small, Too Large, Just Right

1. Usually, several forces act on an object at one time. How will balanced and unbalanced forces affect the motion of characters or objects in your game?

2. Write a short statement that describes what happens in your game.

3. Sketch what will happen in your game when the forces are too small, too large, and just right.

QUEST CHECK OFF

Solar Sailing

Suppose you wanted to travel an extremely long distance, such as to another solar system. You would need a lot of fuel. But maybe there is another way to move your vehicle. Scientists at NASA are modeling a new system based on a technology from long ago—the sailing ship.

Light and other particles rushing out from the sun cause a slight force on objects in space. The force is not large, and it decreases as the object in space travels farther from the sun. However, little friction acts in space, so the force of this solar wind could cause a large sail to accelerate.

Right now, NASA is testing sails as small as 10 meters on each side. The sails are made of plastic with an aluminum coating and are about as thick as a human hair. These sails could be useful inside the solar system. To travel into deep space, a spaceship would need a very large sail. A sail that size might measure many kilometers or even hundreds of kilometers on each side.

Identify Why would the sail in space travel much farther than it would if a force of the same size acted on it on Earth?

____

____

____

____

____

Quest Findings

INTERACTIVITY

Use a table to organize the cause and effect relationships in your Quest.

STEM Forces in Outer Space Game

How can you apply forces in a space-based video game?

Relate Cause and Effect

When you used forces in your game, you related the cause of a change in motion to its effect.

Discuss how your video game applies Newton's laws of motion so that the player understands the cause and effect relationships in the game. Are there any things that you should change to make the action of the game better?

Evaluate a Model

Present your video game as a slide presentation or as a series of drawings. Ask other students to provide feedback on how well the game models forces and motion. Also have them rate the game for its fun and playability. Make notes below. Record suggestions for improvements on the card.

My Video Game

____

____

____

____

____

____

____

____

____

QUEST CHECK OFF

Career Connection

Video Game Designer

Video game designers are part of a larger team that creates video games. They play an important part in the planning and design of a video game. They work on developing the storyline, the environment, and the characters as well as the overall software programming.

Video game designers are talented in both the creative and technical end of video game design. They are able to visualize a concept for the game with both the programming and creative concerns in mind.

Video game design has become a popular industry and can lead to careers with game developers or in specialized positions for software design. The opportunities to work in video game design have increased over the years. Some design companies have even been granted the opportunity to partner with the military or NASA.

Reflect What do you think is the most challenging part about being a video game designer?

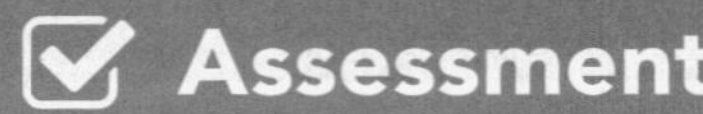

Assessment

Read each question and choose or write the best answer.

1. **Explain** What causes a friction force to act on a moving object?

2. **Analyze** Which statement correctly describes the forces acting on the water in this photo?

   A. Gravity and friction are the two forces acting on the water.

   B. The total force on the water equals zero.

   C. The electrical force acting on the water is greater than the force of gravity acting on the water.

   D. The forces acting on the water are unbalanced.

3. **Infer** A car is travelling down a straight road. The driver presses on the accelerator but the car does not change speed. How is this possible?

4. **Explain Phenomena in Terms of Concepts** Which scenarios demonstrate the action-reaction forces described by Newton's Third Law? Check all that apply.

   - [ ] Theo's hands ache after playing the bongo drums for a long concert.
   - [ ] Amanda has to use her whole body to push a very heavy crate across the carpet.
   - [ ] A dropped ball bounces.
   - [ ] A table exerts an upward force on a book.
   - [ ] A roller coaster must use an engine to pull the cars up the first hill.

SC.5.P.13.1, SC.5.P.13.2, SC.5.P.13.3, SC.5.P.13.4

5. **Use Models** How could you use a yo-yo to model how Earth's gravity acts on the moon to keep it in orbit around Earth?

______

______

______

______

______

______

6. **Summarize** What is the total force acting on the ball in the diagram? How would you describe its velocity?

______

______

______

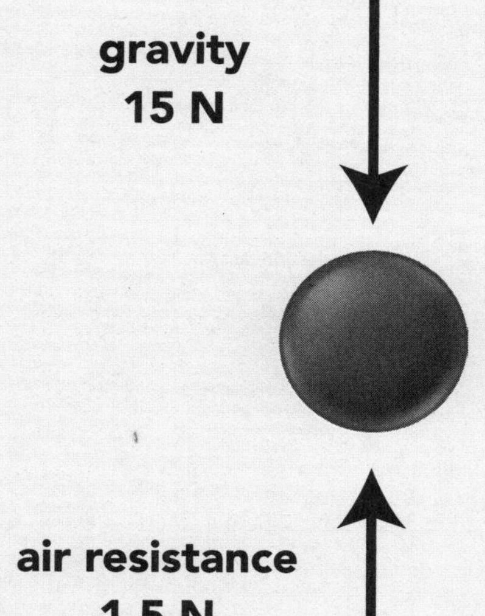

7. **Describe** How is a noncontact force different from a contact force?

A. A noncontact force is stronger.

B. A noncontact force acts at a distance.

C. A noncontact force changes motion.

D. A noncontact force is in one direction.

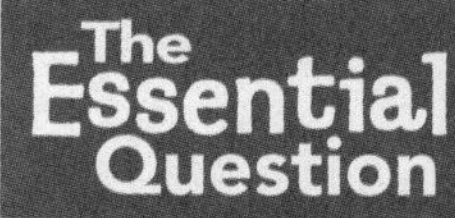

What affects the motion of objects?

Show What You Learned

How do forces affect the motion of objects?

______

______

______

______

______

______

______

Science Assessment Practice

Read the scenario and answer questions 1–2.

Two students are conducting an investigation to study the relationship between mass and force. They found the masses of three balls that they will use in their investigation. The masses are shown in the table.

Ball	Mass (g)
A	68
B	72
C	64

1. **Analyze Data** Which ball would have the greatest acceleration if the students applied an upward force of the same magnitude on each ball?

   Ⓐ Ball A

   Ⓑ Ball B

   Ⓒ Ball C

   Ⓓ The acceleration would be the same for all three balls.

2. **Identify** Which two forces act on each ball as it moves upward?

   Ⓕ gravity and electricity

   Ⓖ gravity and air resistance

   Ⓗ magnestism and friction

   Ⓘ friction and electricity

3. **Assess** Which scenario is explained by inertia?

   Ⓐ A car slows to a stop.

   Ⓑ A ball bounces.

   Ⓒ A train moves at a constant rate.

   Ⓓ A heavy box is hard to push.

SC.5.P.13.1, SC.5.P.13.2, SC.5.P.13.3, SC.5.P.13.4

Read the scenario and answer questions 4–5.

Raj draws a diagram to show the forces that act on an airplane when it is in flight. The air moving past the plane provides an upward force called lift. Lift opposes the pull of gravity on the plane. Engines push exhaust out of the rear of the plane, and in response, the exhaust pushes the plane forward. This is caused thrust. Some planes are built with pointy noses to reduce air resistance, also called drag, that acts on the plane.

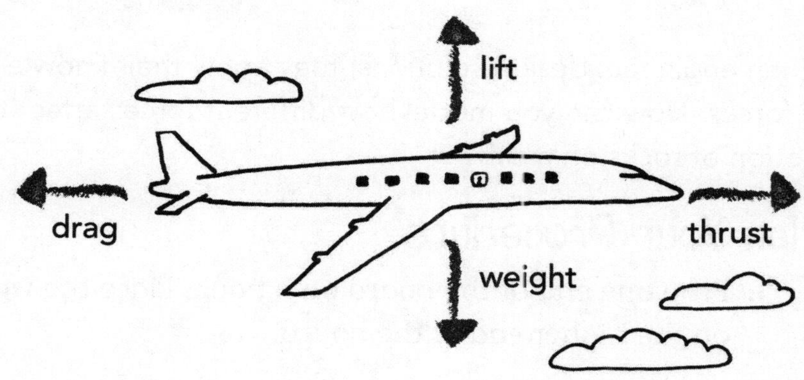

4 **Apply** The plane in the diagram is accelerating forward and parallel to the ground. Which statement about the forces acting on the plane is correct?

Ⓕ Drag is greater than thrust.

Ⓖ Lift is greater than weight.

Ⓗ Thrust is greater than drag.

Ⓘ Weight is greater than thrust.

5 **Explain** Raj wants to explain how Newton's laws apply to the plane's motion. Which explanation should he choose?

Ⓐ Newton's third law explains how the engine can move the plane forward.

Ⓑ Newton's first law explains how the plane stays in the air instead of falling to the ground.

Ⓒ Newton's second law explains why the exhaust pushes back on the plane.

Ⓓ Newton's third law explains why lift cancels out the weight of the plane.

uDemonstrate Lab

Why do things move?

When engineers design solutions, they apply their knowledge of forces. How can you model how different forces affect the motion of rocks on a cliff?

Materials

- board
- wooden block
- books
- tape
- sandpaper

Suggested Materials

- plastic wrap
- wax paper
- ruler

Plan Your Procedure

☐ **1.** Prop one end of the board on a book. Place the wooden block on the higher end of the board.

☐ **2.** Observe and record the motion of the block. Write a hypothesis explaining how forces will be affected if the end of the board is raised to different heights or if different surface materials are used.

____

____

____

____

____

Engineering Practice

Engineers **investigate** to identify cause and effect relationships.

☐ **3.** Write a procedure to test your hypothesis. In your procedure, describe the data you will collect. Show your procedure to your teacher before you begin.

____

____

____

____

____

____

____

☐ **4.** Draw your observations. Your drawings and their labels should display evidence that relates to your hypothesis.

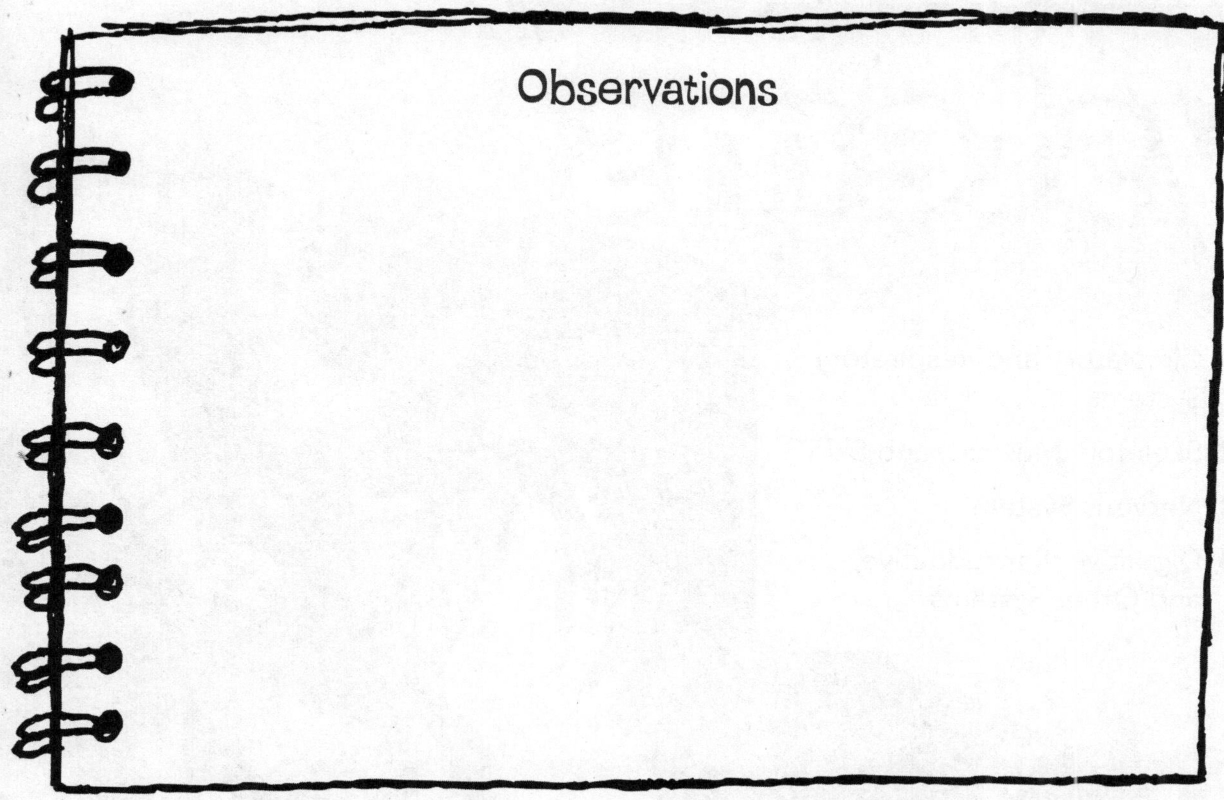

Communicate Your Plan

5. Interpret Data How do changes in board angle and surface type affect the block? What can you infer from this evidence about rock movement on a cliff?

Topic 7

Human Body Systems

Lesson 1 Circulatory and Respiratory Systems
Lesson 2 Skeleton, Muscles, and Skin
Lesson 3 Nervous System
Lesson 4 Digestive, Reproductive, and Other Systems

SC.5.L.14.1 Identify the organs in the human body and describe their functions, including the skin, brain, heart, lungs, stomach, liver, intestines, pancreas, muscles and skeleton, reproductive organs, kidneys, bladder, and sensory organs. (Also **SC.5.N.1.1, SC.5.N.1.5, LAFS.5.RI.1.2**)

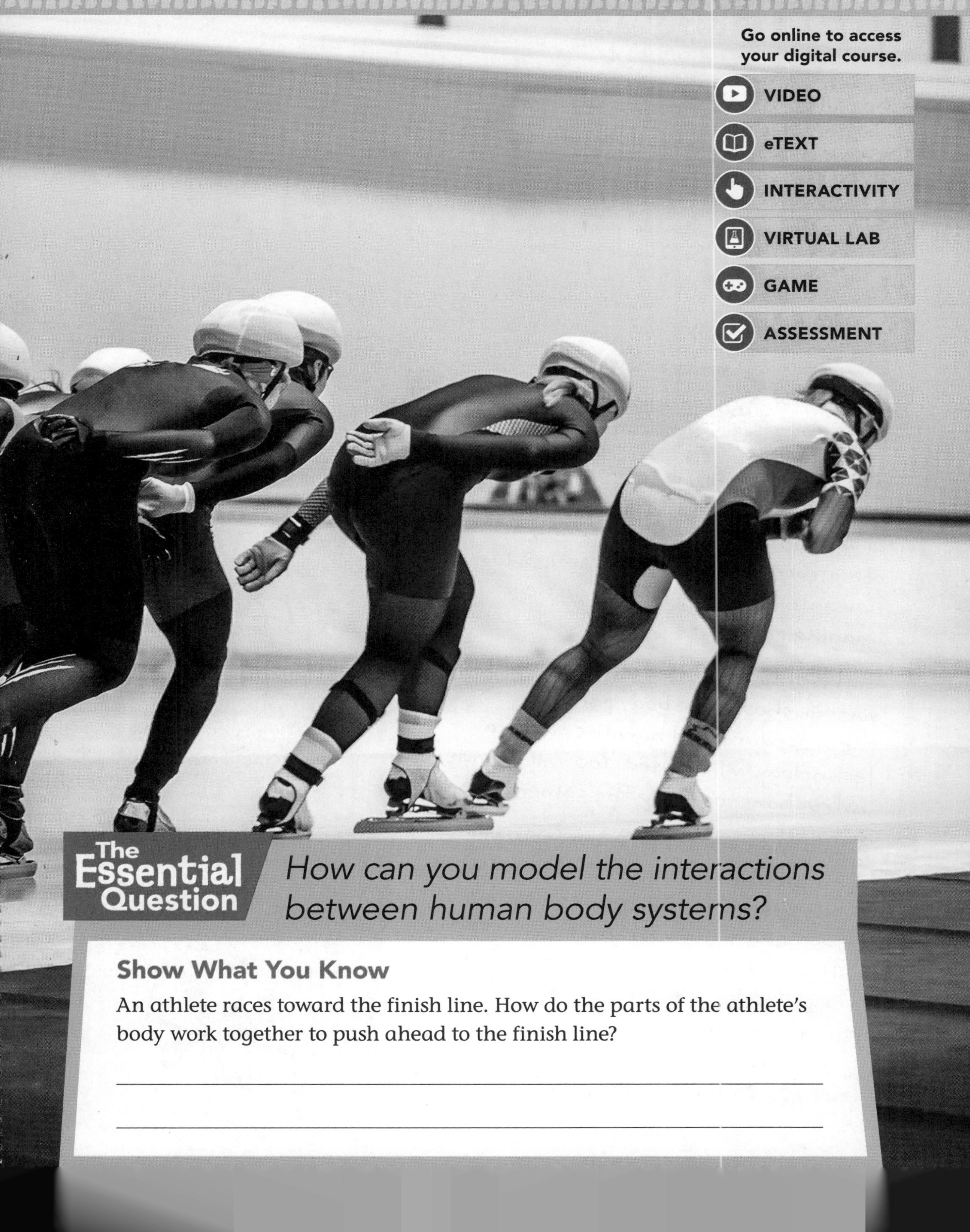

The Essential Question How can you model the interactions between human body systems?

Show What You Know

An athlete races toward the finish line. How do the parts of the athlete's body work together to push ahead to the finish line?

____

____

Quest Kickoff

STEM

Make a Human Body Road Map

How can you help a tiny camera navigate the human body?

Hi, I'm Warren Snyder, a medical imaging technician. I would like you to provide guidance for creating a remote-controlled micro-camera to navigate inside the body for a new imaging procedure.

In this problem-based learning activity, you will choose the body part for the procedure and how the camera technology will be used. You will provide instructions for using the camera.

Follow the path to learn how you will complete the Quest. The Quest activities in the lessons will help you complete the Quest! Check off your progress on the path when you complete an activity with a QUEST CHECK OFF. Go online for more Quest activities.

Quest Check-In 1

Lesson 1

Learn about the circulatory system to help you determine how to navigate the remote-controlled camera through the blood vessels of the body.

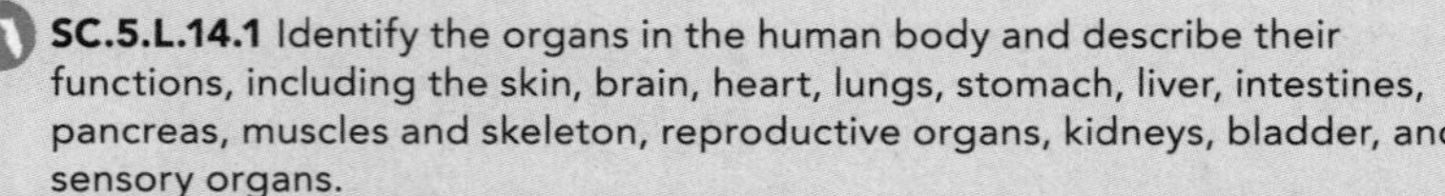

SC.5.L.14.1 Identify the organs in the human body and describe their functions, including the skin, brain, heart, lungs, stomach, liver, intestines, pancreas, muscles and skeleton, reproductive organs, kidneys, bladder, and sensory organs.

 VIDEO

Watch a video about a medical imaging technician.

Quest Check-In 2

Lesson 2

Use what you learn about the skeleton, muscles, and skin to find out how your camera can travel to a broken bone.

Quest Check-In Lab 3

Lesson 3

Learn how signals travel through the body. Apply what you learn to determine how to guide your camera with messages.

Quest Check-In 4

Lesson 4

Find out about the immune system, and then tell how to track the path of germs as they enter the body and affect body parts.

Quest Findings

You've finished your tour of the human body. Choose one body system and write or draw instructions to complete your Quest.

uConnect Lab

HANDS-ON LAB

SC.5.L.14.1, SC.5.N.1.1

Which body parts work together to do a task?

When scientists investigate a question, they base their arguments on their observations. How can you observe your body parts working together as you do a simple task?

Suggested Materials

- books
- stopwatch
- basketball
- 2 rubber balls
- yo-yo

Science Practice

Scientists use evidence to answer scientific questions.

Do not perform any physical activities if you have a health problem.

Procedure

☐ **1.** Choose a simple task you can perform using any of the materials.

☐ **2.** As you perform the task, observe which body parts are involved. Record your observations.

☐ **3.** Choose a second task, and repeat step 2.

Task	Body Parts Involved

Analyze and Interpret Data

4. Compare and Contrast Were the body parts you used for both tasks the same? Why do you think that is so?

____

____

5. Did your observations provide evidence of body parts working together? How?

____

____

Main Idea and Details

LAFS.5.RI.1.2

The main idea in a text is the overall message an author is trying to share. The specific details in the text help to support the main idea.

Here are some strategies for identifying the main idea and details:

- Underline any text that supports a similar idea or provides new information about the same subject.
- Use the text you underline to infer what the author wants the reader to take away from this reading.

Read the following information about chimpanzees.

GAME

Practice what you learn with the Mini Games.

Chimpanzees and Humans

Like humans, chimpanzees are intelligent animals that can communicate with actions. But there are plenty of differences between chimpanzees and humans. Humans walk differently than chimpanzees, and we use language to communicate.

Many people would also include the difference of strength. That is true, but not in the way you might think. While chimpanzee muscles are similar to those of humans, chimpanzees are actually two to three times stronger than humans. Humans have more control as they move muscles, but this also limits the amount of power we can exert. Because chimpanzees do not have the same kind of muscle control, they are much more powerful when they take action.

READING CHECK **Main Idea and Details** What did the author want you to take away from this text? Underline the details that helped you come to this conclusion.

____

____

Lesson 1

Circulatory and Respiratory Systems

I can...

Explain how the heart helps move blood through the body.
Explain how the circulatory and respiratory systems interact to move oxygen through the body.

Literacy Skill
Main Idea and Details

Vocabulary
organ system
organ
tissue
lungs
diaphragm
heart

Academic Vocabulary
function

VIDEO

Watch a video about the circulatory and respiratory systems.

SC.5.L.14.1 Identify the organs in the human body and describe their functions, including the skin, brain, heart, lungs, stomach, liver, intestines, pancreas, muscles and skeleton, reproductive organs, kidneys, bladder, and sensory organs. (Also **SC.5.N.1.5, LAFS.5.RI.1.2**)

CURRICULUM Connection

Think about how you are breathing right now. You feel the air move in through your nose or mouth. Your rib cage rises and falls as air moves in and out of your body. If you take a deep breath, you might feel your belly rise. But how does the breathing change when you talk or sing? Many professional singers learn and practice useful breathing methods while singing. These methods improve the quality of their voices. Singers practice expanding their rib cage to produce sound. When they breathe out, they control the air to help them hit high and low notes, as well as maintain long, slow phrases.

Compare and Contrast Besides singing and talking, when do you take deeper breaths? Why do you think that is so?

___

___

___

uInvestigate Lab

How can you model how you breathe?

SC.5.L.14.1, SC.5.N.1.5

Scientists often build models to study how something works. What pulls air into your body when you breathe?

Materials
- top of plastic bottle with bottom cut off
- 2 balloons
- tape
- safety goggles
- scissors

Be careful handling scissors and with sharp edges on plastic bottles.

Wear safety goggles.

Procedure

☐ **1.** Sit quietly and observe what happens in your body as you breathe in and out. Use all the materials. Plan a model to show how air gets in and out of your body.

☐ **2.** Draw your model. Ask your teacher for permission before you begin to build your model.

Analyze and Interpret Data

3. How does your model demonstrate what happens when you breathe?

____

____

____

____

Science Practice
Scientists **develop models** to understand scientific concepts.

My Model

4. Based on your model, how might you explain how air gets in and out of your lungs?

____

____

____

____

____

Tissues, Organs, and Organ Systems

If you are sitting quietly in a chair, you might think that not much is happening in your body. But a lot goes on in your body all the time. Your heart pumps, and your brain receives and sends messages. Muscles and bones work together so that you can move. All the parts of your body work together as organ systems to do a specific **function**, or job. An **organ system** is made up of a group of organs that do a particular job.

Organs are body parts that perform specific functions. Your heart, for example, is an organ that is part of the circulatory system. The function of this system is to move materials throughout the body in the blood. All the body's systems work together to help the cells of your body meet their needs for survival.

Organs are made up of **tissues**, groups of cells of the same kind that have a specific function. Your heart is an organ that contains muscle tissue. The cells that make up heart muscle tissue work together to make the heart pump.

READING CHECK **Main Idea and Details** Underline the sentences that tell how tissues, organs, and organ systems are related. Then match the labels with the parts of the diagram.

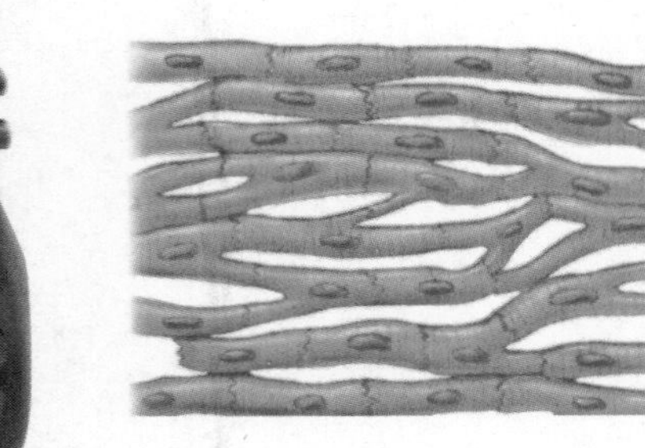

cell | tissue | organ | organ system

Respiratory System

Air in, air out—again and again. A person must breathe in and out for an entire lifetime. Cells in the body need a steady supply of oxygen to function properly. Oxygen is a part of air. The respiratory system takes in oxygen from the air so that it can be delivered to all body cells. It also gets rid of gaseous wastes produced by body cells.

Air enters your body through the nose or the mouth. It flows through the throat into a hard tube called the trachea, or windpipe. The trachea divides into two smaller tubes. Each tube leads to one of the two main parts of the **lungs**, the main organs of the respiratory system. Inside the lungs, these tubes branch out into smaller and smaller tubes until they form tiny sacs. In the sacs, oxygen is added to the blood, and wastes are removed from the blood.

The lungs cannot expand on their own to move air into the body. The **diaphragm**, a muscle located below the lungs, causes air to flow in and out of your lungs.

Interpret Diagrams Use what you have learned to label the parts of the respiratory system.

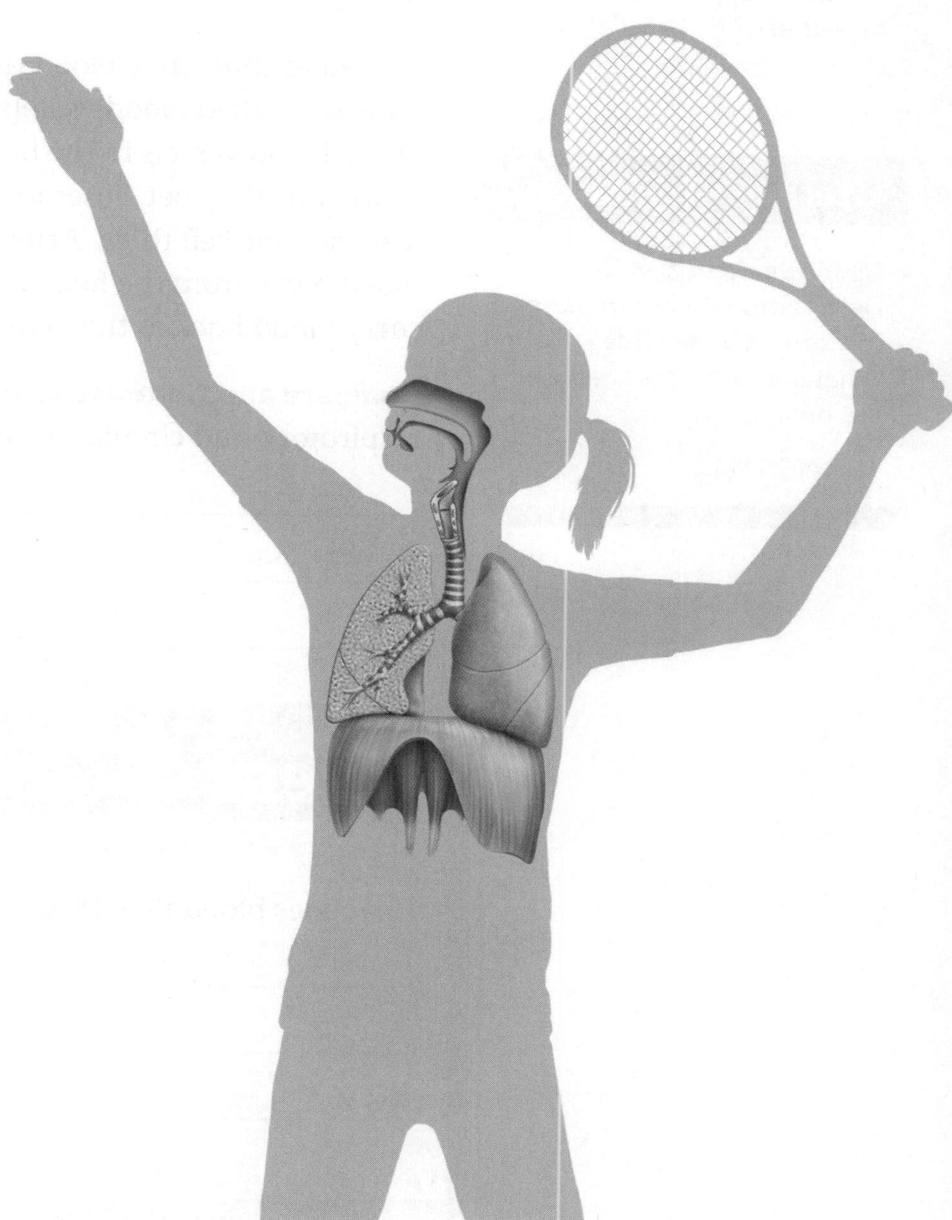

uBe a Scientist

Investigate Your Heartbeat
Find your pulse. Place two fingers under your jawbone. Count the number of times your heart beats in 1 minute. What will happen to your pulse when you exercise? Write a hypothesis. Do jumping jacks for 30 seconds. Record your pulse. Does the data support your hypothesis?

Literacy ▸ Toolbox

Main Idea and Details
Details provide information to support a main idea. What are two details about the heart?

 LAFS.5.RI.1.2

Circulatory System

If you place two fingers below your jawline on your neck, you can feel your pulse. Your pulse is your heart rate, or how many times a minute your heart beats. The **heart** is a muscular organ that pumps blood throughout your body. The heart is part of the circulatory system, a network made up of the heart, blood, and blood vessels. Follow the path of blood through the heart in the picture. When the chambers of the heart relax, they fill up with blood. Then, the chambers squeeze the blood to force it out. With each heartbeat, blood is pumped through tubes to all parts of the body.

The tubes that carry blood throughout every part of the body are called blood vessels. The diagram shows only a few of the blood vessels in the body. The vessels get smaller and smaller as they get closer to the body's cells, until their walls are only one cell thick. Arteries are blood vessels that carry blood away from the heart. Veins are blood vessels that carry blood back to the heart.

Compare and Contrast Contrast the functions of the respiratory and circulatory systems.

____

____

____

Quest Connection

How does blood flow through the body?

____

____

____

Identify On the heart diagram, label where the blood is going and coming from. Draw arrows to show the path of blood through the heart.

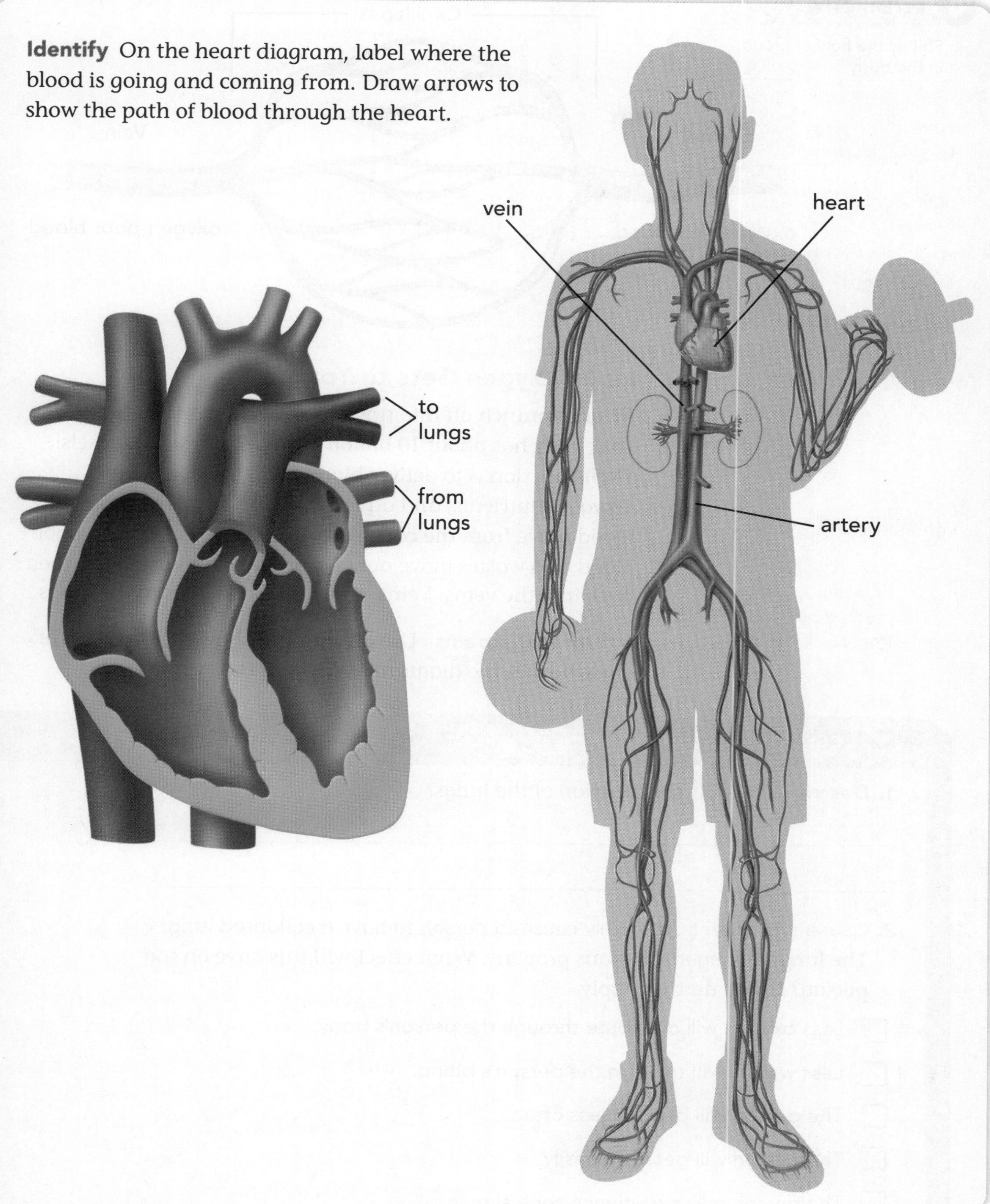

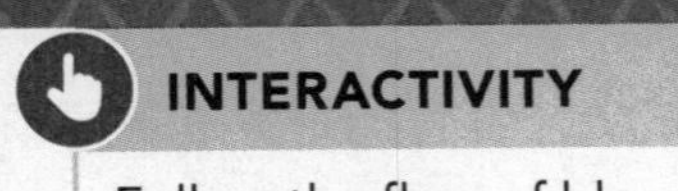

Follow the flow of blood in the body.

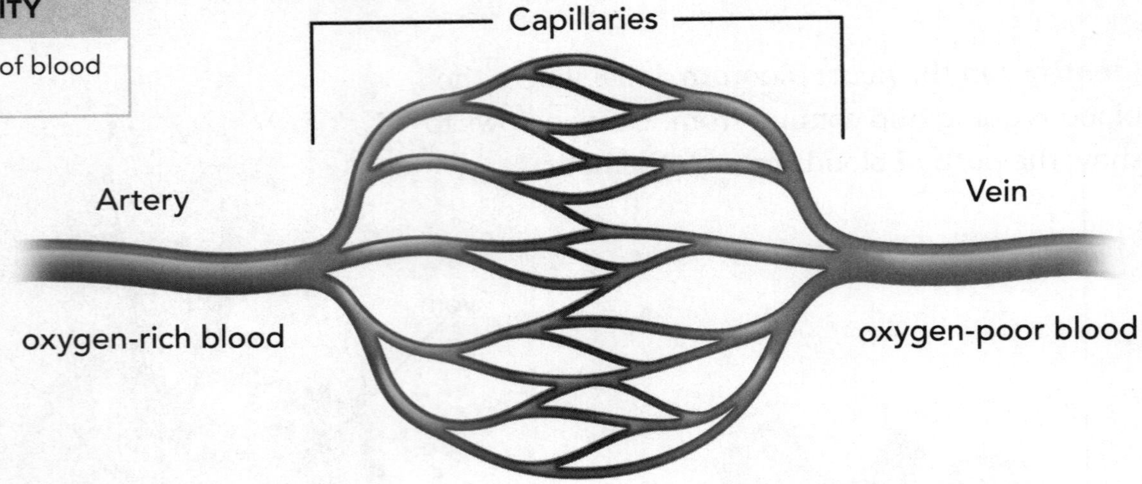

How Oxygen Gets to Your Cells

Arteries branch off into tiny blood vessels called capillaries. Your body has about 10 billion of these tiny blood vessels! Their function is to deliver blood to all the body's cells. Oxygen, nutrients, and other materials that are carried by blood move from the capillaries into the cells. Oxygen-poor blood and wastes move out of cells into capillaries, and then back into the veins. Veins carry the blood back to the lungs.

Interpret Diagrams Use an arrow to show the direction of bloodflow in the diagram of capillaries.

Lesson 1 Check

1. **Describe** What is the function of the lungs?

____

____

2. **Cause and Effect** An injury causes a person to have a collapsed lung. The lung no longer functions properly. What effect will this have on the person? Check all that apply.

- [ ] Less oxygen will distribute through the person's body.
- [ ] Less wastes will travel in the person's blood.
- [ ] The person will breathe less often.
- [ ] The person will get tired easily.
- [ ] The person may experience confusion.

Go with the Flow

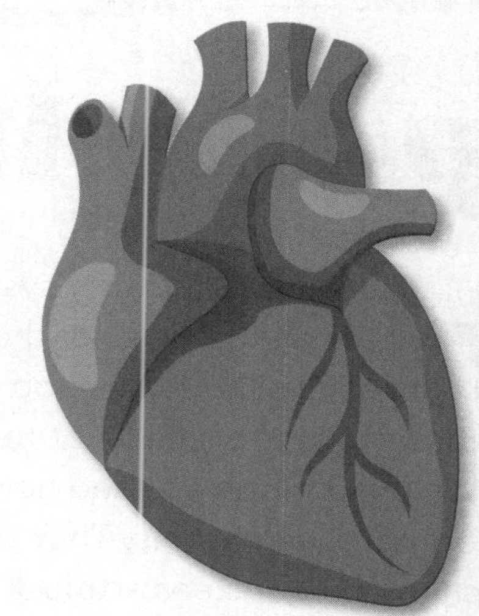

It is time to think about how you can use your remote-controlled camera. Sometimes arteries and veins become blocked. You can use your camera to check whether certain blood vessels are blocked.

One thing you should think about as you plan is that the force with which the blood flows in blood vessels is stronger than the force you will be able to apply to move the camera forward. So the camera must move in the same direction as the blood.

Where will the path of your camera begin? Explain.

____

____

____

Draw a path that shows how the camera will flow through the circulatory system.

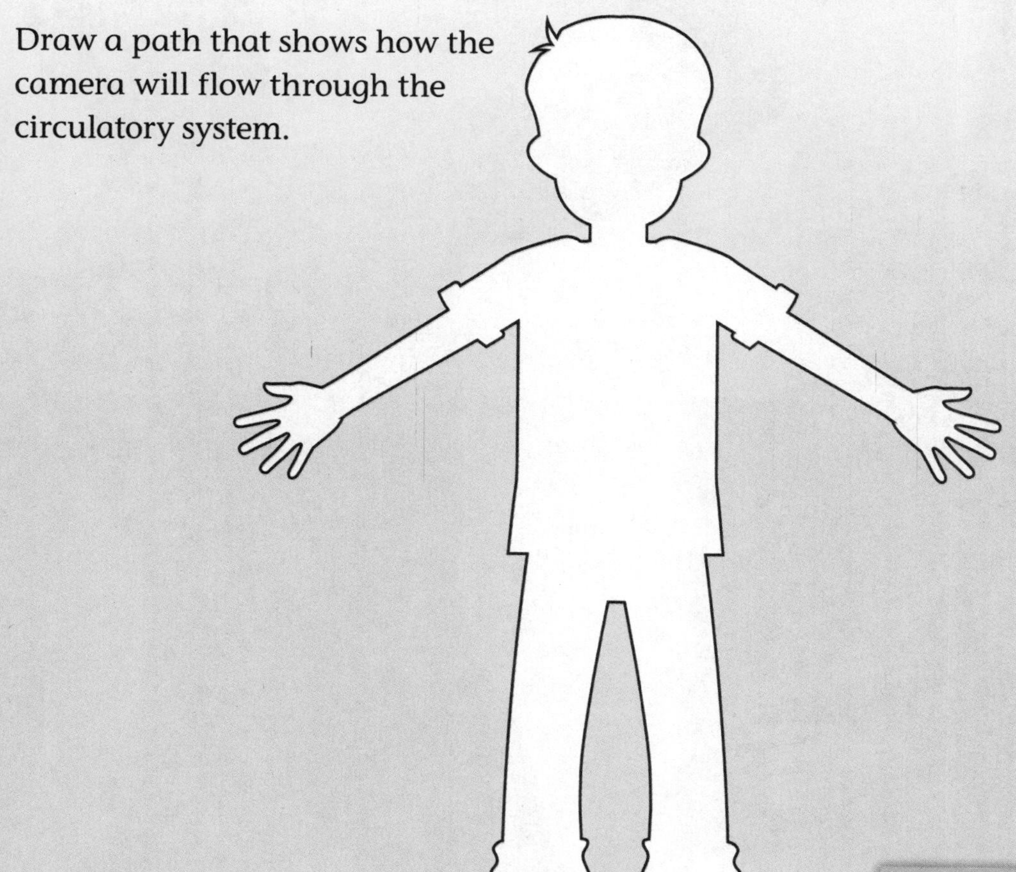

QUEST CHECK OFF

uEngineer It! Build STEM

INTERACTIVITY

Go online to evaluate and suggest improvements for models.

Pump It Up!

How the circulatory system works is not easy to observe. Not only are all the parts of the system inside the body, some parts, such as capillaries, are too tiny to see without a microscope. When something is too small—or too large—to see, engineers and scientists often build models to see how systems work. Scientists can observe the action of their models. They might use their observations to develop technologies such as artificial hearts and mechanical heart valves. They might even use a 3D printer to make a model of a particular person's organ. They can practice on the model before a surgery.

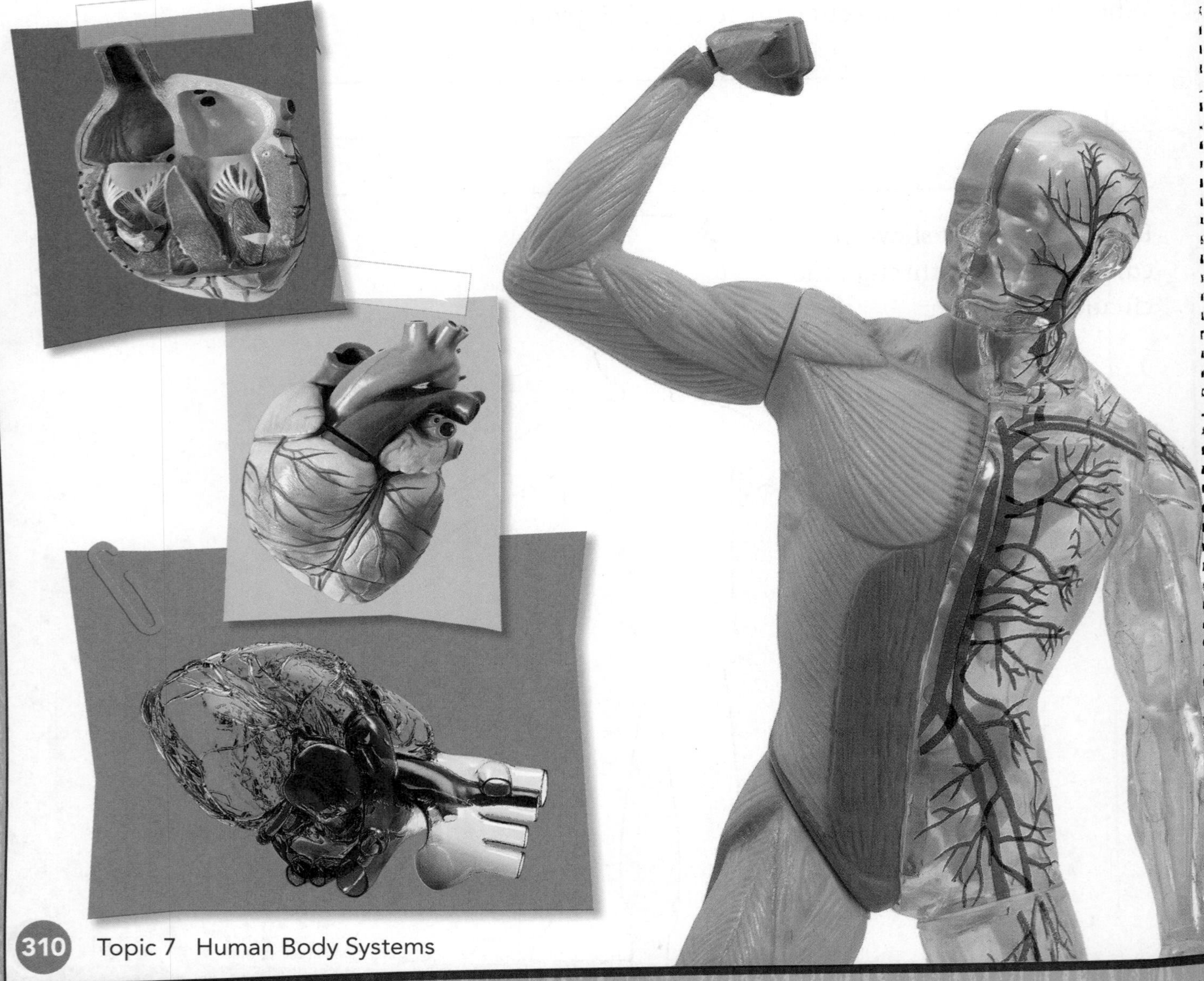

Build It

You will build a model of the circulatory system. Your model should show how blood flows through the four parts of the heart and how it flows to and from other parts of the body.

- ☐ Plan your model. Decide which materials you will use for each part. How will the model work? Make a drawing to show your plan.
- ☐ Show your plan to your teacher before you begin. Then build your model.
- ☐ Test your model. Identify any problems. Make any necessary changes.
- ☐ Share your model with others.

Lesson 2

Skeleton, Muscles, and Skin

I can...

Describe the functions of the skeleton, muscles, and skin.
Explain how the skeletal and muscular systems interact to allow movement.

Literacy Skill

Main Idea and Details

Vocabulary

skeletal system
muscle
skin

Academic Vocabulary

extend

VIDEO

Watch a video about the functions of the skin.

SC.5.L.14.1 Identify the organs in the human body and describe their functions, including the skin, brain, heart, lungs, stomach, liver, intestines, pancreas, muscles and skeleton, reproductive organs, kidneys, bladder, and sensory organs. (Also **SC.5.N.1.1**)

SPORTS Connection

Imagine whizzing along on a skateboard or inline skates. Suddenly you find yourself upside down in the air. You land on your head. OUCH! It's a good thing you are wearing a helmet to protect your skull from injury. Each year, more than 3.5 million children under the age of 14 are injured in sports activities. About half of all injuries occur while bicycling, skateboarding, or rollerskating. Injuries to the skull are especially dangerous because the skull protects the brain. Helmets, eye goggles, knee pads, and elbow pads all help to reduce injuries, such as broken bones, cuts, and bruises. Remember to reduce serious injuries by wearing protective gear!

Communicate For what other sports should a person wear protective gear?

____

____

____

____

uInvestigate Lab

HANDS-ON LAB

SC.5.L.14.1, SC.5.N.1.1

How can you test the strength of a bone?

Suggested Materials
- construction paper
- cardboard
- hole puncher
- scissors
- books
- tape

Be careful using scissors.

People who play many sports need healthy bones to support their body as they play. How can you compare the strength of different bones?

Procedure

☐ **1.** Make a plan to make and use models to answer the question. Tell how you will test your model bones. Show your plan to your teacher before you begin.

☐ **2.** Build your models.

☐ **3.** Test your models. Record your observations.

Science Practice

Scientists **construct arguments** that are supported by models.

Analyze and Interpret Data

4. Use Evidence How does the structure of a bone affect its strength? Cite evidence from the data you collected.

____

____

____

____

____

____

____

____

____

____

____

Observations

uBe a Scientist

Test a Weak Bone

Place a chicken bone in a glass of vinegar. Allow the bone to soak for several days. Remove the bone. Bend it. How does the vinegar affect the bone?

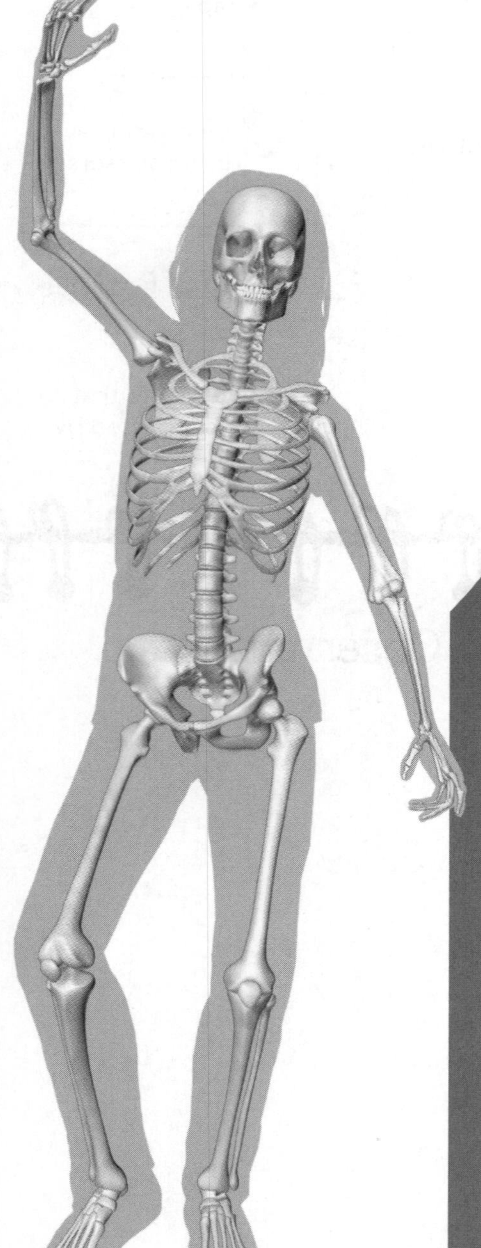

Skeletal System

What do you think would happen if your bones suddenly disappeared? You would fall onto the floor in a blob! Your body has 206 bones that make up the **skeletal system.** The skeletal system supports your body and gives it shape. Your bones also protect your internal organs.

Identify Mark an X on the bones you think protect your internal organs. Circle the bones that help your body stand upright.

Bones are made up of living tissues. They also contain nonliving materials called minerals. Calcium is a mineral that is important for strong, healthy bones. Bones contain a bendable material called cartilage. Feel your nose and ears. They can bend. That is because parts of your nose and ears are made of cartilage. Cartilage also acts as a cushion between bones that meet, such as where your leg bones meet at the knee.

Main Idea and Details Underline the sentences that tell the main idea about the skeletal system.

Quest Connection

How could a remote-controlled camera be used to identify an injury inside the human body?

____

____

____

____

____

____

Muscular System

The bones in your body would not be able to move without muscles. **Muscles** are organs that contract, or shorten, and relax, or lengthen, to move bones. Three kinds of muscles make up the muscular system: smooth muscle, cardiac muscle, and skeletal muscle. Body organs, such as the stomach, are made up of smooth muscle. Cardiac muscle makes up the heart. Muscles need oxygen to perform their tasks.

Connecting Concepts ▸ Toolbox

Structure and Function The structure of skeletal muscles allows them to contract. How is this structure related to the the function of muscles?

Skeletal muscles are attached to your bones by tough rope-like tissues called tendons. Skeletal muscles can only pull on bones. They cannot push bones. So they work in pairs to move bones. For example, bend your arm at the elbow. You can feel the muscle on the top of your upper arm contract, or shorten. This action causes bones to move so that your arm bends at the elbow. Now **extend**, or straighten, your arm. Feel the muscle underneath your arm. When this opposite muscle contracts, your arm straightens.

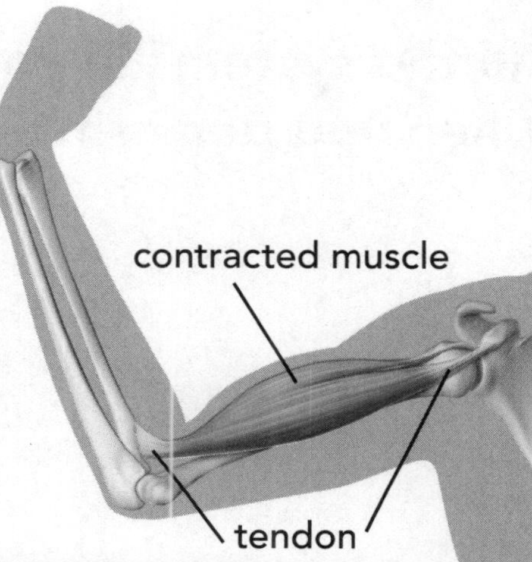

Draw a design that you could use to make a model that shows how muscle pairs work together to move a bone.

Visual Literacy Connection

How do we SKATE ON ICE?

All the systems in your body work together when you perform a task or activity.

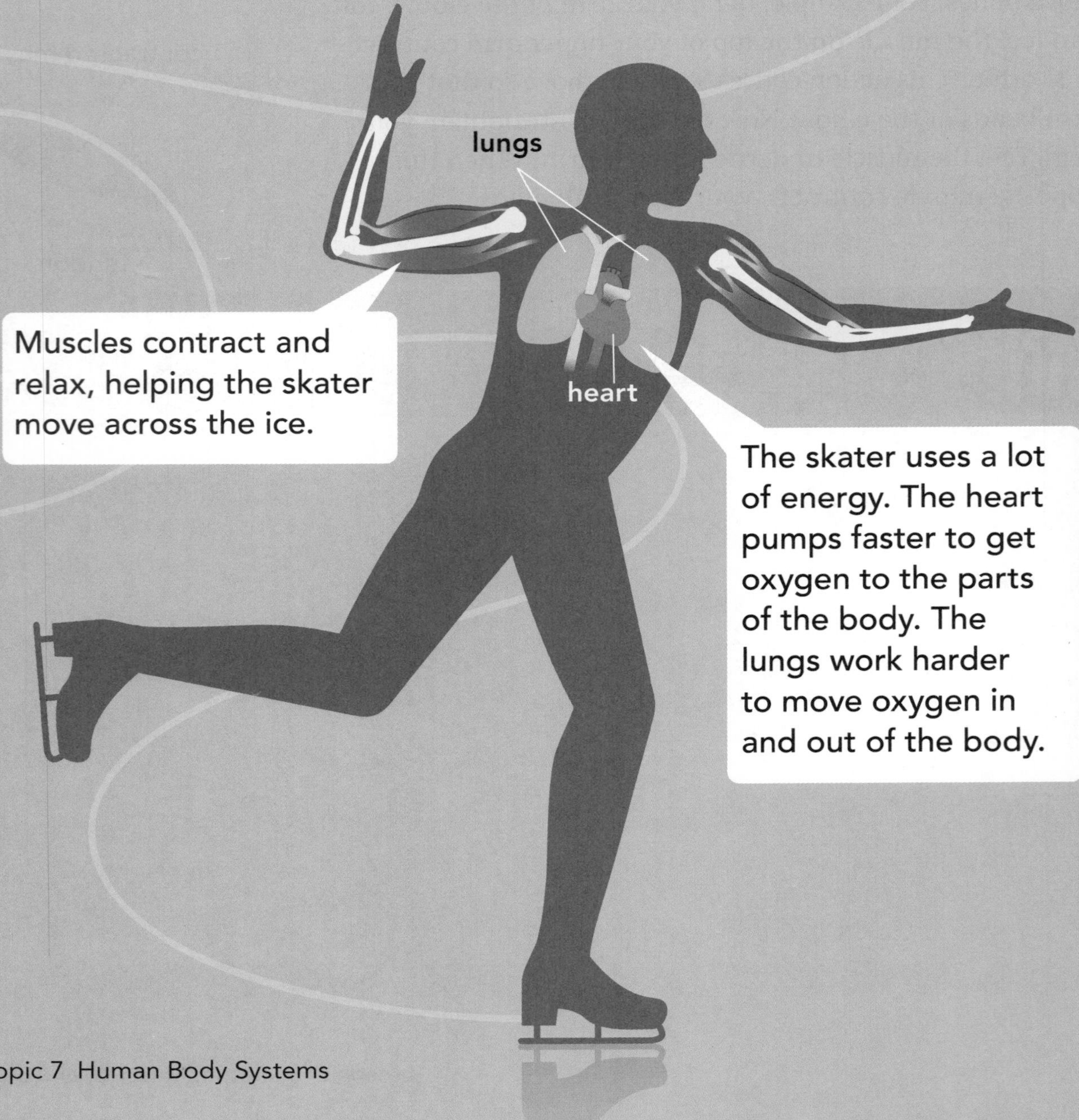

lungs

heart

Muscles contract and relax, helping the skater move across the ice.

The skater uses a lot of energy. The heart pumps faster to get oxygen to the parts of the body. The lungs work harder to move oxygen in and out of the body.

Complete an activity about systems that help you move.

The skater begins to sweat as he reaches the end of the performance.

The bones of the skater support the body as the skater jumps in the air and lands.

Write your own caption. Describe how the body systems work together to help the skater move on ice.

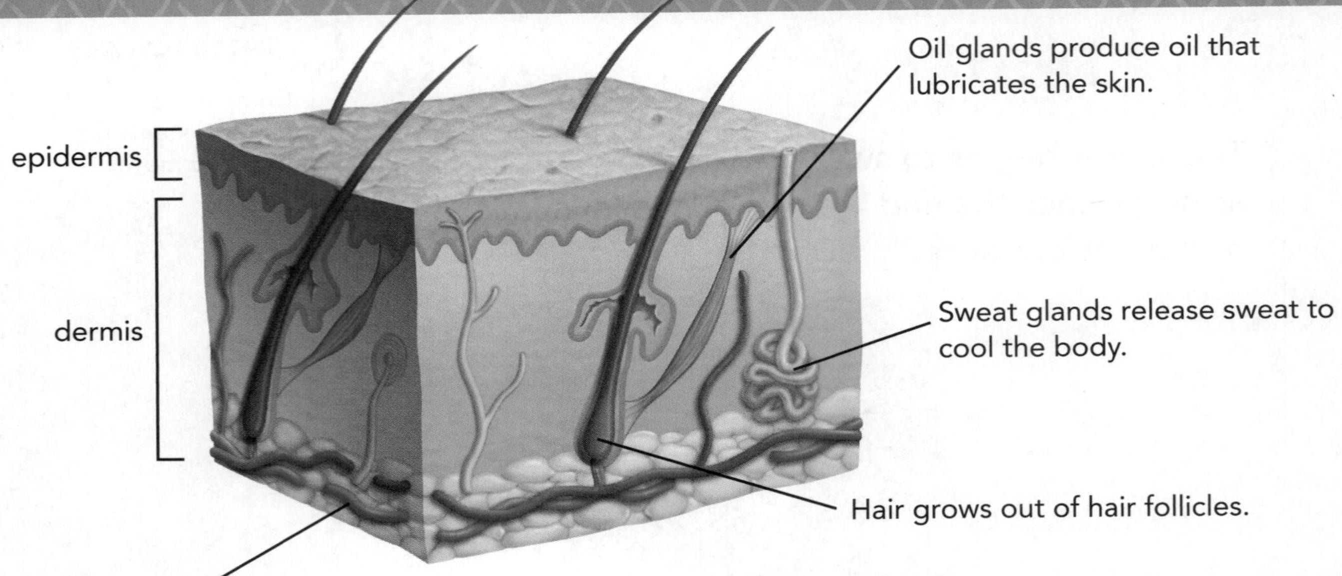

Skin

Your **skin** is your largest organ. It covers and protects your internal organs. It also protects your body from disease-causing germs and helps keep you cool by sweating. The skin has two layers. When you look at your skin, you see the thin outer layer, the epidermis. Pinch some skin on your arm. You can feel the dermis beneath the epidermis. The dermis layer is thick with structures that have different functions. Below the dermis are layers of fat, blood vessels, and muscles.

Make Meaning In your science notebook, write about why taking care of the skin is important. List ways you take care of your skin.

Lesson 2 Check

SC.5.L.14.1

1. **Summarize** Where are the three types of muscles found?

____

____

2. **Assess** Can both ends of a muscle be attached to a bone that is responsible for movement? Why or why not?

____

____

Injury Search

Suppose someone just had a cast placed on her leg. The cast must stay on for several weeks while a broken bone below the knee mends. During that time, the person will not be able use her lower leg muscles.

What might happen to the muscles attached to the leg bones? You can use the remote-controlled camera to find out! The camera can be injected through a short needle. What path must the camera follow to check on the health of the muscle? Draw the path of the camera.

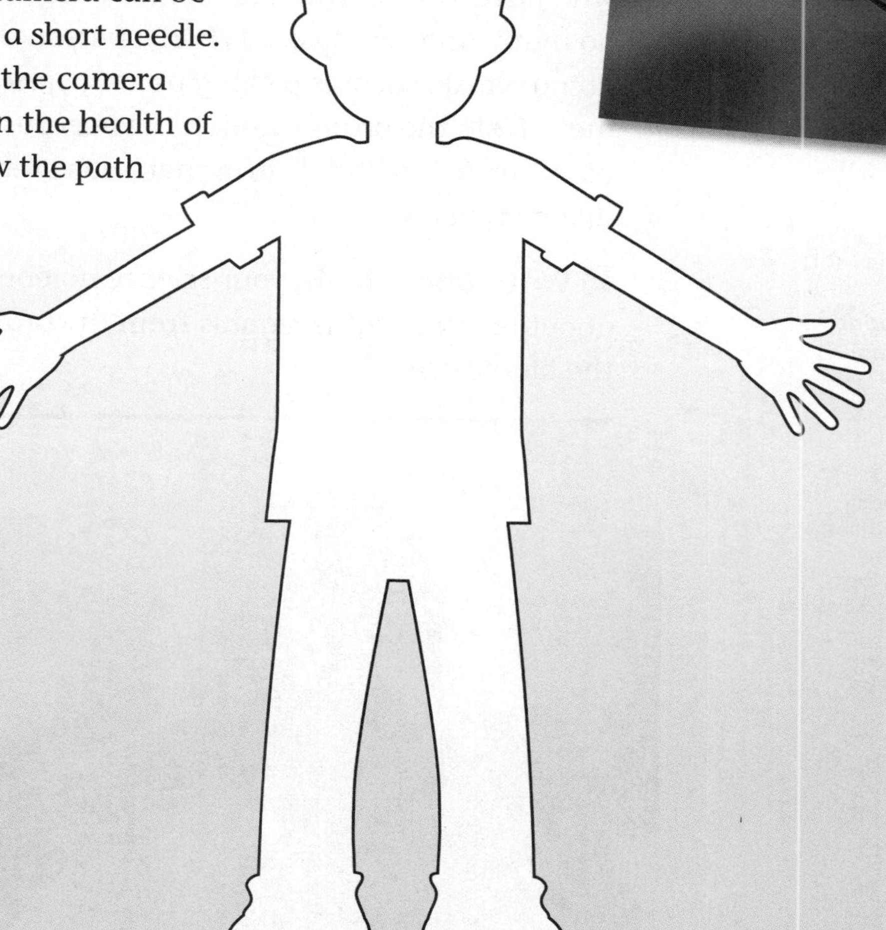

What might your camera discover about the health of the muscle?

____

____

QUEST CHECK OFF

Lesson 3

Nervous System

I can...

Describe the functions of the brain and sensory organs.

Literacy Skill
Main Idea and Details

Vocabulary
sensory organ
brain

Academic Vocabulary
respond

VIDEO

Watch a video about the sensory organs.

SC.5.L.14.1 Identify the organs in the human body and describe their functions, including the skin, brain, heart, lungs, stomach, liver, intestines, pancreas, muscles and skeleton, reproductive organs, kidneys, bladder, and sensory organs. (Also **SC.5.N.1.1**)

ENGINEERING Connection

Do you think about how you move your arm? Or do you just move it without giving it much thought? How does the brain send signals to cause parts to move? That is something that scientists and engineers have been learning more about. They have used what they know to develop a "bionic" arm. A bionic arm is an artificial arm that people can control with their thoughts. People who have lost an arm due to injury use bionic arms to do many different tasks. When a person thinks about doing a task, such as picking up an object, messages move from the brain through the nervous system to the bionic arm. The bionic arm then interprets the message and completes the task.

Write About It In your science notebook, write about how you think signals from the brain can reach the bionic arm.

uInvestigate Lab

HANDS-ON LAB

SC.5.L.14.1, SC.5.N.1.1

Which parts of the body are more sensitive?

Materials
- metric ruler
- erasers
- tape

A medical imaging technician might make images that show nerves in your body. How can you find out whether the nerves in different body parts are more sensitive to touch?

Science Practice

Scientists develop and **use models** to test interactions.

Procedure

☐ **1.** Is your fingertip, arm, or ankle the most sensitive to touch? Write your prediction.

____

☐ **2.** Plan a procedure to test your prediction. Show your plan to your teacher before you begin. Record your observations.

Analyze and Interpret Data

3. Model Draw a picture to show how you think the numbers of nerves in the three areas you tested are different.

Observations	How Number of Nerves Compare

Visual Literacy Connection

What are sensory organs?

Your body connects to the world through the sensory organs. Each sensory organ gathers specific kinds of information. The information is sent to your brain, which is the control center of the body. The brain interprets the information and then tells the body how to react to the information.

Eye

The eye allows us to **see**. Light enters the eye through a small opening called the pupil. A lens behind the pupil focuses the light onto the back of the eye. From there a nerve sends signals to the brain. The brain interprets the signals to form a visual image.

Ear

You can **hear** because of your ears. Sound waves enter the ear and cause the eardrum to vibrate. The ear changes the vibrations into nerve signals. A nerve carries the signals to the brain. The brain interprets the signals as words, music, or other sounds.

Tongue

The sense of **taste** comes from the tongue. It has small structures called taste buds. They send signals to your brain. The brain interprets the signals as taste—sweet, salty, bitter, or sour.

Nose

The nose detects **smell**. Small structures in the tongue pick up chemicals in the air. They change the chemicals into nerve signals that are sent to the brain. The brain identifies these signals as various smells. Your sense of smell also helps you taste things.

Skin

The sense of **touch** comes from nerve endings in the skin. They help you feel pressure, pain, hot, and cold. Some parts of the body, such as the fingertips, have more nerve endings than other parts of the body.

Choose one of the senses. Draw something you detect with that sense.

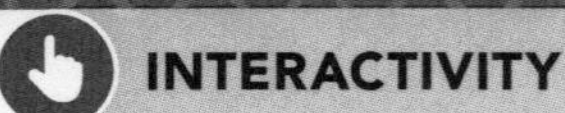

Do an activity about the nervous system.

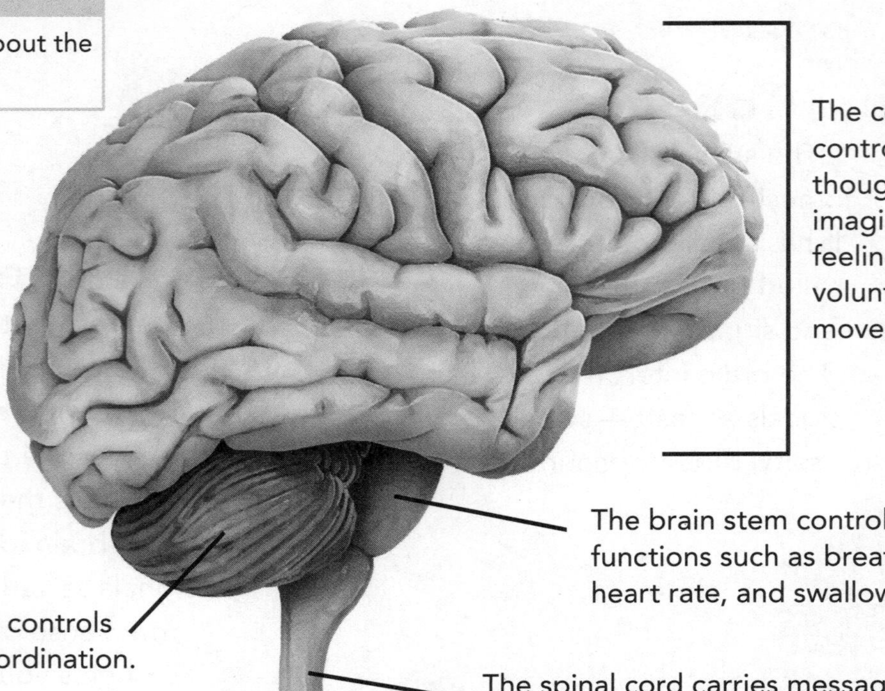

uBe a Scientist

Reaction Time

The time it takes you to react to something is called reaction time. With a partner, design a way to test your reaction time. Make a prediction. Does your reaction time improve with practice?

Brain

The nervous system sends messages throughout your body. Your brain is your body's most complex organ. It does more than just think! It interprets the information it receives about conditions inside and outside the body. Then it sends messages telling the body how to **respond**, or react. The brain is made up of nerve cells. Nerve cells also carry messages through the spinal cord to and from all parts of the body.

Quest Connection

To what kinds of messages might the brain respond to keep you balanced on one foot?

____

____

____

Nerves

The brain and the spinal cord make up the central nervous system. The spinal cord is made up of a thick bundle of nerves. Messages to and from your brain travel through the nerves of your spinal cord. These nerves branch out to other parts of the body. Some of these nerves are motor nerves that carry messages from the brain to other parts of the body. Other nerves are sensory nerves that carry messages from sense organs and other body parts to the spinal cord.

Connecting Concepts ▸ Toolbox

Structure and Function The way a structure is shaped is closely related to its function. How does the shape of the nervous system enable the brain to get messages from all parts of the body?

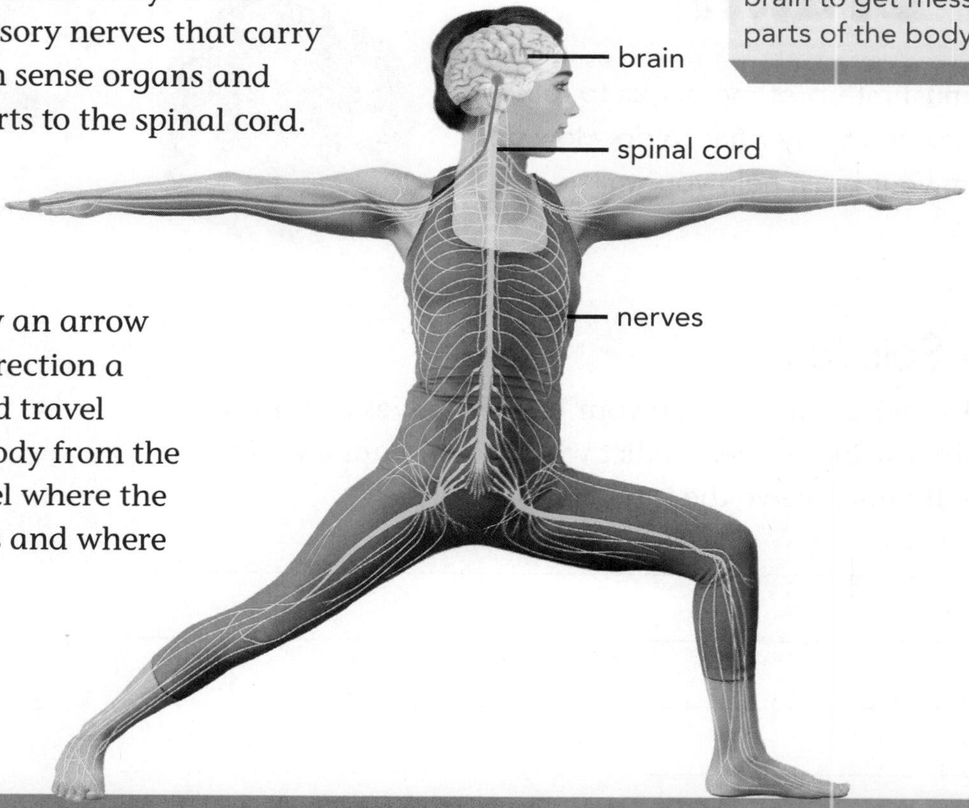

brain

spinal cord

nerves

Identify Draw an arrow to show the direction a message would travel through the body from the fingertip. Label where the message starts and where it ends.

Lesson 3 Check

SC.5.L.14.1

1. **Explain Phenomena** What evidence can you use to prove that different nerves carry information from the fingertips to the brain?

___

___

___

2. **Main Idea** Write a main idea statement about the nervous system.

___

___

___

STEM Quest Check-In Lab

How can you test signals to and from your brain?

Materials

- masking tape

The brain must interpret messages to tell other parts of the body what to do. How do signals from your brain help you walk in a straight line?

Engineering Practice

Engineers **communicate a design idea** to others.

Design a Solution

☐ **1.** Think of what information your brain receives to help you walk in a straight line. Predict what would happen if your brain did not receive the information.

☐ **2.** Use the materials to help you test your prediction. Show your plan to you teacher before you start. Record your observations.

☐ **3.** Think of how your signals travel in your body. How is that similar to the remote-controlled micro-camera? Draw a model that shows the path a signal must travel from the technician to the camera and back.

My Design

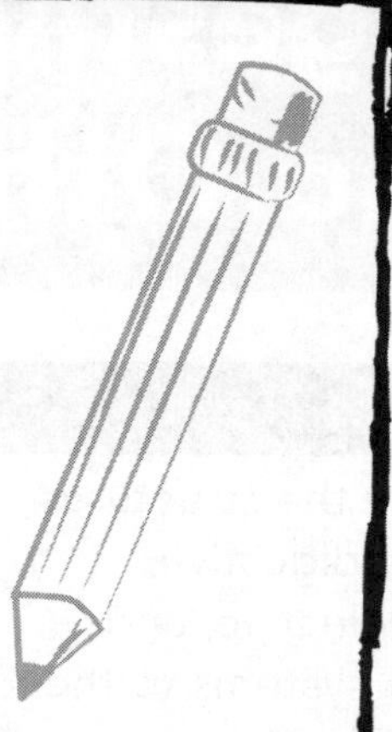

Communicate Your Solution

4. Explain Does your model show how the model remote-controlled camera will stay on the correct path through the body? Explain.

5. Analyze Show your model to another pair of students. Compare the path that you made with that of other students. Discuss any differences.

QUEST CHECK OFF

Lesson 4

Digestive, Reproductive, and Other Systems

I can...

Relate the structures in the digestive, reproductive, and other systems to their functions.

Literacy Skill
Main Idea and Details

Vocabulary
small intestine
large intestine
pancreas
liver
stomach
excretory system
kidneys
bladder

Academic Vocabulary
connect

VIDEO

Watch a video about the digestive system.

SC.5.L.14.1 Identify the organs in the human body and describe their functions, including the skin, brain, heart, lungs, stomach, liver, intestines, pancreas, muscles and skeleton, reproductive organs, kidneys, bladder, and sensory organs. (Also **SC.5.N.1.1**)

LOCAL-TO-GLOBAL Connection

Yikes! Your body has bacteria! Some of the bacteria helps keep you healthy. For example, the digestive system contains bacteria that help to digest food. However, not all people have the same digestive bacteria. In Japan, people have bacteria with a substance that helps them digest seaweed. These bacteria are not found in people from North America. Scientists think the bacteria got into Japanese intestines over many generations as a result of eating the seaweed in many Japanese meals. The bacteria live on the seaweed that people eat.

Explain Why are these bacteria found only in Japanese people?

____

____

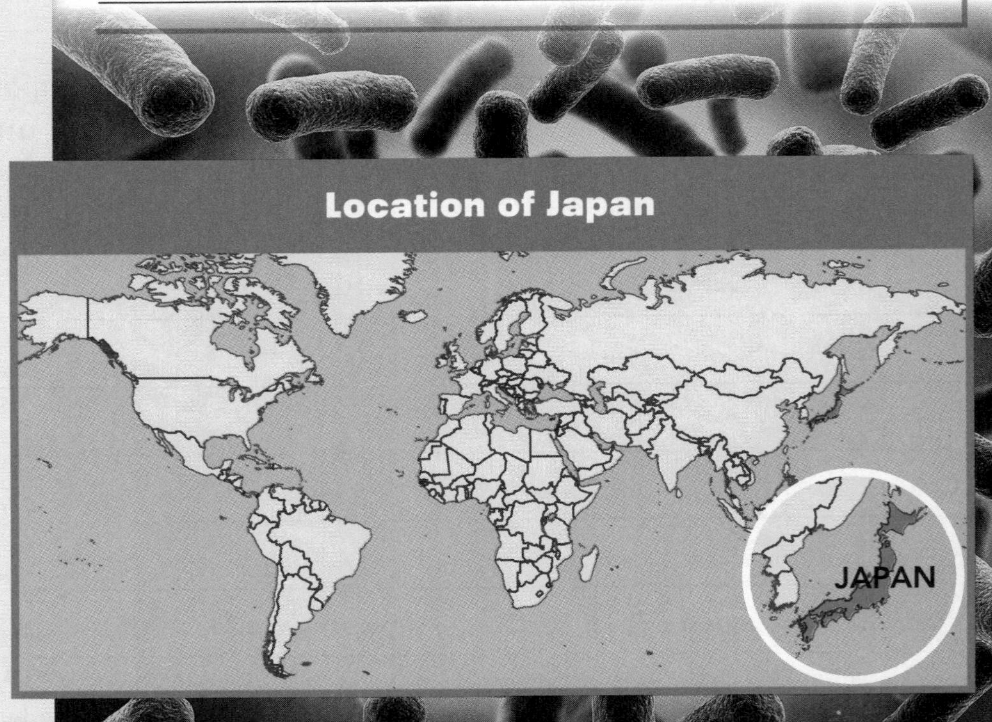

uInvestigate Lab

HANDS-ON LAB

SC.5.L.14.1, SC.5.N.1.1

How are intestines arranged inside your body?

Scientific data shows that the small intestine is very long. How can something so long fit inside your body?

Materials
- large sheet of paper
- tape measure

Suggested Materials
- string
- rope
- yarn
- glue
- scissors

Be careful using scissors.

Procedure

☐ 1. Trace the outline of another student's body on the large sheet of paper.

☐ 2. Your small intestine is about 3.5 times your height. Calculate in meters the length of the small intestine of the student you outlined. Record your data.

____

____

☐ 3. Choose a material to represent the small intestine. Use the material to model how the intestine might be arranged in the outlined body. Draw how your model looks.

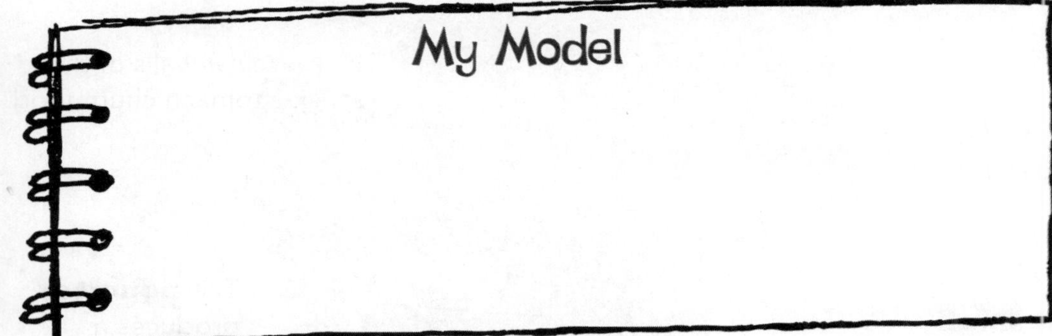

Science Practice

Scientists use evidence to construct an argument.

Analyze and Interpret Data

4. **Use Evidence** How do you think the small intestine is arranged to fit into a small space? Provide evidence from your observations.

____

____

____

Connecting Concepts ▸ Toolbox

Structure and Function Look in a mirror to see how your teeth are shaped. Contrast the front teeth and the back teeth. How are they different? How are these two kinds of teeth used differently?

Digestive System

What did you eat for breakfast today? Once you swallowed the food, where did it go? It entered the digestive system. The digestive system breaks down food into nutrients and other substances that the body can use. Cells use these substances for energy, growth, and repair. Food undergoes many changes as it passes through the digestive system.

Digestion begins in the mouth, where your teeth tear and crush food. Saliva, the liquid in your mouth, begins to chemically break down some food. Study the diagram to see how food is broken down and absorbed as it passes through the rest of the digestive system.

Identify Label the missing part of the diagram.

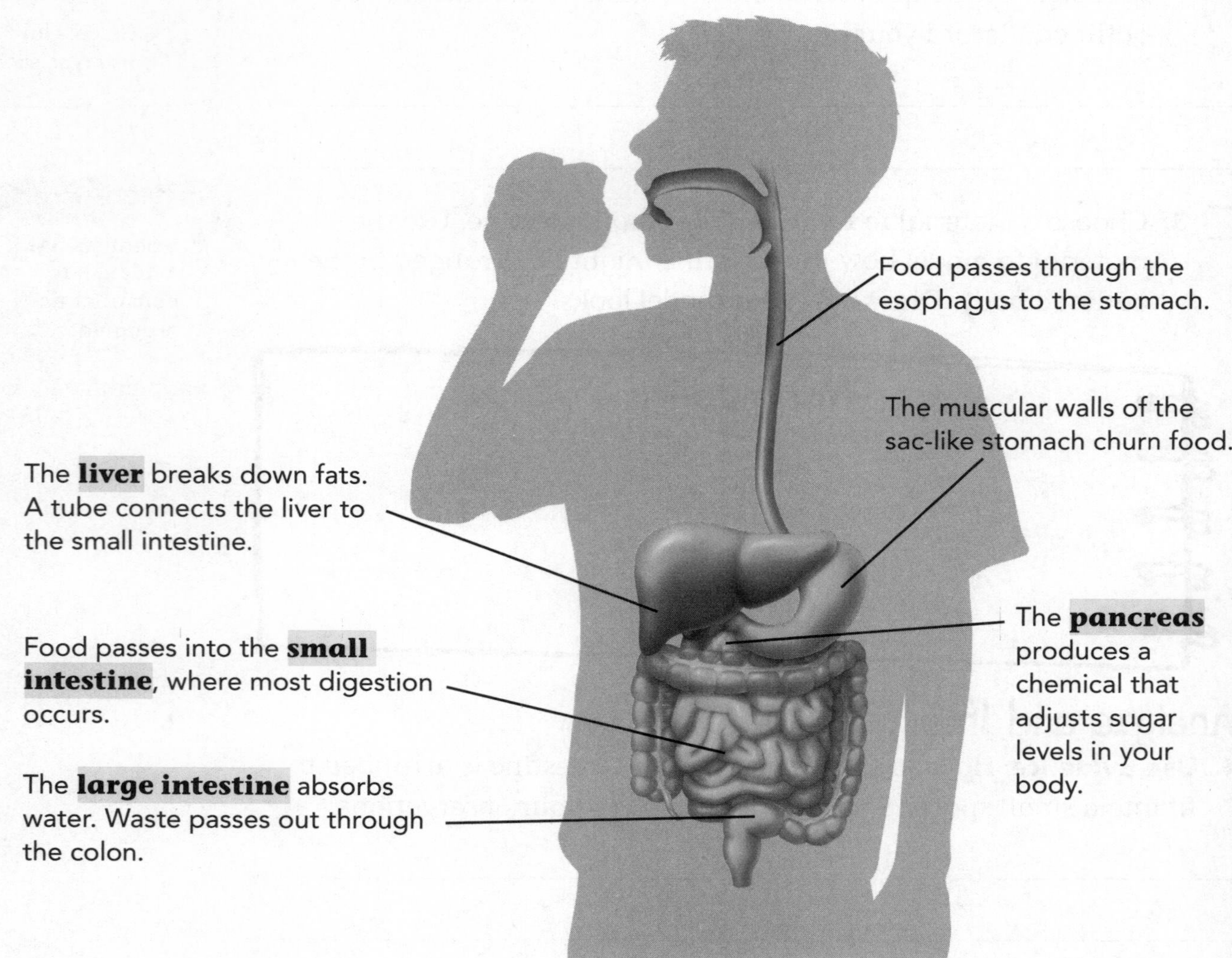

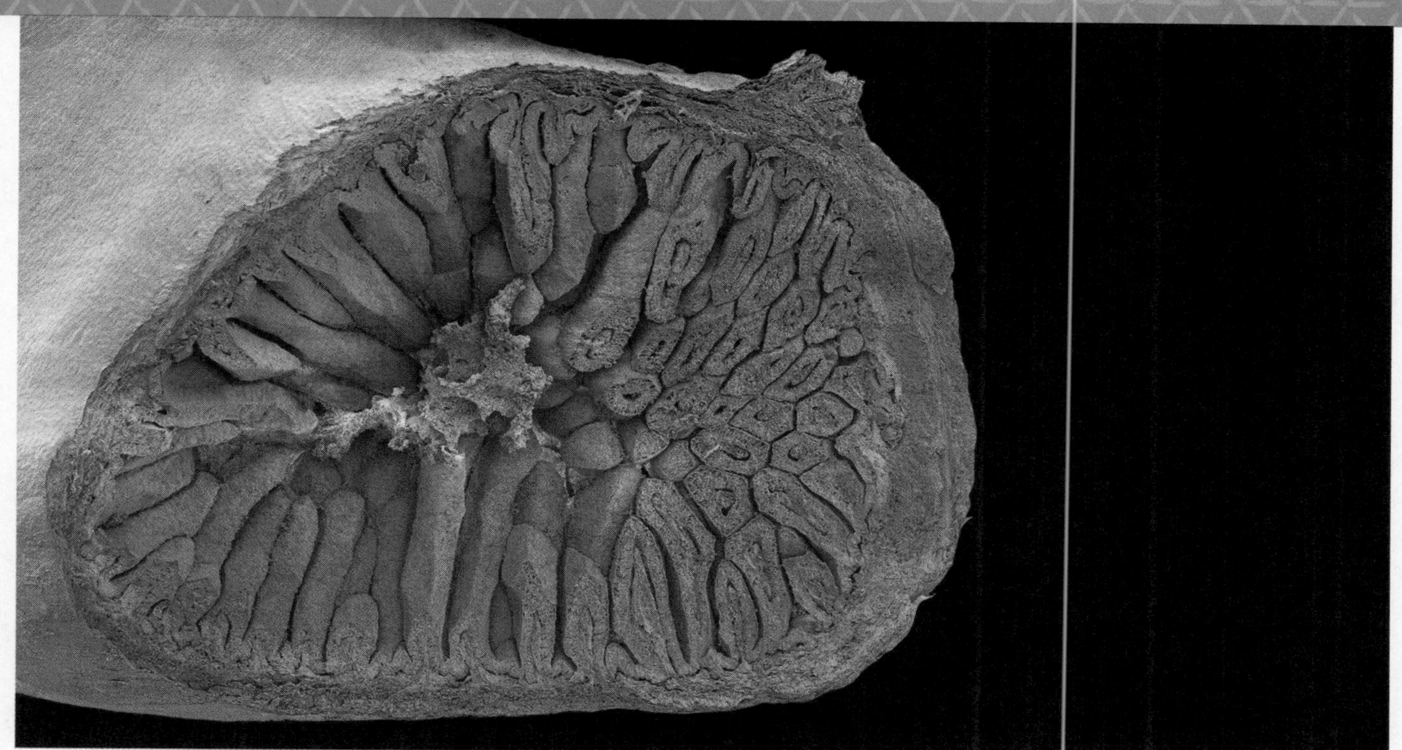

How Nutrients Get to Parts of the Body

We often think of the stomach as the organ that digests our food. But the **stomach** is involved in the digestion of only certain kinds of food. Most digestion takes place in the small intestine. In addition to the digestive juices produced by the intestine, the liver and the pancreas send chemicals to the small intestine to break down food.

Find the small fingerlike structures in the cross-section photo of the small intestine. They are the villi on the inside of the small intestine. Capillaries line the walls of villi. Food that is completely digested is absorbed through the walls of the villi into the capillaries. The capillaries **connect**, or attach, with larger blood vessels that carry nutrients to all parts of the body.

Relate Why is it important for the villi to absorb digested food into the blood?

____

____

____

uBe a Scientist

Digestion in the Mouth

Put a saltine in your mouth and observe how it tastes. Then chew the saltine for about a minute. What change do you notice in its taste? Why do you think the taste changed?

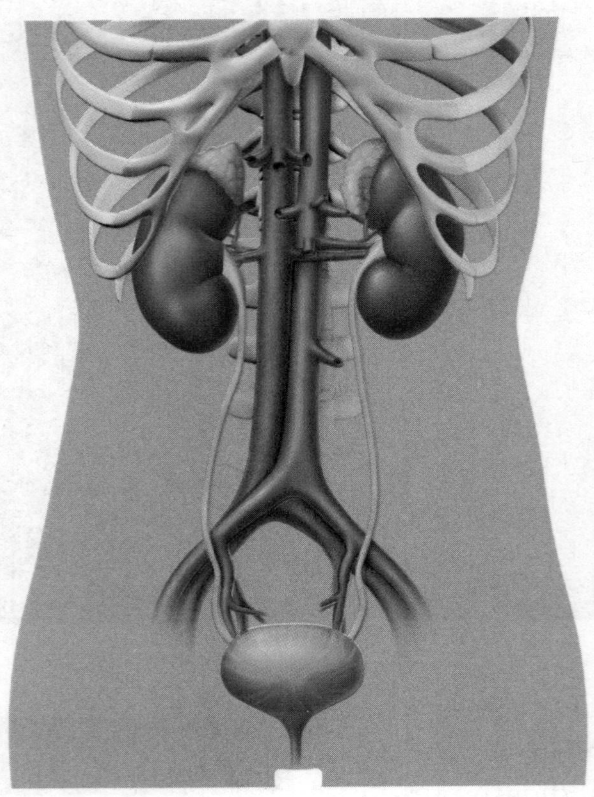

Excretory System

Cells absorb nutrients from the blood, but in return they produce wastes. These wastes are removed from the body by the **excretory system**. Several organs help with this process. They include the lungs, the liver, and the skin, but mostly the kidneys, the bladder, and the urethra.

The **kidneys** are a pair of bean-shaped organs that filter wastes from the blood. As blood passes through the kidneys, capillaries remove these wastes. The wastes combine with water to form urine. The urine travels through tubes called ureters to a muscular sac called the **bladder**, where it is stored until it is released from the body.

Identify Label the kidneys, the bladder, and the ureters.

Quest Connection

How could a remote-controlled camera be used to find an unhealthy kidney?

___

___

___

___

___

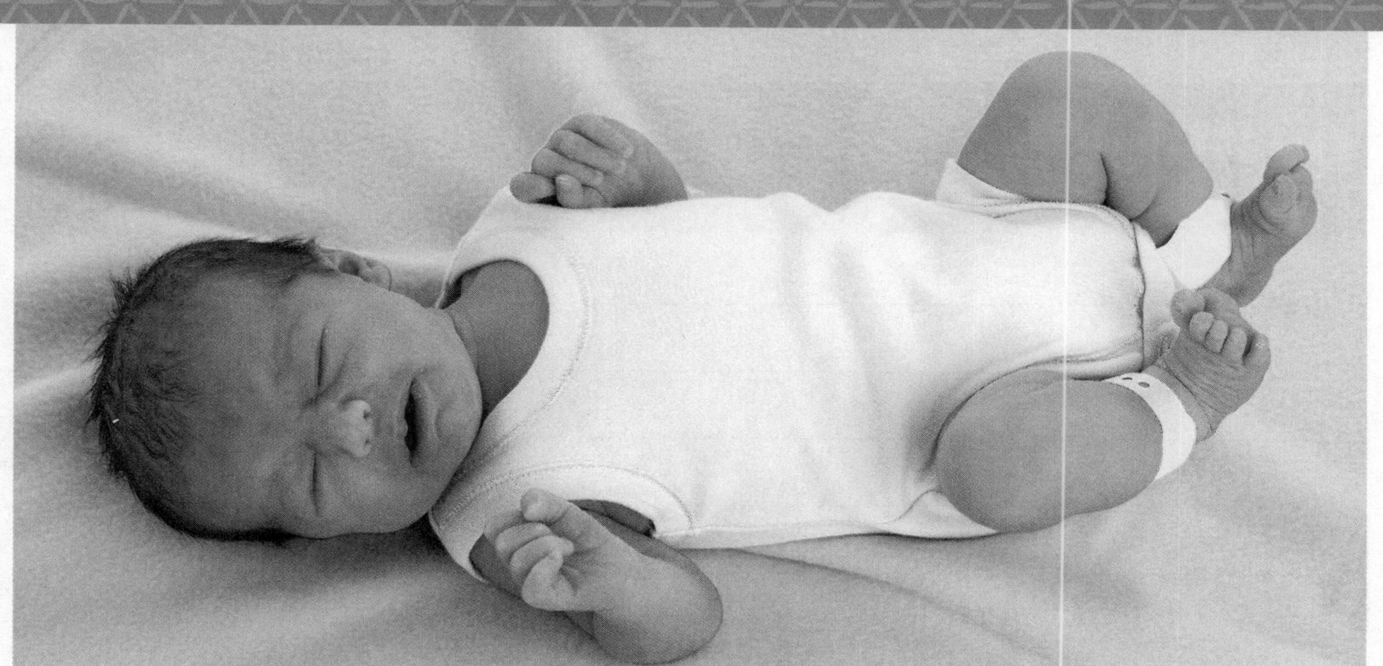

Reproductive System

The baby in the picture is very young. Its body will go through many stages. When it reaches a stage called adolescence, the body becomes able to reproduce, or produce offspring. The reproductive system is made up of organs that allow people to reproduce.

The female body has organs called ovaries that produce eggs. Once a month, an egg will burst out of one ovary and travel down a tube. If the egg is joined by a sperm cell, it travels to a muscular sac inside the lower belly. Here, the egg develops and grows into a baby.

The male reproductive system produces sperm in sac-like organs. The sperm mix with other fluids. These materials travel through a long, thin tube that carries them to the outside of the body.

Reproduction can only happen if a male sperm cell joins with a female egg cell. When the sperm joins with an egg, the two cells form a single cell. This cell divides and grows and eventually becomes a newborn baby.

READING CHECK **Main Idea and Details** Underline the main idea about what happens during adolescence.

Question It!

Suppose you work at a medical testing lab. You received a sample of an unknown germ. What questions would you ask to help you identify it?

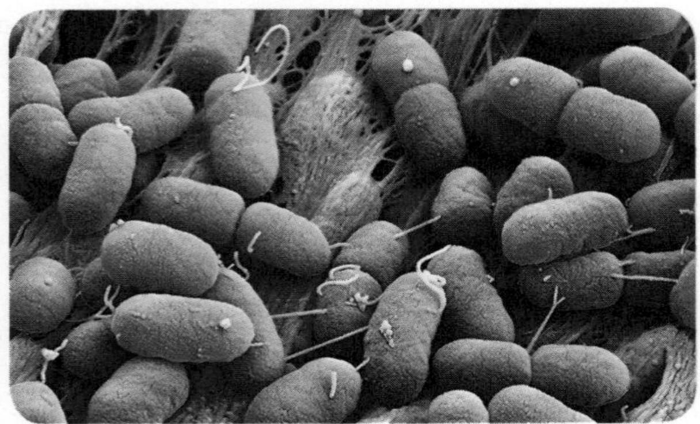

Some bacteria can cause illness, but most bacteria are harmless. Helpful bacteria in your intestines aid in digesting food.

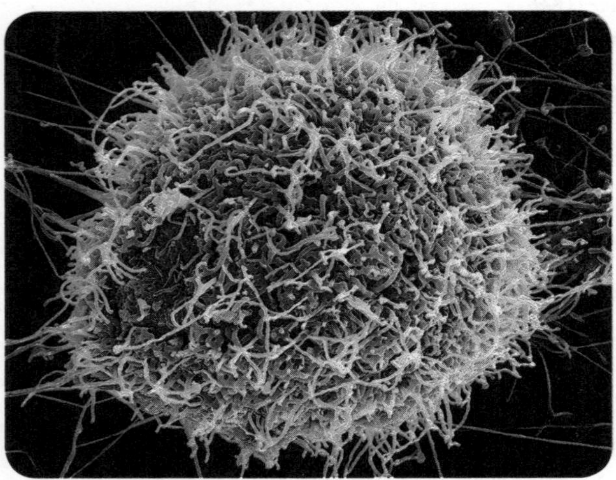

Viruses are germs that cause colds and flu.

Immune System

Have you ever missed school with a cold or flu? If so, your body was invaded by germs. Germs, such as some bacteria, cause diseases that prevent the body from staying healthy. Your immune system protects your body against diseases. It has an army of defenses that can destroy germs or prevent them from entering the body.

One of the first lines of defense, or protection, in the body's army is the tiny hairs and mucus in the nose and windpipe. The hairs and mucus trap germs you may breathe in. Saliva, another defense, kills germs that enter the mouth.

READING CHECK Main Idea and Details Circle two details about how the immune system protects the body.

Fever is another defense. Sometimes when you are ill, you get a fever. The rise in body temperature kills the invading germs. If germs get into the stomach, digestive juices destroy the germs.

Do an activity about the human body.

The skin is another line of defense. It acts like a wall to stop germs from getting inside the body. If you cut yourself, germs can enter the body through the cut and get into your blood. The picture shows one kind of blood cell that fights germs. These white blood cells surround and engulf the germs.

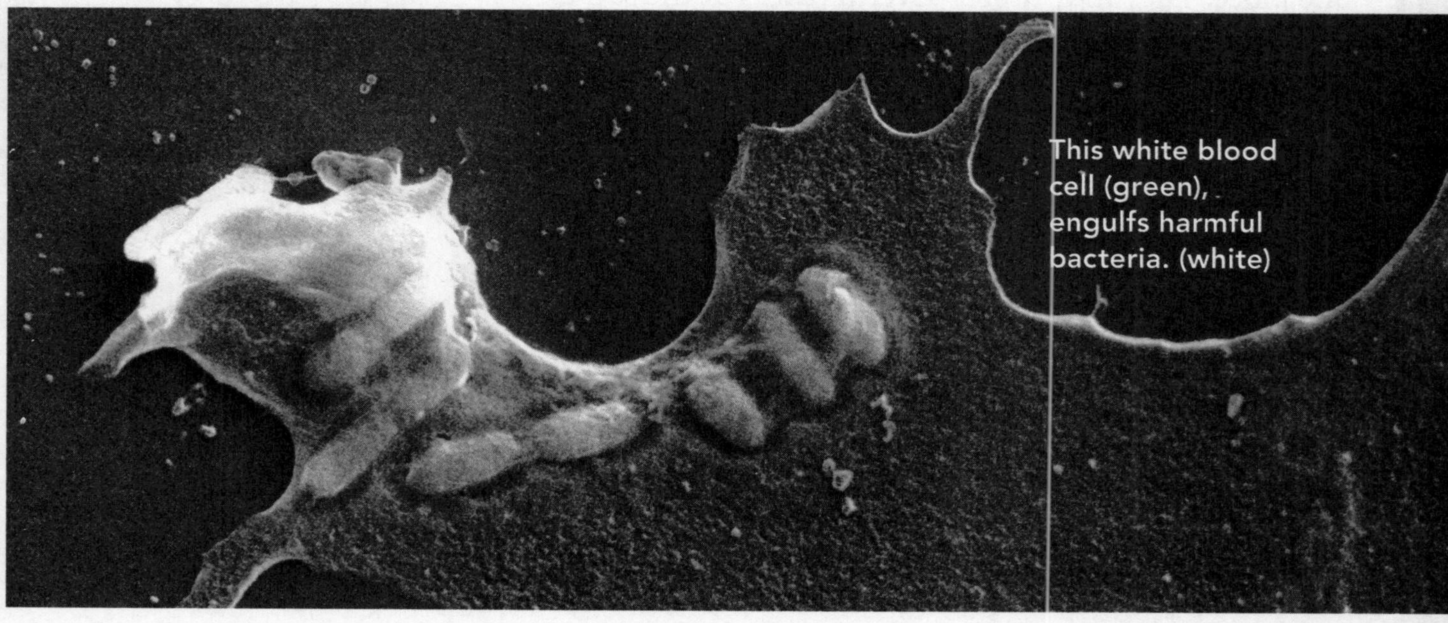

This white blood cell (green), engulfs harmful bacteria. (white)

Lesson 4 Check

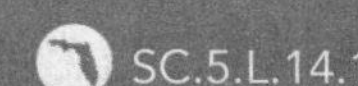

1. **Formulate** Donovan claims that the immune system works with other body systems. Is he correct? Explain.

____

____

____

2. **Relate** How does the digestive system work with the blood vessels of the circulatory system?

____

____

____

Tracking Germs

When germs enter the body, they can attack more than one place. They may attack several places at the same time. Or they may move from one place to another. How can you use your remote-controlled camera to follow germs that invade your body?

Identify where the germs enter the body.

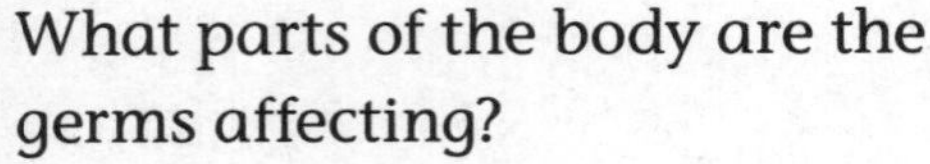

____

____

What parts of the body are the germs affecting?

____

____

Draw the path the camera will follow. Label the organs it will travel through.

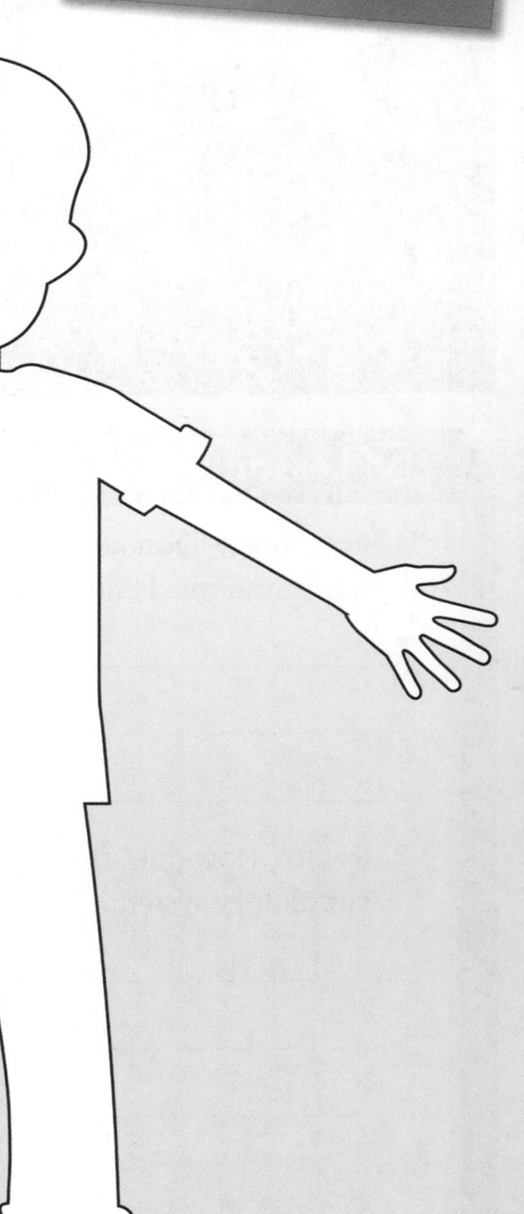

Lines of Symmetry

If you fold the figures in half along the black line, both sides of each figure will be the same. The two halves of each figure will have the same size and shape. The figures have symmetry. Each fold represents a line of symmetry that separates the two identical parts.

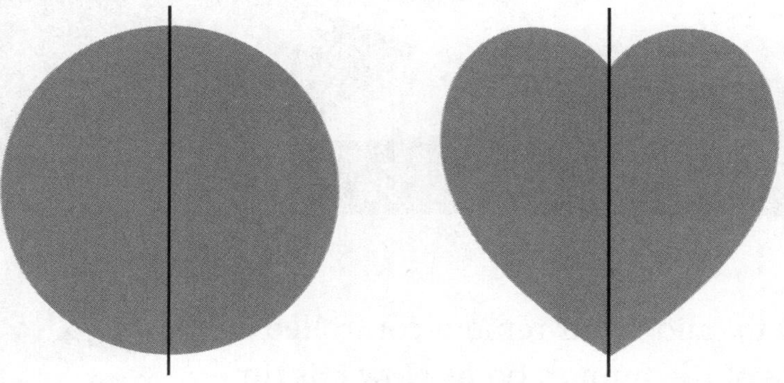

The human body has symmetry. Draw a picture of your face. Then draw a line of symmetry. Do the parts match?

Identify a body system that has a line of symmetry. Explain.

Quest Findings

INTERACTIVITY

Organize data to support your Quest Findings.

STEM Make a Human Body Road Map

How can you make a tiny camera navigate the human body?

Make a Plan

You have determined how to guide your remote-controlled camera to view some parts of the human body. Now it is time to provide guidance for a way the camera can be used for a specific part of the body during a medical checkup.

Choose a body organ or system that you have studied. Think about the parts of that organ or system and how they function together.

What specifically will be checked using the camera?

How will the camera be used during the checkup procedure?

You should explain how the camera will be used and where it needs to go. Decide how different forms of communication can help you guide users. You can write instructions, draw maps and diagrams, and even make "road signs."

How will you show a path on a map through the body system you have chosen? Write your ideas.

____

____

____

Present your plan to the class.

Career Connection

Medical Imaging Technician

A medical imaging technician works with challenging cases and specialized medical equipment. A medical imaging technician helps to capture images through a variety of tests, including MRIs, X-rays, and ultrasounds. These tests help diagnose, treat, or track patients with a variety of symptoms.

For instance, when a medical imaging technician does a CT scan, the technician can capture the right details. The computer technology the technician uses combines several X-ray images to provide more detail and information about the condition of a patient that may not have been easy to see in a regular X-ray or other testing.

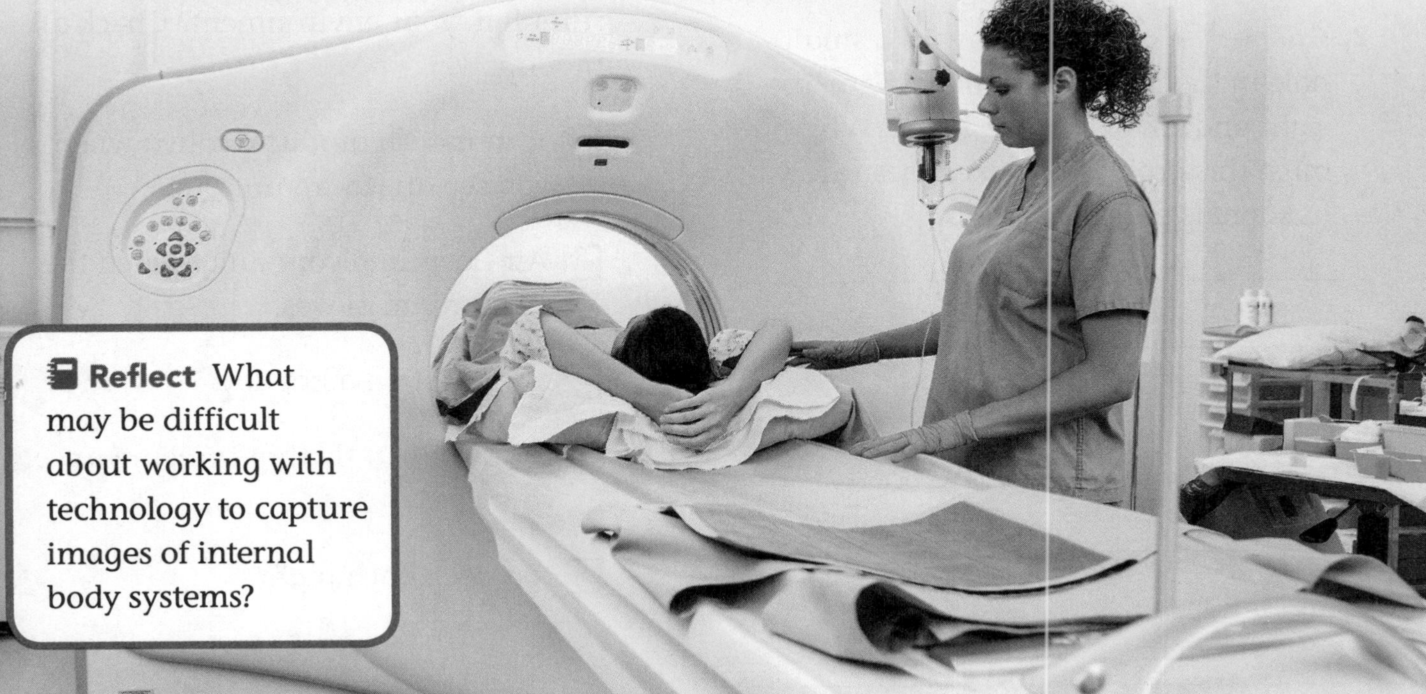

Reflect What may be difficult about working with technology to capture images of internal body systems?

Assessment

Read each question and choose or write the best answer.

1. **Use a Diagram** Match the labels to the correct area of the digestive system.

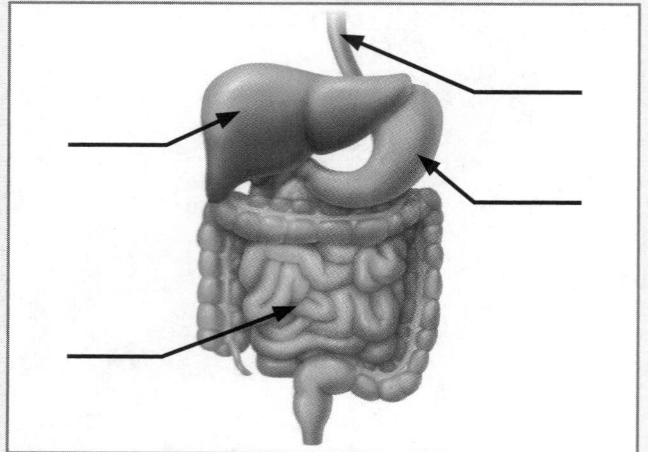

A. esophagus

B. liver

C. small intestine

D. stomach

2. **Connect** A child is born with a small hole in the muscular wall between the right and left side of the heart. Why must this problem be fixed by surgery as soon as possible?

3. **Assess** Explain how digestive organs depend upon each other to provide nutrients to the body.

4. **Apply Concepts** Which events are evidence that your brain responds to stimuli in your environment? Check all that apply.

- ☐ Your mouth produces saliva when you see an ice cream cone.
- ☐ Air flows into your lungs when the diaphragm moves.
- ☐ You sweat on a hot day.
- ☐ You swat at a fly that comes near your eyes.
- ☐ You sleep each night.

5. **Use Reasoning** A woman donates one of her kidneys to a person who needs a transplant. To stay healthy, she might need to:

A. exercise more

B. avoid foods that are difficult to digest

C. drink less water throughout the day

D. avoid medicines that are difficult to remove from the body

6. **Interpret a Diagram** Which structure would most likely respond if a person is running a 5-kilometer race?

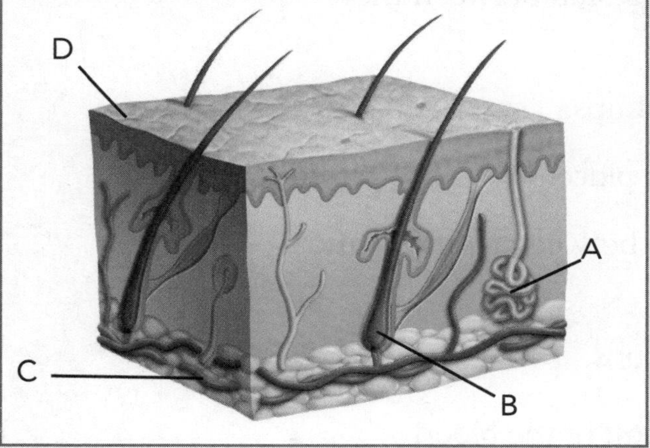

A. A

B. B

C. C

D. D

7. **Analyze** Amara injures her knee during a soccer game and is having a lot of trouble bending it. What might cause this problem?

____

____

____

____

____

____

____

The Essential Question *How can you model the interactions among human body systems?*

Show What You Learned

Choose two organ systems that you studied. Describe how you would make a model to show how the two systems interact with each other.

____

____

____

____

____

____

____

Science Assessment Practice

Read the scenario and answer questions 1–2.

A group of students conducted an investigation to see how heart and breathing rates change with exercise. Students measured and recorded their heart and breathing rates for one minute while resting. Then they performed various physical activities for 2 minutes and measured their heart and breathing rates again. They recorded their data in the table.

Activity	Heart rate before exercise	Heart rate after exercise	Breathing rate before exercise	Breathing rate after exercise
running in place	78	102	17	23
push ups	72	95	15	22
balancing an egg on a spoon	75	75	14	14

1 **Use Tables** Suppose that the students first ran in place and then did pushups. What evidence do you see that they rested between these activities?

Ⓐ They were breathing faster before the pushups.

Ⓑ The heart rate was faster after running in place.

Ⓒ The students balanced an egg on a spoon between running and pushups.

Ⓓ The heart rate was slower before the pushups.

2 **Use Reasoning** What would happen if only half of the blood returning to the heart from the body was pumped to the lungs as students ran in place?

Ⓕ The heart rate would decrease.

Ⓖ The lungs would exchange less oxygen and carbon dioxide with the air.

Ⓗ Exercise would become less tiring.

Ⓘ The breathing rate would decrease.

Read the scenario and answer questions 3–4.

Dogs can be trained to sit or stay in response to spoken commands. They can also be trained to produce saliva, or salivate, in response to a command. The diagrams show how this training happens.

The dog salivates in response to seeing food.

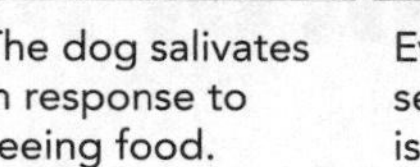

Every time the dog sees food, a bell is rung.

The dog salivates in response to a bell being rung.

3 **Use Evidence** What evidence from the diagram shows that dogs respond to information from their environment?

Ⓐ The bell is rung every time the dog sees food.

Ⓑ The dog sits in front of the food.

Ⓒ The dog salivates when it sees the food and when it hears the bell.

Ⓓ The dog sits even when the food is not present.

4 **Evaluate** Jane thinks that saliva production is controlled only by the mouth. She thinks that the mouth releases saliva when it detects food. According to the diagram, is Jane correct? Why or why not?

Ⓕ Yes, she is correct. The dog salivates when food is present.

Ⓖ Yes, she is correct. The dog salivates when the bell rings.

Ⓗ No, she is not correct. The dog only salivates when food is present and the bell is rung.

Ⓘ No, she is not correct. The dog salivates when it thinks about food.

5 **Synthesize** Which body response shows a connection between the respiratory system, the nervous system, and the muscular system?

Ⓐ shivering caused by cold

Ⓑ coughing to prevent choking

Ⓒ crying after chopping onions

Ⓓ sweating on a hot day

uDemonstrate Lab

How do your sensory organs gather information?

Scientists study how different parts of a system work together to explain how the system functions. What evidence can you use to explain how your sensory organs work as a system?

Suggested Materials

- blindfold
- scented candle
- feather
- paper tube
- soap

Be aware of physical safety!

Do not taste any thing in lab.

Science Practice

Scientists use evidence to answer scientific questions.

Procedure

☐ **1.** Choose two sensory organs to learn more about how they work. Think of a way to test how your eyes, ears, nose, or skin gather information.

☐ **2.** Make a plan. Show your plan to your teacher before you begin. Conduct your investigation.

☐ **3.** Record your observations.

Observations

SC.5.L.14.1, SC.5.N.1.1

Analyze and Interpret Data

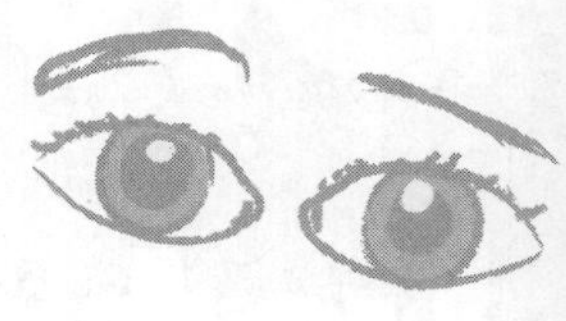

4. **Explain** What did the tests you conducted show about how sensory organs works as a system? Use your observations to support your explanation.

5. **Present an Argument** Use evidence to explain how having more than one sensory organ helps humans. What would happen if one did not work?

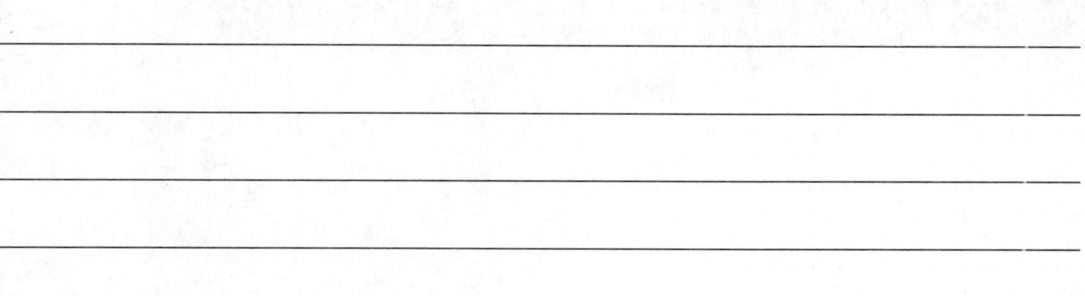

Topic 8

Diversity and Interdependence

SC.5.L.14.2 Compare and contrast the function of organs and other physical structures of plants and animals, including humans, for example: some animals have skeletons for support—some with internal skeletons others with exoskeletons—while some plants have stems for support.
SC.5.L.15.1 Describe how, when the environment changes, differences between individuals allow some plants and animals to survive and reproduce while others die or move to new locations.
SC.5.L.17.1 Compare and contrast adaptations displayed by animals and plants that enable them to survive in different environments such as life cycles variations, animal behaviors and physical characteristics. (Also **SC.5.N.1.1, SC.5.N.2.1, LAFS.5.RI.2.5,** and **MAFS.5.MD.1.1**)

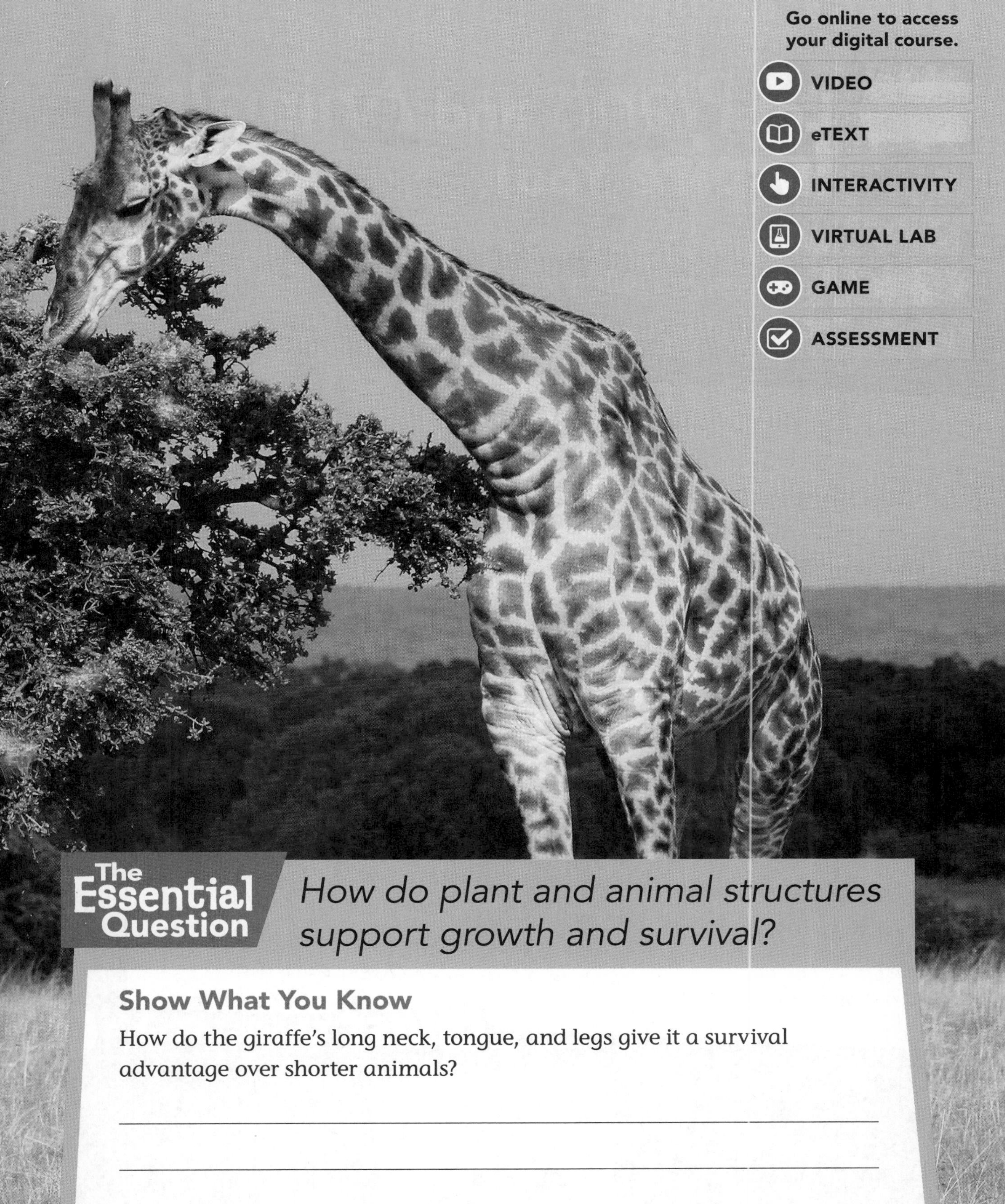

The Essential Question *How do plant and animal structures support growth and survival?*

Show What You Know

How do the giraffe's long neck, tongue, and legs give it a survival advantage over shorter animals?

____

____

____

Quest Kickoff

STEM

Let Plants and Animals Inspire You!

Which human problem can you help solve using what you learn about plants and animals?

Hi! I am Leigh Meredith, and I am a nature photographer. Have you ever noticed the many different shapes, sizes, and colors of both plants and animals? Wouldn't it be fun to see how a plant or animal uses these features? You can do just that! In this problem-based learning activity, you will use what you learn about plant and animal features to solve a human problem of your choosing.

Many products we use every day were inspired by plants and animals. For example, cats have pads on the bottoms of their paws, so when they jump, their fall is cushioned. Similarly, shoes have padding, or soles, on the bottom so our feet do not hurt when we walk on the hard ground.

Follow the path to learn how you will complete the Quest. The Quest activities in the lessons will help you complete the Quest! Check off your progress on the path when you complete an activity with a QUEST CHECK OFF. Go online for more Quest activities.

Quest Check-In Lab 1

Lesson 1

Examine the internal structure of a stem, and apply what you learn to solving a human problem.

SC.5.L.17.1 Compare and contrast adaptations displayed by animals and plants that enable them to survive in different environments such as life cycles variations, animal behaviors and physical characteristics. (Also **SC.5.L.14.2**)

VIDEO

Watch a video about a nature photographer.

Quest Check-In 4

Lesson 4

How can lobster claws inspire a solution to a human problem?

Quest Check-In 3

Lesson 3

Think of a product that could be designed based on what you learn about the swim bladder of a fish.

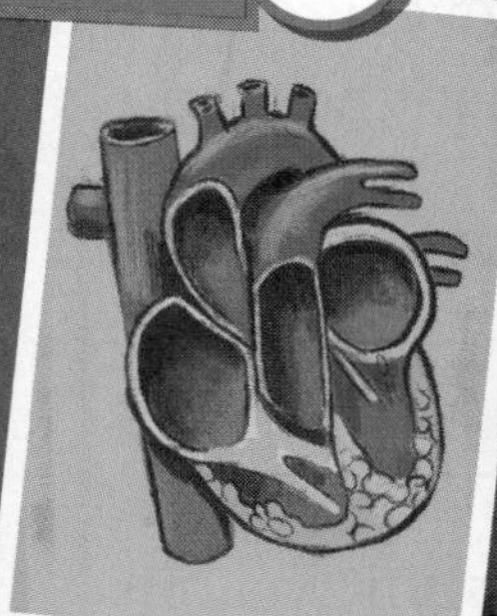

Quest Check-In 5

Lesson 5

Explore how bats observe their environment and how their process might apply to a human product.

Quest Check-In 2

Lesson 2

Examine the structures of seeds, and identify how they might be used to solve a human problem.

Quest Findings

Complete the Quest! Choose a plant or animal structure to inspire your own design solution for a human problem. Build a model to help communicate your solution.

uConnect Lab

HANDS-ON LAB

SC.5.L.17.1, SC.5.N.1.1

How do your eyes respond to differences in lighting?

Scientists analyze how a system changes in response to a variable. How can you investigate how the human eye reacts to light?

Materials

- flashlight
- white paper
- tape

Do not shine the flashlight directly into the eyes.

Procedure

☐ **1.** Look closely at the eyes of another student. Find the pupil, which is the dark circle in the middle of the eye. Predict what will happen to the pupil when the environment has more and less light.

____

____

☐ **2.** Make a plan to test your prediction without shining light directly into the eye. Show your plan to your teacher before you begin.

☐ **3.** Conduct your investigation. Record your observations.

Science Practice

Scientists **analyze information** from investigations.

Analyze and Interpret Data

4. Use Data Was your prediction right? How do you think the pupil helps humans adapt to different environments?

____

____

____

____

____

____

Observations

Compare and Contrast

LAFS.5.RI.2.5

GAME

Practice what you learn with the Mini Games.

Scientists compare and contrast structures of plants. When they compare, they find out what is the same. When they contrast, they find out what is different. Read the text to learn about the trunk of an oak tree and the trunk of a white birch tree.

Oak Tree

The trunk of an oak tree is sturdy, large, and dark brown. The bark covering its trunk is thick. The trunk supports the tree. Branches grow from the trunk. The internal structures of the trunk take water to all parts of the tree.

White Birch Tree

The trunk of a white birch tree is narrow and white. The bark covering the trunk is thin. The trunk supports the tree. The trunk has branches growing from it. The internal structures of the trunk take water to all parts of the tree.

READING CHECK **Compare and Contrast** Complete the chart.

Oak tree trunk	Both trunks	White birch tree trunk

Lesson 1

Internal Structures and Functions of Plants

I can...

Describe some internal structures that help plants survive and reproduce.

Literacy Skill
Compare and Contrast

Vocabulary
structure
function
ovary
vascular system

Academic Vocabulary
external
internal

VIDEO

Watch a video about plant functions and structures.

SC.5.L.14.2 Compare and contrast the function of organs and other physical structures of plants and animals, including humans, for example: some animals have skeletons for support some with internal support—some with exoskeletons—while some plants have stems for support.

SC.5.L.17.1 Compare and contrast adaptations displayed by animals and plants that enable them to survive in different environments such as life cycles variations, animal behaviors and physical characteristics. (Also, **SC.5.N.1.1, SC.5.N.2.1, LAFS.5.RI.2.5**)

CURRICULUM Connection

Have you ever made a delicious fruit salad for a picnic? A fruit salad might contain watermelon, oranges, kiwi, papaya, peaches, apricots, nectarines, and bananas. One of the hardest parts about making a fruit salad is avoiding all the seeds that fruits contain.

You may have eaten an orange and a peach. They are both round fruits, but on the inside the orange has small seeds and the peach has one giant pit.

Look at the cross section of an orange and a peach. The peach pit actually contains a seed.

Infer Why do you think the peach seed is enclosed in such a hard pit? Explain.

____

____

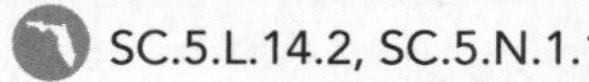

uInvestigate Lab

HANDS-ON LAB

SC.5.L.14.2, SC.5.N.1.1

What parts are inside a flower?

Scientists make observations and collect evidence to understand how nature works. How can you dissect a flower to see its parts?

Materials
- flower
- forceps
- toothpick
- hand lens

Wash your hands when done.

Dispose of materials properly.

Science Practice

Scientists **make observations** to answer questions.

Procedure

☐ **1.** Remove the petals of a flower. Describe what you see at the base of the flower. Predict what you might find inside this part.

____

____

☐ **2.** What do you think is the best way to observe what is inside this part? Write a procedure. Show your plan to your teacher before you begin.

____

____

☐ **3.** Record your observations by drawing what you observe. Include any important notes on your diagram.

Observations

Analyze and Interpret Data

4. Analyze Information Do your observations support your prediction? Explain.

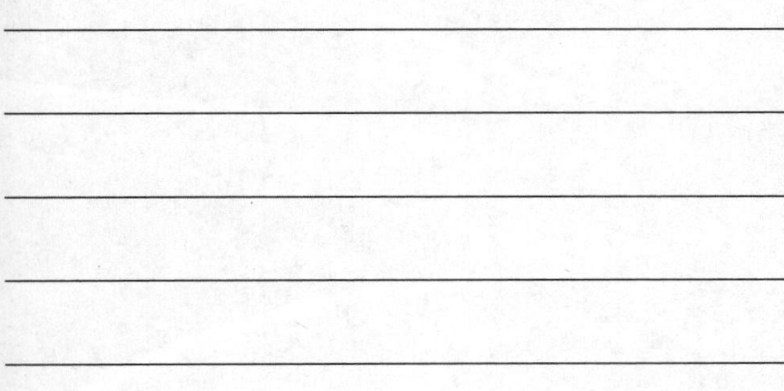

Literacy ▸ Toolbox

Compare and Contrast
You can understand plants better if you know how they are alike and different. Underline the parts of the definitions that describe the difference between external and internal structures in a plant.

 LAFS.5.RI.2.5

Plant Systems

Each organism is a system. The system is made of different **structures**, or organized parts, that work together to help the organism survive.

Plants have **external**, or outer, structures that are easy to see. The plant system also has structures that are **internal**, or inside the plant. These internal structures can best be seen and understood by cutting, or dissecting, the plant. When you cut open an aloe plant, which has a stiff, green exterior, you find a clear gel inside. Internal structures can be surprising like this.

Internal structures in plants take on many shapes. They can be large or so small that you can see them only with a microscope. Each kind can be in just one part of the plant or throughout many parts of the plant. The kinds of internal structures plants have depend on their environment.

Reflect What is your favorite plant? What structures does it have that make it different from other kinds of plants?

Functions of Plant Structures

Each structure of a plant has a **function**, or particular job. Some of the most important functions are survival, growth, protection, and reproduction. The internal structures of a plant function to help the plant survive and remain healthy. They may aid in protection or help with growth and reproduction. The functions of each kind of internal structure are more specific. For example, the **ovary** of a flower is the female reproductive part that helps the plant reproduce. Its specific function is to produce eggs and provide a place for seeds to develop. The seeds inside a tomato start out as eggs in the ovary of a tomato flower.

INTERACTIVITY

Complete an activity on the structure of flowers.

READING CHECK Compare and Contrast
Each plant's system has internal structures that help it survive. How would the functions of a plant system be different between a plant living in a desert and one living in a forest?

____

____

____

____

____

Question It! Fruits develop when a protective layer grows around a seed. What questions would you ask to determine which fresh produce you eat is a fruit?

____

____

____

Visual Literacy Connection

What are some functions of internal leaf structures?

Plants need to make food to survive. Plants use a process called photosynthesis to make food, or sugar. Three internal structures of the plant help in this process.

The veins of a plant draw water from the soil up into its leaves. The leaves use the water and carbon dioxide in the air to produce sugar.

Infer **What do you think would happen to a plant that does not have chloroplasts?**

____

____

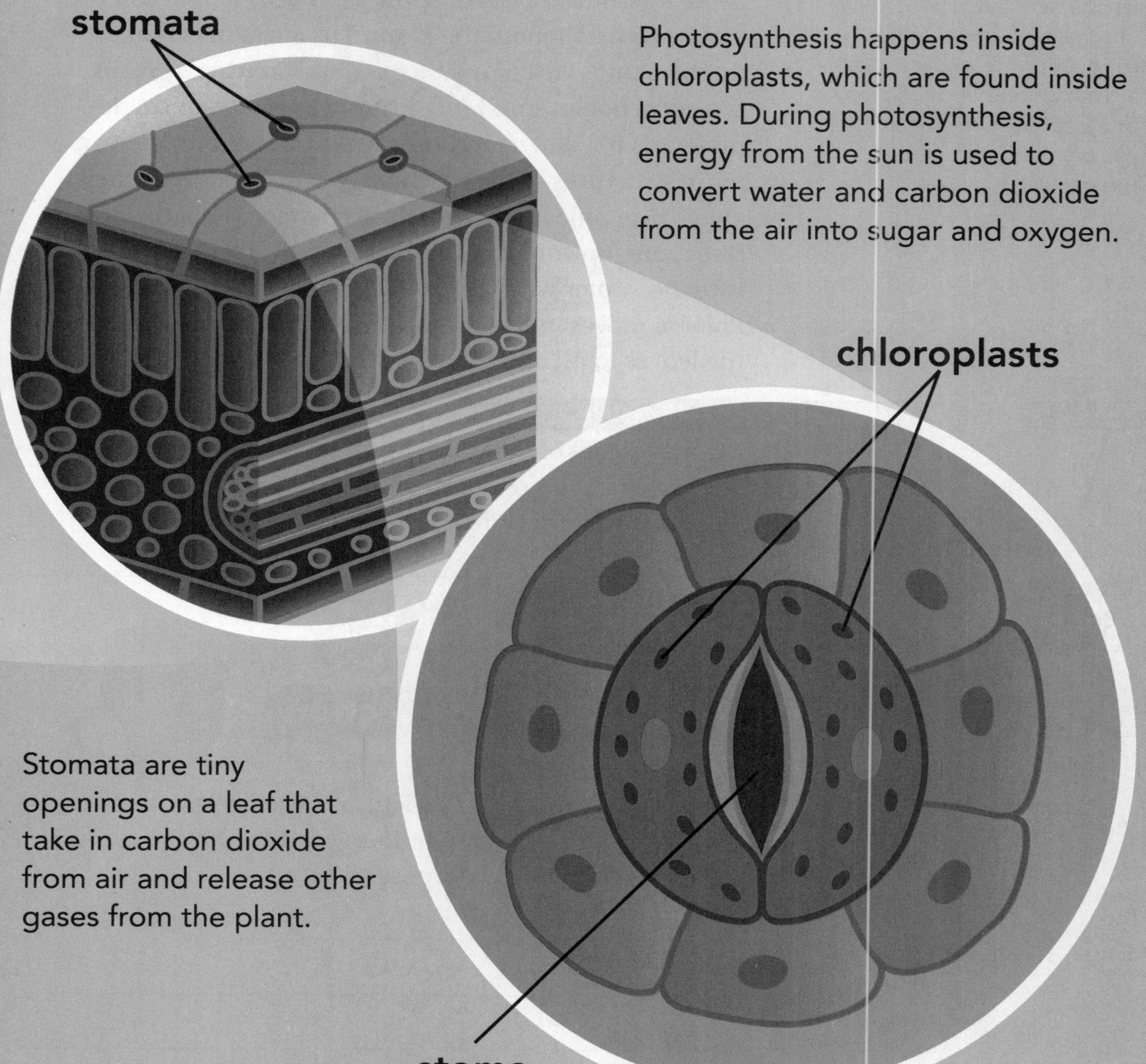

Photosynthesis happens inside chloroplasts, which are found inside leaves. During photosynthesis, energy from the sun is used to convert water and carbon dioxide from the air into sugar and oxygen.

Stomata are tiny openings on a leaf that take in carbon dioxide from air and release other gases from the plant.

uBe a Scientist

Make a Plant Collection

With an adult, go outside and collect three plant parts. Try to pick parts that have already separated from the plant. Safely cut or break the parts open, and use a magnifying lens to search for internal structures. Some suggestions to observe are a twig, a stem of dandelion, or a big leaf. Draw what you see, and try to label the parts.

The Structure and Function of Stems

Plants make their own food using the process of photosynthesis. During photosynthesis, a plant needs sunlight, carbon dioxide, and water. These materials must reach the plant's leaves. In addition, the food that the leaves make must reach the other parts of the plant. Without this food, the plant's cells would not have a source of energy and would die.

Some internal structures of the stem help move these materials throughout the plant. The structures make up the plant's vascular system. The **vascular system** is a collection of small tubes that transports, or carries, materials up, down, and throughout the plant. The two main structures of the vascular system are tubes called xylem and phloem. Xylem moves materials in only one direction—upward from the roots to all the plant parts. It carries water with dissolved nutrients from the roots. Phloem moves in many directions. It transports food from the leaves to all other parts of the plant.

READING CHECK **Compare and Contrast** Contrast the movement of materials in xylem and phloem by drawing arrows beside each label on the diagram. Then write one way they are the same.

____

Quest Connection

Choose a plant. Find a structure of the plant with an interesting shape. What human products have a similar shape with a similar purpose?

____

____

____

Plant Adaptations to Their Environment

One group of plants that has adapted to its environment is the cactus. The cactus must survive in the desert, where little rain falls. The internal structures of the cactus take in water when it rains and store it for a long time. This process takes place in the cactus stem, which is larger than stems in most kinds of plants. With these internal structures, the cactus can survive in very dry weather.

Lesson 1 Check

SC.5.L.14.2, SC.5.L.17.1

1. **Define** Fill in the missing spaces in the table to summarize two internal plant structures and their functions.

Structure	Function
xylem	
	transports sugars throughout the plant

2. **Investigate** The Venus fly trap is an unusual flowering plant that obtains some of its nutrients from insects. How would you investigate the structures that the plant uses to eat insects?

____

____

____

Quest Check-In Lab

How can you observe a plant's vascular system in action?

Scientists use dyes to highlight certain structures of a plant. The celery that you buy in a grocery store is the stem of the plant. How can you observe how the stem moves materials?

Materials
- celery stalk with leaves
- plastic knife
- food coloring
- water
- clear containers
- plastic gloves
- apron

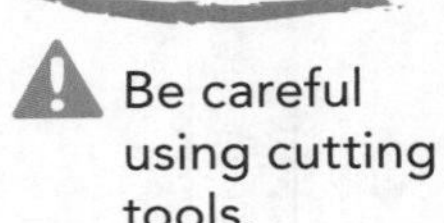

Be careful using cutting tools.

Do not taste.

Wash your hands when finished.

Wear plastic gloves and apron.

Procedure

☐ 1. What internal structures do you think are in the stem? Describe their functions.

____

____

☐ 2. How can you use the materials to observe the function of the celery stem? Make a plan. Show your plan to your teacher before you begin. Record your observations.

Science Practice

Scientists use evidence to construct an argument.

Observations

SC.5.L.14.2, SC.5.N.2.1

Analyze and Interpret Data

4. **Use Evidence** Make an argument about where the xylem is in the celery stem. What evidence from your investigation supports this argument?

5. **Apply Concept** Xylem transports water. What human products can you think of that transport water? What human problem do they solve?

Lesson 2

External Structures and Functions of Plants

I can...

Describe some external structures that help plants survive and reproduce.

Literacy Skill
Compare and Contrast

Vocabulary
cuticle
sepal
stamen
pistil

Academic Vocabulary
classify

SC.5.L.14.2 Compare and contrast the function of organs and other physical structures of plants and animals, including humans, for example: some animals have skeletons for support—some with internal skeletons others with exoskeletons—while some plants have stems for support. **SC.5.L.17.1** Compare and contrast adaptations displayed by animals and plants that enable them to survive in different environments such as life cycles variations, animal behaviors and physical characteristics. (Also **SC.5.N.1.1**)

ENGINEERING Connection

Have you ever gone apple picking? Most apples that are sold in supermarkets today are picked by hand, and most workers pick thousands of apples a day. Handpicking can be slow and tiring. Engineers tried to make the process faster by developing a machine that shook the apple tree to make the apples fall off. The problem was that when the apples fell, they would bruise.

Engineers designed another machine called the apple vacuum harvester. One part of the machine is a tube with a slippery lining inside it. A worker stands on the edge of the machine, handpicks the apple, and puts it in the tube. The tube carries the apple to a large bin where a fanlike structure gently arranges the apples. The machine eliminates the need for ladders and prevents the workers from having to carry all the apples.

Write About It In your science notebook, tell how you think the apple vacuum harvester helps orchard owners and people who buy apples.

VIDEO

Watch a video about external reproductive structures.

uInvestigate Lab

HANDS-ON LAB

SC.5.L.17.1, SC.5.N.1.1

How are leaf coverings different?

Scientists collect evidence to understand plant structures and functions. How do leaf coverings help plants survive in different environments?

Materials
- 2 plant leaves
- water
- dropper
- hand lens
- crayons
- gloves

Procedure

☐ **1.** Observe the leaves. Describe how they are different.

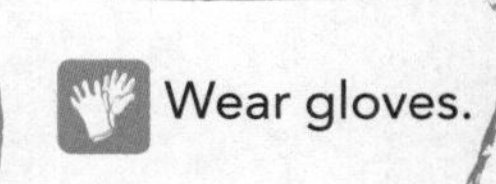

☐ **2.** Plan a procedure to investigate what happens to water on each leaf covering. Show your plan to your teacher before you begin. Record your observations.

Science Practice

Scientists gather evidence to defend conclusions.

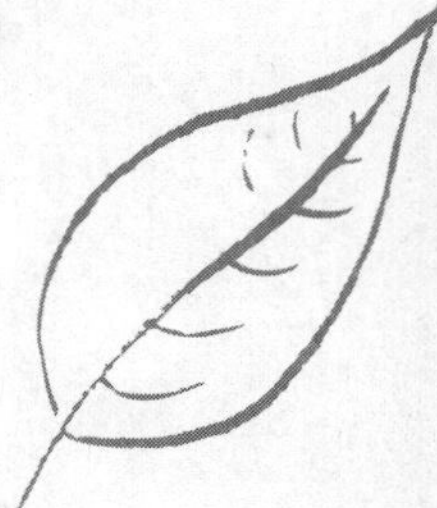

Analyze and Interpret Data

3. Use Evidence Which type of leaf do you think would function best in a dry climate? Support your conclusion with the evidence you gathered.

uBe a Scientist

Plant Comparison
Identify two plants you are familiar with. Develop a diagram that explains how two of their external structures are alike and different. Present your diagram to classmates.

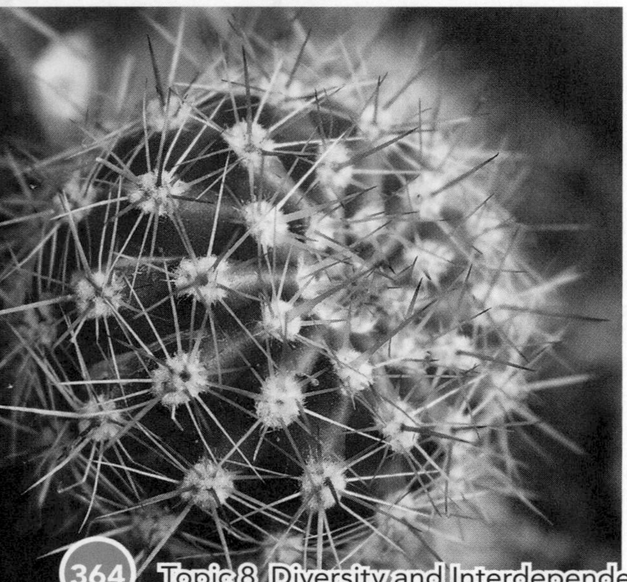

External Structures of a Plant

The external structures of plants are probably the ones you are most familiar with—the leaf, stem, roots, and flowers. You might also be familiar with two other external features—bark and thorns. Just like internal structures, the external parts of plants help them survive, grow, and reproduce.

Plants lose water through their leaves. The leaves have a **cuticle**, or a waxy outer covering. The cuticle helps limit the amount of water a plant loses. Plants that live in a desert environment often have thick leaves with a smooth, waxy cuticle. The thick, waxy coating gives the plant extra protection against water loss. The thick leaves help the plant store water. The same process also works in reverse. The waxy cuticle prevents unwanted water from entering the plant leaf. While water is good for a plant, it is best taken in through the roots of the plant and not the leaves. The cuticle cannot completely seal the plant leaf. It must work with the stomata to make sure that air can enter the plant.

Plants often attract animals for help with reproduction. When animals eat the red berries on the plant, they help scatter the seeds inside the berries. Plants also need to prevent the animal from eating them. One way to do this is with thorns, which are sharp, pointy structures on plant leaves or stems. Cacti contain a lot of water, and thirsty animals would want to eat them. Thorns like those on this cactus, help keep animals away. Roses have prickles, which are similar to thorns.

READING CHECK Compare and Contrast Even though they look different, how are a leaf cuticle and a thorn the same?

____

____

Stems and Their Coverings

Stems come in many forms. Some stems are green. Other stems are woody. Scientists can **classify**, or group, stems according to their structures and functions. The type of stem a certain kind of plant has depends on the environment in which it must survive.

Tree trunks, for example, are covered in bark. This outside barrier protects the tree from harmful materials or organisms in its environment. The bark of some kinds of trees is thick. Other kinds of trees have thin bark. The bark on this Scots pine tree is very thick. The thick bark protects it from the fires that often happen in its environment. Trees with thin bark are more likely to die when fires happen.

Model It! Diagrams are one kind of model. Draw the trunk of a tree that must survive in a windy environment. Next, draw the trunk of a tree that has no wind in its environment. Focus on how the trunk might change because of the wind.

Quest Connection

Tree bark protects the trunk of a tree. Humans also need protection. What are some kinds of body covering that humans use for protection?

____

____

Visual Literacy Connection

Which structures do flowering plants use to REPRODUCE?

Flowering plants have external structures that help them reproduce.

Petals have a variety of colors, patterns, shapes, and odors that attract pollinators. Pollinators are animals that transfer pollen from a stamen to a pistil.

The **stamen** is the male part of a flower that makes pollen. Pollen is the male reproductive cell.

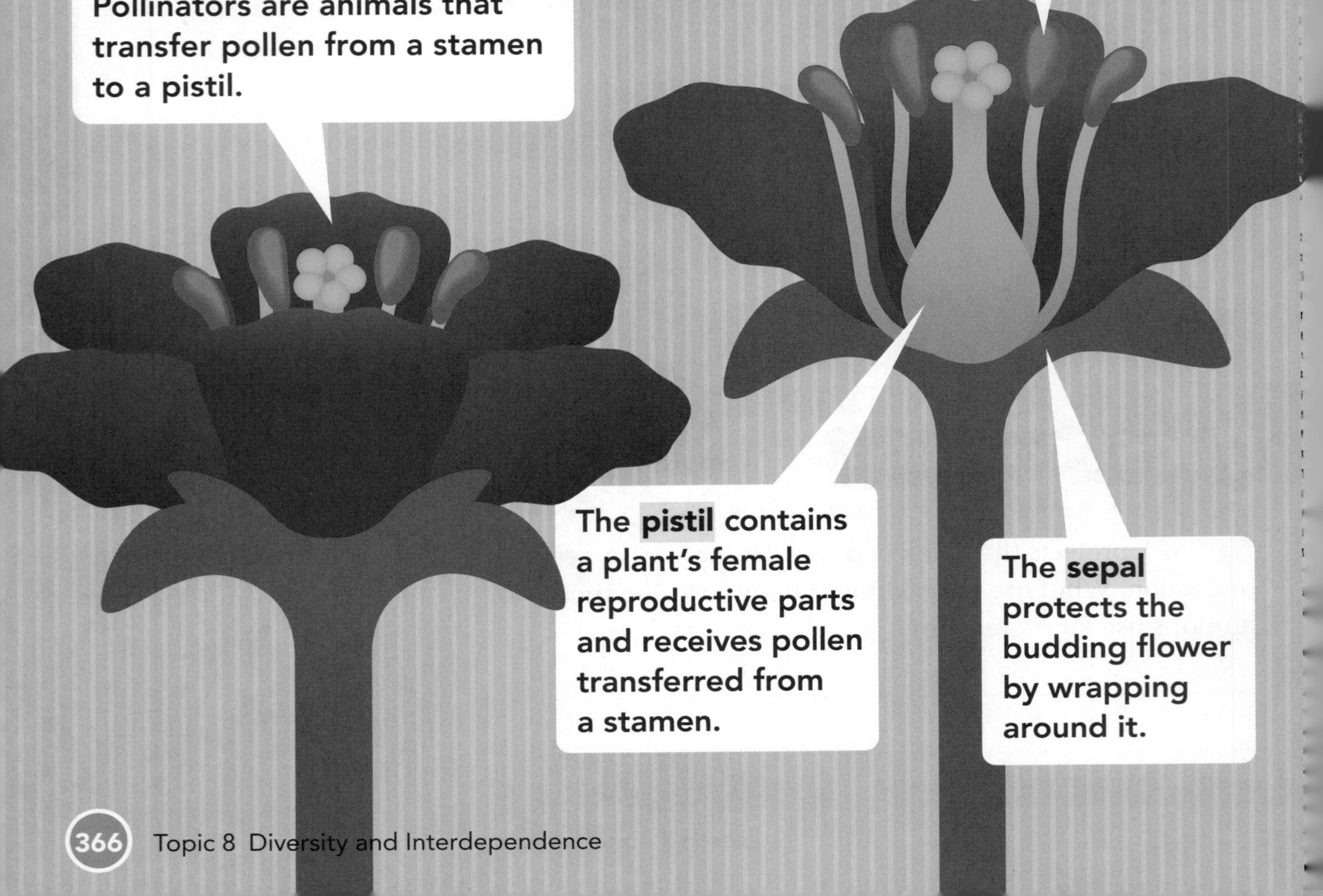

The **pistil** contains a plant's female reproductive parts and receives pollen transferred from a stamen.

The **sepal** protects the budding flower by wrapping around it.

INTERACTIVITY

Complete an activity on external structures of plants.

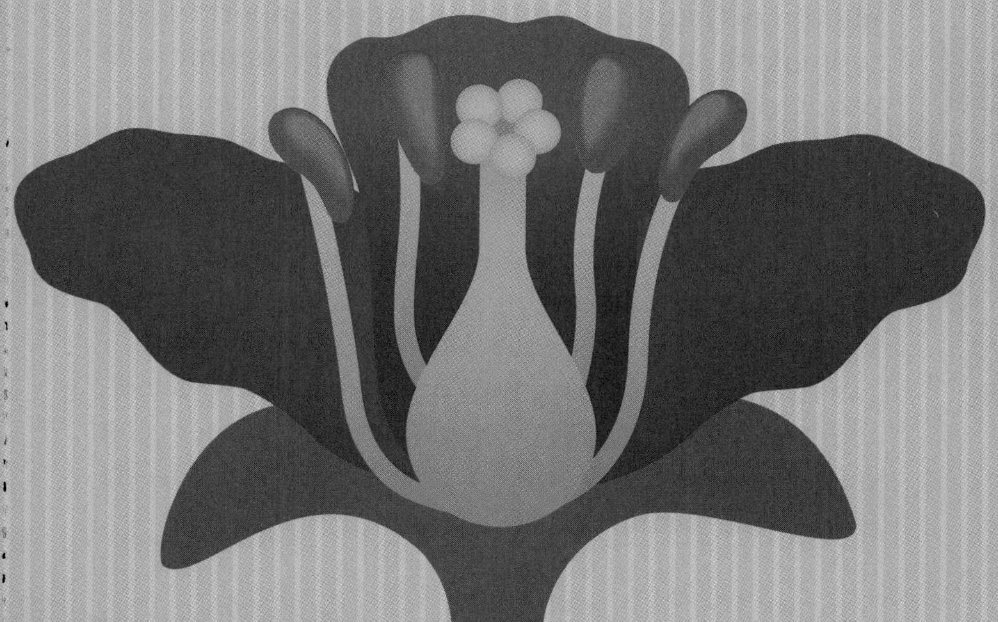

Infer How do you think petals protect the internal structures of a plant?

Compare How do the numbers of male and female reproductive structures of this flower compare?

Adaptations of Flowers

Why do flowers come in so many different colors? Over time, some kinds of flowers have developed colors, patterns, shapes, and odors that certain kinds of animals like. These adaptations are important for making sure that the right kind of pollinator is attracted to the flower. For example, birds that take nectar from a flower need a flower structure that they can perch on.

A bee is one very important pollinator of flowering plants. Many people think bees are attracted to the bright flower colors we see. However, scientific tests have provided evidence that bees are also attracted to ultraviolet light, which we cannot see. Flower colors and ultraviolet light often make patterns that direct bees to the location of the nectar.

Lesson 2 Check

SC.5.L.14.2, SC.5.L.17.1

1. **Predict** Suppose a disease caused the cuticle on a plant's leaves to disappear. What would most likely happen to the plant? Why?

____

____

2. **Explain** How are the functions of a flower's stamen and pistil related to reproduction?

____

____

____

____

Throwing Seeds Around

Plants have developed many different ways to scatter their seeds. If seeds are scattered, they are more likely to survive when they sprout because they do not compete as much for things they need.

The photos show structures that plants have developed to help them disperse their seeds.

The female pine cone stores the seeds until they are ready to be dispersed.

The milkweed seed pod explodes, flinging its seeds great distances.

The coconut can float for long periods because its covering traps air.

The light fluffy seeds of the dandelion are easily blown by the wind.

Interpret Photos Choose one of the seeds and explain how it might be used to solve a human problem.

____

____

____

____

____

QUEST CHECK OFF

Lesson 3

Internal Structures and Functions of Animals

I can...

Describe some internal structures that help animals survive.

Literacy Skill

Compare and Contrast

Vocabulary

skeleton
heart
lungs
gills
brain

Academic Vocabulary

interpret

SC.5.L.14.2 Compare and contrast the function of organs and other physical structures of plants and animals, including humans, for example: some animals have skeletons for support—some with internal skeletons others with exoskeletons—while some plants have stems for support. **SC.5.L.17.1** Compare and contrast adaptations displayed by animals and plants that enable them to survive in different environments such as life cycles variations, animal behaviors and physical characteristics. (Also **SC.5.N.1.1, MAFS.5.MD.1.1**)

VIDEO

Watch a video about internal structures of animals.

STEM Connection

Have you heard of catgut? Sounds gross! However, it is not really the guts of a cat. Catgut is made from the intestines of other animals. For a long time, medical sutures were made from catgut. Sutures are the stitches that are used to close up a wound. To make the material of catgut, the animal intestines were twisted into a cord shape. They were sterilized to make them safer to use on wounds. Today, other materials, such as cotton, are commonly used to make sutures. These materials are cheaper to make, and they cause fewer infections.

Identify What are two advantages of using newer materials rather than catgut?

____

____

uInvestigate Lab

HANDS-ON LAB

SC.5.L.14.2, SC.5.N.1.1

How can you compare the stomachs of cows and dogs?

Materials
- Cow and Dog Stomachs sheet
- metric ruler

Scientists compare similar structures in different animals to help them understand how structures are unique to each kind of animal. How can you compare the stomach of a cow and a dog?

Science Practice

Scientists **use evidence** to support an argument.

Procedure

☐ **1.** Observe the diagrams of the cow and dog stomachs. What are three features that you can use to compare and contrast the stomachs?

☐ **2.** Make a table to record your observations of the features of the two stomachs.

Feature	Cow stomach	Dog stomach
Location in body		
Shape		
Number of pouches		

Analyze and Interpret Data

3. Compare A cow is bigger than a dog. How does the size of the animal compare to the size of its stomach?

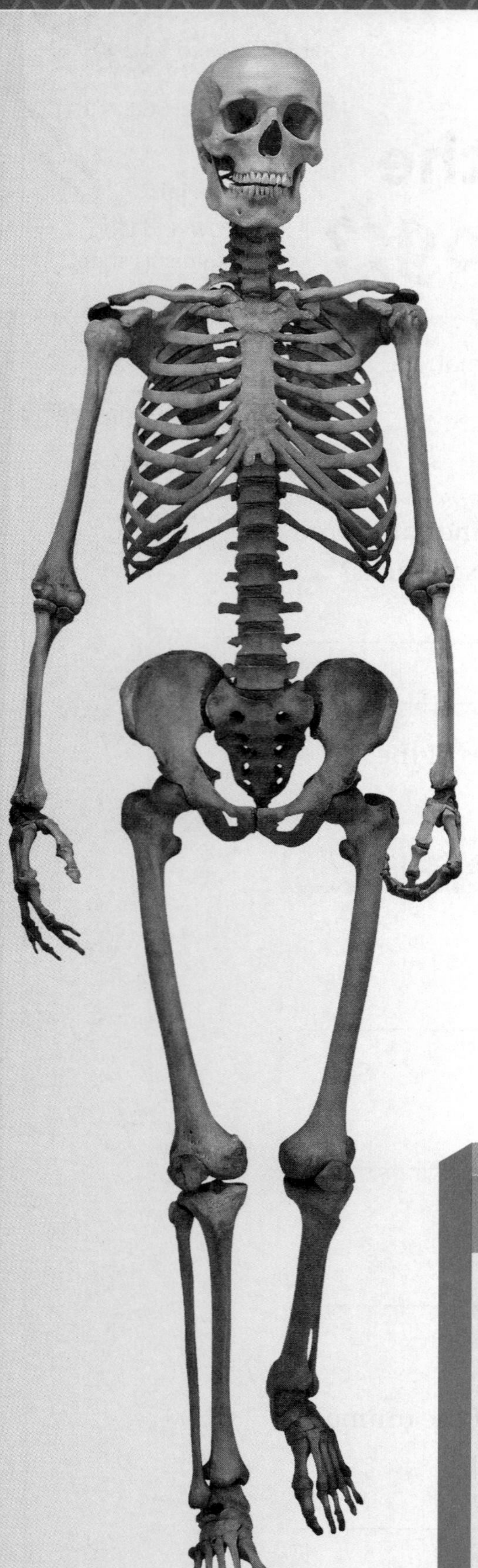

Animal Structures for Support

Like plant bodies, animal bodies need support. Because most animals move, they need a different kind of support system than plants need. All mammals, including humans and dogs, have a **skeleton**—a rigid support system that includes bones that connect to the soft structures of the body. Without a skeleton, a mammal would have little shape and be unable to move. Animals with an internal bony skeleton are called vertebrates. They include mammals, fish, frogs, snakes, and birds.

READING CHECK **Compare and Contrast** Label the parts of the human skeleton with the same labels shown on the dog skeleton.

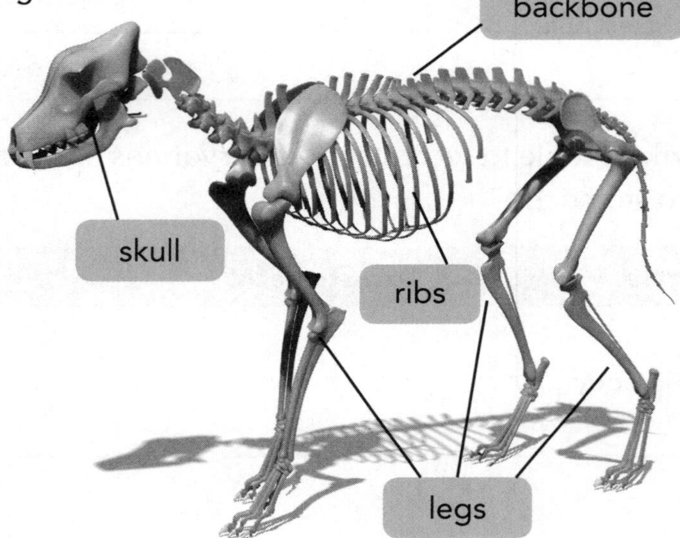

Quest Connection

Identify a situation in which a human might need something strong and sturdy for support. What product would you suggest?

____

____

____

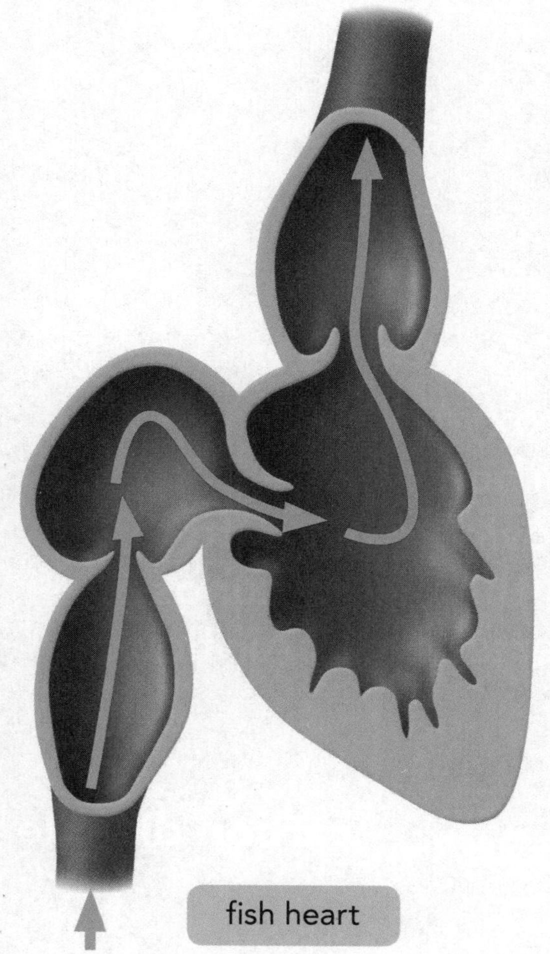

fish heart

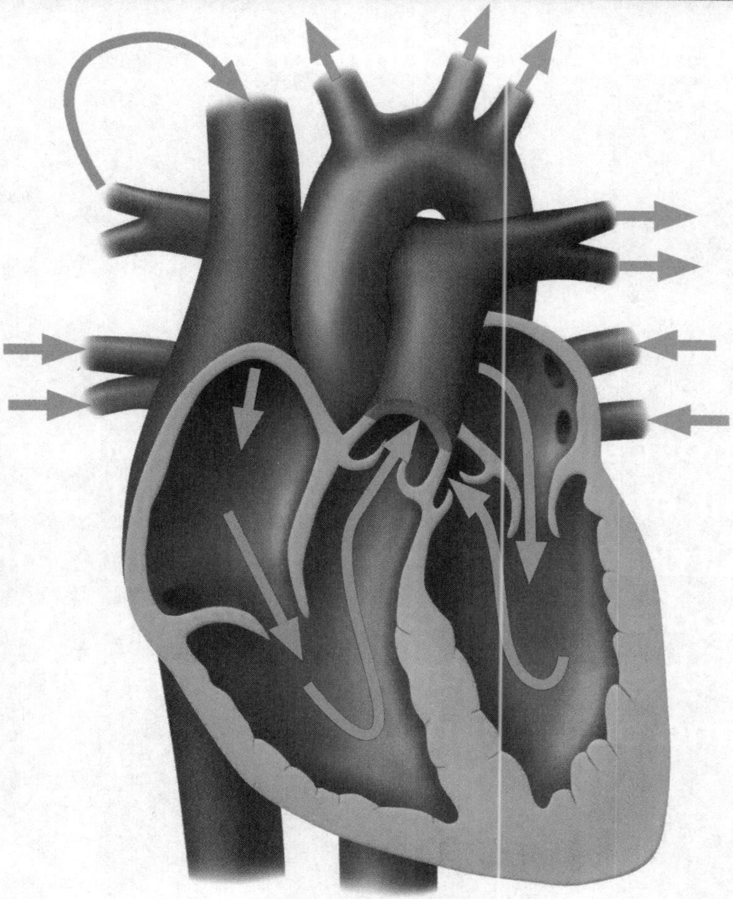

mammal heart

Structure of the Animal Heart

Vertebrates rely on blood to carry many of the materials they need to all parts of the body. For blood to move through the body, something must pump it. In vertebrate animals, the **heart** is the internal organ that pumps blood. It usually is located near the center of the body. The ribs of the skeleton protect it.

Most vertebrates that live in water have hearts that pump blood around the body in one circular motion. Vertebrates that live on land usually have hearts that pump blood in two different circles. One side of the heart pumps blood from the heart to and from the lungs. The other side of the heart pumps blood from the lungs to all parts of the body.

READING CHECK **Compare and Contrast** Underline the differences between the hearts of vertebrates that live in water and the hearts of vertebrates that live on land. Circle the similarities.

Math ▸ Toolbox

Compare Amounts An adult heart pumps about 5 L of blood each minute. An athlete's heart can pump as much as 35 L a minute. How much more blood does an athlete's heart pump per minute when compared to an average adult heart?

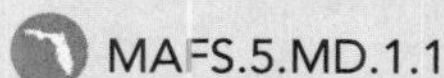
MAFS.5.MD.1.1

Visual Literacy Connection

How do lungs and gills compare?

Almost all living things must take in oxygen gas from their environments and get rid of carbon dioxide gas that their bodies produce. **Lungs** provide oxygen to the blood and take carbon dioxide from the blood. Lungs are the paired breathing organ of vertebrates. Air flows in and out of lungs.

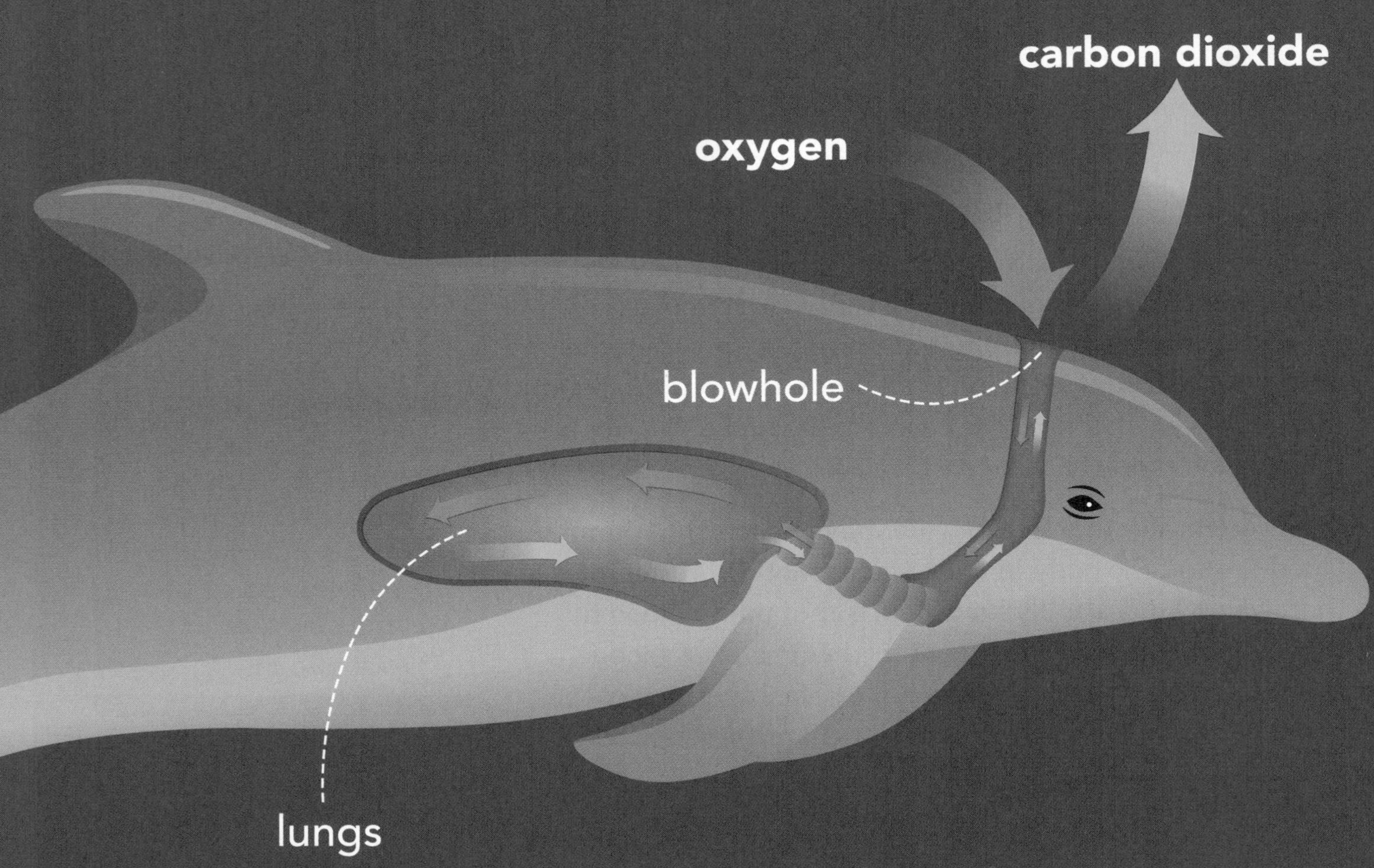

INTERACTIVITY

Complete an activity on the structures and functions of internal animal parts.

In fish, the process happens in the gills. **Gills** are organs that take in oxygen from water as it flows over them.

Infer Why do you think fish and mammals, such as dolphins, have different structures to perform the same function?

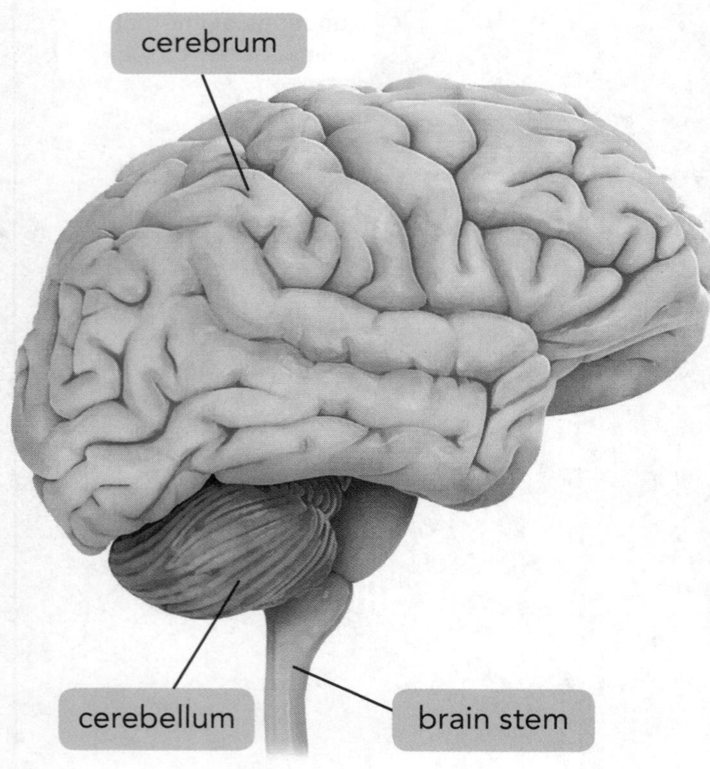

Structure of the Animal Brain

The **brain** is the structure that receives information about an animal's environment. It **interprets**, or figures out the meaning of, the information it receives and tells the body how to respond. In vertebrates, the brain is located inside the protective skull. Different parts of the brain are involved in different functions. For example, the cerebrum is the thinking part of the brain. It gets the information about an animal's environment. The cerebellum coordinates the animal's movement. The brain stem controls how many internal structures function.

Infer People sometimes say that serious thinkers are *cerebral*. Why do you think they use that word?

Lesson 3 Check

1. **Infer** Suppose a classmate told you that vertebrates do not need a skeleton. Explain how lacking a skeleton would affect vertebrates.

2. **Evaluate** How are lungs and gills adapted for different types of environments?

Fish Float and Sink

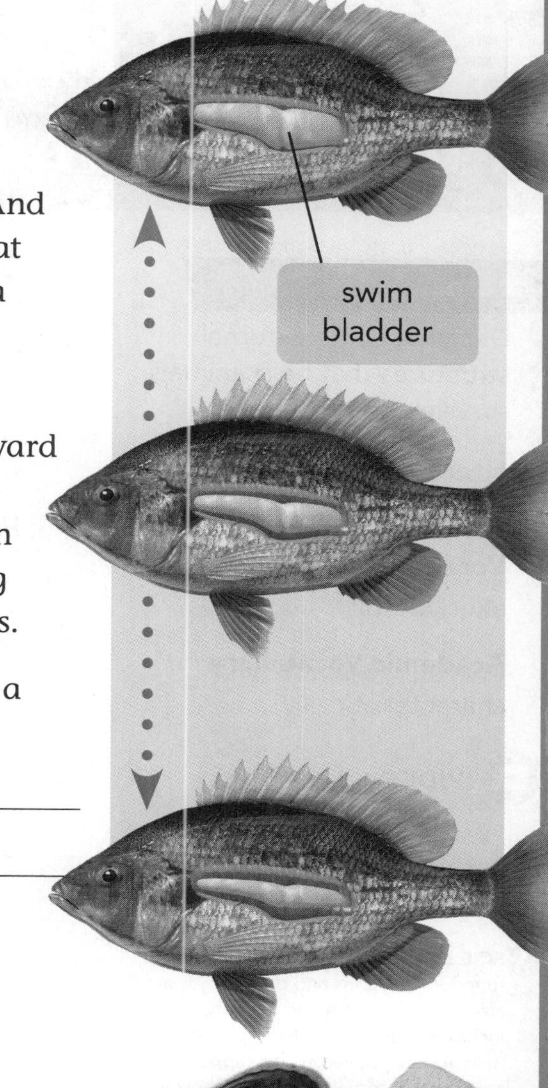

Did you ever wonder why a fish can float day after day? And how does it move upward or downward? The reason is that some fish have a swim bladder. The swim bladder is like a balloon inside the fish. The more gas that is in the swim bladder, the higher the fish will float.

The swim bladder is surrounded by muscles. To move upward in the water, the fish relaxes the muscles around the bladder, and it fills with more air. To move deeper, the fish tightens the muscles, and the air is pushed out. By sinking and floating, the fish can gather food and avoid predators.

Identify Which existing human inventions are similar to a fish's swim bladder?

____

____

Brainstorm Think of an invention based on a fish's swim bladder that could solve a human problem. Identify the problem in your response.

____

____

____

QUEST CHECK OFF

Lesson 4

External Structures and Functions of Animals

I can...

Describe some external structures that help animals survive and reproduce.

Literacy Skill
Compare and Contrast

Vocabulary
exoskeleton

Academic Vocabulary
characteristic

VIDEO

Watch a video about external structures of animals.

SC.5.L.14.2 Compare and contrast the function of organs and other physical structures of plants and animals, including humans, for example: some animals have skeletons for support—some with internal skeletons others with exoskeletons—while some plants have stems for support. **SC.5.L.17.1** Compare and contrast adaptations displayed by animals and plants that enable them to survive in different environments such as life cycles variations, animal behaviors and physical characteristics. (Also **SC.5.N.1.1**)

CURRICULUM Connection

A horse's tail is surrounded by long, flowing hair. The long hair has a useful function of swatting away flies that bite the horse. Humans use the hair of the horse's tail in a different way. If you have ever seen someone play the violin, you have seen one way humans use horsehair. It is used in the bow of the string instrument. The horsehair is stretched into a thin ribbon to serve as the bow. When it glides across the violin strings, it makes a sound that we hear as music. People have been using horsehair this way for more than 400 years.

Infer Why do you think horsehair is preferred for bows over dog hair ?

STEM uInvestigate Lab

HANDS-ON LAB

SC.5.L.14.2, SC.5.N.1.1

How can you design a protective insect shell?

Scientists design models to find solutions to problems. How can you design a model insect with a protective shell that helps the insect survive?

Suggested Materials

- aluminum foil
- paper
- tape
- small foam balls
- toothpicks
- pipe cleaners
- cardboard
- crayons
- pieces of plastic

Design and Build

☐ 1. Consider the scenario your teacher has provided. What criteria must the outer shell of your insect meet to protect the insect?

____

____

____

Science Practice

Scientists **develop and use models** to test interactions.

☐ 2. Draw a design for your insect. Plan how you will test your insect to see whether it meets the criteria. Show your drawing and plan to your teacher before you begin. Record your observations.

My Insect

Evaluate Your Design

3. **Evaluate Models** Compare your design with those of others. Which design met the criteria best? Why do you think that is so?

____

____

____

____

____

____

____

Visual Literacy Connection

What do exoskeletons do?

Not all animals have support systems similar to those of vertebrates. The support structure for some animals is an **exoskeleton**, a hard external covering that is waterproof. The exoskeleton protects the soft body parts underneath. Large exoskeletons are called shells.

Snail

A snail's shell protects the snail from the sun and water loss. The shell also acts as a way for the snail to camouflage itself in its environment.

INTERACTIVITY

Complete an activity on external structures of organisms.

Ladybug

A ladybug's exoskeleton helps to protect its wings. Ladybugs have two pairs of wings, a set of wings that are hard like their exoskeleton, and then a set of flying wings that are softer.

Crab

A crab's shell helps protect its internal structures from its aquatic environment. Its shell is waterproof, which helps crabs survive.

Other External Structures of Animals

For animals that do not have an exoskeleton, other external structures provide protection.

Skin Skin protects the animal body and acts as a barrier against harmful materials. Skin can be different colors or textures. Rhinoceroses have thick, rough skin to protect them from the hot African sun and biting insects. Naked mole rats have soft, thin skin because they live underground where the soil is cool and dark.

Fur, Feathers, and Scales Some animals have fur, feathers, or scales for protection. The bear's fur is thick to keep it warm in cold weather. Bird feathers protect against temperature changes. Feathers also enable most birds to fly. Birds can fly to avoid predators, to look for food, and to migrate. The scales of reptiles and fish are a rough covering that protects and insulates the body.

Claws Claws are sharp, pointy structures on the feet of mammals, reptiles, and birds. They are used for capturing, carrying, and tearing apart prey.

READING CHECK **Compare and Contrast** Underline the words that show how the skin of a naked mole rat and the scales of a fish are alike. Circle how they are different.

Quest Connection

Fur covers some animals and helps them regulate their body temperature in different climates. What is a product for humans that can regulate body temperature? How does it work?

___

___

___

Animal Characteristics

A **characteristic** is a quality or trait. Some characteristics of animal structures include color, size, and shape. Animals of the same kind share most characteristics, but sometimes the characteristics of the same structures are a bit different. An animal's characteristics enable the animal to survive and reproduce in its environment. For example, when male tree frogs are looking for a mate, they croak loudly by using special folds of skin that they can inflate, or blow up. Female tree frogs are usually attracted to the loudest sound because it often means that this male frog is the healthiest among other males.

Make Meaning In your science notebook, identify some characteristics you share with other humans. Which of your characteristics are unique to you?

Lesson 4 Check

SC.5.L.14.2, SC.5.L.17.1

1. **Identify** What are two external structures of the frogs in the picture? How do they help the frogs survive?

2. READING CHECK **Compare and Contrast** How is an exoskeleton similar to the skeleton of vertebrates?

Lobster Claws

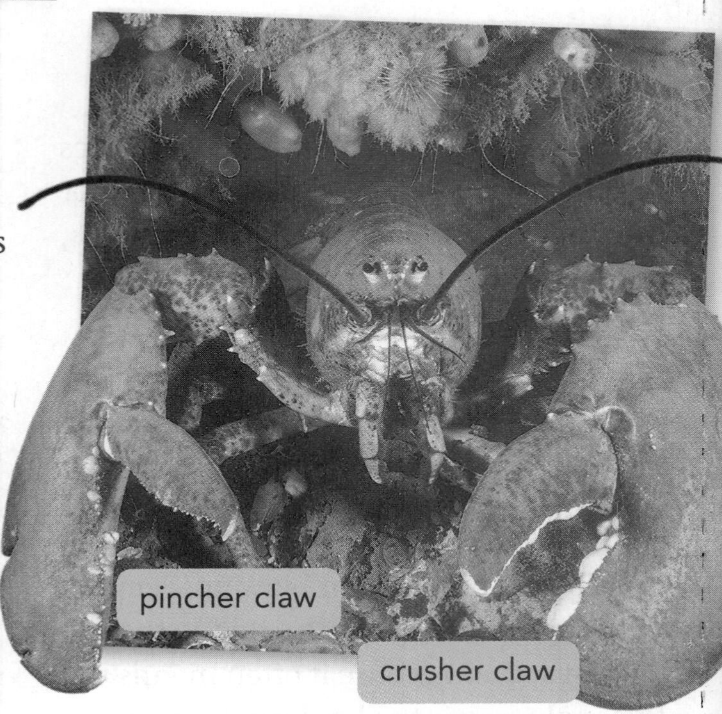

One external structure that all lobsters share is their claws. A lobster has two types of claws—crusher claws and pincher claws. The crusher claw is larger and used to crush prey. The pincher claw has small "teeth" that help the lobster capture and open the shells of its prey.

Brainstorm Can you think of an invention that would help humans and is inspired by one type of lobster claw? How would the invention help humans?

____

____

____

Design a Model Draw a design of your invention.

My Model

SOLVE it WITH Science

Why do animals shed their exoskeletons?

Did you ever need new clothes because you outgrew your old ones? As your body grows, your clothes do not grow with it. In some ways, a rigid exoskeleton is similar to the clothes that humans wear. When an animal sheds its exoskeleton, the exoskeleton separates from its body, and the animal leaves it behind. A new exoskeleton then forms around the animal.

Why does the praying mantis in the photo need to shed its exoskeleton? Use evidence from the text as you consider these questions.

- What are some functions of exoskeletons?
- How does an exoskeleton limit an animal?
- What do you think might happen if the insect did not shed its exoskeleton?

Use what you considered to write a **science-based explanation** to answer the question in the title.

____

____

____

____

____

____

Lesson 5

Plant and Animal Responses to the Environment

I can...

Explain how animals use sensory information to respond to their environments.

Describe how plants and animals can survive in different environments because of adaptations.

Literacy Skill
Compare and Contrast

Vocabulary
extinct

Academic Vocabulary
stimulus

VIDEO

Watch a video about animal responses.

SC.5.L.15.1 Describe how, when the environment changes, differences between individuals allow some plants and animals to survive and reproduce while others die or move to new locations. (Also **SC.5.N.1.1**)

ENGINEERING Connection

Dogs have heightened senses and can often hear and smell things that a human cannot. For this reason, dogs are often used to detect particular odors. For example, at airports, dogs are used to sniff for bombs and drugs. The dogs help keep people safe so that nothing harmful gets on a plane. Dogs are also often sent on search parties to find people who are missing. They will smell a shirt that has the scent of a person on it. Then they will search for a similar scent. When they get on the trail of a scent, dogs will follow it with their nose until they find the missing person. Engineers are working to design an artificial, or human-made, nose that can act like a dog's nose. They have analyzed the way a dog detects a scent and have begun to mimic it in their designs.

Apply If you had a keen sense of smell like that of a dog, what do you think you would smell that you cannot smell now?

____

uInvestigate Lab

HANDS-ON LAB

SC.5.N.1.1

How can you locate an object using only sound?

Scientists use models to answer questions about how animals sense the world around them. How can you find an object using only the sound it makes?

Suggested Materials

- blindfold
- bucket
- bell
- cooking pot

Procedure

☐ **1.** Choose any object that makes a sound. Make a plan to model an animal that relies on sound to locate what they need.

☐ **2.** Show your plan to your teacher before you begin. Record your observations.

Science Practice

Scientists use models to better understand how something works.

Analyze and Interpret Data

3. Model How successful were you in locating the sound? Explain.

Visual Literacy Connection

How do elephants respond to stimuli?

When animals receive a **stimulus**, or a nerve signal, the signal is sent to their brain. The brain interprets the signal. It then sends messages telling the body how to respond. Elephants receive information through their sense of sight, hearing, and touch.

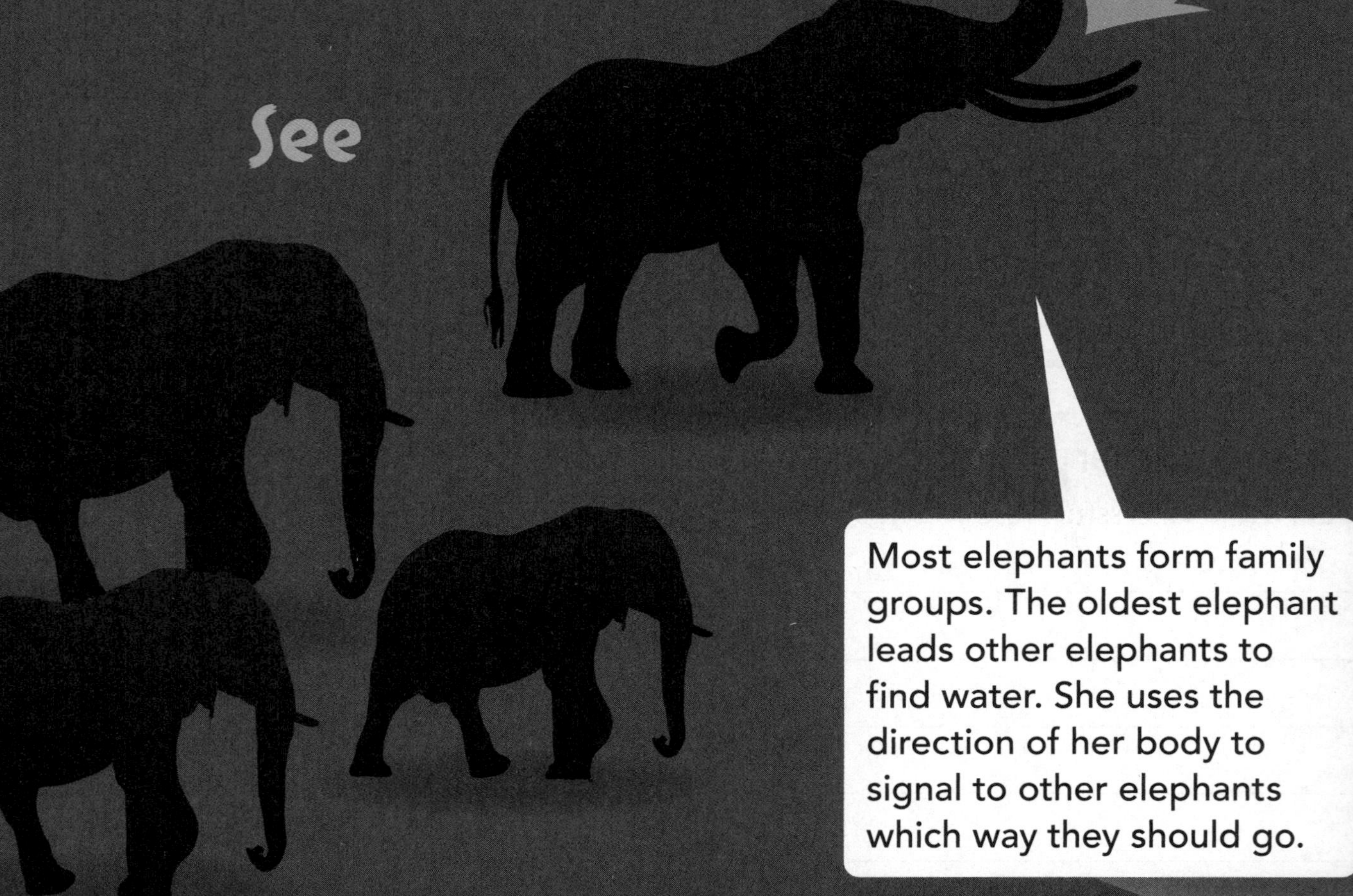

Most elephants form family groups. The oldest elephant leads other elephants to find water. She uses the direction of her body to signal to other elephants which way they should go.

Hear

Elephants use their trunks to make loud calls to signal the other elephants of danger in their environment. Usually, the older elephants will form a circle around the younger elephants to protect them.

Feel

Elephants make low rumbling sounds to communicate with each other. Elephants feel the vibrations of the sound on the ground with their feet. Humans cannot hear these sounds.

Describe **How do your senses help you respond to different stimuli you encounter in your environment?**

Complete an activity on repsonding to the environment.

uBe a Scientist

Test Your Senses
Plan an investigation that will test your sense of smell. Write a procedure, and share it with an adult before you begin. Present your results to your classmates.

Animal Responses to Smell

Some animals have a sense of smell that is much stronger than that of humans. Animals with a keen sense of smell include bears, sharks, dogs, and snakes. These animals use their keen sense to find food or to observe that another animal is nearby. If they identify the approaching animal as an enemy, they can flee or hide. Snakes collect scent through their nostrils, though their tongue is better.

Apply How might the sense of smell help a mother protect her offspring?

____

____

Quest Connection

How could you study an animal's senses to design a product for humans who are missing one of their senses?

____

____

____

Changing Environments and Survival

Environments can change, and plants and animals must be able to survive in those changed environments. Plants and animals that have adaptations to live in the new environment will survive. If an environment changes and a particular kind of plant or animal cannot survive there, that kind of organism may become extinct. When a kind of organism becomes **extinct**, no more of that kind of organism lives on Earth. Once a kind of organism is gone, it is gone forever.

Analyze What changes in the environment could cause a plant or animal to become extinct?

____

____

____

Science Practice ▸ Toolbox

Ask Questions Suppose a kind of animal is in danger of becoming extinct. What questions would you ask to find out how you could help save the animal?

Behaviors and Survival

Many animal behaviors help animals survive. Some animals, such as deer, form groups for safety. Animals that stick together are often better able to communicate that a predator is near. Bears hibernate in cold weather when food is scarce. While it hibernates, a bear does not need as much energy from food. Penguins do not hibernate, so they form huddles to survive cold winter climates. Some animals that are not adapted to the cold migrate. Many birds fly south for the winter to avoid colder temperatures and fly north again when it is warmer.

Reflect In your science notebook, tell how you survive changes in your environment.

Lesson 5 Check

1. **Analyze** An animal is not able to see in a dark environment. What other ways could the animal gather information about its surroundings to find food in the dark?

____

____

2. **READING CHECK Compare and Contrast** How are seasonal behaviors of bears and penguins alike and different?

____

____

____

Quest Check-In

Sound Off!

Bats are nocturnal, which means they are awake at night and asleep during the day. They live in dark environments, such as caves. Because there is little light when they hunt insect prey, they rely on their sense of hearing. They do this through a process called echolocation.

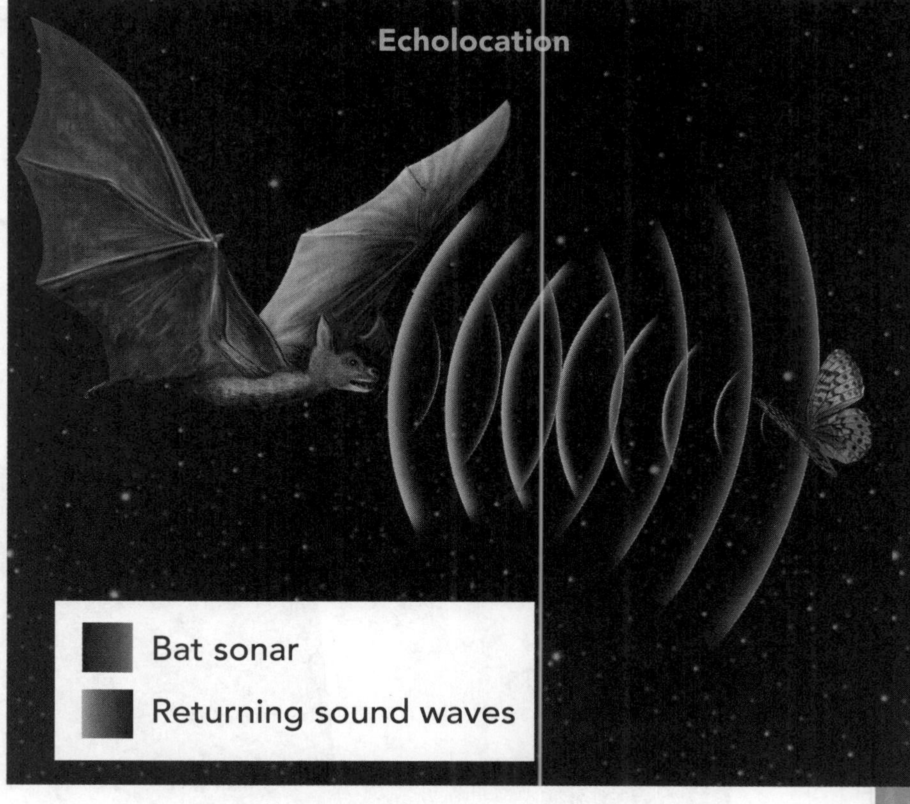

When a bat emits, or lets out, a sound, the sound bounces off the wall of the cave, an insect, or other objects in its environment. The bounced sounds reach the bat's ears. These bounced sounds give the bat information about the objects in its environment. The information allows the bat to know how close or how large an object is. This helps the bat locate its prey.

Summarize How does a bat use sound to find an insect?

____

____

____

Relate In which situations do you think it could be helpful for humans to locate objects using sound?

____

____

____

____

SC.5.L.17.1

uEngineer It! Model STEM

Eye See You!

VIDEO

Watch a video about optical detection technology and how it was modeled after an animal eye.

Animal eyes are unique and extraordinary. Different kinds of animals can see in different environmental conditions, such as dark and light. Nature photographers use different kinds of cameras that can produce good images in different conditions. Cameras function the same way eyes do—both have a lens that focuses the light that comes into the eye. When animals need to see prey at night, the pupils of their eyes allow more light to come in so that their vision is enhanced.

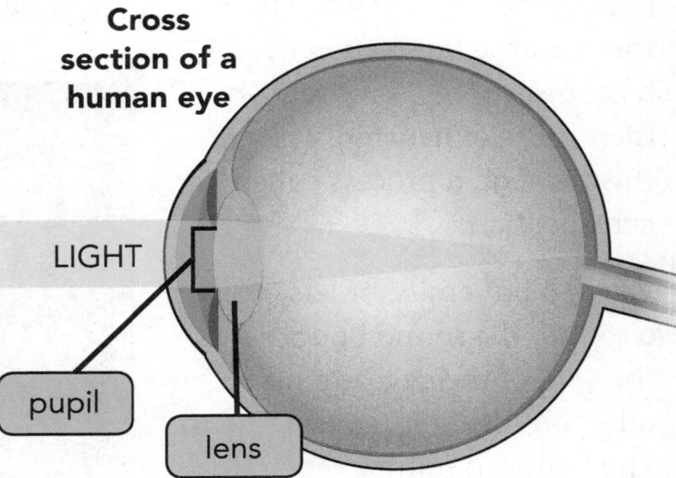

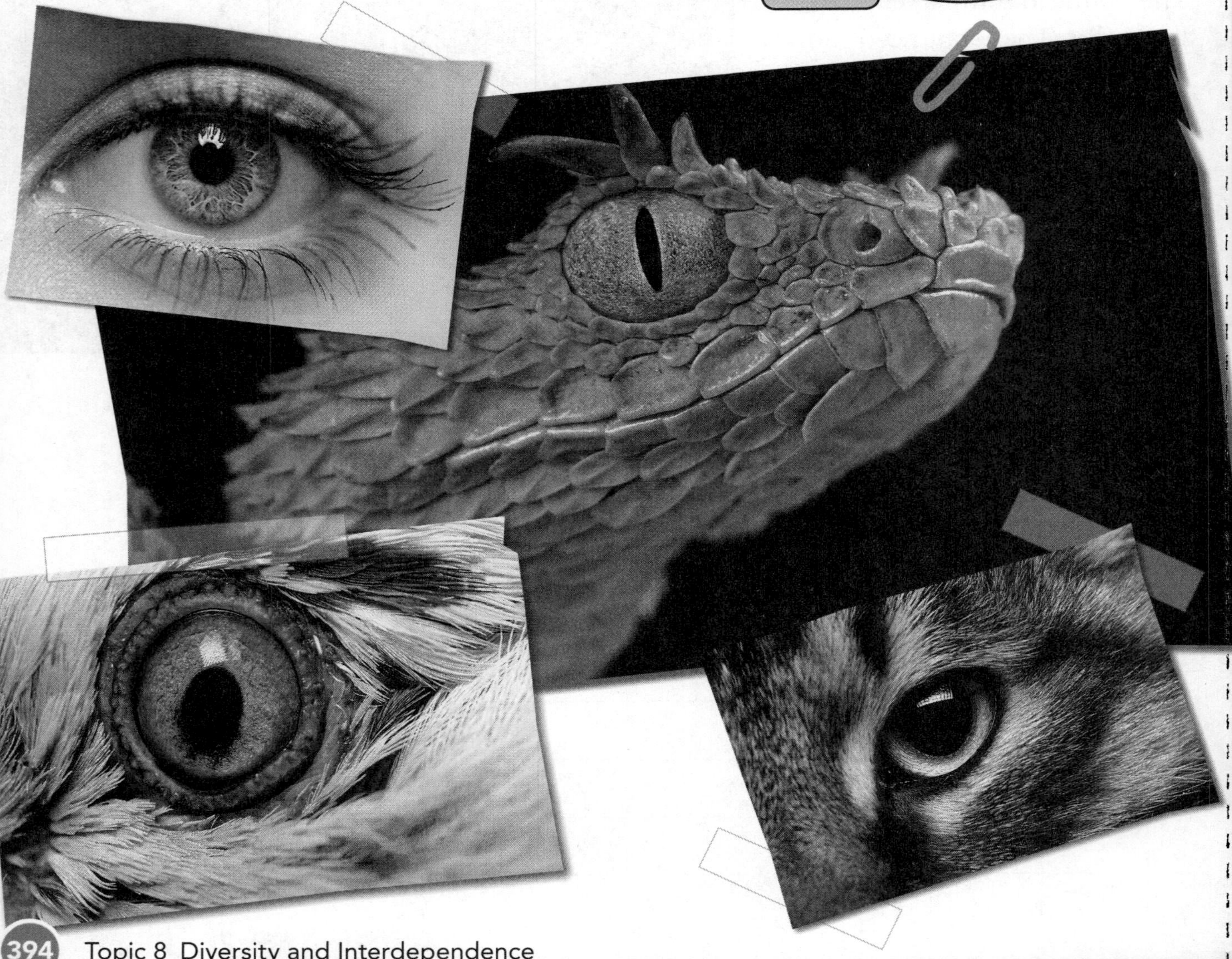

Model It

Suppose you want to make a model that you could use to teach younger students about animal eyes.

- ☐ Choose an animal and research how it sees.
- ☐ In your model, what stimulus will the eye receive? For example, will it see food or a prey animal?

____

____

- ☐ What are the conditions of the environment—dark, light, hot, cold?

____

____

- ☐ Think about how to show all the parts of the eye in your model.
- ☐ Draw and label your model animal eye. Show how light travels when it enters the eye.

Quest Findings

INTERACTIVITY

Organize your information to build your model.

STEM

Let Plants and Animals Inspire You!

Which human problem can you help solve using what you learn about plants and animals?

You explored many plant and animal structures that have useful functions. Now it is time to choose a plant or animal structure to inspire a product that will solve a human problem of your choosing. It can be an internal or an external structure. Be creative!

Explain

Choose one plant or animal structure. Decide how you will use this structure to create a product that could solve a human problem. What problem will it solve?

____

____

____

____

____

____

Design and Build Your Model

Draw your design. Present your design idea to the class, and ask for feedback to improve your design. Then build your model!

QUEST CHECK OFF

Career Connection

Nature Photographer

A nature photographer takes pictures of scenes and objects in nature. These include flowers, rocks, trees, mountains, grass, and rock formations. A nature photographer also photographs animals in their natural habitats. The animals can be as common as birds, insects, and prairie dogs, or as exotic as cheetahs, pythons, and lions.

The tools nature photographers use are a camera with film or a digital photo card and the photographer's creative mind. They capture different angles of objects. Their photos are used for scientific research about plants and animals. Pictures are also used in textbooks, on Internet Web sites, in travel brochures, and sometimes just for fun!

You can be a nature photographer no matter where you live because nature is everywhere, but you have to like working outdoors! Also, sometimes travel is involved because different nature scenes may be in another state or country.

The job of nature photographers is rewarding because people are often inspired by their photos. Without nature photographers, we would know less about what certain plants and animals look like in places we do not visit.

Write About It
Do you think you could be a nature photographer? What are things in nature you would like to photograph?

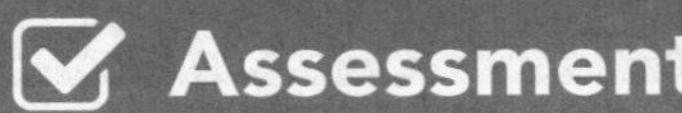

Assessment

Read each question and choose or write the best answer.

1. **Identify** Which structure helps the vascular system in plants perform its primary function?

   A. broad leaves

   B. long tubes

   C. stomata

   D. prickly spines

2. **Describe** The picture shows some of the internal structures of a certain animal. What is the name of the internal structure shown and what is its most important function?

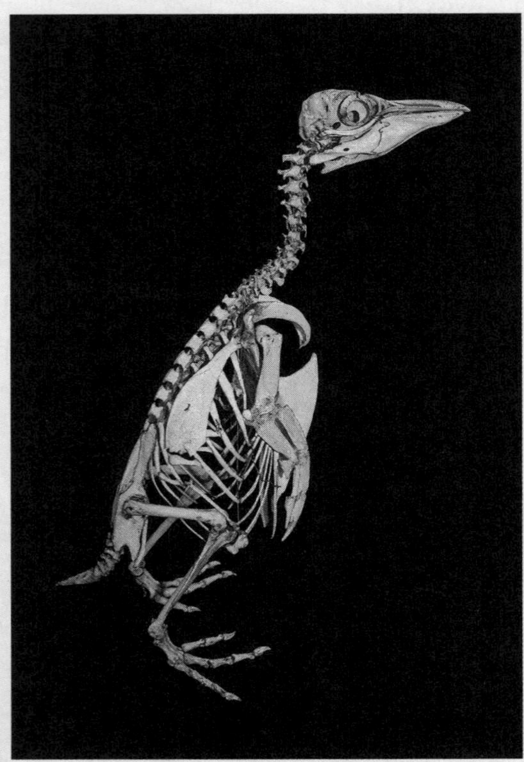

3. **Use Evidence** Do you think the organism in the photo spends most of its time in water or on land? Use structure and function evidence from the photo to support your claim.

4. **Use Reasoning** In a field of flowering plants, each plant competes with the others for sunlight, water, and soil nutrients. Use this information to explain why the fluffy, floating seeds of dandelion plants provide survival advantages.

5. **Interpret Diagrams** Scientists studied the behavior of migrating birds in different amounts of light. They estimated the number of birds in an area. Then they turned on two beams of light and estimated the number of birds again.

Effect of Large Light Display on Bird Density

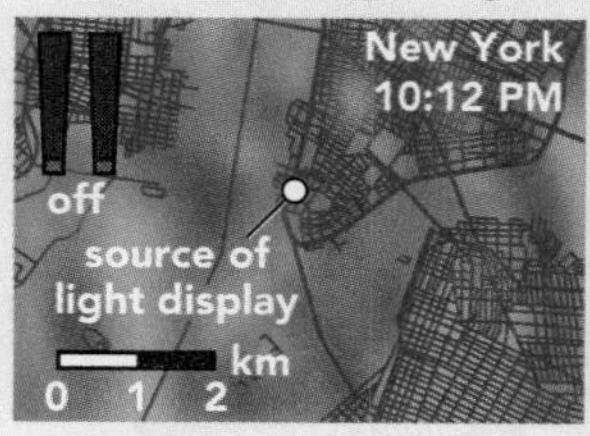

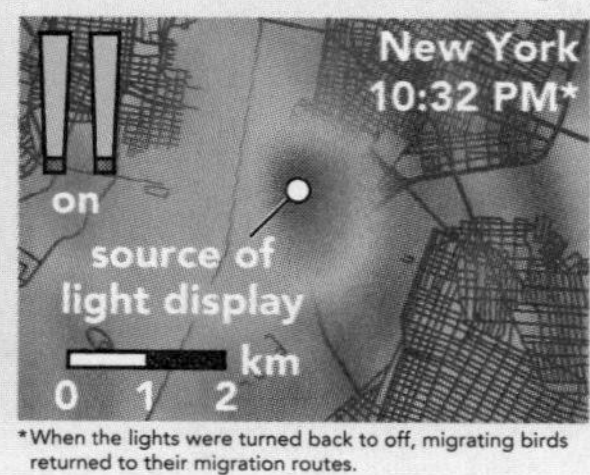

*When the lights were turned back to off, migrating birds returned to their migration routes.

What evidence from the diagrams supports this claim: Birds respond to stimuli in their environment.

6. **Observe Patterns** To increase the likelihood of reproduction, many flowering plants have _______.

A. flowers with a ring of petals around the stamen and pistil

B. seed pods that burst to spread seeds

C. clusters of flowers on long stems

D. flowers with long pistils and stamens that extend past the flower's petals

7. **Apply** Which sentence describes a behavior that helps an animal survive?

A. An animal goes into hibernation during winter.

B. The heart pumps blood through an animal's body.

C. Animals become tired after running long distances.

D. Fur coloration helps an animal blend into its environment.

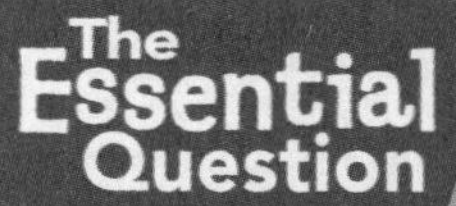

How do plant and animal structures support growth and survival?

Show What You Learned

How do plant and animal structures help them survive in different environments?

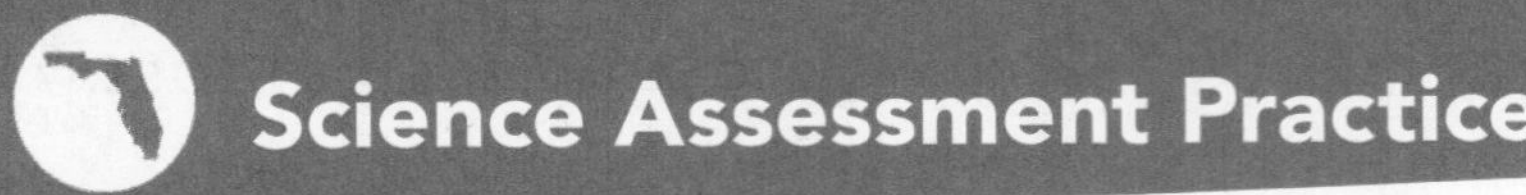

Science Assessment Practice

Read the scenario and answer questions 1–2.

Plants have specialized cells called stomata on the underside of their leaves. During the day, the stomata close to prevent water loss. The stomata open and take in carbon dioxide at night and store it until the daytime when photosynthesis can take place. Cells use the movement of water to open and close the stomata.

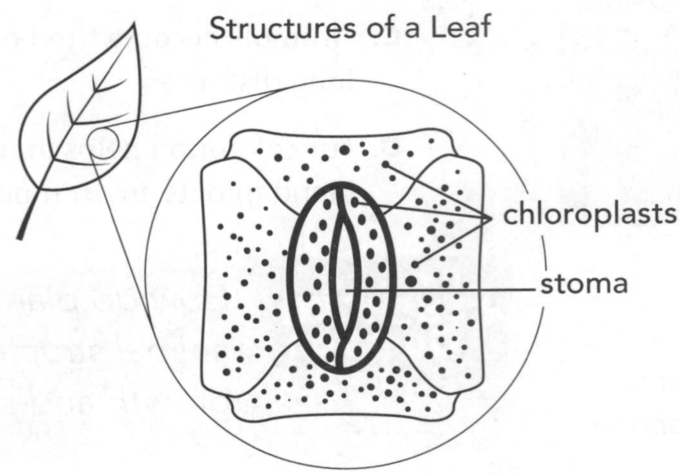

1 **Connect** Which statement **best** describes a similarity between stomata and human sweat glands?

Ⓐ Stomata and sweat glands take in materials from the environment.

Ⓑ Stomata and sweat glands help an organism respond to changes in its environment.

Ⓒ Stomata and sweat glands help control body temperature.

Ⓓ Stomata and sweat glands are controlled by nerves.

2 **Formulate** Think about the function of the leaf structure shown in the diagram. What kind of plant is **more likely** to survive if the amount of carbon dioxide in the air decreases?

Ⓕ a plant that has many of these structures on every leaf

Ⓖ a plant where these structures can close very tightly

Ⓗ a plant where these structures absorb more oxygen

Ⓘ a plant that does not perform photosynthesis

Read the scenario and answer questions 3–4.

A flying insect was looking for food. It landed on this flower twice and then flew away.

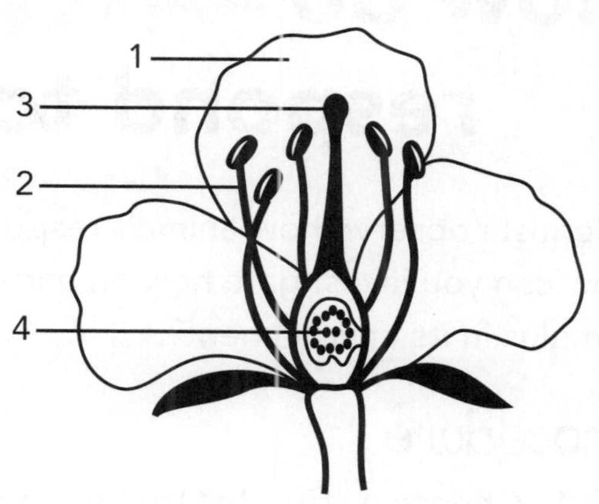

3 **Draw Conclusions** As a result of the insect's visit, the flower produced seeds. Where did the insect most likely touch the flower?

Ⓐ first 2, then 3

Ⓑ first on 1, then on 3

Ⓒ first on 3, then on 4

Ⓓ twice on 3

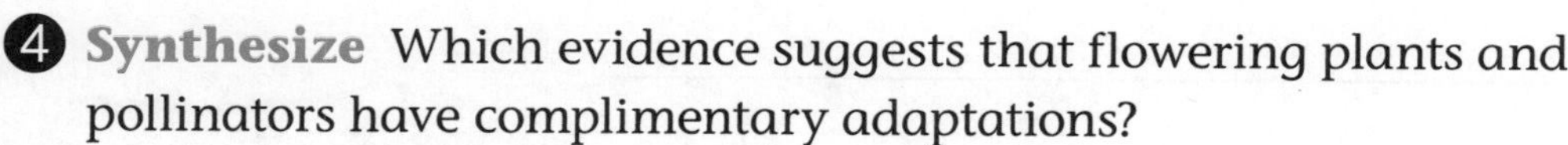

4 **Synthesize** Which evidence suggests that flowering plants and pollinators have complimentary adaptations?

Ⓕ Butterfly wings are made of many overlapping scales, not stretched skin.

Ⓖ Plants with long-tube flowers attract hummingbirds with long, needle-like beaks.

Ⓗ Hummingbirds must feed frequently on plant nectar to have enough energy.

Ⓘ Bees tend to avoid red flowers.

5 **Explain Phenomena** Zebras are grazing animals that live in herds. Which statement correctly explains why herding behavior provides the zebra with a survival advantage?

Ⓐ Zebras living in a herd are less likely to compete for resources.

Ⓑ Living in herds reduces competition for mates.

Ⓒ Living in herds reduces the spread of disease.

Ⓓ In a herd, each zebra is less likely to get caught by a predator.

uDemonstrate Lab

How do earthworms respond to stimuli?

Scientists observe how animals respond to different situations. How can you investigate how an earthworm responds to a stimulus in its environment?

Materials
- earthworm
- plastic gloves

Suggested Materials
- container
- spray bottle with water
- water dropper
- soil
- warm and cold water
- paper towels
- aluminum foil

Procedure

☐ **1.** Choose a stimulus that you want to test with your earthworm. Predict how an earthworm will react to this stimulus.

____

____

____

____

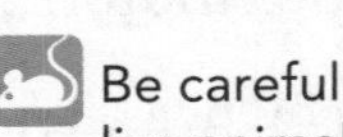

Be careful with live animals.

Wash your hands when done.

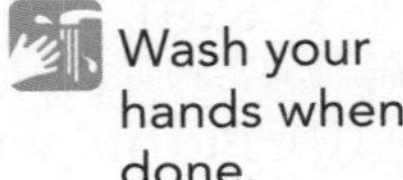

Wear plastic gloves.

☐ **2.** Make a plan to test the stimulus you chose. Remember to control your variables. Show your plan to your teacher before you begin.

____

____

____

____

____

____

____

Science Practice

Scientists **analyze information** from investigations.

☐ **3.** Conduct your investigation and record your results.

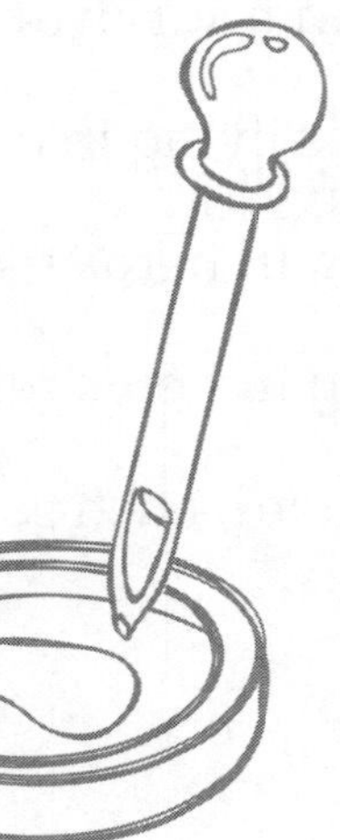

Observations

Analyze and Interpret Data

4. **Analyze Data** Does your data support your prediction? Explain.

____

____

____

____

5. **Draw Conclusions** What conclusion can you draw from your observations?

____

____

____

____

How do scientists ask and answer questions?

Questions and Investigations

Science is the study of the natural world using scientific tools and methods. The natural world includes things like matter, energy, the planets, and living things.

A scientist asks questions and then tries to answer them. For example, a scientist might wonder what causes ocean waves to move. The scientist could first study what others have already learned. Then the scientist could investigate, or look carefully at, questions that have not been answered.

Scientists look for answers by doing experiments and making observations. They keep records to share what they learn. They use their results to form explanations. A scientific explanation is an answer based on evidence. Evidence is what scientists gather from experiments and observations. For example, a scientist studying waves in the ocean might measure wind speed and wave sizes in an area. The data the scientist collects is evidence.

Ask Questions What questions would you ask about waves?

____

Reference Materials

Scientists use reference materials to learn more about their subjects. Reference materials include encyclopedias, books, journals, and certain websites on the Internet.

Scientists write articles in scientific journals to share what they learned. Other scientists read the articles to learn what others have already discovered.

Creativity

Science is focused on answering new questions. That often means that scientists must come up with new ways to answer questions. Designing a good experiment requires them to think of new ways to solve problems. They need to think about what could go wrong and how to fix it. For example, a scientist who studies tiny organisms in the ocean could use a machine that was first used in hospitals to count blood cells.

Plan Investigations Think about measuring the temperature of ocean water at different depths. How would you do it quickly and safely?

____

____

____

These researchers are investigating nature to answer their questions.

How do scientists work together?

Comparing Results

When a scientific investigation is repeated in exactly the same way, the results should be the same. Scientists compare their results. For example, a scientist may observe that the water pressure in the ocean increases as the water gets deeper. If someone else measures the water pressure at the same locations, the results should be similar.

After an investigation is done, other scientists repeat the investigation. They use the same tools and the same conditions. Then they compare their results with the results of the first investigation. Usually the results are the same. If the results are different, it is important to find out why. Sometimes, a very small change in conditions can cause a big change in the results. Sometimes, more than one tool can be used in an investigation. The results should be the same. If not, the scientists will compare results and try to find the reason for the difference.

Ask Questions You and a classmate get different results in an investigation. What question should you ask to find out why?

Keeping Records

During an investigation, scientists keep records of what they observe. Records can be written notes, drawings, charts, or graphs. Sometimes, scientists write their records in a notebook. Other records are on a computer. These records show exactly what was done in the investigation.

Scientists record their observations.

Records should be accurate. If records are complete and accurate, someone else can use them to do the investigation in the same way. Good records can help find what was different if two investigations give different results.

Communication

Scientists communicate with other scientists to share what they learned. The words that scientists use sometimes have different meanings than the same words in everyday communication. *Current, heat,* and *record* are examples of words that have a specific meaning in science. In science, for example, heat refers to the flow of thermal energy. In everyday use, heat may refer to the temperature on a warm day.

Communicate Scientists communicate in different ways. How could a scientist use a computer to communicate with another scientist?

____

____

____

How do scientists use evidence?

Empirical Evidence

Scientists use empirical evidence when they study nature. Empirical evidence is information that can be verified or disproven. It includes measurements and observations. Scientific conclusions are always based on evidence that can be tested.

For example, sea water tastes salty everywhere. Measurements and observations have shown that it contains different amounts of salt at different locations. It is usually less salty where rivers flow into the ocean.

These measurements can help answer questions about how water from a river mixes with water in the sea.

Measure Your friend thinks it is a hot day, but you think it is not hot. How could you get empirical evidence about the temperature of the air? Why is this empirical evidence?

____

____

____

SC.5.N.1.6 Recognize and explain the difference between personal opinion/interpretation and verified observation. **SC.5.N.2.1** Recognize and explain that science is grounded in empirical observations that are testable; explanation must always be linked with evidence.

Opinion

Scientific observations are different from opinions. An opinion is a personal belief and is not always based on facts. An example of an opinion is that tuna tastes better than salmon. There are no facts to support the opinion. An example of a fact is that salmon lay their eggs in fresh water. This statement can be supported by observation.

Which fish tastes better? That is a matter of opinion.

Support Claims with Evidence

Scientists use evidence to support their conclusions. For example, the conclusion that whales migrate is based on evidence. Whales can be seen in some areas but not in others, depending on the season. Scientists can also track individual whales to see where they go.

Evaluate You read in an advertisement that sandy beaches are more beautiful than rocky cliffs. Can you prove whether that claim is true? Why or why not?

____

____

Scientists can recognize an individual whale by the unique marks on its tail.

What are scientific models?

Models

Scientists often use models to help them understand something. You may be familiar with models like toy boats. A toy boat looks like a real boat, only smaller. It does not work like a real boat though. Models are objects or ideas that represent other things. A model shows only part of the object or system that it represents.

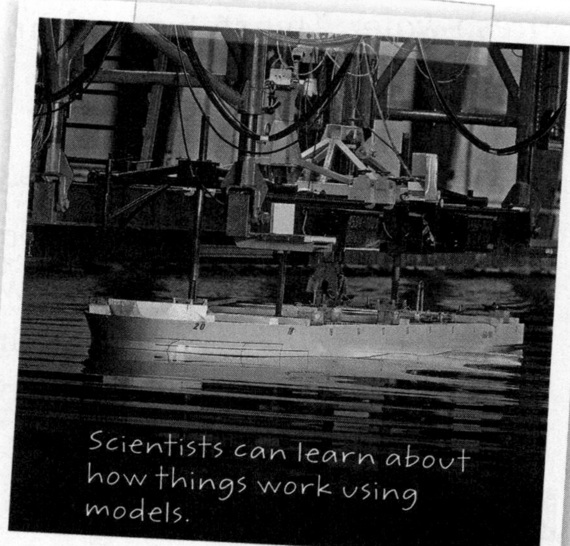
Scientists can learn about how things work using models.

Models can help scientists understand things that are too big or too small to observe. A map of the ocean floor is a model that shows how underwater mountains and plains are arranged. We cannot see these features from the surface.

Models can be two-dimensional or three-dimensional. A map of the ocean floor is a two-dimensional model. It shows some things about the ocean floor, but it cannot show the exact shape of the ocean's features. A toy boat is a three-dimensional model of a full-sized boat.

Scientists also use computers to make models. For example, a computer model can show how fast the water in an ocean current is moving and which way it flows.

SC.5.N.1.2 Explain the difference between an experiment and other types of scientific investigation. **SC.5.N.1.4** Identify a control group and explain its importance in an experiment.

Investigations and Experiments

Scientists observe the natural world to learn about how it works. There are different ways to learn about nature. One way to learn is through observation. When scientists make observations, they do not change anything. For example, a scientists who want to learn about changes in climate can observe the ice near the North Pole. The scientists do not change anything about the ice. Instead, they look at how the ice changes over time and draw conclusions based on evidence from their observations.

Scientists also investigate the world using experiments. In an experiment, scientists make a change to the thing they are observing. Scientists who want to find out how quickly salt dissolves in water at different temperatures might do an experiment. They might put identical amounts of salt and water in several containers. One container is left at room temperature and stirred to dissolve the salt; this is the control. To do the experiment, the scientists will need to change something. The thing that they change is called the variable. In this case, the variable is temperature. Scientists change the temperature of other containers to see if this makes the salt dissolve more easily.

Plan Investigations You want to learn how far the water is moving in an ocean current. Would you do an experiment or make an observation? Why?

____

____

____

____

How do scientists investigate?

Scientific Investigations

Scientists use scientific methods as they work in the many different fields of science. Scientific methods are an organized way to answer questions and solve problems. They are also a way of discovering cause and effect. Scientific methods often include some or all of the steps on the card.

- Ask a question and form a hypothesis.
- Use reference materials.
- Plan and carry out investigations.
- Collect and organize data in charts, tables, and graphics.
- Analyze and interpret data.
- Draw conclusions based on evidence.
- Report results.

These steps enable scientists to perform investigations, but not every investigation follows all of these steps. All scientific investigations include collecting data. Scientific conclusions are always based on evidence.

Plan an Investigation A scientist is investigating life cycles of lobsters. What are some things the scientist should observe?

____

____

____

SC.5.N.1.1 Define a problem, use appropriate reference materials to support scientific understanding, plan and carry out scientific investigations of various types such as: systematic observations, experiments requiring the identification of variables, collecting and organizing data, interpreting data in charts, tables, and graphics, analyze information, make predictions, and defend conclusions. **SC.5.N.1.3** Recognize and explain the need for repeated experimental trials. **SC.5.N.1.5** Recognize and explain that authentic scientific investigation frequently does not parallel the steps of "the scientific method." **SC.5.N.2.2** Recognize and explain that when scientific investigations are carried out, the evidence produced by those investigations should be replicable by others.

Evaluate Investigations

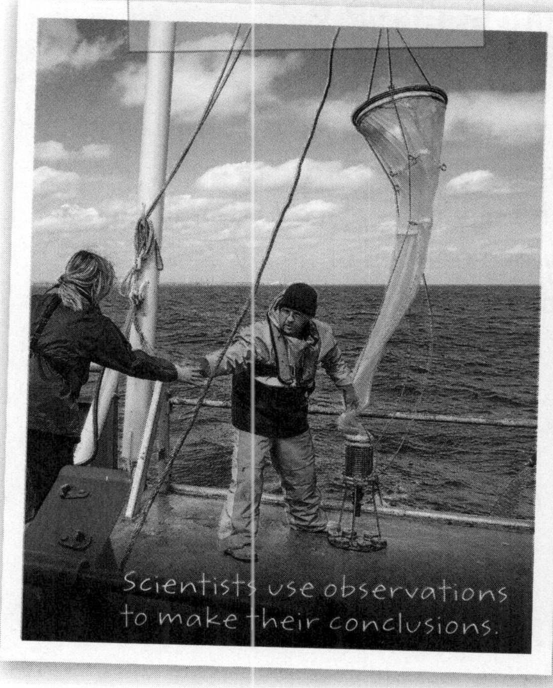
Scientists use observations to make their conclusions.

Scientists do not perform a single observation or experiment and then come to a conclusion. The results of a scientific investigation must be repeatable. Scientists perform investigations many times and compare the results before they draw a conclusion. If the results cannot be repeated, then some of the observations may include an error.

It is also important that scientific observations can be repeated by other researchers. Sometimes, other researchers cannot get the same result. Then the scientists compare their methods to find out what is different. It is possible that there is an error in one of the methods.

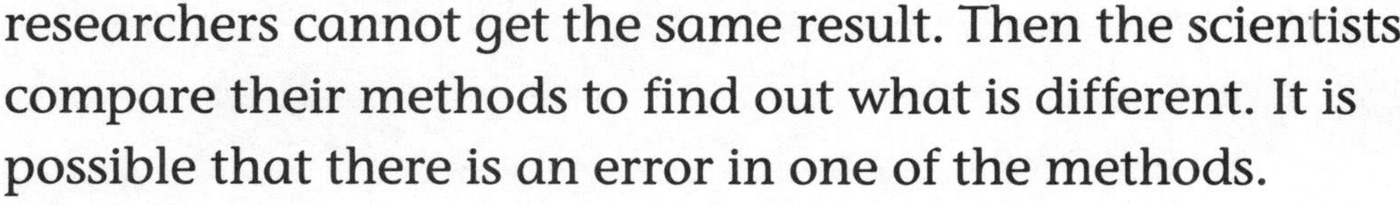

Being able to repeat results makes the conclusion more reliable, so communication among scientists is important. Scientists communicate their methods and results so other scientists can repeat and then compare them.

Evaluate A scientist repeats an experiment and gets a different result. What should the scientist do next?

Glossary

The glossary uses letters and signs to show how words are pronounced. The mark " is placed after a syllable with a primary or heavy accent. The mark ʹ is placed after a syllable with a secondary or lighter accent.

Pronunciation Key

a	in hat, cap	k	in kind, seek	th	in thin, both
ā	in age, face	l	in land, coal	TH	in then, smooth
â	in care, fair	m	in me, am	u	in cup, butter
ä	in father, far	n	in no, in	u̇	in full, put
b	in bad, rob	ng	in long, bring	ü	in rule, move
ch	in child, much	o	in hot, rock	v	in very, save
d	in did, red	ō	in open, go	w	in will, woman
e	in let, best	ȯ	all, caught	y	in young, yet
ē	in equal, be	ô	in order	z	in zero, breeze
ėr	in term, learn	oi	in oil, voice	zh	in measure, seizure
f	in fat, if	ou	in house, out	ə a	in about,
g	in go, bag	p	in paper, cup	e	in taken,
h	in he, how	r	in run, try	i	in pencil,
i	in it, pin	s	in say, yes	o	in lemon,
ī	in ice, five	sh	in she, rush	u	in circus
j	in jam, enjoy	t	in tell, it		

acceleration (ak selʹ ə rā" shən) a change in an object's direction or speed

air pressure (âr presh" ər) the downward force of air that affects weather

aquifer (ak" wə fər) large supplies of underground water

apparent (ə par" ənt) how something looks

asteroid (as" tə roidʹ) chunks of rocks in space

atom (at" əm) a particle that is the smallest and most basic part of an element

atomic theory (ə tom" ik thē" ər ē or ə tom" ik thir" ē) the idea that everything is made of small particles

balanced (bal" ənst) when two equal forces acting on an object cancel out each other's effect on the object

bladder (blad" ər) an organ that stores urine in the body

brain (brān) an organ that can recognize senses and causes the rest of the body to react

characteristic (kârʹ ik tə ris" tik) a trait that can help identify something

chemical change (kem" ə kəl chānj) the process where one or more kinds of matter changes into one or more different kinds of matter

chemical reaction (kem" ə kəl rē ak" shen) a change where one or more substances are turned into one or more different substances, usually caused by heat or mixing new substance

circulation (air) (sėr′ kyə lā" shen) air moving heat in a circular motion

circulation (water) (sėr′ kyə lā" shen) a swirling movement that moves ocean water around the globe

classify (klas′ ə fī) to sort objects or living things into groups based on shared traits

climate (kli" mit) the average weather patterns of a place found by studying years of weather

comet (kom" it) chunks of rock and ice that orbit the sun

compound (kom" pound) a matter made of two or more elements, such as water, oxygen, and salt

compute (kəm pyüt") to find or calculate

conclude (kən klüd") to make a statement with data and facts

condensation (kon′ den sā" shən) the process where a gas cools and becomes a liquid

conductor (kən duk" tər) a material that energy can easily flow through

connect (kə nekt") to attach or put together

conservation of matter (kon′ sər vā" shən ov mat" ər) the scientific law that matter cannot be made or destroyed, only transferred and changed

contact force (kon" takt fôrs) a push or pull that moves or changes an object when two objects touch

convection current (kən vek" shən kėr" ənt) a circular motion created when air rises and sinks because of heating and cooling

cuticle (kyü" tə kəl) a waxy outer coating on leaves that helps a plant store water

cycle (si" kəl) a series of events that repeats itself

deduce (di düs") to form an idea based on evidence

determine (di tėr" mən) to control or cause something

diaphragm (di" ə fram) a muscle below the lungs that helps lungs take air in and push it out

differentiate (dif′ ə ren" shē āt) to identify the differences between two or more objects

distribution (dis′ trə byü" shən) how something is spread out

Glossary

electric charge (i lek" trik chärj) a force caused by the movement of negative and positive particles

electric current (i lek" trik kėr" ənt) a flow of particles caused by negative and positive charges

elevation (el′ ə vā" shən) the height above sea level

energy (en" ər jē) the ability to do work or cause a change

establish (e stab" lish) to show an idea

evaporation (i vap′ ə rā" shən) the process where a substance warms and changes from a liquid into a gas

evident (ev" ə dənt) describes something easily observed that can be used to confirm or deny an idea

excretory system (ek" skrə tôr′ ē sis" təm) the organs that remove waste from the human body.

exoskeleton (ek′ sō skel" ə tən) a hard covering on invertebrates used to maintain their shape and protect their organs

extend (ek stend") to stretch

external (ek stėr" nl) something that is on the outside of an organism or object

extinct (ek stingkt") the death of all organisms in a species

force (fôrs) a push or pull that can act on or change an object

formula (fôr" myə lə) a math problem that shows a scientific fact

friction (frik" shən) an opposing force caused by two objects touching each other

function (fungk" shən) the main action that something is made to do

galaxy (gal" ək sē) a massive group of stars, gas, and dust in space

gas (gas) a form of matter that does not have a definite shape or volume

gills (gils) the organ in fish and young amphibians that takes in oxygen from water

glacier (glā shər) snow and ice gathered in one area over many years

gravity (grav" ə tē) a force that pulls masses toward large objects, such as the Earth and the sun

hail (hāl) precipitation formed when rain is repeatedly blown back up into the cloud and freezes in layers

heart (härt) an organ that moves blood to and from different areas of the body

humidity (hyü mid" ə tē) the amount of water vapor in the air

hypothesize (hī poth" ə sīz) to form a scientific idea that is often tested in an experiment

illustrate (il" ə strāt or i lus" trāt) to explain with an example

impact (im" pakt) to directly affect something

inertia (in ėr" shə) an object's ability to oppose a change in motion

inner planets (in" ər plan" it) the four rocky planets closest to the sun

insulator (in" sə lā' tər) a material that stops the flow of electricity

internal (in tėr" nl) something that is on the inside of an organism or object

interpret (in tėr" prit) to explain an idea

kidneys (kid" nēs) two organs that filter waste

kinetic energy (ki net" ik en" ər jē) the energy of motion

large intestine (lärj in tes" tən) the organ that takes in water from food and helps get rid of waste

latitude (lat" ə tüd) parallel lines on a map or globe that shows how far away from the equator a place is

liquid (lik" wid) matter with a definite mass but no definite volume where particles easily slide around each other

liver (liv" ər) an organ that breaks down fats and helps with digestion

lungs (lung) an organ that takes in and releases air

mass (mas) the amount of matter an object has

milky way (mil" kē wā) the galaxy that our solar system is in

mixture (miks" chər) a substance where different materials are put together but each keeps its own properties

molecule (mol" ə kyül) the smallest particle of a compound that is made out of atoms

moon (mün) a large, round piece of rock that revolves around a planet

Glossary

muscle (mus" əl) a tissue that helps make a body move

natural disaster (nach" ər əl də zas" tər) a destructive change that is not caused by people

non-contact force (non" kon′ takt fôrs) a force that does not need to touch an object to affect it, such as gravity

orbit (ôr" bit) the circular movement of an object, such as a planet or moon, around an object that can hold it in place with gravity, such as a sun or large planet

organ (ôr" gən) parts of a body that make a body live and move

organ system (ôr" gən sis" təm) a group of organs that work together to take care of a specific need of the body

organize (ôr" gə nīz) to arrange something to make it easier to understand

outer planet (ou" tər plan" it) the four large planets farthest from the sun that are made of ice and gases

ovary (ō" vər ē) the part of the flower that holds the eggs needed for a flower to make seeds

pancreas (pan" krē əs) the organ that manages sugar in the body

parallel circuit (par" ə lel sėr" kit) a path for an electric current that has multiple loops

pattern (pat" ərn) an observable event that happens in the same way again and again

physical change (fiz" ə kəl chānj) a change in traits—such as color, size, and shape—that does not change what the substance is made of

pistil (pis" tl) the part of a flower that receives pollen to make a seed

potential energy (pə ten" shəl en" ər jē) stored energy

precipitation (pri sip′ ə tā" shən) water in the atmosphere that falls to earth as rain, sleet, snow, or hail

primary (pri" mer′ ē) the original or most important part

reservoir (rez" ər vwär) a place to store water made by humans

respond (ri spond") to react to a change or action

salinity (sə lin" ə tē) the amount of salt in water

sensory organ (sen" sər ē ôr" gən) an organ that collects information about the body's surroundings, such as eyes, ears, nose, skin, and tongue

sepal (sē" pəl) green, leaf-like structures that protect a flower before it blooms

series circuit (sir" ēz sėr" kit) a path for electric energy made out of a single loop

severe weather (sə vir" weTH" ər) dangerous weather, such as tornadoes and hurricanes

skeletal system (skel" ə təl sis" təm) the bones in the human body that interact to move, protect the body, and give it shape

skeleton (skel" ə tən) an inner support in vertebrates made of bones

skin (skin) the organ that surrounds and protects the body

sleet (slēt) raindrops that freeze before they land

small intestine (smȯl in tes" tən) the organ where most of digestion occurs

solar system (sō" lər sis" təm) the planets, asteroids, and comets that orbit the sun, as well as the planets' moons

solid (sol" id) matter with a definite shape and volume that is made of vibrating particles

solution (sə lü shən) a mixture where the substances are evenly spread out

sound energy (sound en" ər jē) energy that can be heard

stamen (stā" mən) the part of the flower that makes pollen

star (stär) a giant ball of hot, glowing gases

stimulus (stim" yə ləs) an action or change that causes a certain reaction in an animal

stomach (stum" ək) the organ that breaks down food for the body to use

strategy (strat" ə jē) a plan

structure (struk" chər) an arrangement of particles for a specific purpose

supports (sə pôrts") to back up a theory with evidence or data

temperature (tem" pər ə chər) the measure of how hot or cold something is

tides (tīd) a pattern of rising and falling movement in the ocean caused by gravity

tissue (tish" ü) cells that make up an organ

trace (trās) a small amount

vascular system (vas" kyə lər sis" təm) tube-like parts of a plant that transport water and sugar around the plant

volume (vol" yəm) the amount of space an object takes up

water cycle (wȯ" tər si" kəl) the pattern of water moving on earth from the ocean, to the sky, to rain, to a river, and back to the ocean

weather (weTH" ər) the conditions in a place's atmosphere, such as sunny, rainy, or snowy

Index

*Page numbers for charts, graphs, maps,and pictures are printed in *italics*.

Q

R

S

U

V

W

X

Z

Credits

Illustrations

Articulate Graphics/IllustrationOnline.com; Aaron Ashley Illustration; Peter Bull Art Studio; Dan Crisp/The Bright Agency; Stuart Holmes/Illustration Inc.; Melissa Manwill/Shannon Associates, LLC; Mapping Specialists, Ltd.; Bojan Orešković; Pronk Media Inc.; Rob Schuster; Geoffrey P. Smith; Jim Steck/Steck Figures; Symmetry Creative Productions; Sam Valentino/Bumblecat Design & Illustration, LLC; Ralph Voltz/IllustrationOnline.com

Photographs

Photo locators denoted as follows: Top (T), Center (C), Bottom (B), Left (L), Right (R), Background (Bkgd)

Front Cover: Alex Mustard/Nature Picture Library;
Back Cover: Marinello/DigitalVision Vectors/Getty Images;

FM

iv: Tanarch/Shutterstock; vi: Wavebreakmedia/Shutterstock; vii: Monkey Business Images/Shutterstock; viii: Tracy Whiteside/Shutterstock; ix: A and N photography/Shutterstock; x: Warren Goldswain/Shutterstock; xi: Paul Hakimata Photography/Shutterstock; xii: Medioimages/Photodisc/Getty Images; xiii: Racorn/Shutterstock; xiv Bkgrd: Iakov Kalinin/Fotolia; xiv TR: Barry Tuck/Shutterstock; xv B: Pearson Education; xv TL: Pearson Education

T01

000: Vadim Sadovski/Shutterstock; 002: Wavebreakmedia/Shutterstock; 005 R: ESA/NASA; 005 TR: National Geographic Creative/Alamy Stock Photo; 006: Engel Ching/Alamy Stock Photo; 007 BR: Elina Li/Shutterstock; 007 CR: Dmitriy Eremenkov/Shutterstock; 008: Oliver Taylor/Alamy Stock Photo; 009 BC: Wavebreakmedia/Shutterstock; 009 TR: Subaru Telescope (NAOJ), Hubble Space Telescope/Robert Gendler/NASA; 012 CL: 1973kla/Shutterstock; 012 TL: Suat Gursozlu/Shutterstock; 013 B: Kidsada Manchinda/Alamy Stock Photo; 013 TL: Wavebreakmedia/Shutterstock; 014 BL: Egyptian Studio/Shutterstock; 014 CR: Alex Tudorica/Shutterstock; 014 TR: Taborsky/Shutterstock; 016: Krista Long/Moment Open/Getty Images; 017: MisterElements/Shutterstock; 020 C: Science Source; 020 BR: Wavebreakmedia/Shutterstock; 021: Dedek/Shutterstock; 022: Wavebreakmedia/Shutterstock; 024: Lebrecht Music and Arts Photo Library/Alamy Stock Photo; 025: Raquel Lonas/Moment Open/Getty Images; 026: Wavebreakmedia/Shutterstock; 027 BR: Imagenavi/Fotolia; 027 TR: Vadim Sadovski/Shutterstock; 030: 123RF; 031 CR: Science Source; 031 TR: 123RF; 032: Wavebreakmedia/Shutterstock; 034 Bkgrd: Mezzotint_alamy/Alamy Stock Photo; 034 TR: Wavebreakmedia/Shutterstock; 035 B: Science Source; 035 TR: Monty Rakusen/Cultura/Getty Images; 037: 123RF

T02

042: Durk Talsma/Shutterstock; 044: Monkey Business Images/Shutterstock; 047 BR: NASA Earth Observatory images/U.S. Geological Survey; 047 CR: NASA Earth Observatory images/U.S. Geological Survey; 047 R: NASA Earth Observatory images/U.S. Geological Survey; 048: Vbaleha/Fotolia; 050: Bonita R. Cheshier; 054: Monkey Business Images/Shutterstock; 055: Monkey Business Images/Shutterstock; 056 B: Alexander/Fotolia; 056 CL: Kavram/iStock/Getty Images Plus/Getty Images; 056 CR: Mariusz_prusaczyk/iStock/Getty Images Plus/Getty Images; 058: Chicago History Museum/Archive Photos/Getty Images; 062 B: Scott London/Alamy Stock Photo; 062 BR: Monkey Business Images/Shutterstock; 066: Sergey Nivens/Shutterstock; 068 CR: Monkey Business Images/Shutterstock; 068 BL: Somchai Som/Shutterstock; 073: Avalon/Photoshot License/Alamy Stock Photo; 074: Monkey Business Images/Shutterstock; 075 B: B.A.E. Inc./Alamy Stock Photo; 075 TR: Tristan3D/Alamy Stock Photo; 076 Bkgrd: Aronaze/iStock /Getty Images Plus/Getty Images; 076 TR: Monkey Business Images/Shutterstock; 077 B: Starman963/Fotolia; 077 TR: Hero Images/Getty Images

T03

084: James BO Insogna/Shutterstock; 086: Tracy Whiteside/Shutterstock; 089: Peter Titmuss/Shutterstock; 090: Bikeriderlondon/Shutterstock; 091 BR: Hchjjl/Shutterstock; 091 CR: Christopher Hall/Shutterstock; 093 BC: Tracy Whiteside/Shutterstock; 093 TR: ChiccoDodiFC/Alamy Stock Photo; 097 BL: Trek6500/Shutterstock; 097 CL: Ian Dagnall/Commercial Collection/Alamy Stock Photo; 097 TCL: Vaclav P3k/Shutterstock; 097 TL: Tracy Whiteside/Shutterstock; 098 B: Martina Vaculikova/Shutterstock; 098 CL: Roman Kadarjan/Alamy Stock Photo; 098 CR: Feng Yu/Shutterstock; 099: LHF Graphics/Shutterstock; 100 B: Kichigin/Shutterstock; 100 BL: Ruben Alexander/The Wanderer's Eye Photography/Moment Open/Getty Images; 101: Lemonade Serenade/Shutterstock; 102: Richard Smith Alamy Stock Photo; 103 BC: Tracy Whiteside/Shutterstock; 103 BR: Tomislav Stefanac/Alamy Stock Photo; 106: EPA European Pressphoto Agency b.v./Alamy Stock Photo; 107: Tracy Whiteside/Shutterstock; 108 B: Mark Pearson/Alamy Stock Photo; 108 CR: Joel Sartore/National Geographic/Getty Images; 110 C: Natasha Ethrington/Alamy Stock Photo; 110 CR: Mary Lane./Shutterstock; 111: Tracy Whiteside/Shutterstock; 114 CL: Leonard Zhukovsky/Shutterstock; 114 TL: Anton Foltin/Shutterstock; 115 B: AfriPics.com/Alamy Stock Photo; 115 TL: Tracy Whiteside/Shutterstock; 116: Pixdeluxe/iStock/Getty Images Plus; 118: Christopher Wood/Shutterstock; 119: Tracy Whiteside/Shutterstock; 121: Hopewell/Shutterstock; 122 CR: Nikolaeva/Shutterstock; 122 TC: Tracy Whiteside/Shutterstock; 122 TR: Vagabond54/Shutterstock; 123: Hchjjl/Shutterstsock; 124: Bettmann/Getty Images; 125: Lemonade Serenade/Shutterstock; 126: Jason Persoff Stormdoctor/Cultura Creative/Alamy Stock Photo; 127: SpiffyJ/Stock/Getty Images Plus; 130 BCR: Tracy Whiteside/Shutterstock; 130 C: Skodonnell/E+/Getty Images; 131 : Daniel Padavona/Shutterstock; 132 B: Heiko Kueverling/Shutterstock; 132 TR: Photka/Fotolia; 133 BR: LilKar/Shutterstock; 133 TR: Denis Burdin/Shutterstock; 134 Bkgrd: Jat306/Fotolia; 134 CR: Tracy Whiteside/Shutterstock; 135 Bkgrd: Ryan McGinnis/Alamy Stock Photo; 135 TR: Steve Morgan/Alamy Stock Photo; 136: Leonard Zhukovsky/Shutterstock; 141: Astarina/Shutterstock

T04

142: Milosz Maslanka/Shutterstock; 144: A and N photography/Shutterstock; 147 CR: U.S. Department of Energy/Science Source; 147 R: Leonid Ikan/Fotolia; 148 B: apiguide/Shutterstock; 148 CR:

Mark Baigent Life/Alamy Stock Photo; 150 B: Kinn Deacon/Alamy Stock Photo; 150 BL: Alexey V Smirnov/Shutterstock; 151 BC: A and N photography/Shutterstock; 151 C: Molekuul/123RF; 154: Photo5963_shutter/Shutterstock; 155 BR: Alexeysun/Shutterstock; 155 TR: A and N photography/Shutterstock; 156 BL: dod/Fotolia; 156 BR: Jay Beaumont/Fotolia; 156 C: Barry Tuck/Shutterstock; 156 CL: RGtimeline/Shutterstock; 158: Schankz/Shutterstock; 159 BCR: Lineartestpilot/Shutterstock; 159 BR: BeatWalk/Shutterstock; 161 BL: Education Images/Universal Images Group North America LLC/Alamy Stock Photo; 161 TR: Goss Images/Alamy Stock Photo; 162: A and N photography/Shutterstock; 163 CR: Aksenenko Olga/Shutterstock; 163 TR: Dmitr1ch/Fotolia; 164 BR: Viktor1/Shutterstock; 164 CR: A and N photography/Shutterstock; 166: Antantarctic/Fotolia; 170 B: Antonina Sotnykova/Shutterstock; 170 BR: Aukarawatcyber/Shutterstock; 170 CL: Tim UR/Shutterstock; 171 C: A and N photography/Shutterstock; 171 R: Sara Winter/Fotolia; 172: Calek/Shutterstock; 173 TL: A and N photography/Shutterstock; 173 TR: Anne Gilbert/Alamy Stock Photo; 174: Cyran/Shutterstock; 176 CR: A and N photography/Shutterstock; 176 TL: Lersan Moomueansri/123RF; 177 B: Nati Harnik/AP Images; 177 TR: David Taylor/Science Source; 178 Bkgrd: Santiparp Wattanaporn/Shutterstsock; 178 BL: Foto Images/Fotolia; 178 CL: Kichigin/Shutterstock; 180 C: Tibet Saisema/Shutterstock; 180 TL: A and N photography/Shutterstock; 181 B: Jeff Smith/Alamy Stock Photo; 181 CR: Njnightsky/123RF; 182: Lukas Gojda/Fotolia; 185 C: galichstudio/Fotolia; 185 CL: galichstudio/Fotolia; 187 C: A and N photography/Shutterstock; 187 CR: ahavelaar/Fotolia; 187 TR: mexrix/Shutterstock; 190 B: Mushy/Fotolia; 190 BC: Magnago/Shutterstock; 190 BCL: ajt/Shutterstock; 190 BL: Lizard/Shutterstock; 190 BR: Daxiao Productions/Shutterstock; 191 TCR: Andrew Kurcan/EyeEm/Getty Images; 191 TR: Steve Carroll/123RF; 192 BC: Scott Bolster/Shutterstock; 192 BR: Pearson Education; 192 TR: A and N photography/Shutterstock; 194: Joannawnuk/Shutterstock; 196 CL: Hemera Technologies/PhotoObjects.net/Getty Images Plus/Getty Images; 196 TL: Slava_Kovtun/Shutterstock; 197 B: Sergieiev/Shutterstock; 197 C: A and N photography/Shutterstock; 200: Richard Megna/Fundamental Photographs; 201: Donfiore/Shutterstock; 202 Bkgrd: Severija/Shutterstock; 202 C: A and N photography/Shutterstock; 204 Bkgrd: Yatra/Shutterstock; 204 CR: A and N photography/Shutterstock; 205 B: Jean-Marie Guyon/123RF; 205 CR: Jiri Hera/Fotolia; 205 TR: Nd3000/Fotolia; 207 BCL: Aleksandar Grozdanovski/Shutterstock; 207 BL: Mark Prytherch/Shutterstock; 207 TCL: Gudz Sofiya/Shutterstock; 207 TL: HUANG Zheng/Shutterstock

T05

212: Rostislav Glinsky/Shutterstock; 214: Warren Goldswain/Shutterstock; 217 CR: Scanrail/123RF; 217 R: Itestro/Fotolia; 218: Sergey Novikov/Shutterstock; 222: Jeff Hinds/Shutterstock; 223 BC: Warren Goldswain/Shutterstock; 223 B: Yorik/Shutterstock; 224 B: Senohrabek/Fotolia; 224 CL: Steve Byland/Shutterstock; 225 BC: Mwpenny/iStock/Getty Images Plus/Getty Images; 225 BL: David Arky/Getty Images; 225 BR: Fuse/Corbis/Getty Images; 226: iStock/Getty Images Plus/Getty Image; 227 BR: MG-PicturesProd/Shutterstock; 227 BL: Andy Roberts/Caiaimage/Getty Images; 227 TR: Gabbro/Alamy Stock Photo; 227 TL: Warren Goldswain/Shutterstock; 228: S.E.A. Photo/Alamy Stock Photo; 232: IE008/Image Source/Alamy Stock Photo; 233 C: Warren Goldswain/Shutterstock; 233 TR: Petr Malyshev/Alamy Stock Photo; 234 : Warren Goldswain/Shutterstock; 235 B: Images-USA/Alamy Stock Photo; 235 T: Tetsuo Wada/Aflo/Getty Images; 236 BC: Matej Kastelic/Shutterstock; 236 CL: imageBROKER/Alamy Stock Photo; 236 CR: Baranozdemir/E+/Getty Images; 238: TebNad/Shutterstock; 240: Vladyslav Danilin/Shutterstock; 241 BC: Warren Goldswain/Shutterstock; 241 TR: Haryigit/Shutterstock; 244: Warren Goldswain/Shutterstock; 246 Bkgrd: Flegere/Shutterstock; 246 TR: Warren Goldswain/Shutterstock; 247 BL: Mouse in the House/Alamy Stock Photo; 247 CL: Hitandrun/Ikon Images/Alamy Stock Photo; 247 TR: Image Source/Getty Images; 248: Rick Partington/Shutterstock

T06

254: Sarah Jessup/Shutterstock; 256: Paul Hakimata Photography/Shutterstock; 259 C: Upslim/Shutterstock; 259 R: Mmac72/E+/Getty Images; 260: Technotr/E+/Getty Images; 261: LHF Graphics/Shutterstock; 262: Ron S Buskirk/Alamy Stock Photo; 263: Comstock/Stockbyte/Getty Images; 266: Paul Hakimata Photography/Shutterstock; 267: Dmitry Berkut/123RF; 268: Paul Hakimata Photography/Shutterstock; 270: NASA; 271: Lineartestpilot/Shutterstock; 272 CL: Gary Wainwright/Alamy Stock Photo; 272 TL: Andi Duff/Alamy Stock Photo; 273 BC: NASA; 273 BR: NASA/JPL; 276 CR: Paul Hakimata Photography/Shutterstock; 276 TL: Jacob Lund/Shutterstock; 277: Paul Hakimata Photography/Shutterstock; 278 TC: Puruan/Shutterstock; 278 TR: Sudowoodo/Shutterstock; 278 CR: NASA Archive/Alamy Stock Photo; 280: Gari Wyn Williams/Alamy Stock Photo; 284 CR: Paul Hakimata Photography/Shutterstock; 284 L: Marka/Universal Images Group/Getty Images; 285: JohnatAPW/Alamy Stock Photo; 286: Paul Hakimata Photography/Shutterstock; 287 BR: Paul Wootton/Science Source; 287 TR: NASA; 288 Bkgrd: Stocktrek Images/Getty Images; 288 CR: Paul Hakimata Photography/Shutterstock; 289 B: NASA/Dmitri Gerondidakis; 289 TR: FabioBalbi/iStock/Getty Images Plus/Getty Images; 290: Sciencephotos/Alamy Stock Photo; 294: Lubenica/Shutterstock

T07

296: Sportpoint/Shutterstock; 298: Medioimages/Photodisc/Getty Images; 301 C: Penny Tweedie/Alamy Stock Photo; 301 R: Praweena style/Shutterstock; 302: Highwaystarz/Fotolia; 306: Medioimages/Photodisc/Getty Images; 309: Medioimages/Photodisc/Getty Images; 310 BL: Medical_IllustrationCorner/Alamy Stock Photo; 310 BR: lady_in_red13/Shutterstock; 310 CL: Komsan Loonprom/Shutterstock; 312: Angela Hampton Picture Library/Alamy Stock Photo; 319: Medioimages/Photodisc/Getty Images; 320: Erik Tham/Alamy Stock Photo; 326: Medioimages/Photodisc/Getty Images; 328: Jezperklauzen/iStock/Getty Images Plus/Getty Images; 331: Steve Gschmeissner/Science Source; 333: Roddy Paine/Pearson Education Ltd; 334 BL: Callista Images/Cultura/Getty Images; 334 CL: Eye of Science/Science Source; 335: Biophoto Associates/Science Source; 336: Medioimages/Photodisc/Getty Images; 338 Bkgrd: Science Photo Library/Brand X Pictures/Getty Images; 338 CR: Medioimages/Photodisc/

Getty Images; 339 Bkgrd: Tyler Olson/Shutterstock; 339 TR: Echo/Cultura/Getty Images

T08

346: Scotty/Fotolia; 348: Racorn/Shutterstock; 351 CR: JG Photography/Alamy Stock Photo; 351 R: Alvis Upitis/Photographer's Choice RF/Getty Images; 351 TR: Chris Baynham/Alamy Stock Photo; 352 BL: RuslanHoroshko/iStock/Getty Images Plus/Getty Images; 352 BR: Adriana Marteva/EyeEm/Getty Images; 354 B: Lubilub/E+/Getty Images; 354 CL: Sabine Scheckel/Photodisc/Getty Images; 355: Patrick Walchshofer/EyeEm/Getty Images; 358: Racorn/Shutterstock; 359: Jerry Horbert/Shutterstock; 360 BCR: Anastacia azzzya/Shutterstock; 360 BR: Elina Li/Shutterstock; 360 TC: Racorn/Shutterstock; 361: Syaber/iStock/Getty Images Plus/Getty Images; 362 BL: David Palos/EyeEm/Getty Images; 362 B: Westend61/Getty Images; 363: Elina Li/Shutterstock; 364 BL: Akshit Ughade/EyeEm/Getty Images; 364 CL: Chris Hiscoke/Alamy Stock Photo; 365 BC: Racorn/Shutterstock; 365 R: Judith320/iStock/Getty Images Plus/Getty Images; 368 Bkgrd: Jasmina81/iStock/Getty Images Plus/Getty Images; 368 TL: Jgareri/iStock/Getty Images Plus/Getty Images; 369 BL: Brian A Jackson/Shutterstock; 369 BR: 123RF; 369 CL: Mike Truchon/Alamy Stock Photo; 369 CR: Thomas & Pat Leeson/Science Source; 369 TL: Racorn/Shutterstock; 370 BL: Mihail Syarov/Hemera/Getty Images Plus; 370 BR: Hemera Technologies/PhotoObjects/Getty Images Plus; 371: Bukhavets Mikhail/Shutterstock; 372 BR: Racorn/Shutterstock; 372 L: Potapov Alexander/Shutterstock; 377 B: 123RF; 377 TL: Racorn/Shutterstock; 378 B: Karen Patterson/Alamy Stock Photo; 378 BR: Phekthong Lee/Hemera/Getty Images Plus; 382 bear:

Sergey Uryadnikov/Shutterstock; 382 bird: Boonchuay Promjim/Shutterstock; 382 iguana: Stayer/Shutterstock; 382 mole: Dorling Kindersley ltd/Alamy Stock Photo; 382 paw: Pongsathon; 382 rhino: Eric Nathan Alamy Stock Photo; 382 talons: Studybos/Fotolia; 382 BR: Racorn/Shutterstock; 383 C: Gary Retherford/Science Source; 383 TR: Millard H. Sharp/Science Source; 384 TL: Racorn/Shutterstock; 384 TR: Andrew J. Martinez/Science Source; 385: Scott Camazine/Science Source; 386: Ttempus fugit1980/Fotolia; 390 Bkgrd: VisionDive/Shutterstock; 390 BR: Racorn/Shutterstock; 390 CR: Gnagel/Fotolia; 391: Nature Source/Science Source; 392 Bkgrd: Malcolm Schuyl/ lamy Stock Photo; 392 TL: 123RF; 393: Racorn/Shutterstock; 394 BL: Preobrajenskiy/Shutterstock; 394 BR: DC Studio/Fotolia; 394 C: Mgkuijpers/Fotolia; 394 CL: Piotr Krzeslak/Shutterstock; 396 Bkgrd: Dariush M./Shutterstock; 396 TR: Racorn/Shutterstock; 397 B: Ueuaphoto/Shutterstock; 397 TR: Rafael Ben-Ari/Alamy Stock Photo; 398: Sabena Jane Blackbird/Alamy Stock Photo; 402: Mhatzapa/Shutterstock; 404: AlinaMD/Shutterstock

EM

EM1: Goodluz/Shutterstock; EM3: Alexis Rosenfeld/Science Source; EM4: ImageBROKER/Alamy Stock Photo; EM5: Elvira Sa/Shutterstock; EM6: Axel Heimken/AP Photo; EM8: DmitriMaruta/iStock/Getty Images Plus/Getty Images; EM9: Monty Rakusen/Cultura/Getty Images

My Notes and Designs

Draw, Write, Create

My Notes and Designs

Draw, Write, Create

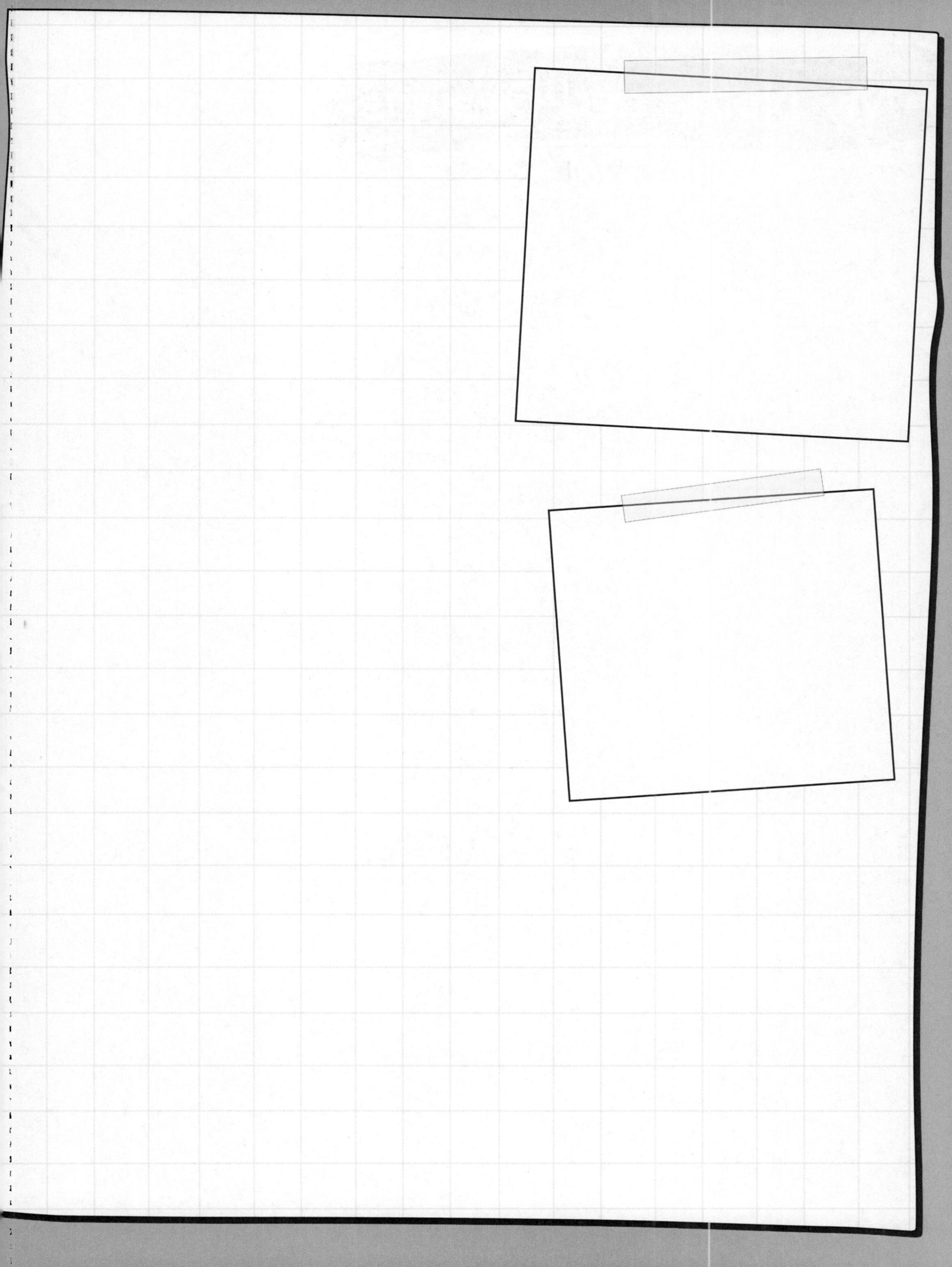

My Notes and Designs

Draw, Write, Create

My Notes and Designs

Draw, Write, Create

My Notes and Designs

Draw, Write, Create

My Notes and Designs

Draw, Write, Create